CICERO, Marcus Tullius.

DE ORATORE

IN TWO VOLUMES
I
BOOKS I, II

WITH AN ENGLISH TRANSLATION BY
E. W. SUTTON, B.C.L., M.A.
FORMERLY EXHIBITIONER OF TRINITY COLLEGE, OXFORD

COMPLETED, WITH AN INTRODUCTION, BY
H. RACKHAM, M.A.
FELLOW OF CHRIST'S COLLEGE, CAMBRIDGE

CAMBRIDGE, MASSACHUSETTS
HARVARD UNIVERSITY PRESS
LONDON
WILLIAM HEINEMANN LTD
MCMLIX

First printed 1942
Revised and reprinted 1948, 1959

Printed in Great Britain

CONTENTS

PREFACE

Though his name does not appear on the title-page, any merit discoverable in the translation of *De Oratore*, Book I is largely due to my friend Mr. Charles Stuttaford, sometime of Amersham Hall School. Originally entrusted with the execution of both these volumes, he had done much preliminary work on the text and translation of Book I, when reasons of health compelled him to relinquish his task. I most gratefully acknowledge my heavy indebtedness to his labours.

E. W. S.

25th February 1939

The late Mr. E. W. Sutton left at his death only the ms. and proof of his translation of *De Oratore*, Book I, and three-quarters of Book II, at various stages of correction. I have completed the volume.

An index will be found in Volume Two, which contains *De Oratore*, Book III, *De Fato*, *Paradoxa Stoicorum*, and *De Partitione Oratoria*.

H. R.

January 1942

INTRODUCTION

DATE AND PURPOSE OF THE WORK

THE circumstances in which Cicero wrote his essay *On the Orator* and the object that he had in view can be inferred from the following three passages in his letters :

Ad Atticum iv. 13. 2 (November 55 B.C.). De libris oratoriis factum est a me diligenter : diu multumque in manibus fuerunt.

Ad Fam. i. 9. 23 (September 54 B.C.). Scripsi etiam— nam ab orationibus diiungo me referoque ad mansuetiores Musas, quae me nunc maxime sicut iam a prima adu- lescentia delectarunt—scripsi igitur Aristotelio more, quemadmodum quidem volui, tres libros in disputatione ac dialogo de oratore, quos arbitror Lentulo tuo non fore inutiles ; abhorrent enim a communibus praeceptis atque omnium antiquorum, et Aristoteliam et Isocratiam, rationem oratoriam complectuntur.

Ad Atticum xiii. 19. 4 (45 B.C.). Sunt etiam de oratore nostri tres (libri), mihi vehementer probati. In eis quoque eae personae sunt ut mihi tacendum fuerit, Crassus enim loquitur, Antonius, Catulus senex, C. Iulius frater Catuli, Cotta, Sulpicius. Puero me hic sermo inducitur, ut nullae esse possent partes meae. Quae autem his temporibus [*i.e.* 45 B.C.] scripsi Aristotelium morem habent, in quo sermo ita inducitur ceterorum ut penes ipsum sit princi- patus.

We thus learn that Cicero finished the book in the early winter of 55 B.C., when he had been working on

ix

it for some time ; and we infer that he published it soon afterwards, since in the following September he promises to send a copy to his friend Lentulus for the use of his son. He remarks to Lentulus that he has now almost entirely given up composing speeches, and has returned to his youthful love, the humane letters.

He had indeed for some time lived entirely withdrawn from public life, where even previously he had lost all power of influencing the course of affairs. In 63 B.C. the oligarchical party had been glad to make use of his legal and oratorical talents in the suppression of the conspiracy of Catiline ; but they were not willing to make any sacrifices in order to repay him for his services, and in 58 B.C. they allowed Clodius to procure his banishment in punishment for the alleged illegality of his procedure in the Catilinarian affair. A year later Pompeius, finding Clodius more dangerous, again required Cicero's assistance, and procured his recall from exile. He was warmly welcomed back by the public, but he was no longer of any political importance, although he still appeared in the law-courts, where he delivered some considerable speeches. In 55 B.C. however, when the *imperium* of the triumvirs was prolonged for five years, he withdrew from the courts as well as from the senate, and devoted his leisure to study, the first fruits being the present treatise.

Of its merits he himself took a high view ; the tone in which he writes of it to Atticus (in the third extract above) is very different from the apologetic way in which ten years later he spoke about his philosophical works : these he referred to as ἀπόγραφα, mere transcripts from Greek originals, that cost him

INTRODUCTION

little labour. The present work is indeed worthy
of the greatest of Roman orators, who regards oratory as of supreme practical importance in the guidance of affairs, and who resolves, while his mind is still
vigorous and powerful, to devote his enforced leisure
to placing on record the fruits of his experience, for
the instruction of future statesmen.

The treatise is composed in the form of a conversation, though its method is very different from that
of the dialogues of Plato. In those the conversational
form is employed to convey the feeling of corporate
research into complicated abstract questions, pro-
gressing towards the truth but not attaining it with
sufficient certainty and completeness to justify its
being expounded dogmatically ; the positive results,
so far as any can be elicited, are merely tentative.
In Cicero's dialogues on the contrary the facts in
respect to the matter under consideration are regarded as already ascertained ; doctrines are expounded as dogmatic truths, the dialogue form being
adopted as a vivid method of exhibiting the many-
sided nature of the subject and the departments into
which a systematic treatment of it falls. If differing
opinions about it are introduced, the parts of them
that are valid are accepted and put together in a
single system.

In the second of the passages quoted above Cicero
describes the work as written 'in the Aristotelian
manner.' Its manner is extremely unlike that of
the works of Aristotle that have come down to us,
which are rigidly scientific expositions, in places
hardly more than outlines and enumerations of
arguments, and which have been conjectured to be
the Master's actual notes for his lectures. We know

however that Aristotle also wrote dialogues, in which he published his doctrines in a more popular form, but all of them have now been lost.[a] It is this group of Aristotle's works the method of which, *disputatio et dialogus*, Cicero claims to have adopted in the present treatise, as a vehicle by which to convey the oratorical system of Aristotle himself and that of Isocrates. Some difficulty has been felt to be raised by the third passage quoted, which is ten years later in date ; in it Cicero contrasts *De Oratore* with his later philosophical dialogues, on the ground that in the former he is not himself one of the party, the scene being laid in the time of his boyhood, whereas in the latter he follows the Aristotelian plan of assigning the principal part in the discussion to himself (a feature in Aristotle's dialogues of which we have no other evidence, but which we must accept on Cicero's authority). But in point of fact there is no discrepancy. The comparison with Aristotle in the latter passage relates to the assignment of the parts : that in the former refers to the dialogue form. Also it must be noticed that in the former passage Cicero claims to have adopted the Aristotelian method ' at all events as far as I thought fit ' : this qualification may well hint at the difference from Aristotle consisting in the author's taking no part in the dialogue himself.

SCENE AND DATE OF THE DIALOGUE

Details are given by the author in the introductory passages at the beginning of each of the

[a] The recently recovered *Athenian Constitution* does not fall exactly into either class ; it is not a dialogue, but a straightforward exposition in a fully finished form.

INTRODUCTION

three Books; they will be found in the outline below, pp. xv, xix, xxi.

Persons of the Dialogue

L. Licinius Crassus was born in 140 B.C., and was therefore forty-nine years old at the date when the discussion is supposed to take place, September 91 B.C. He died only a few days after that date. He was a leading figure among the moderate and judicious optimates, though it is true that he gave his name to an unwise law checking the movement to strengthen Rome by extending the citizenship to the Latins. He passed through the *cursus honorum*, becoming consul in 95 B.C. He was the most illustrious Roman orator before Cicero, and when Cicero was a boy he acted as his tutor in rhetoric. In the present dialogue he is the mouthpiece of Cicero's own opinions.

M. Antonius, the grandfather of the triumvir, was Crassus's senior by three years.[a] As praetor 103 B.C. he put down piracy in Cilicia and was awarded a triumph. Six years later he was a vigorous censor. Four years after the supposed date of the dialogue he fell a victim to Marius, whose minions murdered him when at supper at a friend's house.

In colloquy with these two great orators Cicero introduces two of the most distinguished of their younger followers.

P. Sulpicius Rufus was now thirty-three years old. He was one of the chief hopes of the optimate party, being a moderate conservative and following Drusus in his movement for limited reform. Later however he swung over to Marius and the extremists, and when (ten years after the date of the dialogue) Sulla

[a] Cic. *Brutus* 161 *triennio*.

made himself master of Rome, he with Marius was proscribed, and soon after murdered.

C. Aurelius Cotta, a young man of less vigorous character, of the same age as Sulpicius, attached himself in a similar manner to Antonius. He also belonged to the party of conservative reform, but unlike Sulpicius he remained a moderate and never joined the extreme reformers. Sulla therefore allowed him to return from exile in 82 B.C. and resume his career. He rose to be consul in 75 B.C., and died the next year, after achieving some minor military successes as proconsul in Gaul.

These four characters take part in the whole of the dialogue. Q. Mucius Q. F. Scaevola the Augur figures in Book I only. He was nearly or quite seventy years old at the time, having been consul 117 B.C. He was a learned lawyer, and an adherent of the Stoic philosophy, being a member of the Hellenizing 'Scipionic circle.' In extreme old age he refused to figure as an adherent of Sulla. Cicero tells Atticus (*ad Att.* iv. 16. 3) that he thought it suitable to his character and interests to introduce him at the beginning of the discussion, but due to his years to spare him the τεχνολογία of the later part. He is represented as displaying great legal knowledge and experience of the world ; he somewhat disparages the value of rhetoric, and questions the need of a wide literary and philosophic education for an orator.

Books II and III introduce two others, Q. Lutatius Catulus and his half-brother C. Julius Caesar Strabo Vopiscus. Catulus first appears in history as colleague of Marius in the consulship, 102 B.C. In the next year as proconsul he failed to check the Cim-

brians from invading Gallia Transpadana, but with
Marius defeated them at Vercellae : according to
Plutarch the greater part of the credit was due
to Catulus. They celebrated a triumph together.
Fourteen years later on Marius's return to Rome he
made Catulus one of his victims : ' moriatur ' was
his instruction. Catulus was an officer and gentleman of spotless integrity ; he also had considerable
literary gifts.

Vopiscus early won a position at the bar, and was
aedile in the year after the date of the dialogue.
He too fell a victim to Marius.

Outline of Contents

Book I (§§ 1-23) Introduction : (§§ 1-5) Cicero sub-
stitutes this essay for his earlier writings on rhetoric,
in order to satisfy his brother Quintus's desire for
a discussion of the functions of the orator, and to
justify his own view that the orator requires a wide
liberal education. (§§ 6-15) Great orators are rare,
not owing to dearth of ability, but because of the
difficulty of the art, and in spite of its attractions.
(§§ 16-23) It calls for wide knowledge, command of
language, psychological insight, wit and humour, a
good delivery and a good memory—even if we only
aim at the eloquence requisite for public life, and
consider it not theoretically but in the light of
practical experience.

(§§ 24-29) Scene of the dialogue. The treatise gives
an account of a discussion held in September 91 B.C.
at the Tusculan villa of Antonius, between him and
Crassus, a minor share being taken by Scaevola,
Sulpicius and Cotta. The discussion was as follows :

INTRODUCTION

(§§ 30-95) Oratory, its nature and range.

(§§ 30-34) Crassus praises oratory as of primary importance to society and the state : the orator's position is eminent, gratifying and powerful for good ; he excels in the very gift wherein man is superior to animals, ' discourse of reason.'

(§§ 35-44) Scaevola objects that Crassus overrates the political influence of orators and exaggerates the range of their powers : they are often incapable of dealing with questions of law, philosophy and science. Their proper sphere is the law-courts and political debates.

(§§ 45-57) Crassus replies that this is indeed the Greek view, but it puts the function of oratory too low. Yet even if thus limited to politics it calls for wide knowledge, and on the other hand men of science and philosophers borrow style from oratory, although style is not as essential for them as a command of matter is essential for the orator, especially in order to control the emotions of the audience. (§§ 58-68) Eloquence does not itself bestow political knowledge, but the orator must be well versed in political and also moral science. (§§ 69-73) In power of expression and range of subject he compares with the poet ; and his style will reveal whether he has had a wide education.

(§§ 74-79) Scaevola repeats that such a range of knowledge is beyond the reach of most orators. Crassus disclaims it himself, but maintains it as the ideal.

(§§ 80-95) Antonius thinks that so much knowledge is unattainable in a practical career, and also likely to form a style too abstract to be useful. He reports a debate at Athens between a Stoic, Menedemus,

who disparaged rhetoric altogether, and an Academic, Charmadas, who held that it should be based on philosophy, giving examples; Charmadas denied any science of rhetoric, saying that oratory depends merely on natural aptitude and practice, and has to go to philosophy for matter. Antonius says that he has never heard real eloquence, though it may be a possibility.

(§§ 96-112) Crassus is urged to expound his views more fully, and with reluctance consents to do so. (§§ 102-109) He asks, is there an art [a] of rhetoric ? This is a question rather for a Greek. But when pressed he says that there is none, in the strict sense, although if one reduces the results of observation and experience to a system one may produce a sort of art. He is urged to give the results of his own experience.

(§§ 113-262) The requirements of the orator.

(§§ 113-128) Natural gifts are essential for high success, although the ideal is hard to attain. Antonius agrees : orators are more exposed to criticism than even actors. (§§ 129-136) Crassus concurs, as every defect is noticed at once. He praises the natural gifts of Sulpicius and the zeal of Cotta ; they only need training, so he will describe his own method.

(§§ 137-147) He began by taking the school course in rhetoric, treating (1) the purpose of oratory, (2) the classification of subjects, (3) the determination of the point at issue, (4) the three kinds of oratory, forensic, deliberative and panegyric ; (5) its five divisions, invention, arrangement, style, memory

---

[a] It must be remembered that *ars* means a systematic treatment of a subject and conveys the sense that we attach rather to the word ' science.' *Cf.* Book II, § 30.

and delivery ; (6) the division of a speech into the proper parts ; (7) rules of diction. Such a system though useful has not in fact been the guide of the ablest orators. Practice is all-important; it includes (§§ 148-159) speaking on cases taken from real life, occasionally impromptu ; writing compositions, for training both in style and in matter; making paraphrases of poetry, especially Greek poetry, and prose, from memory ; training voice and gesture ; *memoria technica* ; speaking in public ; critical reading of literature ; debating *pro* and *contra* ; study of history, law and politics ; collecting notes. Wide knowledge is essential. The true orator possesses dignity and force (160-204).

(§§ 205-209) Sulpicius asks for further detail, and Antonius consents to give his own views. (§§ 209-218) He challenges Crassus's definition : an orator must be able to speak agreeably and convincingly on public questions, but does not require wide general culture : that is a matter belonging to some other art. (§§ 219-233) In order to work on the emotions he needs shrewdness, experience and knowledge of the world, but not philosophy—some effective lines of pleading might be disapproved of by philosophers. (§§ 234-239) Wide knowledge of law is also unnecessary : it is eloquence that wins cases, and on hard points of law even the experts disagree. (§§ 240-250) Nor is law an easy or attractive study. A general acquaintance with its principles is all that a busy man can or need attain; details should be got up for the occasion. (§§ 251-262) Similarly voice-control, history, antiquities must be studied to some extent, but not so far as to encroach on the time needed for practice in speaking —practice is the important thing.

INTRODUCTION

(§§ 263-265) Crassus hints that Antonius has only been displaying his skill in refutation, and requests him to set out his own view of the matter in the next day's debate.

Book II (§§ 1-11) Introduction : Crassus and Antonius were not unlearned, as is usually supposed ; such eloquence as theirs must have been based on wide study. The dialogue following will constitute a treatise on rhetoric based on more practical experience than that possessed by previous authors.

(§§ 12-27) The second day's debate. Catulus and Caesar arrive, and after some conversation about the employment of leisure, Antonius begins to state his own case. (§§ 28-38) He says that oratory cannot be made into a science, but some rules for speakers can be derived from observation and experience ; oratory covers all good speaking and all subjects. (§§ 39-73) He proceeds to consider the proper sphere of rhetoric. Demonstration needs no special rules ; nor does history—he gives a survey of the chief Greek historians. The rhetoricians formulate no rules for writing history, nor for the other forms of literature that require eloquence. The same is true of the discussion of abstract subjects, for which no rules of style are needed. Any student who has mastered the more difficult problems will need no directions as to the easier ones. Forensic oratory is really the most difficult kind of oratory.

(§§ 74-89) Catulus tells a story illustrating the uselessness of theory without practical experience. Antonius criticizes some superfluous or misleading rules of rhetoric. The first requisite is natural endowment, as the instance of Sulpicius shows. (§§ 90-98) There must be constant practice, largely in writing,

a good model being chosen to copy—the Greek schools of oratory are enumerated. But men of originality can dispense with a model. (§§ 99-113) To master first of all the facts of the case will at once make clear the point at issue, which will be either one of fact or of nature or of definition. (§§ 114-151) The facts are established by evidence or by argument. The handling of these methods needs practice. Antonius offers to treat of the invention of arguments, but on request consents to deal with the method of stating them. The case should be considered under some general proposition (*locus*); it is a mistake to labour the distinction between general propositions and particular instances, since the vast majority of cases can all be brought under a few general heads. The sources of arguments for dealing with these should be familiar by nature, theory and particularly study.

(§§ 152-161) Catulus says that this agrees largely with Aristotle. He develops the Roman attitude to philosophy. Antonius holds that the Stoic system is of no use to the orator, but he praises the acuteness of Aristotle and the dialectic of Carneades.

(§§ 162-177) The doctrine of 'topics'—but for this purpose attention and natural acumen, together with care for variety, will nearly suffice. (§§ 178-184) It is important to win the favour of the audience; modes of doing this. (§§ 185-216) It is also important to inspire them with suitable emotions; these the speaker must himself feel—instances from Antonius's own career. But in some cases to excite emotion is a mistake; and when done it must be done in the proper manner, and without exaggeration or hurry, and interspersed with conciliatory passages. Argu-

ments must be met by argument, and appeals to
emotion by exciting the opposite emotion.

(§§ 217-234) Caesar discusses wit. It is of two
kinds ; it cannot be taught ; its effectiveness illustrated from speeches of Crassus ; rules for its
criticism. (§§ 235-247) The laughable—its nature ;
its origin the unseemly, treated in a neat style ;
where applicable and where not ; (a) wit of form and
(b) wit of matter—illustrations of the latter. (§§ 248-
263) (a) Seven kinds of verbal wit, defined and illustrated. (§§ 264-290) (b) Nine kinds of wit of thought,
subdivided and illustrated. (§§ 291-332) Antonius
resumes from § 216, and discusses his own and his
opponent's case. Arrangement : put your strongest
argument at the beginning or at the end. Rules for
the various parts of a speech. (§§ 333-340) Speeches
of advice derive effect from the character of the
speaker and his political experience ; errors to avoid.
(§§ 341-349) Panegyric, Greek masters of ; praise
should be given to the subject's character as displayed
in his attitude towards circumstances ; compare him
with illustrious examples.

(§§ 350-367) Antonius sketches a *memoria technica*,
originating from observations made by Simonides.

The debate is adjourned to the afternoon.

Book III (§§ 1-10) Death of Crassus soon after
he had delivered an important speech. Fate of the
other characters in this dialogue.

(§§ 17-24) The discussion resumed : Crassus begins
his exposition of style. Style is not really separable
from matter. (§§ 25-37) Our senses differ, but each
gives pleasure ; and the same is the case with works
of art. Similarly various styles of oratory are all
admirable.

INTRODUCTION

(§§ 38-52) The first requisite is pure and clear diction. (§§ 53-96) Ornate style, its true conception and proper compass. (§§ 56-73) The relation of eloquence to philosophy, especially in the post-Socratic schools. (§§ 97-148) Embellishment should be produced by continuous grace, avoiding extravagance, studying light and shade, and based on general culture. (§§ 149-208) Detailed theory of the ornate style : choice of words ; their combination, in point of order and rhythm ; figures of speech.

(§§ 208-227) Oratory must be adapted to the occasion. Delivery (*actio*), including gesture and voice. Conclusion : Hortensius complimented.

EDITIONS

De Oratore was first printed at Subiaco about 1415, and three other Italian editions followed in fifteen years.

All subsequent editions have been supplanted by that of A. S. Wilkins, Oxford, 1892, the earliest containing a commentary in English. Its introduction is a mine of information on the text and contents of the book and the earlier history of rhetoric in Greece and Rome.

TEXT

The present edition has been printed from the text of V. Bétolaud, Paris, no date. A few corrections have been introduced from the text and notes of Wilkins, and a few variants are noted at the foot of the page.

For an exhaustive account of the MSS. the student

can refer to Wilkins. It may be noted here that the accepted text is based on two primary MSS. of the ninth century and one of the tenth, which clearly come from a single not very much older copy. Though full of obvious errors in copying, they are free from deliberate corrections ; all three however are mutilated, and they leave considerable gaps in the text unattested. The same is the case with a more numerous second set, of the fourteenth and fifteenth centuries, which are manifestly based on one or other of the above or on their common source. A third set, all of a later date, give a complete text ; but they do not show the same amount of agreement as the two earlier groups, and also their value is even more reduced by the probability that they have been largely corrupted by conjectural emendation.

DE ORATORE

BOOKS I, II

M. TULLI CICERONIS

AD QUINTUM FRATREM
DIALOGI TRES

DE ORATORE

DIALOGUS SEU LIBER PRIMUS

1   I. Cogitanti mihi saepenumero, et memoria vetera repetenti, perbeati fuisse, Quinte frater, illi videri solent, qui in optima republica, cum et honoribus, et rerum gestarum gloria florerent, eum vitae cursum tenere potuerunt, ut vel in negotio sine periculo, vel in otio cum dignitate esse possent. Ac fuit quidem, cum mihi quoque initium requiescendi, atque animum ad utriusque nostrum praeclara studia referendi, fore iustum et prope ab omnibus concessum arbitrarer, si infinitus forensium rerum labor, et ambitionis occupatio, decursu honorum, 2 etiam aetatis flexu, constitisset. Quam spem cogitationum et consiliorum meorum, cum graves communium temporum, tum varii nostri casus fefellerunt.

ª The metaphors are borrowed from the Circus. *Decursu honorum = decursis honoribus* : Cicero had been successively augur, quaestor, aedile, praetor, consul and proconsul.

MARCUS TULLIUS CICERO

ON

THE MAKING OF AN ORATOR

IN THREE BOOKS
ADDRESSED TO HIS BROTHER QUINTUS

BOOK THE FIRST

1 I. WHEN, as often happens, brother Quintus, I
think over and recall the days of old, those men
always seem to me to have been singularly happy
who, with the State at her best, and while enjoying
high distinctions and the fame of their achievements,
were able to maintain such a course of life that they
could either engage in activity that involved no risk
or enjoy a dignified repose. And time was when I
used to imagine that I too should become entitled,
with wellnigh universal approval, to some opportunity of leisure and of again directing my mind to
the sublime pursuits beloved of us both, when once,
the career of office complete and life too taking the
turn towards its close,[a] the endless toil of public speaking and the business of canvassing should have come
2 to a standstill. The hopes so born of my thoughts
and plans have been cheated, alike by the disastrous
times of public peril and by my manifold personal

Nam qui locus quietis et tranquillitatis plenis-
simus fore videbatur, in eo maximae moles molestia-
rum, et turbulentissimae tempestates exstiterunt.
Neque vero nobis cupientibus atque exoptantibus
fructus otii datus est ad eas artes, quibus a
pueris dediti fuimus, celebrandas, inter nosque
3 recolendas. Nam prima aetate incidimus in ipsam
perturbationem disciplinae veteris ; et consulatu
devenimus in medium rerum omnium certamen
atque discrimen ; et hoc tempus omne post consula-
tum obiecimus eis fluctibus, qui, per nos a communi
peste depulsi, in nosmet ipsos redundarunt. Sed
tamen in his vel asperitatibus rerum, vel angustiis
temporis, obsequar studiis nostris ; et, quantum mihi
vel fraus inimicorum, vel causae amicorum, vel
respublica tribuet otii, ad scribendum potissimum
4 conferam. Tibi vero, frater, neque hortanti deero,
neque roganti, nam neque auctoritate quisquam
apud me plus valere te potest, neque voluntate.

II. Ac mihi repetenda est veteris cuiusdam
memoriae non sane satis explicata recordatio, sed,
ut arbitror, apta ad id, quod requiris, ut cognoscas
quae viri omnium eloquentissimi clarissimique sen-
5 serint de omni ratione dicendi. Vis enim, ut mihi
saepe dixisti, quoniam quae pueris aut adolescentulis
nobis ex commentariolis nostris inchoata ac rudia
exciderunt, vix hac aetate digna, et hoc usu, quem

---

[a] Cicero was about eighteen years old at the outbreak of
the civil strife between Marius and Sulla.

[b] The reference is to the juvenile *De Inventione* of Cicero,
in two books.

misfortunes. For the time of life which promised
to be fullest of quiet and peace proved to be that
during which the greatest volume of vexations and the
most turbulent tempests arose. And notwithstanding my desire, and indeed my profound longing, no
enjoyment of leisure was granted me, for the cultivation and renewed pursuit, in your company, of those
arts to which from boyhood you and I have been
3 devoted. For in my early years [a] I came just upon
the days when the old order was overthrown; then
by my consulship I was drawn into the midst of
a universal struggle and crisis, and my whole time
ever since that consulship I have spent in stemming
those billows which, stayed by my efforts from ruining
the nation, rolled in a flood upon myself. But none
the less, though events are thus harassing and my
time so restricted, I will hearken to the call of our
studies, and every moment of leisure allowed me by
the perfidy of my enemies, the advocacy of my friends
and my political duties, I will dedicate first and fore-
4 most to writing. And when you, brother, exhort
and request me, I will not fail you, for no man's
authority or wish can have greater weight with me
than yours.

II. And now I must bring back to mind the recollection of an old story, not, I admit, as clear in detail
as it might be, but, to my thinking, suited to what
you ask; so that you may learn what men renowned
above all others for eloquence have thought about
5 the whole subject of oratory. For it is your wish, as
you have often told me, that—since the unfinished
and crude essays,[b] which slipped out of the notebooks
of my boyhood, or rather of my youth, are hardly
worthy of my present time of life and of my experi-

Education of the orator.

5

ex causis, quas diximus, tot tantisque consecuti sumus, aliquid eisdem de rebus politius a nobis perfectiusque proferri : solesque nonnunquam hac de re a me in disputationibus nostris dissentire, quod ego prudentissimorum hominum artibus eloquentiam contineri statuam ; tu autem illam ab elegantia doctrinae segregandam putes, et in quodam ingenii atque exercitationis genere ponendam.

6 Ac mihi quidem saepenumero in summos homines, ac summis ingeniis praeditos intuenti, quaerendum esse visum est, quid esset, cur plures in omnibus artibus, quam in dicendo admirabiles exstitissent. Nam, quocumque te animo et cogitatione converteris, permultos excellentes in quoque genere videbis, non

7 mediocrium artium, sed prope maximarum. Quis enim est, qui, si clarorum hominum scientiam rerum gestarum vel utilitate vel magnitudine metiri velit, non anteponat oratori imperatorem ? Quis autem dubitet, quin belli duces praestantissimos ex hac una civitate paene innumerabiles, in dicendo autem ex-

8 cellentes vix paucos proferre possimus ? Iam vero, consilio ac sapientia qui regere ac gubernare rempublicam possent, multi nostra, plures patrum memoria, atque etiam maiorum exstiterunt, cum boni perdiu nulli, vix autem singulis aetatibus singuli

6

ence gained from the numerous and grave causes in
which I have been engaged—I should publish something more polished and complete on these same
topics ; and generally you disagree with me, in our
occasional discussions of this subject, because I hold
that eloquence is dependent upon the trained skill
of highly educated men, while you consider that it
must be separated from the refinements of learning
and made to depend on a sort of natural talent and
on practice.

6 And for my own part, when, as has often happened, Great
I have been contemplating men of the highest emin- orators—
ence and endowed with the highest abilities, it has why rare.
seemed to me to be a matter for inquiry, why it was
that more of them should have gained outstanding
renown in all other pursuits, than have done so in
oratory. For in whatever direction you turn your
mind and thoughts, you will find very many excelling
in every kind, not merely of ordinary arts, but of such
7 as are almost the greatest. Who, for instance, in
seeking to measure the understanding possessed by
illustrious men, whether by the usefulness or the
grandeur of their achievements, would not place the
general above the orator ? Yet who could doubt
that, from this country alone, we could cite almost
innumerable examples of leaders in war of the
greatest distinction, but of men excelling in oratory
8 a mere handful ? Nay further, among the men who
by their counsel and wisdom could control and direct
the helm of state, many have stood out in our own
day, and still more in the history of our fathers and
even of our remoter ancestors, and yet through
lengthy ages no good orator is to be found, and in
each successive generation hardly a single tolerable

7

tolerabiles oratores invenirentur. Ac, ne quis forte
cum aliis studiis, quae reconditis in artibus, atque in
quadam varietate litterarum versentur, magis hanc
dicendi rationem, quam cum imperatoris laude, aut
cum boni senatoris prudentia comparandam putet,
convertat animum ad ea ipsa artium genera, circum-
spiciatque, qui in eis floruerint, quamque multi : sic
facillime, quanta oratorum sit semperque fuerit
paucitas, iudicabit.

9   III. Neque enim te fugit, artium omnium lauda-
tarum procreatricem quamdam, et quasi parentem
eam, quam φιλοσοφίαν Graeci vocant, ab hominibus
doctissimis iudicari ; in qua difficile est enumerare,
quot viri, quanta scientia, quantaque in suis studiis
varietate et copia fuerint, qui non una aliqua in
re separatim elaborarint, sed omnia, quaecumque
possent, vel scientiae pervestigatione, vel disserendi
10 ratione, comprehenderint.   Quis ignorat, ei, qui
mathematici vocantur, quanta in obscuritate rerum,
et quam recondita in arte, et multiplici subtilique
versentur ? quo tamen in genere ita multi perfecti
homines exstiterunt, ut nemo fere studuisse ei
scientiae vehementius videatur, quin, quod voluerit,
consecutus sit.   Quis musicis, quis huic studio litterarum, quod profitentur ei, qui grammatici vocantur,
penitus se dedidit, quin omnem illarum artium paene
infinitam vim et materiam scientiae cogitatione
comprehenderit ?

11   Vere mihi hoc videor esse dicturus, ex omnibus eis,

one. And that no one may think that other pursuits, which have to do with abstruse branches of study, and what I may call the varied field of learning, should be compared with this art of oratory, rather than the merits of a commander or the wisdom of a statesman-like senator, let him turn his attention to these very kinds of art, and look around to see who, and how many, have been distinguished therein; in this way he will most readily judge how scarce orators are now, and ever have been.

9 III. For indeed you cannot fail to remember that the most learned men hold what the Greeks call 'philosophy' to be the creator and mother, as it were, of all the reputable arts, and yet in this field of philosophy it is difficult to count how many men there have been, eminent for their learning and for the variety and extent of their studies, men whose efforts were devoted, not to one separate branch of study, but who have mastered everything they could whether by scientific investigation or by the methods 10 of dialectic. Who does not know, as regards the so-called mathematicians, what very obscure subjects, and how abstruse, manifold, and exact an art they are engaged in? Yet in this pursuit so many men have displayed outstanding excellence, that hardly one seems to have worked in real earnest at this branch of knowledge without attaining the object of his desire. Who has devoted himself wholly to the cult of the Muses, or to this study of literature, which is professed by those who are known as men of letters, without bringing within the compass of his knowledge and observation the almost boundless range and subject-matter of those arts?

11 I think I shall be right in affirming this, that out of

Eminence in all fields rare.

qui in harum artium studiis liberalissimis sint doctrinisque versati, minimam copiam poetarum et oratorum egregiorum exstitisse, atque in hoc ipso numero, in quo perraro exoritur aliquis excellens, si diligenter, et ex nostrorum, et ex Graecorum copia comparare voles, multo tamen pauciores oratores, quam poetae boni

12 reperientur. Quod hoc etiam mirabilius debet videri, quia ceterarum artium studia fere reconditis atque abditis e fontibus hauriuntur ; dicendi autem omnis ratio in medio posita, communi quodam in usu, atque in hominum more et sermone versatur : ut in ceteris id maxime excellat, quod longissime sit ab imperitorum intellegentia sensuque disiunctum, in dicendo autem vitium vel maximum sit a vulgari genere orationis, atque a consuetudine communis sensus abhorrere.

13 IV. Ac ne illud quidem vere dici potest, aut plures ceteris artibus inservire, aut maiore delectatione, aut spe uberiore, aut praemiis ad perdiscendum amplioribus commoveri. Atque ut omittam Graeciam, quae semper eloquentiae princeps esse voluit, atque illas omnium doctrinarum inventrices Athenas, in quibus summa dicendi vis et inventa est et perfecta : in hac ipsa civitate profecto nulla unquam vehementius, quam eloquentiae studia viguerunt.

14 Nam posteaquam, imperio omnium gentium constituto, diuturnitas pacis otium confirmavit, nemo fere laudis cupidus adolescens non sibi ad dicendum

---

a The traditional reading omits the words *et oratorum*, but their insertion seems necessary to the sense, and is supported by O. Hense, Harnecker, Wilkins and Stangl.

all those who have been engaged in the infinitely copious studies and learning pertaining to these arts, the smallest number of distinguished men is found among poets and orators [a]; and even in this small number—within which a man of excellence very rarely emerges—if you will make a careful comparison of our own national supply and that of Greece, far fewer good orators will be found even than
12 good poets. And this should seem even more marvellous because the subjects of the other arts are derived as a rule from hidden and remote sources, while the whole art of oratory lies open to the view, and is concerned in some measure with the common practice, custom, and speech of mankind, so that, whereas in all other arts that is most excellent which is farthest removed from the understanding and mental capacity of the untrained, in oratory the very cardinal sin is to depart from the language of everyday life, and the usage approved by the sense of the community.

13 IV. And yet it cannot truly be said either that more men devote themselves to the other arts, or that those who do so are stimulated to close study by greater pleasure, higher hopes, or more splendid rewards. In fact, to say nothing of Greece, which has ever claimed the leading part in eloquence, and of Athens, that discoverer of all learning, where the supreme power of oratory was both invented and perfected, in this city of our own assuredly no studies have ever had a more vigorous life than those having to do with the art of speaking.

Oratory an attractive but difficult study.

14 For as soon as our world-empire had been established, and an enduring peace had assured us leisure, there was hardly a youth, athirst for fame, who did

11

studio omni enitendum putavit. Ac primo quidem
totius rationis ignari, qui neque exercitationis ullam
viam, neque aliquod praeceptum artis esse arbitrarentur, tantum, quantum ingenio et cogitatione
poterant, consequebantur. Post autem, auditis
oratoribus Graecis, cognitisque eorum litteris, ad-
hibitisque doctoribus, incredibili quodam nostri
15 homines dicendi studio flagraverunt. Excitabat eos
magnitudo et varietas, multitudoque in omni genere
causarum, ut ad eam doctrinam, quam suo quisque
studio assecutus esset, adiungeretur usus frequens,
qui omnium magistrorum praecepta superaret. Erant
autem huic studio maxima, quae nunc quoque sunt,
exposita praemia, vel ad gratiam, vel ad opes, vel
ad dignitatem. Ingenia vero (ut multis rebus possumus iudicare) nostrorum hominum multum ceteris
16 hominibus omnium gentium praestiterunt. Quibus
de causis, quis non iure miretur, ex omni memoria
aetatum, temporum, civitatum, tam exiguum oratorum numerum inveniri ?

Sed nimirum maius est hoc quiddam, quam homines opinantur, et pluribus ex artibus studiisque
collectum.

V. Quis enim aliud, in maxima discentium multitudine, summa magistrorum copia, praestantissimis
hominum ingeniis, infinita causarum varietate, amplissimis eloquentiae propositis praemiis, esse causae
putet, nisi rei quamdam incredibilem magnitudinem,
17 ac difficultatem ? Est enim et scientia comprehen-

not deem it his duty to strive with might and main after eloquence. At first indeed, in their complete ignorance of method, since they thought there was no definite course of training or any rules of art, they used to attain what skill they could by means of their natural ability and of reflection. But later, having heard the Greek orators, gained acquaintance with their literature and called in Greek teachers, our people were fired with a really incredible enthusi-

15 asm for eloquence. The importance, variety, and frequency of current suits of all sorts aroused them so effectually, that, to the learning which each man had acquired by his own efforts, plenty of practice was added, as being better than the maxims of all the masters. In those days too, as at present, the prizes open to this study were supreme, in the way of popularity, wealth, and reputation alike. As for ability again—there are many things to show it— our fellow-countrymen have far excelled the men of

16 every other race. And considering all this, who would not rightly marvel that, in all the long record of ages, times, and states, so small a number of orators is to be found ?

But the truth is that this oratory is a greater thing, and has its sources in more arts and branches of study, than people suppose.

V. For, where the number of students is very great, the supply of masters of the very best, the quality of natural ability outstanding, the variety of issues unlimited, the prizes open to eloquence exceedingly splendid, what else could anyone think to be the cause, unless it be the really incredible vastness and diffi-

17 culty of the subject ? To begin with, a knowledge of very many matters must be grasped, without which

Its wide demands on the student;

13

denda rerum plurimarum, sine qua verborum volu-
bilitas inanis atque irridenda est ; et ipsa oratio
conformanda, non solum electione, sed etiam con-
structione verborum ; et omnes animorum motus,
quos hominum generi rerum natura tribuit, penitus
pernoscendi ; quod omnis vis ratioque dicendi in
eorum, qui audiunt, mentibus, aut sedandis, aut
excitandis expromenda est. Accedat eodem oportet
lepos quidam facetiaeque, et eruditio libero digna,
celeritasque et brevitas et respondendi, et laces-
sendi, subtili venustate, atque urbanitate coniuncta.
18 Tenenda praeterea est omnis antiquitas, exemplo-
rumque vis ; neque legum, aut iuris civilis scientia
neglegenda est. Nam quid ego de actione ipsa plura
dicam ? quae motu corporis, quae gestu, quae vultu,
quae vocis conformatione ac varietate moderanda
est ; quae sola per se ipsa quanta sit, histrionum
levis ars et scena declarat : in qua cum omnes in
oris, et vocis, et motus moderatione elaborent, quis
ignorat, quam pauci sint, fuerintque, quos animo
aequo spectare possimus ? Quid dicam de thesauro
rerum omnium, memoria ? quae nisi custos inventis
cogitatisque rebus et verbis adhibeatur, intellegimus,
omnia, etiam si praeclarissima fuerint in oratore,
peritura.

19 Quam ob rem mirari desinamus, quae causa sit
eloquentium paucitatis, cum ex eis rebus universis
eloquentia constet, quibus in singulis elaborare per-

oratory is but an empty and ridiculous swirl of
biage: and the distinctive style has to be formed, 1.
only by the choice of words, but also by the arrange
ment of the same ; and all the mental emotions, with
which nature has endowed the human race, are to be
intimately understood, because it is in calming or kindling the feelings of the audience that the full power
and science of oratory are to be brought into play. To
this there should be added a certain humour, flashes
of wit, the culture befitting a gentleman, and readiness and terseness alike in repelling and in delivering
the attack, the whole being combined with a delicate
18 charm and urbanity. Further, the complete history
of the past and a store of precedents must be retained
in the memory, nor may a knowledge of statute law
and our national law in general be omitted. And
why should I go on to describe the speaker's delivery ?
That needs to be controlled by bodily carriage,
gesture, play of features and changing intonation of
voice ; and how important that is wholly by itself,
the actor's trivial art and the stage proclaim ; for
there, although all are labouring to regulate the
expression, the voice, and the movements of the
body, everyone knows how few actors there are, or
ever have been, whom we could bear to watch !
What need to speak of that universal treasure-house
the memory ?   Unless this faculty be placed in charge
of the ideas and phrases which have been thought out
and well weighed, even though as conceived by the
orator they were of the highest excellence, we know
that they will all be wasted.

19   Let us therefore cease to wonder what may be the
cause of the rarity of orators, since oratory is the
result of a whole number of things, in any one of which

magnum est ; hortemurque potius liberos nostros,
ceterosque, quorum gloria nobis et dignitas cara est,
ut animo rei magnitudinem complectantur, neque eis
aut praeceptis, aut magistris, aut exercitationibus,
quibus utuntur omnes, sed aliis quibusdam, se id,
quod expetunt, consequi posse confidant.

20 VI. Ac, mea quidem sententia, nemo poterit esse
omni laude cumulatus orator, nisi erit omnium rerum
magnarum atque artium scientiam consecutus.
Etenim ex rerum cognitione efflorescat et redundet
oportet oratio ; quae, nisi subest res ab oratore
percepta et cognita, inanem quamdam habet elocu-
21 tionem, et paene puerilem. Neque vero ego hoc
tantum oneris imponam nostris praesertim oratoribus,
in hac tanta occupatione urbis ac vitae, nihil ut eis
putem licere nescire : quanquam vis oratoris pro-
fessioque ipsa bene dicendi, hoc suscipere ac polliceri
videtur, ut omni de re, quaecumque sit proposita, ab
22 eo ornate copioseque dicatur. Sed quia non dubito,
quin hoc plerisque immensum infinitumque videatur,
et quod Graecos homines non solum ingenio et
doctrina, sed etiam otio studioque abundantes,
partitionem quamdam artium fecisse video, neque in
universo genere singulos elaborasse, sed seposuisse
a ceteris dictionibus eam partem dicendi, quae in
forensibus disceptationibus iudiciorum, aut delibera-

to succeed is a great achievement, and let us rather
exhort our children, and the others whose fame and
repute are dear to us, to form a true understanding
of the greatness of their task, and not to believe that
they can gain their coveted object by reliance on the
rules or teachers or methods of practice employed by
everybody, but to rest assured that they can do this
by the help of certain other means.

20 VI. And indeed in my opinion, no man can be an
orator complete in all points of merit, who has not
attained a knowledge of all important subjects and
arts. For it is from knowledge that oratory must
derive its beauty and fullness, and unless there is such
knowledge, well-grasped and comprehended by the
speaker, there must be something empty and almost
21 childish in the utterance. Not that I am going to
lay so heavy a burden upon orators—least of all upon
our own, amid all the distractions of life in Rome—
as to hold that there is nothing of which it is permissible for them to be ignorant, although the
significance of the term " orator," and the mere act
of professing eloquence, seem to undertake and to
promise that every subject whatsoever, proposed to
an orator, will be treated by him with both distinc-
22 tion and knowledge. But being assured that to most
men this appears a vast and indeed limitless enter-
prise, and perceiving that the Greeks, men not only
abounding in genius and learning, but also amply
endowed with leisure and the love of study, have
already made a sort of division of the arts,—nor did
every student of theirs work over the whole field
by himself, but they separated from other uses of
speech that portion of oratory which is concerned
with the public discussions of the law-courts and of

*even if only
pursued for
practical
purposes, as
at Rome.*

17

tionum versaretur, et id unum genus oratori reliquisse;
non complectar in his libris amplius, quam quod huic
generi, re quaesita et multum disputata, summorum
23 hominum prope consensu est tributum ; repetamque,
non ab incunabulis nostrae veteris puerilisque
doctrinae quemdam ordinem praeceptorum, sed ea,
quae quondam accepi in nostrorum hominum elo-
quentissimorum et omni dignitate principum, disputatione esse versata. Non quod illa contemnam,
quae Graeci, dicendi artifices et doctores, reliquerunt;
sed, cum illa pateant in promptuque sint omnibus,
neque ea interpretatione mea aut ornatius explicari,
aut planius exprimi possint, dabis hanc veniam, mi
frater, ut opinor, ut eorum, quibus summa dicendi
laus a nostris hominibus concessa est, auctoritatem
Graecis anteponam.

24 VII. Cum igitur vehementius inveheretur in
causam principum consul Philippus, Drusique tribunatus, pro Senatus auctoritate susceptus, infringi
iam debilitarique videretur ; dici mihi memini,
ludorum Romanorum diebus, L. Crassum, quasi
colligendi sui causa, se in Tusculanum contulisse ;
venisse eodem, socer eius qui fuerat, Q. Mucius
dicebatur, et M. Antonius, homo et consiliorum in
republica socius, et summa cum Crasso familiaritate
25 coniunctus. Exierant autem cum ipso Crasso adole-

ᵃ For Philippus and Drusus see Index, and for the other
names referred to in this chapter see Introduction.

debate, and left that branch only to the orator—I shall not include in this work more than has been assigned to this type of oratory by the all but unanimous judgement of the most eminent men, after 23 investigation and long argument of the matter ; nor shall I recall, from the cradle of our boyish learning of days gone by, a long string of precepts, but I shall repeat the things I heard of as once handled in a discussion between men who were the most eloquent of our nation, and of the highest rank in distinction of every kind. Not that I despise what the Greek craftsmen and teachers of oratory have left us ; but that is open to the view and ready to the hand of every man, nor could it be more happily set forth or more clearly expounded by any interpretations of my own, so that you will forgive me, brother mine, I do believe, if I prefer to Greek instruction the authoritative judgement of those to whom the highest honours in eloquence have been awarded by our own fellow-countrymen.

Dialogue form appropriate for the present subject.

24 VII. I remember then being told how, at the time when Philippus,[a] though consul, was furiously assailing the policy of the leading men, and the tribuneship of Drusus, undertaken in support of the power of the Senate, had begun to show symptoms of shock and weakness, Lucius Crassus, on the plea of recruiting his energies, betook himself during the days of the Roman Games to his seat at Tusculum, whither (as the story went) there came Quintus Mucius, once his father-in-law, and Marcus Antonius, a partner in the political designs of Crassus, and a man united with him in the closest 25 intimacy. There had also gone out of town, in the company of Crassus, two young men who were very

Date, scene, and persons.

19

scentes duo, Drusi maxime familiares, et in quibus
magnam tum spem maiores natu dignitatis suae
collocarant, C. Cotta, qui tum tribunatum plebis
petebat, et P. Sulpicius, qui deinceps eum magistra-
26 tum petiturus putabatur. Hi primo die de temporibus illis, deque universa republica, quam ob causam
venerant, multum inter se usque ad extremum
tempus diei collocuti sunt. Quo quidem in sermone
multa divinitus a tribus illis consularibus Cotta
deplorata et commemorata narrabat ; ut nihil in-
cidisset postea civitati mali, quod non impendere illi
27 tanto ante vidissent ; eo autem omni sermone con-
fecto, tantam in Crasso humanitatem fuisse, ut, cum
lauti accubuissent, tolleretur omnis illa superioris
tristitia sermonis ; eaque esset in homine iucunditas,
et tantus in iocando lepos, ut dies inter eos Curiae
fuisse videretur, convivium Tusculani.
28   Postero autem die, cum illi maiores natu satis
quiessent, et in ambulationem ventum esset : dicebat
tum Scaevolam, duobus spatiis tribusve factis, dixisse:
Cur non imitamur, Crasse, Socratem illum, qui est
in Phaedro Platonis ? Nam me haec tua platanus
admonuit, quae non minus ad opacandum hunc locum
patulis est diffusa ramis, quam illa, cuius umbram
secutus est Socrates, quae mihi videtur non tam

ᵃ Phaedrus 229 ᴀ, 230 ʙ.

great friends of Drusus, and in whom the older generation at that time reposed high hopes of their maintaining the traditions of their order : they were Gaius Cotta, just then seeking the tribuneship of the commons, and Publius Sulpicius, who was thought likely to become a candidate for that magistracy in 26 succession to him. This party, on the first day and up to a very late hour, held long debate together, concerning the crisis and the state of politics generally, which in fact had been the occasion of their meeting. And Cotta recounted many things which were spoken of in that discussion with deep regret by the three speakers of consular rank, in such inspired fashion that (in his words) no evil had since befallen the community which those men, so long before, had 27 not seen to be hanging over it ; but (he would add) when the colloquy was completely finished, so exquisite was the urbanity displayed by Crassus, that, as soon as they had bathed and settled down to table, the melancholy turn taken by the earlier discussion was wholly banished, and such was the man's pleasantness and so great the charm of his humour that it seemed as though a day in the Senate-house was closing with supper at Tusculum.

28 Then Cotta went on to say how on the morrow, when those older men had rested sufficiently and everyone had come into the garden-walk, Scaevola, after taking two or three turns, observed, " Crassus, why do we not imitate Socrates as he appears in the *Phaedrus* of Plato ? For your plane-tree has suggested this comparison to my mind, casting as it does, with its spreading branches, as deep a shade over this spot, as that one cast whose shelter Socrates sought[a]— which to me seems to owe its eminence less to ' the

21

'ipsa acula,' quae describitur, quam Platonis oratione crevisse : et, quod ille durissimis pedibus fecit, ut se abiceret in herbam, atque ita illa, quae philosophi divinitus ferunt esse dicta, loqueretur, id meis pedibus
29 certe concedi est aequius. Tum Crassum : Immo vero commodius etiam ; pulvinosque poposcisse, et omnes in eis sedibus, quae erant sub platano, consedisse dicebat.

VIII. Ibi, ut ex pristino sermone relaxarentur animi omnium, solebat Cotta narrare, Crassum ser-
30 monem quemdam de studio dicendi intulisse. Qui cum ita esset exorsus, non sibi cohortandum Sulpicium et Cottam, sed magis utrumque collaudandum videri, quod tantam iam essent facultatem adepti, ut non aequalibus suis solum anteponerentur, sed cum maioribus natu compararentur. Neque vero mihi quidquam, inquit, praestabilius videtur, quam posse dicendo tenere hominum coetus, mentes allicere, voluntates impellere quo velit ; unde autem velit, deducere. Haec una res in omni libero populo, maximeque in pacatis tranquillisque civitatibus, praecipue semper floruit, semperque dominata est.
31 Quid enim est aut tam admirabile, quam ex infinita multitudine hominum exsistere unum, qui id, quod omnibus natura sit datum, vel solus, vel cum paucis facere possit ? Aut tam iucundum cognitu atque auditu, quam sapientibus sententiis gravibusque verbis ornata oratio et polita ? Aut tam potens,

22

little rivulet' described by Plato than to the language of his dialogue—and what Socrates did, whose feet were thoroughly hardened, when he threw himself down on the grass and so began the talk which philosophers say was divine,—such ease surely may more 29 reasonably be conceded to my own feet." "Nay," answered Crassus, "but we will make things more comfortable still," whereupon, according to Cotta, he called for cushions, and they all sat down together on the benches that were under the plane-tree.

VIII. In that place, as Cotta was fond of relating, Crassus introduced a conversation on the pursuit of oratory, with a view to relieving all minds from the 30 discourse of the day before. He began by saying that Sulpicius and Cotta seemed not to need exhortation from him but rather commendation, seeing that thus early they had acquired such skill as not merely to be ranked above their equals in age, but to be comparable with their elders. "Moreover," he continued, "there is to my mind no more excellent thing than the power, by means of oratory, to get a hold on assemblies of men, win their good will, direct their inclinations wherever the speaker wishes, or divert them from whatever he wishes. In every free nation, and most of all in communities which have attained the enjoyment of peace and tranquillity, this one art has always flourished above the rest and ever reigned 31 supreme. For what is so marvellous as that, out of the innumerable company of mankind, a single being should arise, who either alone or with a few others can make effective a faculty bestowed by nature upon every man? Or what so pleasing to the understanding and the ear as a speech adorned and polished with wise reflections and dignified language? Or

Thesis: the importance of oratory to society and the state.

23

tamque magnificum, quam populi motus, iudicum
religiones, Senatus gravitatem, unius oratione con-
32 verti ?   Quid tam porro regium, tam liberale, tam
munificum, quam opem ferre supplicibus, excitare
afflictos, dare salutem, liberare periculis, retinere
homines in civitate ?   Quid autem tam necessarium,
quam tenere semper arma, quibus vel tectus ipse
esse possis, vel provocare improbos,[1] vel te ulcisci
lacessitus ?

Age vero, ne semper forum, subsellia, rostra,
Curiamque meditere, quid esse potest in otio aut
iucundius, aut magis proprium humanitatis, quam
sermo facetus ac nulla in re rudis ?   Hoc enim uno
praestamus vel maxime feris, quod colloquimur inter
nos, et quod exprimere dicendo sensa possumus.
33 Quam ob rem quis hoc non iure miretur, summeque
in eo elaborandum esse arbitretur, ut, quo uno
homines maxime bestiis praestent, in hoc hominibus
ipsis antecellat ?   Ut vero iam ad illa summa veniamus ; quae vis alia potuit aut dispersos homines unum
in locum congregare, aut a fera agrestique vita ad
hunc humanum cultum civilemque deducere, aut,
iam constitutis civitatibus, leges, iudicia, iura de-
34 scribere ?   Ac, ne plura, quae sunt paene innumera-

---

[1] improbos *is the reading of Friedrich for the unintelligible*
integros *of the better* MSS.

24

what achievement so mighty and glorious as that the impulses of the crowd, the consciences of the judges, the austerity of the Senate, should suffer transforma-
32 tion through the eloquence of one man? What function again is so kingly, so worthy of the free, so generous, as to bring help to the suppliant, to raise up those that are cast down, to bestow security, to set free from peril, to maintain men in their civil rights? What too is so indispensable as to have always in your grasp weapons wherewith you can defend yourself, or challenge the wicked man, or when provoked take your revenge?

"Nay more (not to have you for ever contemplating public affairs, the bench, the platform, and the Senate-house), what in hours of ease can be a pleasanter thing or one more characteristic of culture, than discourse that is graceful and nowhere uninstructed? For the one point in which we have our very greatest advantage over the brute creation is that we hold converse one with another, and can reproduce our thought in
33 word. Who therefore would not rightly admire this faculty, and deem it his duty to exert himself to the utmost in this field, that by so doing he may surpass men themselves in that particular respect wherein chiefly men are superior to animals? To come, however, at length to the highest achievements of eloquence, what other power could have been strong enough either to gather scattered humanity into one place, or to lead it out of its brutish existence in the wilderness up to our present condition of civilization as men and as citizens, or, after the establishment of social communities, to give shape to laws, tribunals,
34 and civic rights? And not to pursue any further instances—wellnigh countless as they are—I will

25

bilia, consecter, comprehendam brevi ; sic enim
statuo, perfecti oratoris moderatione et sapientia non
solum ipsius dignitatem, sed et privatorum pluri-
morum, et universae reipublicae salutem maxime
contineri. Quam ob rem pergite, ut facitis, adolescentes, atque in id studium, in quo estis, in-
cumbite, ut et vobis honori, et amicis utilitati, et
reipublicae emolumento esse possitis.

35 IX. Tum Scaevola comiter, ut solebat : Cetera,
inquit, assentior Crasso, ne aut de C. Laelii, soceri
mei, aut de huius, generi, aut arte, aut gloria de-
traham ; sed illa duo, Crasse, vereor, ut tibi possim
concedere : unum, quod ab oratoribus civitates et
ab initio constitutas et saepe conservatas esse dixisti ;
alterum, quod, remoto foro, concione, iudiciis, Senatu,
statuisti, oratorem in omni genere sermonis et hu-
36 manitatis esse perfectum. Quis enim tibi hoc concesserit, aut initio genus hominum in montibus ac
silvis dissipatum, non prudentium consiliis com-
pulsum potius, quam disertorum oratione delinitum,
se oppidis moenibusque sepsisse, aut vero reliquas
utilitates, aut in constituendis, aut in conscrvandis
civitatibus, non a sapientibus et fortibus viris, sed
37 a disertis, et ornate dicentibus esse constitutas ? An
vero tibi Romulus ille aut pastores et convenas con-

conclude the whole matter in a few words, for my
assertion is this : that the wise control of the complete orator is that which chiefly upholds not only
his own dignity, but the safety of countless individuals and of the entire State. Go forward
therefore, my young friends, in your present course,
and bend your energies to that study which engages
you, that so it may be in your power to become a
glory to yourselves, a source of service to your
friends, and profitable members of the Republic."

35   IX. Thereupon Scaevola observed, in his courteous
way, "On his other points I am in agreement with
Crassus (that I may not disparage the art or the
renown of my father-in-law Gaius Laelius, or of my
son-in-law here), but the two following, Crassus, I am
afraid I cannot grant you : first your statement that
the orators were they who in the beginning established
social communities, and who not seldom have preserved the same intact, secondly your pronouncement
that, even if we take no account of the forum, of
popular assemblies, of the courts of justice, or of the
Senate-house, the orator is still complete over the
36 whole range of speech and culture. For who is going
to grant you, that in shutting themselves up in walled
cities, human beings, who had been scattered originally over mountain and forest, were not so much convinced by the reasoning of the wise as snared by the
speeches of the eloquent, or again that the other
beneficial arrangements involved in the establishment
or the preservation of States were not shaped by the
wise and valiant but by men of eloquence and fine
37 diction ? Or do you perhaps think that it was by
eloquence, and not rather by good counsel and
singular wisdom, that the great Romulus gathered

*Thesis chal-
lenged : (1)
the achieve-
ment of
oratory
questioned ;*

27

gregasse, aut Sabinorum connubia coniunxisse, aut
finitimorum vim repressisse eloquentia videtur, non
consilio et sapientia singulari ? Quid enim ? in Numa
Pompilio, quid ? in Ser. Tullio, quid ? in ceteris regibus,
quorum multa sunt eximia ad constituendam rempublicam, num quod eloquentiae vestigium apparet ?
Quid ? exactis regibus (tametsi ipsam exactionem
mente, non lingua, perfectam L. Bruti esse cernimus),
sed deinceps omnia, nonne plena consiliorum, inania
38 verborum videmus ? Ego vero si velim et nostrae
civitatis exemplis uti, et aliarum, plura proferre
possim detrimenta publicis rebus, quam adiumenta,
per homines eloquentissimos importata : sed, ut
reliqua praetermittam, omnium mihi videor, exceptis,
Crasse, vobis duobus, eloquentissimos audisse Tib.
et C. Sempronios, quorum pater, homo prudens et
gravis, haudquaquam eloquens, et saepe alias, et
maxime censor, saluti reipublicae fuit. Atque is non
accurata quadam orationis copia, sed nutu atque verbo
libertinos in urbanas tribus transtulit ; quod nisi
fecisset, rempublicam, quam nunc vix tenemus,
iamdiu nullam haberemus. At vero eius filii diserti,
et omnibus vel naturae, vel doctrinae praesidiis
ad dicendum parati, cum civitatem vel paterno
consilio, vel avitis armis florentissimam accepissent,

ᵃ Ti. Sempronius Gracchus, censor 169 B.C., enforced an
existing rule. Freedmen not owning land worth at least
30,000 HS. were limited to the four city tribes. The restriction was removed, probably in 304, but was restored in 220.

together his shepherds and refugees, or brought
about marriages with the Sabines, or curbed the
might of the neighbouring tribes? Is there a trace
of eloquence to be discerned in Numa Pompilius?
Is there a trace in Servius Tullius? Or in the other
kings who have contributed so much that is excellent
to the building-up of the State? Then even after
the kings had been driven forth (and we note that
such expulsion had itself been accomplished by the
mind of Lucius Brutus and not by his tongue), do we
not see how all that followed was full of planning
38 and empty of talking? For my part, indeed, should
I care to use examples from our own and other
communities, I could cite more instances of damage
done, than of aid given to the cause of the State
by men of first-rate eloquence, but putting all else
aside, of all men to whom I have listened except
you two, Crassus, it seems to me that the most
eloquent were Tiberius and Gaius Sempronius, whose
father, a man of discretion and character, but no
speaker whatever, was many a time and most particularly when Censor the salvation of the commonwealth. Yet it was not any studied flow of speech,
but a nod and a word of his that transferred the
freedmen into the city tribes [a]; and had he not done
so, we should long ago have lost the constitution
which, as it is, we preserve only with difficulty. His
sons, on the other hand, who were accomplished
speakers and equipped for oratory with every advantage of nature or training, after they had taken
over a State that was flourishing exceedingly because of their father's counsels and their ancestors'
military achievements, wrecked the commonwealth
by the use of this eloquence to which, according

29

ista praeclara gubernatrice, ut ais, civitatum, eloquentia, rempublicam dissipaverunt.

39 X. Quid ? leges veteres, moresque maiorum ;
quid ? auspicia, quibus et ego, et tu, Crasse, cum
magna reipublicae salute praesumus ; quid ? religiones et caerimoniae ; quid ? haec iura civilia,
quae iampridem in nostra familia sine ulla eloquentiae
laude versantur ; num aut inventa sunt, aut cognita,
40 aut omnino ab oratorum genere tractata ? Equidem
et Ser. Galbam, memoria teneo, divinum hominem
in dicendo, et M. Aemilium Porcinam, et C. ipsum
Carbonem, quem tu adolescentulus perculisti, ignarum legum, haesitantem in maiorum institutis,
rudem in iure civili ; et haec aetas nostra, praeter te,
Crasse, qui tuo magis studio, quam proprio munere
aliquo disertorum, ius a nobis civile didicisti, quod
interdum pudeat, iuris ignara est.

41 Quod vero in extrema oratione, quasi tuo iure
sumpsisti, oratorem in omnis sermonis disputatione
copiosissime posse versari, id, nisi hic in tuo regno
essemus, non tulissem, multisque praeessem, qui aut
interdicto tecum contenderent, aut te ex iure manu
consertum vocarent, quod in alienas possessiones tam
temere irruisses.

42 Agerent enim tecum lege primum Pythagorei
omnes, atque Democritici, ceterique in iure physici

^a See Appendix p. 480. ^b See Appendix p. 480.
^c See Appendix p. 480.

30

to you, civil communities still look for their chief
guidance.

39   X. "What of our ancient ordinances and the cus- (2) other
toms of our forefathers? What of augury, over which factors of
civilization
you and I, Crassus, preside, greatly to the welfare more im-
of the Republic? What of our religious rites and portant;
ceremonies? What of those rules of private law,
which have long made their home in our family,
though we have no reputation for eloquence? Were
these things contrived or investigated or in any way
40 taken in hand by the tribe of orators? Indeed I
remember that Servius Galba, a man who spoke as a
god, and Marcus Aemilius Porcina and Gaius Carbo
himself, whom you crushed in your early manhood,
were all of them ignorant of the statutes, all at a
complete loss among the institutions of our ancestors,
all uninstructed in the law of the Romans; and
except yourself, Crassus, who rather from your own
love of study, than because to do so was any peculiar
duty of the eloquent, have learned the Roman system
from our family, this generation of ours is unversed
in law to a degree that sometimes makes one blush.

41   "But as for the claim you made at the close of your (3) the only
speech, and made as though in your own right—that field of
oratory
whatever the topic under discussion, the orator could the law
deal with it in complete fullness—this, had we not courts and
parliament.
been here in your own domain, I would not have borne
with, and I should be at the head of a multitude who
would either fight you by injunction,[a] or summon you
to make joint seizure by rule of court,[b] for so wantonly
making forcible entry upon other people's possessions.

42   "For, to begin with, all the disciples of Pythagoras
and Democritus would bring statutory process [c]
against you, and the rest of the physicists would assert

31

vindicarent, ornati homines in dicendo et graves, quibuscum tibi iusto sacramento contendere non liceret. Urgerent praeterea philosophorum greges, iam ab illo fonte et capite Socrate ; nihil te de bonis rebus in vita, nihil de malis, nihil de animi permotionibus, nihil de hominum moribus, nihil de ratione vitae didicisse, nihil omnino quaesisse, nihil scire convincerent ; et, cum universi in te impetum fecissent, tum singulae familiae litem tibi intenderent.

43 Instaret Academia, quae, quidquid dixisses, id te ipsum negare cogeret. Stoici vero nostri disputationum suarum atque interrogationum laqueis te irretitum tenerent. Peripatetici autem etiam haec ipsa, quae propria oratorum putas esse adiumenta, atque ornamenta dicendi, ab se peti vincerent oportere ; ac non solum meliora, sed etiam multo plura Aristotelem Theophrastumque de his rebus, quam omnes dicendi magistros, scripsisse ostenderent.

44 Missos facio mathematicos, grammaticos, musicos, quorum artibus vestra ista dicendi vis ne minima quidem societate contingitur. Quam ob rem ista tanta, tamque multa profitenda, Crasse, non censeo. Satis id est magnum, quod potes praestare, ut in iudiciis ea causa, quamcumque tu dicis, melior et probabilior esse videatur ; ut in concionibus et sententiis dicendis ad persuadendum tua plurimum valeat oratio ; denique ut prudentibus diserte stultis

---

their claims in court, elegant and impressive speakers with whom you could not strive and save your stake.[a] Besides this, schools of philosophers, back to great Socrates their fountain-head, would beset you : they would demonstrate that you have learned nothing concerning the good in life, or of the evil, nothing as to the emotions of the mind or of human conduct, nothing of the true theory of living, that you have made no research at all and are wholly without understanding respecting these things ; and after this general assault upon you each sect would launch its

43 particular action against you in detail. The Academy would be at your heels, compelling you to deny in terms your own allegation, whatever it might have been. Then our own friends the Stoics would hold you entangled in the toils of their wranglings and questionings. The Peripatetics again would prove that it is to them that men should resort for even those very aids and trappings of eloquence which you deem to be the special aids of orators, and would show you that on these subjects of yours Aristotle and Theophrastus wrote not only better but also much more than all the teachers of rhetoric put together.

44 I say nothing of the mathematicians, men of letters or devotees of the Muses, with whose arts this rhetorical faculty of yours is not in the remotest degree allied. And so, Crassus, I do not think you should make professions so extensive and so numerous. What you are able to guarantee is a thing great enough, namely, that in the courts whatever case you present should appear to be the better and more plausible, that in assemblies and in the Senate your oratory should have most weight in carrying the vote, and lastly, that to the intelligent you should seem to

etiam vere dicere videaris. Hoc amplius si quid poteris, non id mihi videbitur orator, sed Crassus sua quadam propria, non communi oratorum facultate, posse.

45 XI. Tum ille : Non sum, inquit, nescius, Scaevola, ista inter Graecos dici et disceptari solere. Audivi enim summos homines, cum quaestor ex Macedonia venissem Athenas, florente Academia, ut temporibus illis ferebatur, quod eam Charmadas, et Clitomachus, et Aeschines obtinebant. Erat etiam Metrodorus, qui cum illis una ipsum illum Carneadem diligentius audierat, hominem omnium in dicendo, ut ferebant, acerrimum et copiosissimum. Vigebat auditor Panaetii illius tui Mnesarchus ; et Peripatetici Critolai 46 Diodorus. Multi erant praeterea clari in philosophia et nobiles, a quibus omnibus una paene voce repelli oratorem a gubernaculis civitatum, excludi ab omni doctrina rerumque maiorum scientia, ac tantum in iudicia et conciunculas, tanquam in aliquod pistri- 47 num, detrudi et compingi videbam. Sed ego neque illis assentiebar, neque harum disputationum inventori et principi longe omnium in dicendo gravissimo et eloquentissimo, Platoni, cuius tum Athenis cum Charmada diligentius legi Gorgiam : quo in libro in hoc maxime admirabar Platonem, quod mihi

34

speak eloquently and to the ignorant truthfully as
well. If you can achieve anything more than this,
therein you will seem to me not an orator but a
Crassus, who is making use of some talent that is
peculiarly his own and not common to orators in
general."

45   XI. Then Crassus replied, " I know very well, Scae- Reply to
vola, that these views of yours are often put forward challenge:
function of
and discussed among the Greeks. For I listened to oratory
their most eminent men, on my arrival in Athens wider—it
requires
as a quaestor from Macedonia, at a time when science,
the Academy was at its best, as was then asserted, and science
requires
with Charmadas, Clitomachus and Aeschines to up- style.
hold it. There was also Metrodorus, who, together
with the others, had been a really diligent disciple
of the illustrious Carneades himself, a speaker who,
for spirited and copious oratory, surpassed, it was
said, all other men. Mnesarchus too was in his
prime, a pupil of your great Panaetius, and Diodorus,
46 who studied under Critolaus the Peripatetic. There
were many others besides, of distinguished fame as
philosophers, by all of whom, with one voice as it
were, I perceived that the orator was driven from
the helm of State, shut out from all learning and
knowledge of more important things, and thrust
down and locked up exclusively in law-courts and
petty little assemblies, as if in a pounding-mill.
47 But I was neither in agreement with these men, nor
with the author and originator of such discussions,
who spoke with far more weight and eloquence than
all of them—I mean Plato—whose *Gorgias* I read
with close attention under Charmadas during those
days at Athens, and what impressed me most deeply
about Plato in that book was, that it was when making

in oratoribus irridendis ipse esse orator summus videbatur. Verbi enim controversia iamdiu torquet
Graeculos homines, contentionis cupidiores quam
48 veritatis. Nam si quis hunc statuit esse oratorem,
qui tantummodo in iure, aut in iudiciis possit, aut
apud populum, aut in senatu copiose loqui, tamen
huic ipsi multa tribuat et concedat necesse est, neque
enim sine multa pertractatione omnium rerum
publicarum, neque sine legum, morum, iuris scientia,
neque natura hominum incognita, ac moribus, in his
ipsis rebus satis callide versari et perite potest. Qui
autem haec cognoverit, sine quibus ne illa quidem
minima in causis quisquam recte tueri potest, quid
huic abesse poterit de maximarum rerum scientia ?
Sin oratoris nihil vis esse, nisi composite, ornate,
copiose eloqui : quaero, id ipsum qui possit assequi
sine ea scientia, quam ei non conceditis ? Dicendi
enim virtus, nisi ei, qui dicit, ea, de quibus dicit,
49 percepta sint, exstare non potest. Quam ob rem, si
ornate locutus est, sicut fertur, et mihi videtur,
physicus ille Democritus : materies illa fuit physici,
de qua dixit ; ornatus vero ipse verborum, oratoris
putandus est. Et, si Plato de rebus a civilibus controversiis remotissimis divinitus est locutus, quod ego
concedo ; si item Aristoteles, si Theophrastus, si

fun of orators that he himself seemed to me to
the consummate orator. In fact controversy about
word has long tormented those Greeklings, fonder a
48 they are of argument than of truth. For, if anyone
lays it down that an orator is a man whose sole power
is that of speaking copiously before the Praetor or
at a trial, or in the public assembly or the Senate-
house, none the less even to an orator thus limited
such critic must grant and allow a number of attributes, inasmuch as without extensive handling of all
public business, without a mastery of ordinances,
customs and general law, without a knowledge of
human nature and character, he cannot engage, with
the requisite cleverness and skill, even in these restricted activities. But to a man who has learned
these things, without which no one can properly
ensure even those primary essentials of advocacy,
can there be anything lacking that belongs to the
knowledge of the highest matters ? If, on the other
hand, you would narrow the idea of oratory to nothing
but the speaking in ordered fashion, gracefully and
copiously, how, I ask, could your orator attain even
so much, if he were to lack that knowledge whereof
you people deny him the possession ? For excellence in
speaking cannot be made manifest unless the speaker
fully comprehends the matter he speaks about.
49 It follows that, if the famous natural philosopher
Democritus spoke with elegance, as he is reported
and appears to me to have spoken, those notable
subjects of his discourse belonged to the natural
philosopher, but his actual elegance of diction must be
put down to the orator. And if Plato spoke with the
voice of a god of things very far away from political
debate, as I allow that he did, if again Aristotle and

Carneades in rebus eis, de quibus disputaverunt, eloquentes, et in dicendo suaves, atque ornati fuerunt : sint hae res, de quibus disputant, in aliis quibusdam studiis ; oratio quidem ipsa propria est huius unius rationis, de qua loquimur et quaerimus. 50 Etenim videmus, eisdem de rebus ieiune quosdam et exiliter, ut eum, quem acutissimum ferunt, Chrysippum, disputavisse, neque ob eam rem philosophiae non satisfecisse, quod non habuerit hanc dicendi ex arte aliena facultatem.

XII. Quid ergo interest ? aut qui discernes eorum, quos nominavi, ubertatem in dicendo et copiam ab eorum exilitate, qui hac dicendi varietate et elegantia non utuntur ? Unum erit profecto, quod ei, qui bene dicunt, afferant proprium : compositam orationem, et ornatam, et artificio quodam et expolitione distinctam. Haec autem oratio, si res non subest ab oratore percepta et cognita, aut nulla sit necesse est, 51 aut omnium irrisione ludatur. Quid est enim tam furiosum, quam verborum, vel optimorum atque ornatissimorum, sonitus inanis, nulla subiecta sententia, nec scientia ? Quidquid erit igitur quacumque ex arte, quocumque de genere, id orator, si, tanquam clientis causam, didicerit, dicet melius et ornatius, quam ille ipse eius rei inventor atque artifex. 52 Nam si quis erit, qui hoc dicat, esse quasdam ora-

Theophrastus and Carneades, on the themes which they treated, were eloquent and displayed charm of style and literary form, then, granting that the topics of their discourse may be found in certain other fields of research, yet their actual style is the peculiar product of this pursuit which we are now discussing and 50 investigating, and of no other. For we see that sundry authorities dealt with these same subjects in spiritless and feeble fashion, Chrysippus for instance, reputed as he is to have been the most acute of disputants, and not to have failed to meet the requirements of philosophy just because he had not acquired this gift of eloquence from an alien art.

XII. " What then is the difference, or by what means will you discriminate between the rich and copious diction of those speakers whom I have mentioned, and the feebleness of such as do not adopt this variety and elegance of language ? The sole distinction will surely be that the good speakers bring, as their peculiar possession, a style that is harmonious, graceful, and marked by a certain artistry and polish. Yet this style, if the underlying subject-matter be not comprehended and mastered by the speaker, must inevitably be of no account or even become the sport 51 of universal derision. For what so effectually proclaims the madman as the hollow thundering of words —be they never so choice and resplendent—which have no thought or knowledge behind them ? Therefore whatever the theme, from whatever art or whatever branch of knowledge it be taken, the orator, just as if he had got up the case for a client, will state it better and more gracefully than the actual discoverer 52 and the specialist. For if anyone is going to affirm that there are certain ideas and subjects which speci-

39

torum proprias sententias atque causas, et certarum
rerum forensibus cancellis circumscriptam scientiam :
fatebor equidem in his magis assidue versari hanc
nostram dictionem ; sed tamen in his ipsis rebus
permulta sunt, quae isti magistri, qui rhetorici vocan-
53 tur, nec tradunt, nec tenent. Quis enim nescit,
maximam vim exsistere oratoris in hominum mentibus vel ad iram, aut ad odium, aut ad dolorem
incitandis, vel ab hisce eisdem permotionibus ad
lenitatem misericordiamque revocandis? Quare, nisi
qui naturas hominum, vimque omnem humanitatis,
causasque eas, quibus mentes aut incitantur, aut
reflectuntur, penitus perspexerit, dicendo, quod
54 volet, perficere non poterit. Atqui totus hic locus
philosophorum proprius videtur ; neque orator, me
auctore, unquam repugnabit : sed, cum illis cognitionem rerum concesserit, quod in ea solum illi
voluerint elaborare ; tractationem orationis, quae
sine illa scientia nulla est, sibi assumet. Hoc enim
est proprium oratoris, quod saepe iam dixi, oratio
gravis, et ornata, et hominum sensibus ac mentibus
accommodata.

55 XIII. Quibus de rebus Aristotelem et Theo-
phrastum scripsisse fateor : sed vide, ne hoc, Scaevola, totum sit a me ; nam ego, quae sunt oratori cum
illis communia, non mutuor ab illis ; isti, quae de his
rebus disputant, oratorum esse concedunt, itaque

ally belong to orators, and certain matters whereof
the knowledge is railed-off behind the barriers of
the Courts, while I will admit that these oratorical
activities of ours are exercised within this area with
less intermission than elsewhere, nevertheless among
these very topics there are points in abundance which
even the so-called professors of rhetoric neither teach
53 nor understand. Who indeed does not know that the
orator's virtue is pre-eminently manifested either in
rousing men's hearts to anger, hatred, or indignation,
or in recalling them from these same passions to mildness and mercy ? Wherefore the speaker will not be
able to achieve what he wants by his words, unless
he has gained profound insight into the characters of
men, and the whole range of human nature, and
those motives whereby our souls are spurred on or
54 turned back. And all this is considered to be the
special province of philosophers, nor will the orator, if
he take my advice, resist their claim ; but when he
has granted their knowledge of these things, since
they have devoted all their labour to that alone, still
he will assert his own claim to the oratorical treatment of them, which without that knowledge of theirs
is nothing at all. For this is the essential concern of
the orator, as I have often said before,—a style that
is dignified and graceful and in conformity with the
general modes of thought and judgement.
55 XIII. " And while I acknowledge that Aristotle and Rhetoric is
Theophrastus have written about all these things, a science.
yet consider, Scaevola, whether it is not wholly in
my favour, that, whereas I do not borrow from them
the things that they share with the orator, they on
their part grant that their discussions on these subjects are the orator's own, and accordingly they

ceteros libros artis isti suae nomine, hos Rhetoricos
56 et inscribunt, et appellant. Etenim cum illi in
dicendo inciderint loci (quod persaepe evenit), ut
de diis immortalibus, de pietate, de concordia, de
amicitia, de communi civium, de hominum, de gentium iure, de aequitate, de temperantia, de magnitudine animi, de omni virtutis genere sit dicendum,
clamabunt, credo, omnia gymnasia, atque omnes
philosophorum scholae, sua haec esse omnia propria ;
nihil omnino ad oratorem pertinere. Quibus ego,
ut de his rebus omnibus in angulis, consumendi
otii causa, disserant, cum concessero, illud tamen
oratori tribuam et dabo, ut eadem, de quibus illi
tenui quodam exsanguique sermone disputant, hic
57 cum omni gravitate et iucunditate explicet. Haec
ego cum ipsis philosophis tum Athenis disserebam,
cogebat enim me M. Marcellus hic noster, qui nunc
aedilis curulis est ; et profecto, nisi ludos nunc
faceret, huic nostro sermoni interesset ; ac iam tum
erat adolescentulus his studiis mirifice deditus.

58 Iam vero de legibus instituendis, de bello, de pace,
de sociis, de vectigalibus, de iure civili generatim
in ordines aetatesque descripto, dicant vel Graeci,
si volunt, Lycurgum, aut Solonem (quanquam illos
quidem censemus in numero eloquentium reponendos)
scisse melius, quam Hyperidem, aut Demosthenem,
perfectos iam homines in dicendo, et perpolitos ;

---

a The ' curule' *aediles* were distinguished from the *aediles
plebis* by their right to use the *sella curulis* and the *toga
praetexta.*

entitle and designate all their other treatises by some name taken from their distinctive art, but these

56 particular books as dealing with Rhetoric. And indeed when, while a man is speaking—as often happens —such commonplaces have cropped up as demand some mention of the immortal gods, of dutifulness, harmony, or friendship, of the rights shared by citizens, by men in general, and by nations, of fair-dealing, moderation or greatness of soul, or virtue of any and every kind, all the academies and schools of philosophy will, I do believe, raise the cry that all these matters are their exclusive province, and in no way whatever the concern of the orator. But when I have allowed that they may debate these subjects in their holes and corners, to pass an idle hour, it is to the orator none the less that I shall entrust and assign the task of developing with complete charm and cogency the same themes which they discuss in a

57 sort of thin and bloodless style. These points I used to argue at Athens with the philosophers in person, under pressure from our friend Marcus Marcellus, who is now Aedile of the Chair,[a] and assuredly, if he were not at this moment producing the Games, would be taking part in our present colloquy ; indeed even in those days of his early youth his devotion to these studies was marvellous.

58 "But now as regards the institution of laws, as regards war and peace, allies and public dues, and the legal rights assigned to classes of citizens according to variations of rank and age, let the Greeks say, if they please, that Lycurgus and Solon (although I hold that they should be rated as eloquent) were better informed than Hyperides or Demosthenes, who were really accomplished and highly polished

Exposition demands both knowledge and style.

vel nostri decemviros, qui Duodecim Tabulas per-
scripserunt, quos necesse est fuisse prudentes, ante-
ponant in hoc genere et Ser. Galbae, et socero tuo
C. Laelio, quos constat dicendi gloria praestitisse.
59 Nunquam enim negabo, esse quasdam artes proprias
eorum, qui in his cognoscendis atque tractandis
studium suum omne posuerunt ; sed oratorem
plenum atque perfectum esse eum dicam, qui de
omnibus rebus possit varie copioseque dicere.

XIV. Etenim saepe in eis causis, quas omnes proprias esse oratorum confitentur, est aliquid, quod non
ex usu forensi, quem solum oratoribus conceditis, sed
ex obscuriore aliqua scientia sit promendum atque
60 sumendum. Quaero enim, num possit aut contra
imperatorem, aut pro imperatore dici sine rei mili-
taris usu, aut saepe etiam sine regionum terrestrium
aut maritimarum scientia ; num apud populum de
legibus iubendis, aut vetandis ; num in Senatu de
omni reipublicae genere dici sine summa rerum
civilium cognitione, et prudentia ; num admoveri
possit oratio ad sensus animorum atque motus vel
inflammandos, vel etiam exstinguendos (quod unum
in oratore dominatur), sine diligentissima pervestigatione earum omnium rationum, quae de naturis hu-
mani generis ac moribus a philosophis explicantur.

61   Atque haud scio, an minus hoc vobis sim proba-

orators ; or let our own folk prefer in this regard the Ten Commissioners—who wrote out the Twelve Tables and were necessarily men of practical wisdom —to Servius Galba and your father-in-law Gaius Laelius, whose outstanding renown for eloquence is
59 established. For never will I say that there are not certain arts belonging exclusively to those who have employed all their energies in the mastery and exercise thereof, but my assertion will be that the complete and finished orator is he who on any matter whatever can speak with fullness and variety.

XIV. "Indeed in handling those causes which everybody acknowledges to be within the exclusive sphere of oratory, there is not seldom something to be brought forth and employed, not from practice in public speaking—the only thing you allow the orator —but from some more abstruse branch of knowledge.
60 I ask, for instance, whether an advocate can either assail or defend a commander-in-chief without experience of the art of war, or sometimes too without knowledge of the various regions of land or sea ? Whether he can address the popular assembly in favour of the passing or rejection of legislative proposals, or the Senate concerning any of the departments of State administration, if he lack consummate knowledge — practical as well as theoretical — of political science ? Whether a speech can be directed to inflaming or even repressing feeling and passion —a faculty of the first importance to the orator— unless the speaker has made a most careful search into all those theories respecting the natural characters and the habits of conduct of mankind, which are unfolded by the philosophers ?

"And I rather think I shall come short of convincing

The orator must know the facts.

45

turus ; equidem non dubitabo, quod sentio, dicere :
physica ista ipsa, et mathematica, et quae paulo ante
ceterarum artium propria posuisti, scientiae sunt
eorum, qui illa profitentur, illustrare autem oratione si quis istas ipsas artes velit, ad oratoris ei
62 confugiendum est facultatem. Neque enim, si Phi-
lonem illum architectum, qui Atheniensibus arma-
mentarium fecit, constat, perdiserte populo rationem
operis sui reddidisse, existimandum est, architecti
potius artificio disertum, quam oratoris, fuisse. Nec,
si huic M. Antonio pro Hermodoro fuisset de navalium
opere dicendum, non, cum ab illo causam didicisset,
ipse ornate de alieno artificio copioseque dixisset.
Neque vero Asclepiades is, quo nos medico amicoque
usi sumus, tum, cum eloquentia vincebat ceteros
medicos, in eo ipso, quod ornate dicebat, medicinae
63 facultate utebatur, non eloquentiae. Atque illud
est probabilius, neque tamen verum, quod Socrates
dicere solebat, omnes in eo, quod scirent, satis esse
eloquentes ; illud verius, neque quemquam in eo
disertum esse posse, quod nesciat ; neque, si id
optime sciat, ignarusque sit faciundae ac poliendae
orationis, diserte id ipsum posse, de quo sciat, dicere.
64   XV. Quam ob rem, si quis universam et propriam
oratoris vim definire complectique vult, is orator erit,
mea sententia, hoc tam gravi dignus nomine, qui,

you on my next point—at all events I will not hesitate Science and philosophy must come to oratory for style. to speak my mind : your natural science itself, your mathematics, and other studies which just now you reckoned as belonging peculiarly to the rest of the arts, do indeed pertain to the knowledge of their professors, yet if anyone should wish by speaking to put these same arts in their full light, it is to oratorical

62 skill that he must run for help. If, again, it is established that Philo, that master-builder who constructed an arsenal for the Athenians, described the plan of his work very eloquently to the people, his eloquence must be ascribed not to his architectural, but rather to his oratorical ability. So too, if Marcus Antonius here had had to speak on behalf of Hermodorus upon the construction of dockyards, having got up his case from his client, he would then have discoursed gracefully and copiously of an art to which he was not a stranger. Asclepiades also, he with whom we have been familiar both as physician and as friend, at the time when he was surpassing the rest of his profession in eloquence, was exhibiting, in such graceful speak-

63 ing, the skill of an orator, not that of a physician. In fact that favourite assertion of Socrates—that every man was eloquent enough upon a subject that he knew—has in it some plausibility but no truth : it is nearer the truth to say that neither can anyone be eloquent upon a subject that is unknown to him, nor, if he knows it perfectly and yet does not know how to shape and polish his style, can he speak fluently even upon that which he does know.

64 XV. " Accordingly, should anyone wish to define in The orator can get up techni- calities, but he must be a comprehensive manner the complete and special meaning of the word, he will be an orator, in my opinion worthy of so dignified a title, who, whatever

quaecumque res inciderit, quae sit dictione expli-
canda, prudenter, et composite, et ornate, et memoriter dicat, cum quadam etiam actionis dignitate.

65 Sin cuipiam nimis infinitum vidêtur quod ita posui,
'quacumque de re,' licet hinc, quantum cuique videbitur, circumcidat atque amputet : tamen illud te-
nebo, si, quae ceteris in artibus aut studiis sita sunt,
orator ignoret, tantumque ea teneat, quae sint in
disceptationibus, atque in usu forensi ; tamen his de
rebus ipsis si sit ei dicendum, cum cognoverit ab eis,
qui tenent, quae sint in quaque re, multo oratorem
melius, quam ipsos illos, quorum eae sunt artes, esse

66 dicturum.   Ita si de re militari dicendum huic erit
Sulpicio, quaeret a C. Mario affini nostro, et, cum
acceperit, ita pronuntiabit, ut ipsi C. Mario paene
hic melius, quam ipse, illa scire videatur ; sin de iure
civili, tecum communicabit, teque hominem pru-
dentissimum et peritissimum in eis ipsis rebus, quas

67 abs te didicerit, dicendi arte superabit.   Sin quae
res inciderit, in qua de natura, de vitiis hominum,
de cupiditatibus, de modo, de continentia, de dolore,
de morte dicendum sit ; forsitan, si ei sit visum (etsi
haec quidem nosse debet orator), cum Sex. Pompeio,
erudito homine in philosophia, communicarit ; hoc
profecto efficiet, ut, quamcumque rem a quoque

the topic that crops up to be unfolded in discourse, versed in
will speak thereon with knowledge, method, charm political
and retentive memory, combining with these qualifica- and moral
35 tions a certain distinction of bearing. If however science.
someone considers my expression ' whatever the
topic ' to be altogether too extensive, he may clip
and prune it to his individual taste, but to this much
I shall hold fast—though the orator be ignorant of
what is to be found in all the other arts and branches
of study, and know only what is dealt with in debate
and the practice of public-speaking ; none the less,
if he should have to discourse even on these other
subjects, then after learning the technicalities of each
from those who know the same, the orator will speak
about them far better than even the men who are
6 masters of these arts. For example, should our
friend Sulpicius here have to speak upon the art of
war, he will inquire of our relative Gaius Marius, and
when he has received his teachings, will deliver himself in such fashion as to seem even to Gaius Marius
to be almost better informed on the subject than
Gaius Marius himself ; while if his topic is to be the
law of private rights, he will consult yourself and,
notwithstanding your consummate learning and
skill in these very things which you have taught him,
7 he will surpass you in the art of exposition. If again
some matter should confront him wherein he must
speak of human nature, human vices or the passions,
of moderation or self-control, of sorrow or death, then
perhaps if he thinks fit—although an orator must have
knowledge of such things—he will have taken counsel
with Sextus Pompeius, a man accomplished in moral
science ; so much he will assuredly achieve, that
whatever his subject and whoever his instructor, on

cognorit, de ea multo dicat ornatius, quam ille ipse,
68 unde cognorit. Sed si me audierit, quoniam philosophia in tres partes est tributa, in naturae obscuritatem, in disserendi subtilitatem, in vitam atque
mores ; duo illa relinquamus, idque largiamur inertiae nostrae : tertium vero, quod semper oratoris
fuit, nisi tenebimus, nihil oratori, in quo magnus esse
69 possit, relinquemus. Quare hic locus de vita et
moribus totus est oratori perdiscendus : cetera si non
didicerit, tamen poterit, si quando opus erit, ornare
dicendo, si modo erunt ad eum delata, et tradita.

XVI. Etenim si constat inter doctos, hominem
ignarum astrologiae, Aratum ornatissimis atque optimis versibus, de coelo stellisque dixisse ; si de rebus
rusticis hominem ab agro remotissimum, Nicandrum
Colophonium, poetica quadam facultate, non rustica,
scripsisse praeclare : quid est, cur non orator de
rebus eis eloquentissime dicat, quas ad certam
70 causam tempusque cognorit ? Est enim finitimus
oratori poeta, numeris astrictior paulo, verborum
autem licentia liberior, multis vero ornandi generibus
socius, ac paene par ; in hoc quidem certe prope
idem, nullis ut terminis circumscribat aut definiat

that subject he will express himself far more grace-
68 fully than his master himself. Nevertheless, if he
will listen to me, since philosophy is divided into
three branches, which respectively deal with the
mysteries of nature, with the subtleties of dialectic,
and with human life and conduct, let us quit claim
to the first two, by way of concession to our indolence,
but unless we keep our hold on the third, which has
ever been the orator's province, we shall leave the
69 orator no sphere wherein to attain greatness. For
which reason this division of philosophy, concerned
with human life and manners, must all of it be
mastered by the orator ; as for the other matters,
even though he has not studied them, he will still be
able, whenever the necessity arises, to beautify them
by his eloquence, if only they are brought to his
notice and described to him.

XVI. " Indeed if it is agreed in learned circles that
a man who knew no astronomy—Aratus to wit—has
sung of the heavenly spaces and the stars in verse of
consummate finish and excellence, and that another
who was a complete stranger to country life, Nicander
of Colophon, has written with distinction on rural
affairs, using something of a poet's skill and not that
of a farmer, what reason is there why an orator
should not discourse most eloquently concerning
those subjects which he has conned for a specific
70 argument and occasion ? The truth is that the poet
is a very near kinsman of the orator, rather more
heavily fettered as regards rhythm, but with ampler
freedom in his choice of words, while in the use of
many sorts of ornament he is his ally and almost his
counterpart ; in one respect at all events something
like identity exists, since he sets no boundaries or

The orator, like the poet, needs a wide education.

51

ius suum, quo minus ei liceat eadem illa facultate et
71 copia vagari, qua velit. Namque quod illud, Scaevola, negasti te fuisse laturum, nisi in meo regno
esses, quod in omni genere sermonis, in omni parte
humanitatis dixerim oratorem perfectum esse debere,
nunquam mehercule hoc dicerem, si eum, quem fin-
72 go, me ipsum esse arbitrarer. Sed, ut solebat C. Lucilius saepe dicere, homo tibi subiratus, mihi propter
eam ipsam causam minus, quam volebat, familiaris,
sed tamen et doctus, et perurbanus, sic sentio, neminem esse in oratorum numero habendum, qui non
sit omnibus eis artibus, quae sunt libero dignae, per-
politus; quibus ipsis, si in dicendo non utimur,
tamen apparet atque exstat, utrum simus earum
73 rudes, an didicerimus. Ut, qui pila ludunt, non
utuntur in ipsa lusione artificio proprio palaestrae,
sed indicat ipse motus, didicerintne palaestram, an
nesciant; et qui aliquid fingunt, et si tum pictura
nihil utuntur, tamen, utrum sciant pingere, an
nesciant, non obscurum est: sic in orationibus hisce
ipsis iudiciorum, concionum, Senatus, etiamsi proprie
ceterae non adhibentur artes, tamen facile declaratur,
utrum is, qui dicat, tantummodo in hoc declamatorio

limits to his claims, such as would prevent him
from ranging whither he will with the same free-
71 dom and licence as the other. For with regard
to your remark, Scaevola, that, had you not been
in my domain, you would not have endured my
assertion that the orator must be accomplished
in every kind of discourse and in every department of culture, I should certainly never have
made that assertion, did I consider myself to be
72 the man I am endeavouring to portray. But, as
was often said by Gaius Lucilius—who was not
altogether pleased with you, and for that very reason
less intimate with myself than he wished, but for all
that an instructed critic and thorough gentleman of
the city—my opinion is this, that no one should be
numbered with the orators who is not accomplished
in all those arts that befit the well-bred ; for though
we do not actually parade these in our discourse, it
is none the less made clear to demonstration whether
we are strangers to them or have learned to know
73 them. Just as ball-players do not in their game
itself employ the characteristic dexterity of the
gymnasium, and yet their very movements show
whether they have had such training or know nothing
of that art ; and, just as, in the case of those who are
portraying anything, even though at the moment
they are making no use of the painter's art, there is
none the less no difficulty in seeing whether or not
they know how to paint ; even so is it with these
same speeches in the Courts, the popular assembly
and the Senate-house—granting that the other arts
may not be specially brought into play, still it is made
easily discernible whether the speaker has merely
floundered about in this declamatory business or

sit opere iactatus, an ad dicendum omnibus ingenuis
artibus instructus accesserit.

74   XVII. Tum ridens Scaevola : Non luctabor, inquit,
tecum, Crasse, amplius.   Id enim ipsum, quod contra
me locutus es, artificio quodam es consecutus, ut et
mihi, quae ego vellem non esse oratoris, concederes ;
et ea ipsa, nescio quomodo, rursus detorqueres, atque
75 oratori propria traderes.   Haec, cum ego praetor
Rhodum venissem, et cum summo illo doctore istius
disciplinae Apollonio, ea, quae a Panaetio acceperam,
contulissem : irrisit ille quidem, ut solebat, philosophiam, atque contempsit, multaque non tam graviter
dixit, quam facete, tua autem fuit oratio eiusmodi,
non ut ullam artem doctrinamve contemneres, sed
ut omnes comites ac ministras oratoris esse diceres.
76 Quas ego, si quis sit unus complexus omnes, idemque
si ad eas facultatem istam ornatissimae orationis
adiunxerit ; non possum dicere, eum non egregium
quemdam hominem atque admirandum fore, sed is,
si quis esset, aut si etiam unquam fuisset, aut vero
si esse posset, tu esses unus profecto ; qui et meo
iudicio, et omnium, vix ullam ceteris oratoribus
77 (pace horum dixerim) laudem reliquisti.   Verum si
tibi ipsi nihil deest, quod in forensibus rebus, civi-
libusque versetur, quin scias, neque eam tamen
scientiam, quam adiungis oratori, complexus es ;

whether, before approaching his task of oratory, he has been trained in all the liberal arts."

74 XVII. At this point Scaevola smilingly declared : The position challenged; "Crassus, I will strive with you no longer. For, in this very speech you have made against me, you have by some trick so managed matters as both to grant me what I said did not belong to the orator, and then somehow or another to wrest away these things again and hand them over to the orator as his absolute 75 property. And as regards these subjects, when on my arrival in Rhodes as praetor I discussed with Apollonius, that supreme master of this science of rhetoric, the things that I had learned from Panaetius, he as usual jeered at philosophy and expressed contempt for it and talked at large in a vein more graceful than serious ; whereas your argument has been of such a kind that you not only refrained from despising any of the arts or sciences, but described them all as the attendants and handmaids of oratory. 76 And for my own part, if ever any one man should have mastered all of them, and that same man should have united with them this added power of perfectly graceful expression, I cannot deny that he would be a remarkable kind of man and worthy of admiration ; but if such a one there should be, or indeed ever has been, or really ever could be, assuredly you would be that one man, who both in my opinion and in that of everyone else, have left all other orators— if they will pardon my saying so—almost without 77 glory. But if you yourself, while lacking nothing of the knowledge that has to do with law-court speaking and politics, have nevertheless not mastered the further learning which you associate with the orator, let us see whether you may not be

55

videamus, ne plus ei tribuas, quam res et veritas ipsa
concedat.

78 Hic Crassus : Memento, inquit, me non de mea,
sed de oratoris facultate dixisse. Quid enim nos aut
didicimus, aut scire potuimus, qui ante ad agendum,
quam ad cognoscendum venimus ; quos in foro, quos
in ambitione, quos in republica, quos in amicorum
negotiis, res ipsa ante confecit, quam possemus aliquid
79 de rebus tantis suspicari ? Quod si tibi tantum in
nobis videtur esse, quibus etiamsi ingenium, ut tu
putas, non maxime defuit, doctrina certe, et otium,
et hercule etiam studium illud discendi acerrimum
defuit : quid censes, si ad alicuius ingenium vel
maius illa, quae ego non attigi, accesserint ? qualem
illum, et quantum oratorem futurum ?

80 XVIII. Tum Antonius : Probas mihi, inquit, ista,
Crasse, quae dicis ; nec dubito, quin multo locupletior
in dicendo futurus sit, si quis omnium rerum atque
81 artium rationem naturamque comprehenderit. Sed
primum id difficile est factu, praesertim in hac nostra
vita, nostrisque occupationibus ; deinde illud etiam
verendum est, ne abstrahamur ab hac exercitatione,
et consuetudine dicendi populari, et forensi. Aliud
enim mihi quoddam genus orationis esse videtur
eorum hominum, de quibus paulo ante dixisti, quamvis
illi ornate et graviter, aut de natura rerum, aut de
humanis rebus loquantur : nitidum quoddam genus

attributing to him more than the real facts of the case allow."

78 Here Crassus interposed : " Remember that I have but not been speaking of my own skill, but of that of an orator. For what have men like myself either learned or had any chance of knowing, who entered upon practice before ever we reached the study of theory, whom our professional activities in public speaking, in the pursuit of office, in politics, and about the affairs of our friends, wore out ere we could form any conception of the importance of these 79 other matters ? But if you find such excellence in me who, if perhaps—as you hold—I have not been completely wanting in ability, have assuredly been wanting in learning and leisure and (to tell the truth) in the requisite enthusiasm for instruction as well, what think you would be the quality and stature of an orator in whom all that I have not attained should be combined with ability such as my own or greater ? "

but defended as an ideal.

80 XVIII. Thereupon Antonius observed : " Crassus, to my mind you establish your case, and I do not doubt that, if a man has grasped the principles and nature of every subject and of every art, he will in consequence be far better equipped as a speaker. 81 But in the first place such knowledge is hard to win, especially in the life we lead, and amid the engagements that are ours, and then again there is the danger of our being led away from our traditional practice of speaking in a style acceptable to the commonalty and suited to advocacy. For it seems to me that the eloquence of these men, to whom you referred just now, is of an entirely different kind, albeit they speak gracefully and cogently, either upon natural philosophy or upon the affairs of mankind:

This ideal again challenged as unpractical and unattainable.

est verborum et laetum, sed palaestrae magis et olei,
82 quam huius civilis turbae ac fori. Namque egomet,
qui sero, ac leviter Graecas litteras attigissem, tamen
cum pro consule in Ciliciam proficiscens Athenas
venissem, complures tum ibi dies sum propter navi-
gandi difficultatem commoratus : sed, cum quotidie
mecum haberem homines doctissimos, eos fere ipsos,
qui abs te modo sunt nominati, cumque hoc, nescio
quomodo, apud eos increbruisset, me in causis maioribus, sicuti te, solere versari, pro se quisque ut
poterat, de officio et ratione oratoris disputabat.

83 Horum alii, sicut iste ipse Mnesarchus, hos, quos
nos oratores vocaremus, nihil esse dicebat, nisi
quosdam operarios, lingua celeri et exercitata ;
oratorem autem, nisi qui sapiens esset, esse neminem ;
atque ipsam eloquentiam, quod ex bene dicendi
scientia constaret, unam quamdam esse virtutem, et
qui unam virtutem haberet, omnes habere, easque
esse inter se aequales et pares : ita, qui esset
eloquens, eum virtutes omnes habere, atque esse
sapientem. Sed haec erat spinosa quaedam et exilis
oratio, longeque a nostris sensibus abhorrebat.
84 Charmadas vero multo uberius eisdem de rebus
loquebatur : non quo aperiret sententiam suam ; hic
enim mos erat patrius Academiae, adversari semper
omnibus in disputando ; sed cum maxime tamen
hoc significabat, eos, qui rhetores nominarentur, et

---

^a Mnesarchus represents the Stoics, whose fundamental
doctrine of the unity and coequality of all virtues implies
that the philosopher alone can be an orator.

theirs is a polished and flowery sort of diction, redolent rather of the training-school and its suppling-oil 82 than of our political hurly-burly and of the Bar. For —when I think of it—although it was late in life and only lightly that I came into touch with Greek literature, still, when on my journey to Cilicia as proconsul I reached Athens, I tarried there for several days by reason of the difficulty in putting to sea : at any rate, as I had about me daily the most learned men, pretty nearly the same as those whom you have lately mentioned, a rumour having somehow spread among them that I, just like yourself, was usually engaged in the more important causes, every one of them in his turn contributed what he could to a discussion on the function and method of an orator.

83   " Some of them were for maintaining, as did your authority Mnesarchus[a] himself, that those whom we called orators were nothing but a sort of artisans with ready and practised tongues, whereas no one was an orator save the wise man only, and that eloquence itself, being, as it was, the science of speaking well, was one type of virtue, and he who possessed a single virtue possessed all of them, and the virtues were of the same rank and equal one with another, from which it followed that the man of eloquence had every virtue and was a wise man. But this was a thorny and dry sort of language, and entirely out of harmony 84 with anything we thought. Charmadas, however, would speak far more copiously upon the same topics, not that he intended thereby to reveal his own opinion, —it being an accepted tradition of the Academy always and against all comers to be of the opposition in debate—just then, however, he was pointing out that those who were styled rhetoricians and pro-

qui dicendi praecepta traderent, nihil plane tenere,
neque posse quemquam facultatem assequi dicendi,
nisi qui philosophorum inventa didicisset.

85 XIX. Disputabant contra diserti homines, Athenienses, et in republica causisque versati, in quis erat
etiam is, qui nuper Romae fuit, Menedemus, hospes
meus; qui cum diceret esse quamdam prudentiam,
quae versaretur in perspiciendis rationibus constituen-
darum et regendarum rerum publicarum, excitabatur
homo promptus atque omni abundans doctrina, et
quadam incredibili varietate rerum et copia. Omnes
enim partes illius ipsius prudentiae petendas esse a
philosophia dicebat, neque ea, quae statuerentur in
republica dc diis immortalibus, de disciplina iuven-
tutis, de iustitia, de patientia, de temperantia, de
modo rerum omnium, ceteraque, sine quibus civitates
aut esse, aut bene moratae esse non possent, usquam
86 in eorum inveniri libellis. Quod si tantam vim rerum
maximarum arte sua rhetorici illi doctores complecte-
rentur, quaerebat, cur de prooemiis, et de epilogis, et
de huiusmodi nugis (sic enim appellabat) referti
essent eorum libri; de civitatibus instituendis, de
scribendis legibus, de aequitate, de iustitia, de fide,
de frangendis cupiditatibus, de conformandis hominum moribus, littera in eorum libris nulla inveni-
87 retur? Ipsa vero praecepta sic illudere solebat, ut
ostenderet, non modo eos illius expertes esse pru-

---

^a Charmadas of the Academy.

pounded rules of eloquence, had no clear compre-
hension of anything, and that no man could attain
skill in speaking unless he had studied the discoveries
of the philosophers.

85   XIX. " Certain Athenians, accomplished speakers
and experienced in politics and at the Bar, argued on
the other side, among them too being that Menedemus, who was lately in Rome as my guest ; and
when he asserted that there was a special sort of
wisdom, which had to do with investigating the principles of founding and governing political communities,
this roused up a man of quick temper [a] and full to over-
flowing of learning of every kind and a really incredible diversity and multiplicity of facts.   For he
proceeded to inform us that every part of this same
wisdom had to be sought from philosophy, nor were
those institutions in a State which dealt with the immortal gods, the training of youth, justice, endurance,
self-control, or moderation in all things, or the other
principles without which States could not exist or at
any rate be well-conditioned, to be met with any-
86 where in the paltry treatises of rhetoricians.   Whereas, if those teachers of rhetoric embraced within their
art so vast a multitude of the noblest themes, how
was it, he inquired, that their books were stuffed full
of maxims relating to prefaces, perorations and similar
trumpery—for so did he describe them—while concerning the organization of States, or the drafting of
laws, or on the topics of fair-dealing, justice, loyalty,
or the subduing of the passions or the building of
human character, not a syllable was to be found in
87 their pages ?   But as for their actual rules he would
scoff at them by showing that not only were their
authors devoid of that wisdom which they arrogated

Report of
debate at
Athens :
is there a
science of
rhetoric,
or does
oratory
depend on
aptitude
and
practice?

61

dentiae, quam sibi adsciscerent, sed ne hanc quidem ipsam dicendi rationem ac viam nosse. Caput enim esse arbitrabatur oratoris, ut et ipsis, apud quos ageret, talis, qualem se ipse optaret, videretur ; id fieri vitae dignitate, de qua nihil rhetorici isti doctores in praeceptis suis reliquissent : et uti eorum, qui audirent, sic afficerentur animi, ut eos affici vellet orator ; quod item fieri nullo modo posse, nisi cognosceret is, qui diceret, quot modis hominum mentes, et quibus rebus, et quo genere orationis in quamque partem moverentur ; haec autem esse penitus in media philosophia retrusa atque abdita ; quae isti rhetores ne primoribus quidem labris at-

88 tigissent. Ea Menedemus exemplis magis, quam argumentis, conabatur refellere : memoriter enim multa ex orationibus Demosthenis praeclare scripta pronuntians, docebat, illum in animis vel iudicum, vel populi, in omnem partem dicendo permovendis, non fuisse ignarum, quibus ea rebus consequeretur, quae negaret ille sine philosophia quemquam scire posse.

89 XX. Huic ille respondebat, non se negare, Demosthenem summam prudentiam summamque vim habuisse dicendi ; sed sive ille hoc ingenio potuisset, sive, id quod constaret, Platonis studiosus audiendi fuisset ; non, quid ille potuisset, sed quid isti

to themselves, but they were ignorant even of the true principles and methods of eloquence. For he was of opinion that the main object of the orator was that he should both appear himself, to those before whom he was pleading, to be such a man as he would desire to seem (an end to be attained by a reputable mode of life, as to which those teachers of rhetoric had left no hint among their instructions), and that the hearts of his hearers should be touched in such fashion as the orator would have them touched (another purpose only to be achieved by a speaker who had investigated all the ways wherein, and all the allurements and kind of diction whereby, the judgement of men might be inclined to this side or to that) ; but according to him such knowledge lay thrust away and buried deep in the very heart of philosophy, and those rhetoricians had not so much as tasted it with the

88 tip of the tongue. These assertions Menedemus would strive to disprove by quoting instances rather than by arguments, for, while reciting from his ready recollection many magnificent passages from the speeches of Demosthenes, he would demonstrate how that orator, when by his eloquence he was compelling the passions of the judges or of the people to take any direction he chose, knew well enough by what means to attain results which Charmadas would say that no one could compass without the aid of philosophy.

89 XX. " To this Charmadas replied that he did not deny to Demosthenes the possession of consummate wisdom and the highest power of eloquence, but whether Demosthenes owed this ability to natural talent or, as was generally agreed, had been a devoted disciple of Plato, the present question was not what Demosthenes could do, but what those

90 docerent, esse quaerendum. Saepe etiam in eam
partem ferebatur oratione, ut omnino disputaret,
nullam artem esse dicendi : idque cum argumentis
docuerat, quod ita nati essemus, ut et blandiri, et
suppliciter insinuare eis, a quibus esset petendum,
et adversarios minaciter terrere possemus, et rem
gestam exponere, et id, quod intenderemus, confirmare, et id, quod contra diceretur, refellere, et ad
extremum deprecari aliquid, et conqueri ; quibus in
rebus omnis oratorum versaretur facultas ; et quod
consuetudo exercitatioque et intellegendi prudentiam
acueret, et eloquendi celeritatem incitaret : tum
91 etiam exemplorum copia nitebatur. Nam primum,
quasi dedita opera, neminem scriptorem artis ne
mediocriter quidem disertum fuisse dicebat, cum
repeteret usque a Corace nescio quo, et Tisia, quos
artis illius inventores et principes fuisse constaret ;
eloquentissimos autem homines, qui ista nec didicissent, nec omnino scire curassent, innumerabiles
quosdam nominabat ; in quibus etiam (sive ille
irridens, sive quod ita putaret, atque ita audisset),
me in illo numero, qui illa non didicissem, et tamen
(ut ipse dicebat) possem aliquid in dicendo, profere-
bat. Quorum illi alterum facile assentiebar, nihil
me didicisse ; in altero autem me illudi ab eo, aut

---

^a For Corax and Tisias see Index. By using the words
nescio quo Antonius affects ignorance of literary history.

rhetoricians were teaching. More than once too he was carried so far away by his discourse as to argue that there was no such thing as an art of eloquence ; and after showing this by arguments—because, as he said, we were born with an aptitude alike for coaxing and unctuously stealing into favour with those from whom a boon had to be sought, and for daunting our antagonists by threats, for setting forth how a deed was done, and establishing our own charges and disproving the allegations of the other side, and for making, in the closing words of a speech, some use of protest and lamentation (in which operations he declared that every resource of the orator was brought into play), and because habit and practice sharpened the edge of discernment and quickened the fluency of delivery, then he would also support his case by an abundance of instances. For in the first place (he would say) not a single writer on rhetoric—it looked as if of set purpose—had been even moderately eloquent, and he searched all the way back to the days of one Corax[a] and a certain Tisias who, he stated, were acknowledged to have been the founders and first practitioners of this art, while on the other hand he would cite a countless host of very eloquent men who had never learned these rules or been at all anxious to make their acquaintance ; and among these—whether in jest or because he thought so and had even so heard —he went on to mention me in the list, as one who had never studied those matters and yet (according to him) had some ability in oratory. To one of these points of his—that I had never learned anything—I readily agreed, but as to the other I considered that he was either making game of me or was even himself

92 etiam ipsum errare arbitrabar. Artem vero negabat
esse ullam, nisi quae cognitis, penitusque perspectis,
et in unum exitum spectantibus, et nunquam
fallentibus rebus contineretur ; haec autem omnia,
quae tractarentur ab oratoribus, dubia esse et
incerta ; cum et dicerentur ab eis, qui ea omnia
non plane tenerent, et audirentur ab eis, quibus non
scientia esset tradenda, sed exigui temporis aut falsa,
93 aut certe obscura opinio. Quid multa ? sic mihi
tum persuadere videbatur, neque artificium ullum
esse dicendi, neque quemquam posse, nisi qui illa,
quae a doctissimis hominibus in philosophia dicerentur, cognosset, aut callide aut copiose dicere. In
quibus dicere Charmadas solebat, ingenium tuum,
Crasse, vehementer admirans, me sibi perfacilem in
audiendo, te perpugnacem in disputando esse visum.

94 XXI. Tumque ego, hac eadem opinione adductus,
scripsi etiam illud quodam in libello, qui me im-
prudente et invito excidit, et pervenit in manus
hominum, disertos me cognosse nonnullos, eloquentem adhuc neminem : quod eum statuebam disertum,
qui posset satis acute, atque dilucide, apud mediocres
homines ex communi quadam opinione dicere ; eloquentem vero, qui mirabilius et magnificentius augere
posset atque ornare, quae vellet, omnesque omnium
rerum, quae ad dicendum pertinerent, fontes animo
ac memoria contineret. Id si est difficile nobis, qui

92 mistaken. He said, however, that there was no
' art ' which did not consist in the knowledge and
clear perception of facts, all tending to a single conclusion and incapable of misleading ; but everything
with which orators dealt was doubtful and uncertain,
since all the talking was done by men who had no real
grasp of their subject, and all the listening by hearers
who were not to have knowledge conveyed to them,
but some short-lived opinion that was either untrue
93 or at least not clear.   In a word, he then looked like
persuading me that no craft of oratory existed, and
that no one could speak with address or copiously
unless he had mastered the philosophical teachings
of the most learned men.   And in these discussions
Charmadas was wont to speak with warm admiration
of your talents, Crassus, explaining that he found in
me a very ready listener, in yourself a most doughty
antagonist.

94   XXI. " And so, won over by these same views, I *Real
actually wrote down in a little pamphlet—which eloquence
slipped abroad without my knowledge or consent and unknown.*
got into the hands of the public—the statement that
I had known sundry accomplished speakers, but no
one so far who was eloquent, inasmuch as I held anyone to be an accomplished speaker who could deliver
his thought with the necessary point and clearness
before an everyday audience, and in accord with what
I might call the mental outlook of the average human
being, whereas I allowed the possession of eloquence
to that man only who was able, in a style more
admirable and more splendid, to amplify and adorn
any subject he chose, and whose mind and memory
encompassed all the sources of everything that concerned oratory.   If this is a hard matter for ourselves,

67

ante quam ad discendum ingressi sumus, obruimur
ambitione et foro ; sit tamen in re positum atque
95 natura. Ego enim, quantum auguror coniectura,
quantaque ingenia in nostris hominibus esse video,
non despero fore aliquem aliquando, qui et studio
acriore, quam nos sumus atque fuimus, et otio ac
facultate discendi maiore ac maturiore, et labore
atque industria superiore, cum se ad audiendum,
legendum, scribendumque dediderit, exsistat talis
orator, qualem quaerimus ; qui iure non solum
disertus, sed etiam eloquens dici possit : qui tamen,
mca sententia, aut hic est iam Crassus, aut, si quis
pari fuerit ingenio pluraque quam hic et audierit
et lectitarit et scripserit, paulum huic aliquid poterit
addere.

96   Hoc loco Sulpicius : Insperanti mihi, inquit, et
Cottae, sed valde optanti utrique nostrum, cecidit,
ut in istum sermonem, Crasse, delaberemini. Nobis
enim huc venientibus iucundum satis fore videbatur,
si, cum vos de rebus aliis loqueremini, tamen nos
aliquid ex sermone vestro memoria dignum excipere
possemus : ut vero penitus in eam ipsam totius huius
vel studii, vel artificii, vel facultatis disputationem
paene intimam perveniretis, vix optandum nobis
97 videbatur. Ego enim, qui ab ineunte aetate in-
census essem studio utriusque vestrum, Crassi vero

because, before we have entered on the required study, we are overwhelmed by the hunt for office and the business of the Bar, none the less let it be accepted
95 as attainable in fact and in the nature of things. For personally, so far as I can form a prediction, and judging from the vast supply of talent which I see existent among our fellow-citizens, I do not despair of its coming to pass that some day some one, keener in study than we are or ever have been, endowed with ampler leisure and earlier opportunity for learning, and exhibiting closer application and more intensive industry, who shall have given himself up to listening, reading and writing, will stand forth as an orator such as we are seeking, who may rightly be called not merely accomplished but actually eloquent ; and after all, to my mind either Crassus is such a man already, or, should some one of equal natural ability have heard, read and written more than Crassus, he will only be able to improve to some slight extent upon him."

96 At this point, " We never looked for it," exclaimed Sulpicius, " but it has fallen out, Crassus, just as both I and Cotta earnestly hoped, I mean that you two should slip into this particular conversation. For on our way hither we were thinking that it would be delightful enough if, while you and Antonius were talking about anything else, we might still manage to catch from your discourse something worth remembering ; but that you should enter at large upon so real and wellnigh exhaustive a discussion of this whole matter—be it practice, art or natural talent—
97 seemed to us a thing we could hardly hope for. The fact is that I, who from my earliest manhood was aglow with enthusiasm for you both, and a positive

Crassus reluctantly consents to give his views.

69

etiam amore, cum ab eo nusquam discederem,
verbum ex eo nunquam elicere potui de vi ac ratione
dicendi, cum et per memet ipsum egissem, et per
Drusum saepe tentassem : quo in genere tu, Antoni,
(vere loquar) nunquam mihi percunctanti, aut quaerenti aliquid, defuisti, et persaepe me, quae soleres
98 in dicendo observare, docuisti.   Nunc quoniam
uterque vestrum patefecit earum rerum ipsarum
aditum, quas quaerimus, et quoniam princeps Crassus
eius sermonis ordiendi fuit, date nobis hanc veniam,
ut ea, quae sentitis de omni genere dicendi, subtiliter
persequamini.   Quod quidem si erit a vobis impetra-
tum, magnam habebo, Crasse, huic palaestrae et
Tusculano tuo gratiam, et longe Academiae illi ac
Lycio tuum hoc suburbanum gymnasium anteponam.

99   XXII. Tum ille : Immo vero, inquit, Sulpici, roge-
mus Antonium, qui et potest facere id, quod requiris,
et consuevit, ut te audio dicere.   Nam me quidem
fateor semper a genere hoc toto sermonis refugisse,
et tibi cupienti atque instanti saepissime negasse, ut
tute paulo ante dixisti.   Quod ego non superbia,
neque inhumanitate faciebam, neque quo tuo studio
rectissimo atque optimo non obsequi vellem, praesertim cum te unum ex omnibus ad dicendum
maxime natum, aptumque cognossem, sed mehercule

devotion to Crassus—seeing that on no occasion did
I leave his side—could never get a word out of him
respecting the nature and theory of eloquence,
although I pleaded in person, besides making frequent trial of him through the agency of Drusus,
whereas on this subject you, Antonius,—and what I
shall say is true—have never failed me at all in my
probings or interrogatories, and have many a time
explained to me what rules you were wont to
observe in practical oratory. Now then that each
of you has opened up a way of reaching these
very objects of our quest, and since it was Crassus
who led off in this discussion, grant us the favour
of recounting with exactness of detail, your respective opinions upon every branch of oratory.
If we do win this boon from you both, I shall be
deeply grateful, Crassus, to this school in your
Tusculan villa, and shall rank these semi-rural
training-quarters of yours far above the illustrious
Academy and the Lyceum."

XXII. Thereupon the other rejoined, "Nay,
Sulpicius, but let us rather ask Antonius, who both
has the ability to do what you demand, and, as I
understand you to say, has been in the habit of so
doing. For as for me, you yourself have just told us
how I have invariably run away from all discussions
of this sort, and time and again have refused com-
pliance with your desire and indeed your importunity.
This I used to do, not from arrogance or churlishness,
nor because I was unwilling to gratify your entirely
legitimate and admirable keenness—the more so as
I had recognized that you were above all other men
eminently endowed by nature and adapted for oratory
—but in solemn truth it was from want of familiarity

istius disputationis insolentia, atque earum rerum,
quae quasi in arte traduntur, inscitia.

100 Tum Cotta : Quoniam id, quod difficillimum
nobis videbatur, ut omnino de his rebus, Crasse,
loquerere, assecuti sumus ; de reliquo iam nostra
culpa fuerit, si te, nisi omnia, quae percunctati
101 erimus, explicaris, dimiserimus. De his, credo,
rebus, inquit Crassus, ut in cretionibus scribi solet,
Quibus sciam, poteroque. Tum ille : Namque quod
tu non poteris, aut nescies, quis nostrum tam impudens est, qui se scire aut posse postulet ? Iam
vero, ista conditione, dum mihi liceat negare posse,
quod non potero, et fateri nescire quod nesciam, licet,
inquit Crassus, vestro arbitratu percunctemini.
102 Atque, inquit Sulpicius, hoc primum ex te, de quo
modo Antonius exposuit, quid sentias, quaerimus :
existimesne artem aliquam esse dicendi ? Quid ?
mihi nunc vos, inquit Crassus, tanquam alicui Grae-
culo otioso et loquaci, et fortasse docto atque erudito,
quaestiunculam, de qua meo arbitratu loquar,
ponitis ? Quando enim me ista curasse aut cogitasse
arbitramini, et non semper irrisisse potius eorum
hominum impudentiam, qui cum in schola assedis-
sent, ex magna hominum frequentia dicere iuberent,
103 si quis quid quaereret ? Quod primum ferunt
Leontinum fecisse Gorgiam : qui permagnum quid-

---

a For the use of the diminutive to indicate the contempt
felt at Rome for the degenerate Greek of the day *cf.* §§ 47,
221, and Juvenal iii. 78 *Graeculus esuriens.*

with arguments of that kind, and awkwardness in handling those theories set forth in what claims to be an art."

100 Cotta then observed, " Since we have secured what seemed most difficult—that you, Crassus, should say anything at all about these matters—as for what remains, it will now be our own fault if we let you go without explaining to us all that we have been in-

101 quiring about." " Limiting the inquiry, I imagine," answered Crassus, " to those subjects which, as the phrase goes in accepting an inheritance, are within my knowledge and power." " By all means," re-turned Cotta, " for what is beyond your own power or knowledge, who among us is so shameless as to claim to be within his own ? " " In that case," replied Crassus, " provided that I may disclaim powers which I do not possess, and admit ignorance of what I do not know,—put what questions to me

102 you please." " Well then," said Sulpicius, " what we ask you to tell us first is your opinion of the view Antonius advanced just now—whether you hold that there is any such thing as an ' art ' of oratory ? " " How now ? " exclaimed Crassus, " Do you think I am some idle talkative Greekling,[a] who is also perhaps full of learning and erudition, that you propound me a petty question on which to talk as I will ? For when was it, think you, that I troubled myself about these matters or reflected upon them, and did not rather always laugh to scorn the effrontery of those persons who, from their chairs in the schools, would call upon any man in the crowded assemblage to propound any question that he might have to put ?

103 It is related that Gorgias of Leontini was the author of this practice, who was thought to be undertaking

Is there a science of rhetoric?

dam suscipere ac profiteri videbatur, cum se ad
omnia, de quibus quisque audire vellet, esse paratum
denuntiaret. Postea vero vulgo hoc facere coeperunt,
hodieque faciunt ; ut nulla sit res, neque tanta, neque
tam improvisa, neque tam nova, de qua se non omnia,
104 quae dici possunt, profiteantur esse dicturos. Quod
si te, Cotta, arbitrarer, aut te, Sulpici, de eis rebus
audire velle, adduxissem huc Graecum aliquem, qui
vos istiusmodi disputationibus delectaret : quod ne
nunc quidem difficile factu est. Est enim apud
M. Pisonem, adolescentem iam huic studio deditum,
summo hominem ingenio, nostrique cupidissimum,
Peripateticus Staseas, homo nobis sane familiaris,
et, ut inter homines peritos constare video, in illo
suo genere omnium princeps.

105 XXIII. Quem tu, inquit, mihi, Mucius, Staseam,
quem Peripateticum narras ? Gerendus est tibi mos
adolescentibus, Crasse : qui non Graeci alicuius quoti-
dianam loquacitatem sine usu, neque ex scholis
cantilenam requirunt, sed ex homine omnium sapien-
tissimo atque eloquentissimo, atque ex eo, qui non in
libellis, sed in maximis causis, et in hoc domicilio
imperii et gloriae, sit consilio linguaque princeps ;
cuius vestigia persequi cupiunt, eius sententiam sci-
106 scitantur. Equidem te cum in dicendo semper
putavi deum, tum vero tibi nunquam eloquentiae
maiorem tribui laudem, quam humanitatis : qua
nunc te uti vel maxime decet, neque defugere eam

74

and professing something very magnificent when he advertised himself as ready for any topic whatever on which anyone might have a fancy to hear him. Later, however, they began to do this everywhere, and are doing it to this day, with the result of there being no theme so vast, so unforeseen, or so novel, that they do not claim to be prepared to say about it 104 all that there is to be said. But had I supposed that you, Cotta, or you, Sulpicius, wished to listen to anything of the kind, I would have brought some Greek or other here to amuse you with discussions of that sort ; and even now this can easily be managed. For staying with Marcus Piso (a young man, but already given up to this pursuit, possessing talent of the highest order and deeply devoted to myself) there is Staseas the Peripatetic, a man whom I know well enough, and who, as I understand to be agreed among experts, is quite supreme in that department of his."

105 XXIII. " Staseas ! what Staseas ? what Peripatetic are you talking to me about ? " said Mucius. " It is for you, Crassus, to comply with the wishes of young men, who do not want the everyday chatter of some unpractised Greek, or old sing-songs out of the schools, but something from the wisest and most eloquent man in the world, and one who, not in the pages of pamphlets, but in the most momentous causes, and that too in this seat of imperial power and splendour, holds the first place for judgement and eloquence ; they are anxious to learn the opinion of the man whose 106 footsteps they long to follow. Moreover, just as I have always accounted you the ideal orator, even so I have never ascribed to you higher praise for eloquence than for kindliness, which quality it becomes you on the present occasion to exercise to the very utmost,

disputationem, ad quam te duo excellentis ingenii adolescentes cupiunt accedere.

107 Ego vero, inquit, istis obsequi studeo, neque gravabor breviter meo more, quid quaque de re sentiam, dicere. Ac primum illud—quoniam auctoritatem tuam neglegere, Scaevola, fas mihi esse non puto—respondeo, mihi dicendi aut nullam artem, aut pertenuem videri, sed omnem esse contentionem inter homines doctos in verbi controversia positam.

108 Nam si ars ita definitur, ut paulo ante exposuit Antonius, ex rebus penitus perspectis planeque cognitis, atque ab opinionis arbitrio seiunctis, scientiaque comprehensis, non mihi videtur ars oratoris esse ulla. Sunt enim varia, et ad vulgarem popularemque sensum accommodata omnia genera huius forensis

109 nostrae dictionis. Sin autem ea, quae observata sunt in usu ac ratione dicendi, haec ab hominibus callidis ac peritis animadversa ac notata, verbis designata, generibus illustrata, partibus distributa sunt—id quod fieri potuisse video—: non intellego, quam ob rem non, si minus illa subtili definitione, at hac vulgari opinione, ars esse videatur. Sed sive est ars, sive artis quaedam similitudo, non est quidem ea neglegenda; verum intellegendum est, alia quaedam ad consequendam eloquentiam esse maiora.

and not to run away from the discussion into which two young men of eminent ability are desirous of your entering."

107 "For my part," answered the other, "I am anxious to humour your friends, and I shall make no difficulty about saying, in my brief fashion, what I think upon each point. And to that first question— since I do not think it dutiful, Scaevola, for me to disregard your claims—I answer, 'I think there is either no art of speaking at all or a very thin one,' all the quarrelling in learned circles being 108 really based upon a dispute about a word. For if, as Antonius just now explained, an art is defined as consisting in things thoroughly examined and clearly apprehended, and which are also outside the control of mere opinion, and within the grasp of exact knowledge, then to me there seems to be no such thing as an art of oratory. For all the kinds of language we ourselves use in public speaking are changeable matter, and adapted to the general 109 understanding of the crowd. If however the actual things noticed in the practice and conduct of speaking have been heeded and recorded by men of skill and experience, if they have been defined in terms, illuminated by classification, and distributed under subdivisions—and I see that it has been possible to do this—I do not understand why this should not be regarded as an art, perhaps not in that precise sense of the term, but at any rate according to the other and popular estimate. But whether this be an art, or only something like an art, assuredly it is not to be disdained; we must however understand that certain other qualifications are of greater consequence for the attainment of eloquence."

No, there is not a science in the strict sense, but experience can furnish a system of rules.

110 XXIV. Tum Antonius vehementer se assentire Crasso dixit, quod neque ita amplecteretur artem ut ei solerent qui omnem vim dicendi in arte ponerent, neque rursum eam totam, sicut plerique philosophi facerent, repudiaret. Sed existimo, inquit, gratum te his, Crasse, facturum, si ista exposueris, quae putas ad dicendum plus, quam ipsam artem, posse prodesse.

111 Dicam equidem, quoniam institui, petamque a vobis, inquit, ne has meas ineptias efferatis : quanquam moderabor ipse, ne, ut quidam magister atque artifex, sed quasi unus e togatorum numero, atque ex forensi usu homo mediocris, neque omnino rudis, videar, non ipse aliquid a me prompsisse, sed fortuito

112 in sermonem vestrum incidisse. Equidem, cum peterem magistratum, solebam in prensando dimittere a me Scaevolam, cum ei ita dicerem, me velle esse ineptum : id erat petere blandius ; quod nisi inepte fieret, bene non posset fieri. Hunc autem esse unum hominem ex omnibus, quo praesente ego ineptus esse minime vellem : quem quidem nunc mearum ineptiarum testem et spectatorem fortuna constituit. Nam quid est ineptius, quam de dicendo dicere, cum ipsum dicere nunquam sit non ineptum, nisi cum est necessarium ?

113 Perge vero, Crasse, inquit Mucius. Istam enim culpam, quam vereris, ego praestabo.

---

a *Ineptus*, generally equivalent to 'unhappy' or 'incongruous,' is here used loosely as meaning 'silly.' Crassus felt that his talking about oratory was as silly a business as was shaking hands with everybody when canvassing.

10   XXIV. Thereupon Antonius observed that he heartily agreed with Crassus, in that he was neither wedded to Art with the devotion of those for whom the whole virtue of oratory resided in an art, nor on the other hand did he put her away altogether, as did most of the philosophers. "But I think, Crassus," he continued, "that you will be doing these two a favour, if you will set forth those things which in your opinion may be more profitable to oratory than even Art herself."

11   " I will certainly name them," replied Crassus, " as I have once begun, beseeching you however not to publish abroad these trifles of mine ; although I too will restrain myself, so as not to seem a sort of master and professional, volunteering some observations of my own, but just one of all the many Roman citizens, a man modestly qualified through experience of public affairs, and not altogether untrained, who

12 has stumbled by chance upon your discussion. The truth is that, when in quest of an office, I used in canvassing to send Scaevola away from me, explaining to him that I proposed to be silly,[a] that is, to make myself winsome in my wooing, and this required some silliness if it was to be well done, whereas our friend here was of all men the one in whose presence I was least willing to appear silly. Yet he it is whom on the present occasion Fate has appointed to be an eye-witness and observer of my silliness. For what is sillier than to talk about talking, since talking in itself is ever a silly business, except when it is indispensable ? "

" Proceed none the less, Crassus," said Mucius, " for I will take upon myself that reproach you are dreading."

XXV. Sic igitur, inquit Crassus, sentio naturam primum, atque ingenium ad dicendum vim afferre maximam ; neque vero istis, de quibus paulo ante dixit Antonius scriptoribus artis, rationem dicendi et viam, sed naturam defuisse. Nam et animi atque ingenii celeres quidam motus esse debent, qui et ad excogitandum acuti, et ad explicandum ornandumque 114 sint uberes, et ad memoriam firmi atque diuturni. Et si quis est, qui haec putet arte accipi posse, quod falsum est—praeclare enim se res habeat, si haec accendi, aut commoveri arte possint : inseri quidem, et donari ab arte non possunt omnia ; sunt enim illa dona naturae— : quid de illis dicet, quae certe cum ipso homine nascuntur ? linguae solutio, vocis sonus, latera, vires, conformatio quaedam et figura totius 115 oris et corporis ? Neque haec ita dico, ut ars aliquid limare non possit—neque enim ignoro, et quae bona sint, fieri meliora posse doctrina, et quae non optima, aliquo modo acui tamen et corrigi posse—sed sunt quidam aut ita lingua haesitantes, aut ita voce absoni, aut ita vultu, motuque corporis vasti atque agrestes, ut, etiamsi ingeniis atque arte valeant, tamen in oratorum numerum venire non possint. Sunt autem quidam ita in eisdem rebus habiles, ita naturae muneribus ornati, ut non nati, sed ab aliquo deo ficti esse videantur.

116 Magnum quoddam est onus atque munus, sus-

XXV. " This then is my opinion," resumed Cr.
" that in the first place natural talent is the ch.
contributor to the virtue of oratory ; and indeed in _____ gifts
those writers on the art, of whom Antonius spoke essential;
just now, it was not the principles and method of
oratory that were wanting, but inborn capacity.
For certain lively activities of the intelligence and
the talents alike should be present, such as to be
at once swift in invention, copious in exposition
and embellishment, and steadfast and enduring in
114 recollection ; and if there be anyone disposed to
think that these powers can be derived from art, a
false belief—for it would be a glorious state of things
if art could even kindle or waken them into life ;
engrafted and bestowed by art of a certainty they
cannot be, for they are all the gifts of nature,—
what will he say of those other attributes which
undoubtedly are innate in the man himself : the
ready tongue, the ringing tones, strong lungs, vigour,
suitable build and shape of the face and body as
15 a whole ? And, in saying this, I do not mean that
art cannot in some cases give polish,—for well I
know that good abilities may through instruction
become better, and that such as are not of the best
can nevertheless be, in some measure, quickened and
amended—, but there are some men either so tongue-
tied, or so discordant in tone, or so wild and boorish
in feature and gesture, that, even though sound in
talent and in art, they yet cannot enter the ranks
of the orators. While others there are, so apt in
these same respects, so completely furnished with
the bounty of nature, as to seem of more than human
birth, and to have been shaped by some divinity.
6 " Great indeed are the burden and the task that

cipere, atque profiteri, se esse, omnibus silentibus, unum maximis de rebus, magno in conventu hominum, audiendum. Adest enim fere nemo, quin acutius atque acrius vitia in dicente, quam recta videat : ita, quidquid est, in quo offenditur, id etiam

117 illa, quae laudanda sunt, obruit. Neque haec in eam sententiam disputo, ut homines adolescentes, si quid naturale forte non habeant, omnino a dicendi studio deterream. Quis enim non videt, C. Coelio, aequali meo, magno honori fuisse, homini novo, illam ipsam, quamcumque assequi poterit, in dicendo mediocritatem ? Quis vestrum aequalem, Q. Varium, vastum hominem atque foedum, non intellegit illa ipsa facultate, quamcumque habet, magnam esse in civitate gratiam consecutum ?

118 XXVI. Sed quia de oratore quaerimus, fingendus est nobis oratione nostra, detractis omnibus vitiis, orator, atque omni laude cumulatus. Neque enim, si multitudo litium, si varietas causarum, si haec turba et barbaria forensis dat locum vel vitiosissimis oratoribus, idcirco nos hoc, quod quaerimus, omittemus. Itaque in eis artibus, in quibus non utilitas quaeritur necessaria, sed animi libera quaedam oblectatio, quam diligenter, et quam prope fastidiose iudicamus ! Nullae enim lites, neque controversiae

he undertakes, who puts himself forward, when all are silent, as the one man to be heard concerning the weightiest matters, before a vast assembly of his fellows. For there is hardly a soul present but will turn a keener and more penetrating eye upon defects in the speaker than upon his good points. Thus any blunder that may be committed eclipses 117 even those other things that are praiseworthy. Not that I am pressing these considerations with the idea of frightening young men away altogether from the pursuit of oratory, should they possibly lack some natural endowment. For who does not observe that Gaius Coelius, a man of my own time and of new family, reached high renown as the result of that very modest degree of eloquence which—such as it was— he had succeeded in attaining? Who again does not know that Quintus Varius, your own contemporary, a man of wild and repellent aspect, has attained great popularity in public life, through whatever practical ability of that kind he has possessed?

18 XXVI. "But since it is 'The Orator' we are though the seeking, we have to picture to ourselves in our dis- ideal is course an orator from whom every blemish has been attain. taken away, and one who moreover is rich in every merit. For even though the multiplicity of litigation, the diversity of issues, and the rabble of rusticity thronging our public places, give opportunity even to the most faulty speakers, we shall not for that reason lose sight of this our objective. In those arts then, in which we are looking, not for any necessary utility, but some method of freely bringing delight to the intellect, how critical—I had almost said how disdainful—are our judgements! For there are no lawsuits or contentions to compel mankind to sit

sunt, quae cogant homines, sicut in foro non bonos
119 oratores, item in theatro actores malos perpeti. Est
igitur oratori diligenter providendum, non uti illis
satisfaciat, quibus necesse est ; sed ut eis admirabilis
esse videatur, quibus libere liceat iudicare. Ac, si
quaeritis, plane, quid sentiam, enuntiabo apud homines familiarissimos, quod adhuc semper tacui, et
tacendum putavi. Mihi etiam, quique optime dicunt,
quique id facillime atque ornatissime facere possunt,
tamen, nisi timide ad dicendum accedunt, et in ex-
ordienda oratione perturbantur, paene impudentes
120 videntur : tametsi id accidere non potest. Ut enim
quisque optime dicit, ita maxime dicendi difficultatem, variosque eventus orationis, exspectationem-
que hominum pertimescit. Qui vero nihil potest
dignum re, dignum nomine oratoris, dignum hominum auribus efficere atque edere, is mihi, etiamsi
commovetur in dicendo, tamen impudens videtur.
Non enim pudendo, sed non faciendo id quod non
121 decet, impudentiae nomen effugere debemus. Quem
vero non pudet—id quod in plerisque video—, hunc
ego non reprehensione solum, sed etiam poena dignum
puto. Equidem et in vobis animadvertere soleo, et
in me ipso saepissime experior, ut exalbescam in
principiis dicendi, et tota mente, atque omnibus
artubus contremiscam ; adolescentulus vero sic initio

through bad acting on the stage, as they would bear
119 with indifferent oratory in Court. Therefore our
orator must carefully see to it, that he not only
contents those whom it is necessary to satisfy, but
is wonderful as well in the eyes of such as have the
right to judge freely. And now, if you would know
it, among my most familiar friends I will publish in
simple language what I think, on which I have
hitherto always kept silence and deemed silence
fitting. In my view, even the best orators, those
who can speak with the utmost ease and elegance,
unless they are diffident in approaching a discourse
and diffident in beginning it, seem to border on the
shameless, although that can never come to pass.
20 For the better the orator, the more profoundly is
he frightened of the difficulty of speaking, and of
the doubtful fate of a speech, and of the anticipations of an audience. On the other hand, the
man who can do nothing in composition and
delivery that is worthy of the occasion, worthy
of the name of an orator, or of the ear of the
listener, still seems to me to be without shame,
be he never so agitated in his speaking; for it is
not by feeling shame at what is unbecoming, but
in not doing it, that we must escape the reproach
21 of shamelessness. While as for him who is un-
ashamed—as I see is the case with most speakers,—
I hold him deserving not merely of reprimand,
but of punishment as well. Assuredly, just as I
generally perceive it to happen to yourselves, so
I very often prove it in my own experience, that I
turn pale at the outset of a speech, and quake in
every limb and in all my soul; in fact, as a very
young man, I once so utterly lost heart in opening

accusationis exanimatus sum, ut hoc summum bene-
ficium Q. Maximo debuerim, quod continuo consilium
dimiserit, simul ac me fractum ac debilitatum metu
viderit.

122   Hic omnes assensi, significare inter sese, et colloqui
coeperunt. Fuit enim mirificus quidam in Crasso
pudor, qui tamen non modo non obesset eius orationi,
sed etiam probitatis commendatione prodesset.

XXVII. Tum Antonius : Saepe, ut dicis, inquit,
animadverti, Crasse, et te, et ceteros summos oratores,
quanquam tibi par, mea sententia, nemo unquam fuit,
123 in dicendi exordio permoveri. Cuius quidem rei
cum causam quaererem, quidnam esset cur, ut in
quoque oratore plurimum esset, ita maxime is perti-
mesceret, has causas inveniebam duas : unam, quod
intellegerent ei, quos usus ac natura docuisset, nonnunquam summis oratoribus non satis ex sententia
eventum dicendi procedere ; ita non iniuria, quoties-
cumque dicerent, id, quod aliquando posset accidere,
124 ne tum accideret, timere. Altera est haec, de qua
queri saepe soleo : ceterarum homines artium spec-
tati et probati, si quando aliquid minus bene fecerunt,
quam solent, aut noluisse, aut valetudine impediti non
potuisse consequi, id quod scirent, putantur : ' Noluit,' inquiunt, ' hodie agere Roscius ' ; aut, ' Crudior

an indictment, that I had to thank Quintus Maximus
for doing me the supreme service of promptly
adjourning the hearing, the moment he saw that I
was broken-down and unnerved by fear."

122   At this point the whole company began to nod
approval one to another, and to talk together. For
there was a marvellous kind of modesty about
Crassus, though this was so far from being any
disadvantage to his oratory, as positively to help it,
by bearing witness to his integrity.

XXVII. Presently Antonius observed : " I have
often noticed, Crassus, that, as you say, both you
and the other orators of the first rank—although in
my opinion no one has ever been your peer—are
deeply disturbed when you are beginning a speech.

123 Now on investigating the reason of this—how it
was that, the greater an orator's capacity, the
more profoundly nervous he was—I discovered
this twofold explanation : first, that those who had
learned from experience and knowledge of human
nature understood that, even with the most eminent orators, the fate of a speech was sometimes
not sufficiently in accordance with their wish ; wherefore, as often as they spoke, they were justifiably
fearful, lest what could possibly happen sometime

124 should actually happen then.   Secondly there is
something of which I often have to complain, that,
whenever tried and approved exponents of the
other arts have done some work with less than their
wonted success, their inability to perform what they
knew how to perform is explained by their being out
of the humour or hindered by indisposition (people
say, ' Roscius was not in the mood for acting to-day,'
or ' He was a little out of sorts ') ; whereas, if it

*Orators
judged less
leniently
than actors*

87

fuit'; oratoris peccatum, si quod est animadversum,
125 stultitiae peccatum videtur. Stultitia autem excusationem non habet : quia nemo videtur, aut quia
crudus fuerit, aut quod ita maluerit, stultus fuisse.
Quo etiam gravius iudicium in dicendo subimus.
Quoties enim dicimus, toties de nobis iudicatur : et,
qui semel in gestu peccavit, non continuo existimatur
nescire gestum ; cuius autem in dicendo aliquid
reprehensum est, aut aeterna in eo, aut certe diuturna
valet opinio tarditatis.

126   XXVIII. Illud vero, quod a te dictum est, esse
permulta, quae orator nisi a natura haberet, non
multum a magistro adiuvaretur : valde tibi assentior,
inque eo vel maxime probavi summum illum doctorem, Alabandensem Apollonium, qui, cum mer-
cede doceret, tamen non patiebatur, eos, quos
iudicabat non posse oratores evadere, operam apud
sese perdere, dimittebatque ; et ad quam quemque
artem putabat esse aptum, ad eam impellere atque
127 hortari solebat.   Satis est enim ceteris artificiis per-
cipiendis, tantummodo similem esse hominis ; et id,
quod tradatur, vel etiam inculcetur, si quis forte sit
tardior, posse percipere animo, et memoria custodire.
Non quaeritur mobilitas linguae, non celeritas verborum, non denique ea, quae nobis non possumus fin-
128 gere, facies, vultus, sonus.   In oratore autem acumen
dialecticorum, sententiae philosophorum, verba prope

is an orator's shortcoming that is being criticized
25 the same is thought due to stupidity. But stupidity
finds no apology, since no man's stupidity is set down
to his having been ' out of sorts ' or ' that way
inclined.' And so in oratory we confront a sterner
judgement. For judgement is passing upon us as
often as we speak ; moreover one mistake in acting does not instantly convict a player of ignorance
of acting, but an orator, censured on some point
of speaking, is under an established suspicion of
dullness once for all, or at any rate for many a
day.

26 XXVIII. " Now as for that remark of yours that Variety of
there were very many qualifications which an orator gifts ex-
must derive from nature, or he would not be greatly the orator
aided by tuition, I thoroughly agree with you ; and
in this respect I most particularly approved of that
very eminent instructor Apollonius of Alabanda,
who, though teaching for hire, would not for all that
suffer such pupils as, in his judgement, could never
turn out to be orators, to waste their labour with him,
but would send them on their ways, and urge and
exhort them to pursue those arts for which he
27 thought them respectively fitted. It is enough, indeed, for acquiring all other crafts, just to be a man
like other men, and able to apprehend mentally and
to preserve in the memory what is taught, or even
crammed into the learner, should he chance to be
dull beyond the ordinary. No readiness of tongue
is needed, no fluency of language, in short none
of those things—natural state of looks, expression,
and voice—which we cannot mould for ourselves.
28 But in an orator we must demand the subtlety of
the logician, the thoughts of the philosopher, a

poetarum, memoria iurisconsultorum, vox tragoe-
dorum, gestus paene summorum actorum est re-
quirendus.   Quam ob rem nihil in hominum genere
rarius perfecto oratore inveniri potest.   Quae enim
singularum rerum artifices singula si mediocriter
adepti sunt, probantur, ea, nisi omnia summa sunt
in oratore, probari non possunt.

129   Tum Crassus : Atqui vide, inquit, in artificio perquam tenui et levi, quanto plus adhibeatur dili-
gentiae, quam in hac re, quam constat esse maximam.
Saepe enim soleo audire Roscium, cum ita dicat, se
adhuc reperire discipulum, quem quidem probaret,
potuisse neminem : non quo non essent quidam pro-
babiles, sed quia, si aliquid modo esset vitii, id ferre
ipse non posset.   Nihil est enim tam insigne, nec tam
ad diuturnitatem memoriae stabile, quam id, in quo
130 aliquid offenderis.   Itaque ut ad hanc similitudinem
huius histrionis oratoriam laudem dirigamus, videtisne, quam nihil ab eo, nisi perfecte, nihil nisi cum
summa venustate fiat, nihil nisi ita, ut deceat, et uti
omnes moveat atque delectet ?   Itaque hoc iamdiu
est consecutus, ut, in quo quisque artificio excelleret,
is in suo genere Roscius diceretur.   Hanc ego absolu-
tionem perfectionemque in oratore desiderans, a qua
ipse longe absum, facio impudenter : mihi enim volo
ignosci, ceteris ipse non ignosco.   Nam qui non potest,
qui vitiose facit, quem denique non decet, hunc—ut

diction almost poetic, a lawyer's memory, a trage-
dian's voice, and the bearing almost of the consummate actor. Accordingly no rarer thing than a
finished orator can be discovered among the sons of
men. For attributes which are commended when
acquired one apiece, and that in but modest degree,
by other craftsmen in their respective vocations,
cannot win approval when embodied in an orator,
unless in him they are all assembled in perfection."

129   "And yet observe," said Crassus at this point,   Defects are
"how much more care is exercised in an extremely   noticed at
mean and trivial craft than in this art, which is   once.
admittedly the greatest. For again and again do
I hear Roscius declaring that so far he has never
succeeded in finding a single pupil of whom he really
approved ; not that there were not some who were
acceptable, but because, if there was any blemish
whatever in them, he himself could not endure it.
For nothing stands out so conspicuously, or remains
so firmly fixed in the memory, as something in which
130 you have blundered. And so, to take this comparison with this player as our standard of an orator's
merit, do you not see how he does nothing otherwise than perfectly, nothing without consummate
charm, nothing save in the manner befitting the
occasion, and so as to move and enchant everybody ?
Accordingly he has long ago brought it about that,
in whatsoever craft a man excelled, the same was
called a Roscius in his own line. For myself, in
demanding in an orator this absolute perfection,
from which I myself am far removed, I am behaving
shamelessly, since I want forgiveness for myself, but
I do not forgive the others. For the man who is
without ability, who makes mistakes, whose claim—

Apollonius iubebat—ad id, quod facere possit, detru-
dendum puto.

131 XXIX. Num tu igitur, inquit Sulpicius, me, aut
hunc Cottam, ius civile, aut rem militarem iubes
discere ? Nam quis ad ista summa atque in omni
genere perfecta, potest pervenire ? Tum ille : Ego
vero, inquit, quod in vobis egregiam quamdam
ac praeclaram indolem ad dicendum esse cognovi,
idcirco haec exposui omnia ; nec magis ad eos deter-
rendos, qui non possent, quam ad vos, qui possetis,
exacuendos accommodavi orationem meam ; et
quanquam in utroque vestrum summum esse ingenium studiumque perspexi, tamen haec, quae sunt
in specie posita, de quibus plura fortasse dixi, quam
132 solent Graeci dicere, in te, Sulpici, divina sunt. Ego
enim neminem, nec motu corporis, neque ipso habitu
atque forma aptiorem, nec voce pleniorem, aut sua-
viorem mihi videor audisse ; quae quibus a natura
minora data sunt, tamen illud assequi possunt, ut eis,
quae habeant, modice et scienter utantur, et ut ne
dedeceat. Id enim est maxime vitandum, et de hoc
uno minime est facile praecipere, non mihi modo, qui
sicut unus paterfamilias his de rebus loquor, sed etiam
ipsi illi Roscio ; quem saepe audio dicere, caput esse
artis, decere : quod tamen unum id esse, quod tradi
133 arte non possit. Sed, si placet, sermonem alio trans-

in a word—does him discredit, should in my judgement, as Apollonius directed, be thrust down to such
work as he can perform."

31   XXIX. " Would you then," said Sulpicius, " direct The natural
Cotta here, or myself, to be studying the common law gifts of
or the soldier's art ? For who can attain to that and Cotta:
sublime and universal perfection which you demand?"
And the other answered : " For my part, it is
precisely because I recognized in you two a really
remarkable and indeed splendid genius for oratory,
that I have set forth all these considerations, while
to stimulate you men of ability no less than
to discourage the inefficient is the object of my
discourse ; and although I have noted in both of
you talent and industry of the highest order, still
as regards these advantages which depend upon the
outer man, concerning which I have perhaps said
more than the Greeks are wont to do, as manifested
32 in yourself, Sulpicius, they are divine. For never, I
think, did I listen to a speaker better qualified in
respect of gesture, and by his very bearing and
presence, or to one with a voice more resonant and
pleasing ; while those on whom these gifts have been
bestowed by nature in smaller measure, can none the
less acquire the power to use what they have with
propriety and discernment, and so as to show no lack
of good taste. For lack of that is above all else to be
avoided, and as to this particular failing it is especially
difficult to lay down rules, difficult not only for me, who
talk of these matters like papa laying down the law,
but even for the great Roscius himself ; whom I often
hear affirming that the chief thing in art is to observe
good taste, though how to do this is the one thing
33 that cannot be taught by art. But, by your leave,

feramus, et nostro more aliquando, non rhetorico,
loquamur.

Minime vero, inquit Cotta : nunc enim te iam
exoremus necesse est, quoniam retines nos in hoc
studio, nec ad aliam dimittis artem, ut nobis explices,
quidquid est istud, quod tu in dicendo potes ; neque
enim sumus nimis avidi : ista tua mediocri eloquentia
contenti sumus, idque ex te quaerimus—ut ne plus
nos assequamur, quam quantulum tu in dicendo assecutus es—, quoniam, quae a natura expetenda sunt,
ea dicis non nimis deesse nobis, quid praeterea esse
assumendum putes.

134   XXX. Tum Crassus arridens : Quid censes, inquit,
Cotta, nisi studium, et ardorem quemdam amoris ?
sine quo cum in vita nihil quidquam egregium,
tum certe hoc, quod tu expetis, nemo unquam assequetur. Neque vero vos ad eam rem video esse
cohortandos ; quos, cum mihi quoque sitis molesti,
135 nimis etiam flagrare intellego cupiditate. Sed profecto studia nihil prosunt perveniendi aliquo, nisi
illud, quod eo, quo intendas, ferat deducatque,
cognoris. Quare, quoniam mihi levius quoddam onus
imponitis, neque ex me de oratoris arte, sed de hac
mea, quantulacumque est, facultate quaeritis, exponam vobis quamdam, non aut perreconditam, aut
valde difficilem, aut magnificam, aut gravem rationem consuetudinis meae, qua quondam solitus sum

let us shift our conversation to other subjects, and chat at last in our own fashion, and not as rhetoricians."

" On no account whatever," returned Cotta: " for since you keep us in this pursuit and do not send us away to some other art, we must now further beseech you to explain to us your own power in oratory, however much you make it out to be ;—for we are not too greedy : we are quite content with what you call your ' ordinary eloquence '—and (so as not to outstrip that small degree of skill you have attained as a speaker), since you tell us that the qualities to be sought from nature are not excessively deficient in ourselves, the thing we wish to know from you is what further requisite you consider should be acquired."

134   XXX. Crassus smiled at this and replied : " What their need else do you suppose, Cotta, but enthusiasm and some-   of training thing like the passion of love ? without which no man will ever attain anything in life that is out of the common, least of all this success which you covet. Not that I look upon you two as needing incitement in that direction, perceiving as I do, from the trouble you are giving even to myself, that you are aflame 135 with only too fervent a desire. Yet assuredly endeavours to reach any goal avail nothing unless you have learned what it is which leads you to the end at which you aim.   And so, since the burden you lay upon me is a lighter one, and you are not examining me in the art of oratory, but as to this ability of my own, however insignificant it is, I will explain to you my habitual method, nothing particularly mysterious or exceedingly difficult, nothing grand or imposing, just the plan I used to follow in bygone

uti, cum mihi in isto studio versari adolescenti
licebat.

136 Tum Sulpicius : O diem, Cotta, nobis, inquit, op-
tatum ! quod enim neque precibus unquam, nec
insidiando, nec speculando assequi potui, ut, quid
Crassus ageret, meditandi aut dicendi causa, non
modo videre mihi, sed ex eius scriptore et lectore
Diphilo suspicari liceret ; id spero nos esse adeptos,
omniaque iam ex ipso, quae diu cupimus, cognituros.

137 XXXI. Tum Crassus : Atqui arbitror, Sulpici, cum
audieris, non tam te haec admiraturum, quae dixero,
quam existimaturum, tum, cum ea audire cupiebas,
causam cur cuperes, non fuisse. Nihil enim dicam
reconditum, nihil exspectatione vestra dignum, nihil
aut inauditum vobis, aut cuiquam novum. Nam
principio illud, quod est homine ingenuo liberali-
terque educato dignum, non negabo me ista omnium
138 communia et contrita praecepta didicisse : primum
oratoris officium esse, dicere ad persuadendum accommodate ; deinde, esse omnem orationem aut de
infinitae rei quaestione, sine designatione personarum
et temporum, aut de re certis in personis ac tem-
139 poribus locata ; in utraque autem re quidquid in
controversiam veniat, in eo quaeri solere, aut factumne sit, aut, si est factum, quale sit, aut etiam quo
nomine vocetur, aut, quod nonnulli addunt, rectene
140 factum esse videatur ; exsistere autem controversias

times, when I was a young man, with liberty to busy myself in that pursuit of yours."

136 At these words Sulpicius exclaimed: "Cotta, behold our longed-for day! For the thing that by entreaties, or lying in wait, or spying, I could never secure,—I mean a chance of observing what Crassus was doing for the purposes of training or rehearsal, I do not say at first-hand, but at least by getting some hint from Diphilus, his secretary and reader,— this I hope you and I have gained, and we are now to learn from his own lips everything that we have long been desiring."

137 XXXI. "And yet I think, Sulpicius," continued Crassus, "that after hearing them you will be less likely to wonder at my observations than to decide that, when you were longing to hear them, there was no ground for your longing. For I shall tell no mystery, nothing worthy of your waiting, nothing that you have not heard already, or that is new to anyone. For to begin with, in regard to what befits a free-born man of liberal education, I will not deny that I learned those commonplace and 138 well-worn maxims of teachers in general: first, that the duty of an orator is to speak in a style fitted to convince; next, that every speech has to do either with the investigation of a general question, wherein no persons or occasions are indicated, or with a problem that is concerned with specific individuals 139 and times; moreover that in both cases, whatever the subject for debate, it is usual for inquiry to be made in respect thereof, either whether a deed was done or, if it was done, what is its character, or again by what name is it known or, as some add, whether it appears to have been done lawfully;

The school course in rhetoric.

97

etiam ex scripti interpretatione, in quo aut ambigue quid sit scriptum, aut contrarie, aut ita, ut a sententia scriptum dissideat : his autem omnibus partibus 141 subiecta quaedam esse argumenta propria. Sed causarum, quae sint a communi quaestione seiunctae, partim in iudiciis versari, partim in deliberationibus ; esse etiam genus tertium, quod in laudandis aut vituperandis hominibus poneretur ; certosque esse locos, quibus in iudiciis uteremur, in quibus aequitas quaereretur ; alios in deliberationibus, qui omnes ad utilitatem dirigerentur eorum, quibus consilium daremus : alios item in laudationibus, in quibus ad per- 142 sonarum dignitatem omnia referrentur. Cumque esset omnis oratoris vis ac facultas in quinque partes distributa ; ut deberet reperire primum, quid diceret ; deinde inventa non solum ordine, sed etiam momento quodam atque iudicio dispensare atque componere ; tum ea denique vestire atque ornare oratione ; post memoria saepire ; ad extremum agere cum dignitate 143 ac venustate : etiam illa cognoram, et acceperam, antequam de re diceremus, initio conciliandos eorum esse animos, qui audirent ; deinde rem demonstrandam ; postea controversiam constituendam ; tum id, quod nos intenderemus, confirmandum ; post, quae contra dicerentur, refellenda ; extrema autem oratione, ea, quae pro nobis essent, amplificanda et augenda ; quaeque essent pro adversariis, infirmanda atque frangenda.

---

[a] These *loci communes* are the ' stock ' arguments and general reflexions referred to in § 56 *supra.*

140 further that contentions also arise out of the construction of a document, wherein there is some ambiguity or contradiction, or something is so expressed that the written word is at variance with the intention ; and again that to all these kinds certain modes of proof are assigned as appropriate.

41 Again I heard that, of such questions as are distinct from general issues, some have their place in courts of justice, others in deliberations ; while there was yet a third kind, which had to do with the extolling or reviling of particular persons ; and that there were prescribed commonplaces *a* which we were to employ in the law-courts where equity was our aim ; others for use in deliberations, all of which were arranged for the benefit of those to whom we might be giving counsel ; and others again in panegyric, wherein the sole consideration was the greatness of the 42 individuals concerned. And, since all the activity and ability of an orator falls into five divisions, I learned that he must first hit upon what to say ; then manage and marshal his discoveries, not merely in orderly fashion, but with a discriminating eye for the exact weight as it were of each argument ; next go on to array them in the adornments of style ; after that keep them guarded in his memory ; and in the 43 end deliver them with effect and charm : I had also been taught that, before speaking on the issue, we must first secure the goodwill of our audience ; that next we must state our case ; afterwards define the dispute ; then establish our own allegations ; subsequently disprove those of the other side ; and in our peroration expand and reinforce all that was in our favour, while we weakened and demolished whatever went to support our opponents.

144 XXXII. Audieram etiam, quae de orationis ipsius
ornamentis traderentur : in qua praecipitur primum,
ut pure et latine loquamur ; deinde ut plane et
dilucide ; tum ut ornate ; post ad rerum dignitatem
apte et quasi decore : singularumque rerum prae-
145 cepta cognoram. Quin etiam, quae maxime propria
essent naturae, tamen his ipsis artem adhiberi videram : nam de actione et de memoria quaedam brevia,
sed magna cum exercitatione praecepta gustaram.

In his enim fere rebus omnis istorum artificum doctrina versatur, quam ego si nihil dicam adiuvare,
mentiar. Habet enim quaedam quasi ad commonen-
dum oratorem, quo quidque referat, et quo intuens,
ab eo, quodcumque sibi proposuerit, minus aberret.
146 Verum ego hanc vim intellego esse in praeceptis
omnibus, non ut ea secuti oratores, eloquentiae
laudem sint adepti, sed, quae sua sponte homines
eloquentes facerent, ea quosdam observasse atque
collegisse ; sic esse non eloquentiam ex artificio, sed
artificium ex eloquentia natum : quod tamen, ut
ante dixi, non eiicio : est enim, etiamsi minus necessarium ad bene dicendum, tamen ad cognoscendum
147 non illiberale. Et exercitatio quaedam suscipienda
vobis est : quanquam vos quidem iampridem estis in
cursu ; sed eis, qui ingrediuntur in stadium, quique
ea, quae agenda sunt in foro, tanquam in acie, possunt etiam nunc exercitatione quasi ludicra prae-
discere ac meditari.

144   XXXII. "I had listened also to the traditional precepts for the embellishment of discourse itself: that we must speak, in the first place, pure and correct Latin, secondly with simple lucidity, thirdly with elegance, lastly in a manner befitting the dignity of our topics and with a certain grace; and on these several points I had learnt particular 145 maxims. Moreover I had seen art called in to aid even those qualities which are peculiarly the endowment of nature: for example, concerning delivery and the memory, I had taken a taste of certain rules which, though concise, involved much practice.

Rules of diction.

"For it is matters like these that employ nearly all the learning of your professors; and if I were to call this learning useless, I should be lying. For in fact it contains certain reminders, as it were, for the orator, as to the standard he must apply on each occasion, and must keep in mind, if he is not to wander from whatever course he has set himself. 146 But to my thinking the virtue in all the rules is, not that orators by following them have won a reputation for eloquence, but that certain persons have noted and collected the doings of men who were naturally eloquent: thus eloquence is not the offspring of the art, but the art of eloquence: even so, as I said before, I do not reject art, for though perhaps hardly essential to right speaking, still it is no ignoble help towards 147 right knowledge. There is also a certain practical training that you must undergo—though indeed you two are already in full career,—I mean it is for those who are at the start of their race, and can even thus early learn beforehand and practise, by a training like that for the games, what will have to be done in the fighting-line, so to speak, of the Courts."

Practice essential.

148 Hanc ipsam, inquit Sulpicius, nosse volumus :
attamen ista, quae abs te breviter de arte decursa
sunt, audire cupimus, quanquam sunt nobis quoque
non inaudita. Verum illa mox : nunc, de ipsa exercitatione quid sentias, quaerimus.

149 XXXIII. Equidem probo ista, Crassus inquit,
quae vos facere soletis, ut, causa aliqua posita con-
simili causarum earum, quae in forum deferuntur,
dicatis quam maxime ad veritatem accommodate.
Sed plerique in hoc vocem modo, neque eam scienter,
et vires exercent suas, et linguae celeritatem incitant,
verborumque frequentia delectantur. In quo fallit
eos, quod audierunt, dicendo homines, ut dicant,

150 efficere solere. Vere enim etiam illud dicitur, perverse dicere, homines, perverse dicendo, facillime
consequi. Quam ob rem in istis ipsis exercitationibus,
etsi utile est, etiam subito saepe dicere, tamen illud
utilius, sumpto spatio ad cogitandum, paratius atque
accuratius dicere. Caput autem est, quod, ut vere
dicam, minime facimus—est enim magni laboris, quem
plerique fugimus—, quam plurimum scribere. Stilus
optimus et praestantissimus dicendi effector ac magister : neque iniuria. Nam si subitam et fortuitam
orationem commentatio et cogitatio facile vincit ;
hanc ipsam profecto assidua ac diligens scriptura

151 superabit. Omnes enim, sive artis sunt loci, sive
ingenii cuiusdam atque prudentiae, qui modo insunt
in ea re, de qua scribimus, anquirentibus nobis,

148 " This training," said Sulpicius, " is the very thing we wish to understand : and none the less we are longing to hear you on those precepts of the art over which you have briefly run, although those too are not unknown to us. But of them presently ; for the moment we want your opinion on the training itself."

149 XXXIII. " I certainly approve," replied Crassus, Rules for " of what you yourselves are in the habit of doing, preparatory training. when you propound some case, closely resembling such as are brought into Court, and argue it in a fashion adapted as nearly as possible to real life. Most students however, in so doing, merely exercise their voices (and that in the wrong way), and their physical strength, and whip up their rate of utterance, and revel in a flood of verbiage. This mistake is due to their having heard it said that it is by speaking

150 that men as a rule become speakers. But that other adage is just as true,—that by speaking badly men very easily succeed in becoming bad speakers. This is why, in those exercises of your own, though there is a value in plenty of extempore speaking, it is still more serviceable to take time for consideration, and to speak better prepared and more carefully. But the chief thing is what, to tell the truth, we do least (for it needs great pains which most of us shirk),— to write as much as possible. The pen is the best and most eminent author and teacher of eloquence, and rightly so. For if an extempore and casual speech is easily beaten by one prepared and thought-out, this latter in turn will assuredly be surpassed by what has

151 been written with care and diligence. The truth is that all the commonplaces, whether furnished by art or by individual talent and wisdom, at any rate such as appertain to the subject of our writing, appear

omnique acie ingenii contemplantibus ostendunt se
et occurrunt ; omnesque sententiae, verbaque omnia,
quae sunt cuiusque generis maxime illustria, sub
acumen stili subeant et succedant necesse est ; tum
ipsa collocatio conformatioque verborum perficitur in
scribendo, non poetico, sed quodam oratorio numero
et modo.

152   Haec sunt, quae clamores et admirationes in bonis
oratoribus efficiunt ; neque ea quisquam, nisi diu
multumque scriptitarit, etiamsi vehementissime se in
his subitis dictionibus exercuerit, consequetur ; et
qui a scribendi consuetudine ad dicendum venit, hanc
affert facultatem, ut, etiam subito si dicat, tamen illa,
quae dicantur, similia scriptorum esse videantur ;
atque etiam, si quando in dicendo scriptum attulerit
aliquid, cum ab eo discesserit, reliqua similis oratio
153 consequetur.   Ut concitato navigio, cum remiges
inhibuerunt, retinet tamen ipsa navis motum et cursum suum, intermisso impetu pulsuque remorum :
sic in oratione perpetua, cum scripta deficiunt,
parem tamen obtinet oratio reliqua cursum, scriptorum similitudine et vi concitata.

154   XXXIV. In quotidianis autem commentationibus
equidem mihi adolescentulus proponere solebam
illam exercitationem maxime, qua C. Carbonem,
nostrum illum inimicum, solitum esse uti sciebam, ut
aut versibus propositis quam maxime gravibus, aut

and rush forward as we are searching out and surveying the matter with all our natural acuteness; and all the thoughts and expressions, which are the most brilliant in their several kinds, must needs flow up in succession to the point of our pen; then too the actual marshalling and arrangement of words is made perfect in the course of writing, in a rhythm and measure proper to oratory as distinct from poetry.

2 "These are the things which in good orators produce applause and admiration; and no man will attain these except by long and large practice in writing, however ardently he may have trained himself in those off-hand declamations; he too who approaches oratory by way of long practice in writing, brings this advantage to his task, that even if he is extemporizing, whatever he may say bears a likeness to the written word; and moreover if ever, during a speech, he has introduced a written note, the rest of his discourse, when he turns away from the writing, will proceed in unchanging style. Just as when a boat is moving at high speed, if the crew rest upon their oars, the craft herself still keeps her way and her run, though the driving force of the oars has ceased, so in an unbroken discourse, when written notes are exhausted, the rest of the speech still maintains a like progress, under the impulse given by the similarity and energy of the written word.

XXXIV. "For my part, in the daily exercises of youth, I used chiefly to set myself that task which I knew Gaius Carbo, my old enemy, was wont to practise: this was to set myself some poetry, the most impressive to be found, or to read as much of

oratione aliqua lecta ad eum finem, quem memoria
possem comprehendere, eam rem ipsam, quam legis-
sem, verbis aliis quam maxime possem lectis, pro-
nuntiarem. Sed post animadverti, hoc esse in hoc
vitii, quod ea verba, quae maxime cuiusque rei propria, quaeque essent ornatissima atque optima,
occupasset aut Ennius, si ad eius versus me exer-
cerem, aut Gracchus, si eius orationem mihi forte
proposuissem. Ita, si eisdem verbis uterer, nihil
prodesse ; si aliis, etiam obesse, cum minus idoneis
155 uti consuescerem. Postea mihi placuit, eoque sum
usus adolescens, ut summorum oratorum graecas
orationes explicarem. Quibus lectis hoc assequebar,
ut, cum ea, quae legerem graece, latine redderem,
non solum optimis verbis uterer, et tamen usitatis,
sed etiam exprimerem quaedam verba imitando, quae
nova nostris essent, dummodo essent idonea.

156 Iam vocis, et spiritus, et totius corporis, et ipsius
linguae motus et exercitationes, non tam artis in-
digent, quam laboris ; quibus in rebus habenda est
ratio diligenter, quos imitemur, quorum similes velimus esse. Intuendi nobis sunt non solum oratores,
sed etiam actores, ne mala consuetudine ad aliquam
157 deformitatem pravitatemque veniamus. Exercenda
est etiam memoria, ediscendis ad verbum quam
plurimis et nostris scriptis, et alienis. Atque in ea
exercitatione non sane mihi displicet adhibere, si
consueris, etiam istam locorum simulacrorumque

---

[a] The speeches of C. Gracchus (see Index) were studied
as models in the rhetorical schools of the Empire.

[b] Crassus is speaking of some system of mnemonics, such
as Antonius discusses in Book II, lxxxvi.-lxxxviii.

some speech as I could keep in my memory, and then to declaim upon the actual subject-matter of my reading, choosing as far as possible different words. But later I noticed this defect in my method, that those words which best befitted each subject, and were the most elegant and in fact the best, had been already seized upon by Ennius, if it was on his poetry that I was practising, or by Gracchus,[a] if I chanced to have set myself a speech of his. Thus I saw that to employ the same expressions profited me nothing, while to employ others was a positive hindrance, in that I was forming the habit of using
5 the less appropriate. Afterwards I resolved,—and this practice I followed when somewhat older,—to translate freely Greek speeches of the most eminent orators. The result of reading these was that, in rendering into Latin what I had read in Greek, I not only found myself using the best words—and yet quite familiar ones—but also coining by analogy certain words such as would be new to our people, provided only they were appropriate.

6 "To proceed, the control and training of voice, breathing, gestures and the tongue itself, call for exertion rather than art; and in these matters we must carefully consider whom we are to take as patterns, whom we should wish to be like. We have to study actors as well as orators, that bad practice may not lead us into some inelegant or ugly habit. The memory too must be trained by carefully learning by heart as many pieces as possible both from our Latin writers and the foreigner. Moreover in this work I do not altogether dislike the use as well, if you are accustomed to it, of that system of associating commonplaces with symbols[b] which is

rationem, quae in arte traditur. Educenda deinde
dictio est ex hac domestica exercitatione et umbratili
medium in agmen, in pulverem, in clamorem, in
castra, atque in aciem forensem; subeundus usus
omnium, et periclitandae vires ingenii; et illa commentatio inclusa in veritatis lucem proferenda est.

158 Legendi etiam poetae, cognoscenda historia, omnium
bonarum artium scriptores ac doctores et legendi, et
pervolutandi, et exercitationis causa laudandi, inter-
pretandi, corrigendi, vituperandi, refellendi; dis-
putandumque de omni re in contrarias partes, et,
quidquid erit in quaque re, quod probabile videri

159 possit, eliciendum atque dicendum; perdiscendum
ius civile, cognoscendae leges, percipienda omnis antiquitas, senatoria consuetudo, disciplina reipublicae, iura sociorum, foedera, pactiones, causa
imperii cognoscenda est: libandus est etiam ex
omni genere urbanitatis facetiarum quidam lepos;
quo, tanquam sale, perspergatur omnis oratio.

Effudi vobis omnia, quae sentiebam, quae fortasse,
quemcumque patremfamilias arripuissetis ex aliquo
circulo, eadem vobis percunctantibus respondisset.

160 XXXV. Haec cum Crassus dixisset, silentium est
consecutum. Sed quanquam satis eis, qui aderant,
ad id, quod erat propositum, dictum videbatur, tamen
sentiebant celerius esse multo, quam ipsi vellent, ab
eo peroratum. Tum Scaevola: Quid est, Cotta?
inquit, quid tacetis? Nihilne vobis in mentem venit,
quod praeterea a Crasso requiratis?

taught in the profession. Then at last must our Oratory be conducted out of this sheltered training-ground at home, right into action, into the dust and uproar, into the camp and the fighting-line of public debate; she must face putting everything to the proof and test the strength of her talent, and her secluded preparation must be brought forth into the daylight of reality. We must also read the poets, acquaint ourselves with histories, study and peruse the masters and authors in every excellent art, and by way of practice praise, expound, emend, criticize and confute them; we must argue every question on both sides, and bring out on every topic whatever points can be deemed plausible; besides this we must become learned in the common law and familiar with the statutes, and must contemplate all the olden time, and investigate the ways of the senate, political philosophy, the rights of allies, the treaties and conventions, and the policy of empire; and lastly we have to cull, from all the forms of pleasantry, a certain charm of humour, with which to give a sprinkle of salt, as it were, to all of our discourse.

"Well, I have poured out for you all my ideas, and perhaps any chance patriarch, upon whom you had fastened at some party or other, would have given the same replies to your interrogatories."

XXXV. When Crassus had finished these observations, a general silence ensued. But though the company held that he had said enough on the topic propounded to him, yet they felt that he had ended far more speedily than they could have wished. Then Scaevola inquired, "Well, Cotta, why are you two silent? Does nothing come to mind on which you would like to question Crassus further?"

Further detail requested.

161 Immo id mehercule, inquit, ipsum attendo. Tantus
enim cursus verborum fuit, et sic evolavit oratio, ut
eius vim atque incitationem aspexerim, vestigia
ingressumque vix viderim; et tanquam in aliquam
locupletem ac refertam domum venerim, non explicata veste, neque proposito argento, neque tabulis
et signis propalam collocatis, sed his omnibus multis magnificisque rebus constructis ac reconditis : sic
modo in oratione Crassi divitias atque ornamenta eius
ingenii per quaedam involucra atque integumenta
perspexi ; sed ea cum contemplari cuperem, vix
aspiciendi potestas fuit. Ita neque hoc possum
dicere, me omnino ignorare, quid possideat, neque
plane nosse, ac vidisse.

162 Quin tu igitur facis idem, inquit Scaevola, quod
faceres, si in aliquam domum, plenam ornamentorum,
villamve venisses ? Si ea seposita, ut dicis, essent, tu
valde spectandi cupidus esses ; non dubitares rogare
dominum, ut proferri iuberet, praesertim si esses
familiaris. Similiter nunc petes a Crasso, ut eam
copiam ornamentorum suorum, quam constructam
uno in loco, quasi per transennam praetereuntes
strictim aspeximus, in lucem proferat, et suo quidque in loco collocet ?

163 Ego vero, inquit Cotta, a te peto, Scaevola—me
enim, et hunc Sulpicium impedit pudor ab homine
omnium gravissimo, qui genus huiusmodi disputationis semper contempserit, haec, quae isti forsitan

31   " In truth," replied the other, " that is just what I am considering. For so great was the speed of his words, and so swiftly winged his discourse that, while realizing its rushing energy, I could hardly follow the traces of its advance; and just as though I had entered some richly stored mansion, wherein the draperies were not unrolled, nor the plate set forth, nor the pictures and statuary displayed to view, but all these many and splendid things were piled together and hidden away : even so just now, during this discourse of Crassus, I discerned the wealth and magnificence of his talent as through some wrappings and coverings, but though I was longing to scrutinize them, I had hardly the chance of a peep. And so I cannot say either that I know nothing at all of the extent of his possessions, or that I know and have seen them clearly."

2   " Why not do then," said Scaevola, " as you would do, if you had come to some mansion or country-house that was full of objects of art ? If these were laid aside, as you describe, and you had a strong desire to behold them, you would not hesitate to ask the master of the house to order them to be brought out, especially if you were his familiar friend. So too now will you beg Crassus to bring out into the daylight that abundance of his treasures, of which, piled together in one place, we in passing have caught just a glimpse, as through a lattice, and also to set up every piece in its proper position ? "

3   " Nay," replied Cotta, " I beg you, Scaevola, to do so (for modesty hinders myself and Sulpicius here from asking the most eminent of men, and one who has always despised this kind of debate, about things which to him may well seem the elementary con-

puerorum elementa videantur, exquirere—: sed tu
hoc nobis da, Scaevola, et perfice, ut Crassus haec,
quae coarctavit, et peranguste refersit in oratione
sua, dilatet nobis atque explicet.

164   Ego mehercule, inquit Mucius, antea vestra
magis hoc causa volebam, quam mea : neque enim
tantopere hanc a Crasso disputationem desiderabam,
quantopere eius in causis oratione delector. Nunc
vero, Crasse, mea quoque etiam causa rogo, ut,
quoniam tantum habemus otii, quantum iamdiu nobis
non contigit, ne graveris exaedificare id opus, quod
instituisti. Formam enim totius negotii opinione
maiorem melioremque video ; quam vehementer
probo.

165   XXXVI. Enimvero, inquit Crassus, mirari satis
non queo, etiam te haec, Scaevola, desiderare, quae
neque ego teneo, uti ei qui docent ; neque sunt eius
generis, ut, si optime tenerem, digna essent ista
sapientia ac tuis auribus. Ain' tu ? inquit ille. Si
de istis communibus et pervagatis vix huic aetati
audiendum putas, etiamne illa neglegere possumus,
quae tu oratori cognoscenda esse dixisti, de naturis
hominum, de moribus, de rationibus eis, quibus
hominum mentes et incitarentur et reprimerentur,
de historia, de antiquitate, de administratione reipublicae, denique de nostro ipso iure civili ? Hanc
enim ego omnem scientiam, et copiam rerum in
tua prudentia sciebam inesse ; in oratoris vero

cerns of schoolboys) : but do us this favour yourself,
Scaevola, and persuade Crassus to enlarge upon and
develop for us everything that in his discourse he
has compressed and stuffed into the narrowest of
spaces."

64 "Truly for my part," said Mucius, "at first it was
more for your sake than my own that I desired this :
for my anxiety to hear this discourse from Crassus
was not commensurate with the delight afforded me
by his speeches in Court. But now, Crassus, for my
own sake as well I ask you, since we are enjoying
leisure more ample than has been allotted to us
for a long time, not to find it a trouble to complete
the structure you have begun. For I perceive the
design of the undertaking as a whole to be better
and more comprehensive than I looked for ; and one
of which I heartily approve."

5 XXXVI. "Well to be sure," said Crassus, "I
cannot feel surprised enough, Scaevola, that you
too should ask for these things, which I do not understand as do those who teach them, and which are not
of such a nature that, even if I understood them
perfectly, they would be worthy of your wisdom and
your ear." "You don't say so !" answered the
other. "Even if you think these everyday and
hackneyed maxims hardly deserving of the attention
of a man of my years, can we for all that neglect the
truths which, you have told us, the orator must know,
concerning varieties of human nature, ethics, the
methods of kindling and calming the minds of men,
history, ancient times, the government of the State,
and lastly our own science of common law ? For I
knew that all this knowledge and this multitude of
things were to be found in your wisdom ; but I had

Instances of importance of legal knowledge.

113

instrumento tam lautam supellectilem nunquam
videram.

166   Potes igitur, inquit Crassus—ut alia omittam
innumerabilia et immensa, et ad ipsum tuum ius
civile veniam—, oratores putare eos, quos multas
horas exspectavit, cum in campum properaret, et
ridens et stomachans Scaevola, cum Hypsaeus maxima voce, plurimis verbis, a M. Crasso praetore
contenderet, ut ei, quem defendebat, causa cadere
liceret, Cn. autem Octavius, homo consularis, non
minus longa oratione recusaret, ne adversarius causa
caderet, ac ne is, pro quo ipse diceret, turpi tutelae
iudicio, atque omni molestia, stultitia adversarii,
167 liberaretur ?   Ego vero istos, inquit—memini enim
mihi narrare Mucium—, non modo oratoris nomine,
sed ne foro quidem dignos putarim.   Atqui non defuit illis patronis, inquit Crassus, eloquentia, neque
dicendi ratio aut copia, sed iuris civilis prudentia :
quod alter plus, lege agendo, petebat, quam quantum lex in Duodecim Tabulis permiserat ; quod cum
impetrasset, causa caderet : alter iniquum putabat
plus secum agi, quam quod erat in actione ; neque
intellegebat, si ita esset actum, litem adversarium
perditurum.

168   XXXVII. Quid ? his paucis diebus, nonne, nobis

never observed furniture so sumptuous in the outfit of an orator."

66   "Can you then," said Crassus "(to pass over other matters innumerable and of vast importance, and come to your favourite common law itself), can you consider those men to be orators, for whom Scaevola, half laughing and half enraged, waited many hours, though in a hurry to start for the Playing Field, while Hypsaeus, at the top of his voice and with most exuberant verbosity, was struggling to procure from Marcus Crassus the praetor the non-suiting of the party for whom he himself was appearing, and Gnaeus Octavius, though a man of consular rank, was objecting, in a speech every bit as long, to having his opponent cast in his suit, and his own client relieved, by the folly of the other side, from a degrading verdict of dishonest guardianship 7 and from all trouble whatever ? " "No," returned Scaevola, " as for such men (for I remember having the story from Mucius), I should not hold them fit even to appear in Court, much less to bear the title of orators." "And yet," Crassus went on, " it was not eloquence, or the art of speaking, or copiousness that was wanting in those counsel, but knowledge of the common law : for the one was claiming, by action on the statute, more than the provision in the Twelve Tables permitted and, had he carried his point, his action must fail : the other thought it unjust that the claim against him should be for more than the amount in suit ; not observing that, if the issue had been defined in that way, his opponent would lose his case.

XXXVII. "Again, within these last few days, when we were sitting as assessors on the Bench of

in tribunali Q. Pompeii, praetoris urbani, familiaris nostri, sedentibus, homo ex numero disertorum postulabat, ut illi, unde peteretur, vetus atque usitata exceptio daretur, CUIUS PECUNIAE DIES FUISSET ? quod petitoris causa comparatum esse, non intellegebat: ut, si ille infitiator probasset iudici ante petitam esse pecuniam quam esset coepta deberi, petitor, rursus cum peteret, ne exceptione excluderetur, QUOD EA RES

169 IN IUDICIUM ANTEA VENISSET. Quid ergo hoc fieri turpius, aut dici potest, quam eum, qui hanc personam susceperit, ut amicorum controversias causasque tueatur, laborantibus succurrat, aegris medeatur, afflictos excitet, hunc in minimis tenuissimisque rebus ita labi, ut aliis miserandus, aliis irridendus esse videatur ?

170 Equidem propinquum nostrum, P. Crassum, illum Divitem, cum multis aliis rebus elegantem hominem et ornatum, tum praecipue in hoc efferendum et laudandum puto, quod, cum P. Scaevola frater esset, solitus est ei persaepe dicere, neque illum in iure civili satis illi arti facere posse, nisi dicendi copiam assumpsisset—quod quidem hic, qui mecum consul fuit, filius eius, est consecutus—; neque se ante causas amicorum tractare atque agere coepisse, quam ius civile didicisset.

171 Quid vero ille M. Cato ? Nonne et eloquentia tanta fuit, quantam illa tempora, atque illa aetas in hac civitate ferre maximam potuit, et iuris civilis

---

[a] 95 B.C.

our friend Quintus Pompeius, the City praetor, did
not one of our accomplished advocates apply, on
behalf of the defendant in an action of debt, for the
insertion of the ancient and familiar restriction, ' *As
regards such moneys as have already accrued due,*' not
understanding that this clause had been ordained
for the benefit of a plaintiff, to the end that, if a
repudiating defendant should satisfy the judge that
money had been claimed before it had become
payable, the plaintiff should not be barred, on
bringing a fresh action, by the special plea ' *That this*
69 *matter has already been litigated* ' ? Can anything
then more unseemly be done or suggested than this,
that the very man who has undertaken the part of
the champion of the quarrels and interests of his
friends, of their helper in trouble, the healer of their
sufferings, and their upholder when they have fallen,
should blunder so grossly in the most trifling and
insignificant technicalities, as to arouse the pity of
some, and the ridicule of others ?

70   " Assuredly I think that our relative Publius
Crassus, surnamed Dives, while in many other ways
a man of taste and accomplishment, was particularly
to be extolled and eulogized for this that, being the
brother of Publius Scaevola, he used continually to
tell him that in common law he could never do justice
to his art, without acquiring as well a copious diction
(advice certainly followed by this son of his, who was
my colleague in the consulship [a]), and that he himself
had learned the common law, before he began to
handle and conduct the causes of his friends.

1   " And what of the eminent Marcus Cato ?   Did he
not combine eloquence as grand as those times and
that epoch could produce in this State, with an un-

117

CICERO

omnium peritissimus ? Verecundius hac de re iamdudum loquor, quod adest vir in dicendo summus,
quem ego unum oratorem maxime admiror ; sed
172 tamen idem hoc semper ius civile contempsit. Verum,
quoniam sententiae atque opinionis meae voluistis
esse participes, nihil occultabo ; et, quoad potero,
vobis exponam quid de quaque re sentiam.

XXXVIII. Antonii incredibilis quaedam, et prope
singularis et divina vis ingenii videtur, etiamsi hac
scientia iuris nudata sit, posse se facile ceteris armis
prudentiae tueri atque defendere. Quam ob rem hic
nobis sit exceptus ; ceteros vero non dubitabo primum inertiae condemnare sententia mea, post etiam
173 impudentiae. Nam volitare in foro, haerere in iure
ac praetorum tribunalibus, iudicia privata magnarum
rerum obire, in quibus saepe non de facto, sed de
aequitate ac iure certetur, iactare se in causis
centumviralibus, in quibus usucapionum, tutelarum,
gentilitatum, agnationum, alluvionum, circumluvi-
onum, nexorum, mancipiorum, parietum, luminum,
stillicidiorum, testamentorum ruptorum aut ratorum,
ceterarumque rerum innumerabilium iura versentur,
cum omnino, quid suum, quid alienum, quare denique civis aut peregrinus, servus aut liber quispiam sit,
ignoret, insignis est impudentiae.

ᵃ A bench of judges appointed yearly for civil suits,
especially those relating to inheritance.
118

equalled knowledge of the common law? It is with some diffidence that I have been so long discussing this topic, when we have with us the greatest of speakers, a man whom I admire above all others as an unique orator, but who nevertheless has always 172 despised this common law. Since however you have sought to be partakers of my view and my judgement, I will suppress nothing but, so far as lies in my power, will lay before you what I think upon every point.

XXXVIII. "In Antonius what I may call a marvellous and almost unrivalled and godlike power of genius seems, even without the protection of this legal knowledge, to be able easily to guard and defend itself with the rest of the armoury of practical wisdom. Let him then be left out of our indictment but, as for the rest, I shall not hesitate to give my vote for a verdict of 'Guilty,' first of 173 laziness and secondly of effrontery as well. For to flit around the Courts, to loiter about the Bench and judgement-seats of the praetors, to engage in civil proceedings involving weighty interests, in which the dispute is often not as to facts but as to equity and law, to vaunt oneself in cases before the Hundred Commissioners,[a] where are debated the rights concerning long user, guardianship, clanship, relationship through males, alluvial accessions, the formation of islands, obligations, sales, party-walls, ancient lights, rain-drip from the eaves, the revocation or establishment of wills, and all those other matters innumerable, when a man is wholly ignorant as to what is his own and what another's, and even of the essential difference between citizen and foreigner, or between bond and free, this is the mark of no ordinary effrontery.

Only genius can dispense with study.

119

174   Illa vero deridenda arrogantia est, in minoribus navigiis rudem esse se confiteri ; quinqueremes, aut etiam maiores, gubernare didicisse. Tu mihi cum in circulo decipiare adversarii stipulatiuncula, et cum obsignes tabellas clientis tui, quibus in tabellis id sit scriptum, quo ille capiatur ; ego tibi ullam causam maiorem committendam putem ? Citius hercule is, qui duorum scalmorum naviculam in portu everterit, in Euxino ponto Argonautarum navem

175 gubernarit ! Quid, si ne parvae quidem causae sunt, sed saepe maximae, in quibus certatur de iure civili ; quod tandem os est illius patroni, qui ad eas causas sine ulla scientia iuris audet accedere ? Quae potuit igitur esse causa maior, quam illius militis, de cuius morte cum domum falsus ab exercitu nuntius venisset, et pater eius, re credita, testamentum mutasset, et, quem ei visum esset, fecisset heredem, essetque ipse mortuus : res delata est ad centumviros, cum miles domum revenisset, egissetque lege in hereditatem paternam, testamento exheres filius ? Nempe in ea causa quaesitum est de iure civili, possetne paternorum bonorum exheres esse filius, quem pater testamento neque heredem, neque exheredem scripsisset nominatim.

176   XXXIX. Quid ? qua de re inter Marcellos et Claudios patricios centumviri iudicarunt, cum Mar-

120

174 " Derision surely befits his presumption, who owns himself a raw hand in managing smaller barks, while claiming to have learned the piloting of five-banked galleys or vessels larger still. When I see you trapped in a private conference by a quibble of your opponent's, and sealing up your client's deed, such deed containing the words by which he is defeated, can I think that any case of real importance ought to be entrusted to you ? Sooner, I vow, shall he who has upset a pair-oared skiff in harbour navigate the 175 ship of the Argonauts upon the Euxine Sea ! Suppose however that the cases are not even trifling, but often of the greatest moment, involving a dispute about the common law : what cheek, I ask you, has that advocate who, without any legal knowledge, ventures to undertake the conduct of these proceedings ? What case, for example, could be more important than that of the well-known soldier, of whose death false news had arrived home from the army, and whose father, believing the tale, had altered his will, and instituted an heir of his own choosing, and then died himself : the matter came before the Hundred Commissioners, upon the soldier returning home and starting an action on the statute for the recovery of his paternal inheritance, as a son disinherited by will ? Certainly in this case the issue was one of common law, that is to say, whether or not a son could be disinherited in respect of his father's estate, when such father in his will had neither instituted him heir nor disinherited him by name.

XXXIX. "What again of the dispute between the Marcellans and the patrician Claudians, determined by the Hundred Commissioners, the Marcellans

Need of erudition proved by instances.

celli ab liberti filio stirpe, Claudii patricii eiusdem
hominis hereditatem, gente ad se rediisse dicerent;
nonne in ea causa fuit oratoribus de toto stirpis ac
177 gentilitatis iure dicendum? Quid? quod item in
centumvirali iudicio certatum esse accepimus, qui
Romam in exsilium venisset, cui Romae exsulare ius
esset, si se ad aliquem quasi patronum applicuisset,
intestatoque esset mortuus : nonne in ea causa ius
applicationis, obscurum sane et ignotum, patefactum
178 in iudicio atque illustratum est a patrono? Quid?
nuper, cum ego C. Sergii Oratae contra hunc nostrum Antonium iudicio privato causam defenderem;
nonne omnis nostra in iure versata defensio est?
Cum enim Marius Gratidianus aedes Oratae vendidisset, neque, servire quamdam earum aedium
partem, in mancipii lege dixisset ; defendebamus,
quidquid fuisset incommodi in mancipio, id si vendi-
tor scisset, neque declarasset, praestare debere.

179 Quo quidem in genere familiaris noster M. Bucculeius, homo neque meo iudicio stultus, et suo valde
sapiens, et a iuris studio non abhorrens, simili in re
quodam modo nuper erravit. Nam cum aedes L.
Fufio venderet, in mancipio lumina, uti tum essent,
ita recepit. Fufius autem, simul atque aedificari
coeptum est in quadam parte urbis quae modo ex
illis aedibus conspici posset, egit statim cum Buc-

ᵃ For this point of law see Appendix p. 480.
ᵇ Some ambiguity in the conveyancing terms used by
Bucculeius in reserving his ' ancient lights ' enabled Fufius
to interpret the reservation as a grant of an absolute right to
light.

alleging that an inheritance had devolved on them from a freedman's son by lineal descent, while the patrician Claudians claimed it as theirs by reverter through clanship ; did not both counsel in that case have to discuss the entire law of lineal descent and

177 of clanship ? And what of that other contention which we have heard was raised in the Court of the Hundred Commissioners, where a foreigner had come into exile at Rome, having a legal right to dwell there, provided that he had attached himself to someone as a kind of protector, and such foreigner had died intestate : in that case was not the law of vassalage, a truly mysterious and unfamiliar thing,

178 revealed and elucidated by counsel in Court ? Then too, when recently I appeared, in a civil action, on behalf of Gaius Sergius Orata, with our friend here Antonius on the other side, was not our defence concerned solely with matter of law ? For Marius Gratidianus had sold a house to Orata, without stating in the conditions of sale that a certain part of the building was subject to an easement, and we were urging that the vendor must allow compensation for any defect in the property sold, if he had known of its existence and had not disclosed it.[a]

179 "In that kind of action too our friend Marcus Bucculeius, no fool in my opinion, and mightily wise in his own, and a man with no distaste for legal studies, somehow went wrong lately on a similar point. For, on the sale of a house to Lucius Fufius, he made a reservation in his conveyance of all rights to light ' as then enjoyed.'[b] Fufius however, the moment that any building began in some part of the city of which as much as a glimpse could be caught from that house of his, immediately launched an

culeio, quod, cuicumque particulae coeli officeretur,
quamvis esset procul, mutari lumina putabat.

180   Quid vero ? clarissima M'. Curii causa Marcique
Coponii nuper apud centumviros, quo concursu
hominum, qua exspectatione defensa est ! cum
Q. Scaevola, aequalis et collega meus, homo omnium
et disciplina iuris civilis eruditissimus, et ingenio pru-
dentiaque acutissimus, et oratione maxime limatus
atque subtilis, atque, ut ego soleo dicere, iuris peritorum eloquentissimus, eloquentium iuris peritissimus, ex scripto testamentorum iura defenderet,
negaretque, nisi postumus et natus, et, antequam in
suam tutelam venisset, mortuus esset, heredem eum
esse posse, qui esset secundum postumum, et natum,
et mortuum, heres institutus : ego autem defenderem, hac eum tum mente fuisse, qui testamentum
fecisset, ut, si filius non esset, qui in tutelam veniret,
M'. Curius esset heres. Num destitit uterque nostrum in ea causa, in auctoritatibus, in exemplis, in
testamentorum formulis, hoc est, in medio iure civili,
versari ?

181   XL. Omitto iam plura exempla causarum amplis-
simarum, quae sunt innumerabilia : capitis nostri
saepe potest accidere ut causae versentur in iure.
Etenim sic C. Mancinum, nobilissimum atque opti-
mum virum, ac consularem, cum eum propter invidiam Numantini foederis pater patratus ex S. C.

---

a See Book II, §§ 140, 221.

b See Appendix p. 480.   *c* In 137 B.C.

d One of the twenty *fetiales* appointed (*patratus*) with
patria potestas over citizens whom he was delegated to hand
over to the enemy.

action against Bucculeius, because he conceived that his rights to light were affected, if any scrap of his view was blocked, however far away.

180 "Finally, remember the conduct of the famous case [a] of Manius Curius against Marcus Coponius, not long ago before the Hundred Commissioners—the crowd that collected, the anticipations aroused! There was Quintus Scaevola, my contemporary and colleague, of all men the most learned in the science of the common law, the most sagacious by talent and experience, the most highly polished and exquisite in diction, and indeed, as I always say, among lawyers the best orator, among orators the best lawyer : he was arguing the rights of the case on the literal terms of the will, and contending that the person who had been nominated heir in the second grade, as substitute for a posthumous son, who should be born and die, could never inherit, unless such posthumous son had in fact been born and died before becoming his own master [b] : on the other side I was affirming the true intention of the testator to have been that Manius Curius should be heir in the event of no son coming of age. In these proceedings were not both of us unceasingly occupied with decisions, with precedents, with forms of wills, with questions, in fact, of common law all around us ?

181 XL. "I pass over yet further examples of most important cases, countless as they are : it may often happen that actions involving our civil rights turn upon points of law. For in truth such was the experience of Gaius Mancinus, a man of the highest rank and character and a past consul, who under a decree of the Senate had been delivered up [c] to the Numantines by the Priestly Envoy,[d] for con-

Cases involving citizenship.

Numantinis dedidisset, eumque illi non recepissent, posteaque Mancinus domum revenisset, neque in senatum introire dubitasset ; P. Rutilius, M. filius, tribunus plebis, de senatu iussit educi, quod eum civem negaret esse ; quia memoria sic esset proditum, quem pater suus, aut populus vendidisset, aut pater patratus dedidisset, ei nullum esse postliminium.

182   Quam possumus reperire ex omnibus rebus civilibus causam contentionemque maiorem, quam de ordine, de civitate, de libertate, de capite hominis consularis ; praesertim cum haec non in crimine aliquo, quod ille posset infitiari, sed in civili iure consisteret ? Similique in genere, inferiore ordine, si quis apud nos servisset ex populo foederato, seseque liberasset, ac postea domum revenisset ; quaesitum est apud maiores nostros, num is ad suos postliminio rediisset,

183 et amisisset hanc civitatem. Quid ? de libertate, quo iudicium gravius esse nullum potest, nonne ex iure civili potest esse contentio, cum quaeritur, is, qui domini voluntate census sit, continuone, an ubi lustrum conditum, liber sit ? Quid, quod usu, memoria patrum, venit, ut paterfamilias, qui ex Hispania Romam venisset, cum uxorem praegnantem in provincia reliquisset, Romaeque alteram duxisset, neque

---

   a ' Return behind one's threshold,' return home and resumption of former status and privileges.

   b The *lustrum* was the sacrifice of purification, which con-

cluding an unpopular treaty with their nation, and whose surrender they had refused to accept, whereupon he returned home and unhesitatingly came into the Senate-house : Publius Rutilius, son of Marcus and tribune of the commons, ordered him to be removed, affirming that he was no citizen, in view of the traditional rule that a man sold by his father or by the people, or delivered up by the Priestly Envoy, had no right of restoration.[a]

182 "What judicial controversy can we discover, within the whole range of public life, more important than one touching the rank, state-membership, freedom and entire civil rights of a past consul, especially as this issue did not depend upon some accusation of fact, which the defendant might be able to disprove, but upon a point of common law ? And in a similar case, affecting humbler folk, if a member of an allied people, after being a slave in Rome, had acquired his freedom and subsequently returned home; it was a moot point with our forefathers whether by process of restoration he had not reverted to his former nationality and lost his Roman citizenship.

183 Then as to freedom, the most serious issue there can be, may not controversy arise out of the common law, on the question whether a slave, enrolled with his master's consent on the censor's list, is to date his enfranchisement from that moment, or from completion of the lustrum ?[b] And what of a case that really happened, within our fathers' recollection, of the head of a family coming from Spain to Rome, and leaving in the province his wife with child : at Rome he married another wife,

cluded the proceedings of the *census* and brought the new register of citizens into operation for the ensuing five years.

nuntium priori remisisset, mortuusque esset intestato,
et ex utraque filius natus esset ; mediocrisne res
in controversiam adducta est, cum quaereretur de
duobus civium capitibus, et de puero, qui ex pos-
teriore natus erat, et de eius matre ? Quae, si iudi-
caretur, certis quibusdam verbis, non novis nuptiis,
fieri cum superiore divortium, in concubinae locum
duceretur.

184　Haec igitur, et horum similia iura suae civitatis
ignorantem, erectum et celsum, alacri et prompto ore
ac vultu, huc atque illuc intuentem, vagari magna
cum caterva toto foro, praesidium clientibus, atque
opem amicis, et prope cunctis civibus lucem ingenii
et consilii sui porrigentem atque tendentem, nonne in
primis flagitiosum putandum est ?

185　XLI. Et quoniam de impudentia dixi, castigemus
etiam segnitiem hominum atque inertiam. Nam si
esset ista cognitio iuris magna ac difficilis, tamen
utilitatis magnitudo deberet homines ad suscipiendum
discendi laborem impellere. Sed, o dii immortales !
non dicerem hoc, audiente Scaevola, nisi ipse dicere
soleret, nullius artis faciliorem sibi cognitionem videri.

186　Quod quidem certis de causis a plerisque aliter existimatur : primum, quia veteres illi, qui huic scientiae
praefuerunt, obtinendae atque augendae potentiae
suae causa, pervulgari artem suam noluerunt, deinde,
posteaquam est editum, expositis a Cn. Flavio primum actionibus, nulli fuerunt, qui illa artificiose

without having sent notice of divorce to the first, and afterwards died intestate, when each woman had borne a son ; was it but an ordinary dispute that thereupon arose, involving as it did the civil rights of two citizens, the boy born of the second consort, and his mother ? She, if it were held that the first wife could be divorced only by using some specific formula, and not by marrying again, would be regarded as being in the position of a concubine.

184 "Accordingly, that a man, ignorant of these and similar laws of his own community, should roam with a large following from court to court, haughtily and with head upraised, eager and assured in mien and countenance, directing his gaze hither and thither, and holding out and tendering protection to clients, aid to friends, and the illumination of his talent and advice to wellnigh every citizen, is not all this to be considered something supremely scandalous ?

185 XLI. "And since I have spoken of the effrontery of men, let us go on to chastise their slackness and laziness. For even if this legal study were a matter of great difficulty, yet its great utility should urge men to undergo the toil of learning. But, by Heaven, I should not say this with Scaevola listening, were he not himself in the habit of affirming that he thinks

186 no art easier of attainment. As to this indeed most people, for definite reasons, think otherwise : first because those men of old time who presided over this study, in their anxiety to maintain and increase their own authority, would not have their art made common property, and secondly, after the law had been published, and the forms of pleading first set forth by Gnaeus Flavius, there were none able to distribute these matters into their kinds and arrange them

Law not a specially difficult study.

digesta generatim componerent. Nihil est enim,
quod ad artem redigi possit, nisi ille prius, qui illa
tenet, quorum artem instituere vult, habeat illam
scientiam, ut ex eis rebus, quarum ars nondum sit,
187 artem efficere possit. Hoc video, dum breviter
voluerim dicere, dictum a me esse paulo obscurius:
sed experiar, et dicam, si potero, planius.

XLII. Omnia fere, quae sunt conclusa nunc artibus,
dispersa et dissipata quondam fuerunt: ut in musicis,
numeri, et voces, et modi; in geometria, lineamenta,
formae, intervalla, magnitudines; in astrologia, caeli
conversio, ortus, obitus motusque siderum; in gram-
maticis, poetarum pertractatio, historiarum cognitio,
verborum interpretatio, pronuntiandi quidam sonus;
in hac denique ipsa ratione dicendi, excogitare, ornare, disponere, meminisse, agere; ignota quondam
188 omnibus, et diffusa late videbantur. Adhibita est
igitur ars quaedam extrinsecus ex alio genere quodam, quod sibi totum philosophi assumunt, quae rem
dissolutam divulsamque conglutinaret, et ratione
quadam constringeret. Sit ergo in iure civili finis
hic, legitimae atque usitatae in rebus causisque ci-
189 vium aequabilitatis conservatio. Tum sunt notanda
genera, et ad certum numerum paucitatemque revocanda. Genus autem est id, quod sui similes
communione quadam, specie autem differentes, duas
aut plures complectitur partes. Partes autem sunt,

artistically. For nothing can be reduced to an art unless the man who has mastered the subject, of which he would organize an art, already possesses the special knowledge requisite to enable him, out of particulars not yet embodied in an art, to con-187 struct one. I see that, in my desire to be brief, I have spoken a little obscurely, but I will try to express myself, if I can, in clearer terms.

XLII. "Nearly all elements, now forming the con- The nature tent of arts, were once without order or correla- of legal tion: in music, for example, rhythms, sounds and science. measures; in geometry, lines, figures, dimensions and magnitudes; in astronomy, the revolution of the sky, the rising, setting and movement of heavenly bodies; in literature, the study of poets, the learning of histories, the explanation of words and proper intonation in speaking them; and lastly in this very theory of oratory, invention, style, arrangement, memory and delivery, once seemed to all men things unknown and widely separate one from another. 88 And so a certain art was called in from outside, derived from another definite sphere, which philosophers arrogate wholly to themselves, in order that it might give coherence to things so far disconnected and sundered, and bind them in some sort of scheme. Let the goal then of the common law be defined as the preservation, in the concerns and disputes of citizens, of an impartiality founded on statute and 89 custom. We must next designate the general classes of cases, restricting these to a small fixed number. Now a general class is that which embraces two or more species, resembling one another in some common property while differing in some peculiarity. And species are subdivisions, ranged

quae generibus eis, ex quibus emanant, subiciuntur;
omniaque, quae sunt vel generum vel partium nomina,
definitionibus, quam vim habeant, est exprimendum.
Est enim definitio, earum rerum, quae sunt eius rei
propriae, quam definire volumus, brevis et circum-
scripta quaedam explicatio.

190   Hisce ergo rebus exempla adiungerem, nisi, apud
quos haec habetur oratio, cernerem : nunc complectar quod proposui, brevi.   Si enim aut mihi facere
licuerit, quod iamdiu cogito, aut alius quispiam, aut,
me impedito, occuparit, aut mortuo effecerit, ut
primum omne ius civile in genera digerat, quae perpauca sunt ; deinde eorum generum quasi quaedam
membra dispertiat ; tum propriam cuiusque vim
definitione declaret ; perfectam artem iuris civilis
habebitis, magis magnam atque uberem, quam dif-
191 ficilem atque obscuram.   Atque interea tamen, dum
haec, quae dispersa sunt, coguntur, vel passim licet
carpentem, et colligentem undique, repleri iusta iuris
civilis scientia.

XLIII. Nonne videtis, equitem Romanum, hominem acutissimo omnium ingenio, sed minime
ceteris artibus eruditum, C. Aculeonem, qui mecum
vivit, semperque vixit, ita tenere ius civile, ut ei,
cum ab hoc discesseritis, nemo de eis, qui peritissimi
192 sunt, anteponatur ? Omnia enim sunt posita ante
oculos, collocata in usu quotidiano, in congressione
hominum atque in foro ; neque ita multis litteris aut

under those general classes from which they spring ;
while all names, whether of general classes or species,
190 must be so defined as to show the significance of
each. A definition of course I may describe as a
concise and accurate statement of the attributes
belonging to the thing we would define.

"I would therefore append illustrations to what I Project for
have said, were I not mindful of the quality of the a treatise.
hearers of this discourse : as it is, I will briefly
summarize my plan. For if I am permitted to do
what I have long been projecting, or if someone
else anticipates me, preoccupied as I am, or does
the work when I am dead, first dividing the entire
common law into its general classes, which are very
few, and next distributing what I may call the subdivisions of those classes, and after that making plain
by definition the proper significance of each, then
you will have a complete art of the common law,
magnificent and copious but neither inaccessible nor
91 mysterious. And yet in the meantime, while these
disconnected materials are being assembled, a man
may, by culling even at random and gathering from
every quarter, become filled with a tolerable knowledge of the common law.

XLIII. "Do you not notice that Gaius Aculeo, Sources
Roman knight, a man of the keenest intelligence, available.
but of slender accomplishment in any other art,
who dwells and has always dwelt with me, is so
complete a master of the common law, that if you
except our friend here, not one of the most learned
92 is to be placed before him ? The reason is that all
its materials lie open to view, having their setting
in everyday custom, in the intercourse of men, and
in public scenes : and they are not enclosed in so

voluminibus magnis continentur : eadem enim sunt
elata primum a pluribus ; deinde, paucis verbis com-
mutatis, etiam ab eisdem scriptoribus, scripta sunt
193 saepius. Accedit vero, quo facilius percipi cognosci-
que ius civile possit (quod minime plerique arbitrantur), mira quaedam in cognoscendo suavitas et
delectatio. Nam, sive quem haec Aeliana studia
delectant ; plurima est, et in omni iure civili, et in
pontificum libris, et in Duodecim Tabulis, antiquitatis
effigies, quod et verborum prisca vetustas cognoscitur,
et actionum genera quaedam maiorum consuetudinem vitamque declarant : sive quis civilem scientiam contempletur, quam Scaevola non putat oratoris
esse propriam, sed cuiusdam ex alio genere prudentiae ; totam hanc, descriptis omnibus civitatis
utilitatibus ac partibus, Duodecim Tabulis contineri
videbit ; sive quem ista praepotens et gloriosa philosophia delectat, dicam audacius, hosce habebit fontes
omnium disputationum suarum, qui iure civili et legi-
194 bus continentur. Ex his enim et dignitatem maxime
expetendam videmus, cum verus, iustus, atque ho-
nestus labor honoribus, praemiis, splendore decora-
tur ; vitia autem hominum, atque fraudes, damnis,
ignominiis, vinculis, verberibus, exsiliis, morte mul-
tantur; et docemur non infinitis, concertationum-
que plenis disputationibus, sed auctoritate, nutuque
legum, domitas habere libidines, coercere omnes

---

a *Philosophia* means here moral philosophy or ethics.

very many records or in books so very big : for
identical matters were originally published by
numerous authors, and afterwards, with slight
variations in terms, were set down time and again
193 even by the same writers. Another help in facili-
tating the learning and understanding of the common
law (though most people hardly credit this), is the
peculiarly wonderful charm and delight of that study.
For if these pursuits associated with Aelius attract
a man, he has throughout the common law, and in
the priestly books and the Twelve Tables, a complete
picture of the olden time, since a primitive antiquity
of language can be studied there, and certain forms
of pleading reveal the manners and the way of life
of our forerunners ; if he is studying political science,
which Scaevola does not regard as the business of
an orator, but of someone belonging to a different
department of learning, he will find the whole of
this subject dependent upon the Twelve Tables,
wherein are described all the interests and the
entire organization of the State ; if he is a lover of
your most mighty and arrogant philosophy [a]—I shall
speak rather boldly—, he will have here the sources
of all his discussions, since these sources derive from
194 common law and statutes. For from these we both
see that merit is above all else to be coveted,
since true, fitting and reputable exertion wins the
adornment of high office, rewards and honour,
while the misdeeds and knaveries of mankind are
visited with fines, degradation, chains, scourgings,
banishment and death ; and we learn too, not by
debates without end and full of recriminations, but
by the authoritative decision of the laws, to have
our passions in subjection, bridle every lust, hold

cupiditates, nostra tueri, ab alienis mentes, oculos, manus abstinere.

195 XLIV. Fremant omnes licet; dicam quod sentio: bibliothecas mehercule omnium philosophorum unus mihi videtur Duodecim Tabularum libellus, si quis legum fontes et capita viderit, et auctoritatis pondere, 196 et utilitatis ubertate superare. Ac, si nos, id quod maxime debet, nostra patria delectat; cuius rei tanta est vis, ac tanta natura, ut 'Ithacam illam in asperrimis saxulis, tanquam nidulum, affixam,' sapientissimus vir immortalitati anteponeret; quo amore tandem inflammati esse debemus in eiusmodi patriam, quae una in omnibus terris domus est virtutis, imperii, dignitatis! Cuius primum nobis mens, mos, disciplina, nota esse debet; vel quia est patria, parens omnium nostrum, vel quia tanta sapientia fuisse in iure constituendo putanda est, quanta fuit in his tantis opibus imperii comparandis.

197 Percipietis etiam illam ex cognitione iuris laetitiam et voluptatem, quod, quantum praestiterint nostri maiores prudentia ceteris gentibus, tum facillime intellegetis, si cum illorum Lycurgo, et Dracone, et Solone nostras leges conferre volueritis. Incredibile est enim, quam sit omne ius civile, praeter hoc nostrum, inconditum, ac paene ridiculum: de quo multa soleo in sermonibus quotidianis dicere, cum hominum nostrorum prudentiam ceteris hominibus, et maxime Graecis, antepono. His ego de causis dixeram, Scaevola, eis, qui perfecti oratores

---

^a For Calypso's offer of immortality to Odysseus see *Od.* v. 135; for the hero's nostalgia, *Od.* i. 55-59, v. 151-158, and ix. 27-28.

what we have, and keep our thoughts, eyes and hands from what is our neighbour's.

195 XLIV. "Though the whole world grumble, I will speak my mind : it seems to me, I solemnly declare, that, if anyone looks to the origins and sources of the laws, the small manual of the Twelve Tables by itself surpasses the libraries of all the philosophers, in weight of authority and wealth of usefulness alike. 196 And if our own native land is our joy, as to the uttermost it ought to be,—a sentiment of such strength and quality that a hero of consummate prudence gave preference over immortality [a] to ' that Ithaca of his, lodged like a tiny nest upon the roughest of small crags,'—with love how ardent must we surely be fired for a country such as ours, standing alone among all lands as the home of excellence, imperial power and good report ! It is her spirit, customs and constitution that we are bound first to learn, both because she is the motherland of all of us, and because we must needs hold that wisdom as perfect went to the establishment of her laws, as to the acquisition of the vast might of her empire.

197 "You will win from legal studies this further joy and delight, that you will most readily understand how far our ancestors surpassed in practical wisdom the men of other nations, if you will compare our own laws with those of Lycurgus, Draco and Solon, among the foreigners. For it is incredible how disordered, and wellnigh absurd, is all national law other than our own ; on which subject it is my habit to say a great deal in everyday talk, when upholding the wisdom of our own folk against that of all others, the Greeks in particular. On these grounds, Scaevola, did I declare a knowledge of the common law

Interest and rewards of legal studies.

esse vellent, iuris civilis cognitionem esse necessariam.

198 XLV. Iam vero ipsa per sese quantum afferat eis,
qui ei praesunt, honoris, gratiae, dignitatis, quis
ignorat ? Itaque, non, ut apud Graecos infimi homines, mercedula adducti, ministros se praebent in
iudiciis oratoribus, ei, qui apud illos πραγματικοὶ
vocantur, sic in nostra civitate ; contra amplissimus
quisque et clarissimus vir ; ut ille, qui propter hanc
iuris civilis scientiam sic appellatus a summo poeta
est,

Egregie cordatus homo, catus Aeliu' Sextus,

multique praeterea, qui, cum ingenio sibi auctore
dignitatem reperissent, perfecerunt, ut in respon-
dendo iure, auctoritate plus etiam, quam ipso ingenio,
valerent.

199 Senectuti vero celebrandae et ornandae quod
honestius potest esse perfugium, quam iuris interpretatio ? Equidem mihi hoc subsidium iam ab
adolescentia comparavi, non solum ad causarum usum
forensium, sed etiam ad decus atque ornamentum
senectutis ; ut, cum me vires (quod fere iam tempus adventat) deficere coepissent, ista ab solitudine
domum meam vindicarem. Quid est enim praeclarius, quam honoribus et reipublicae muneribus
perfunctum senem posse suo iure dicere idem, quod
apud Ennium dicat ille Pythius Apollo, se esse eum,

---

^a Similar practitioners appeared at Rome under the
Empire, but in Cicero's time the great advocates got their
law from the most eminent jurists.

^b *i.e.* Ennius, *Ann.* x. 326, *Remains of Old Latin* (L.C.L.),
i. 120, 121.

to be indispensable to such as sought to become complete orators.

98   XLV. " Who again does not know how much preferment, credit and authority this study of itself secures for its leaders ? Thus, while among the Greeks the humblest persons, ' attorneys ' [a] as they are called in that country, are induced for a mere pittance to proffer their assistance to advocates in Court, in our own community, on the contrary, all the most honourable and illustrious men have done this work, he for example who, for his knowledge of this common law, was described by the greatest of poets [b] as follows :

Notably wise and shrewd among men there was Aelius Sextus,

and many besides him who, after gaining eminence on the strength of their talent, brought it about that, in advising on law, their strength lay less even in their unaided talent than in their reputation.

" Then too, for giving to old age companionship and grace, what worthier resource can there be than the interpretation of law ? For my part, even from earliest manhood, I laid up for myself this provision, not only with a view to my actual practice in the Courts, but also to be the glory and distinction of my age, to the end that, when my bodily powers should have begun to fail (a time already almost upon me), I might preserve my home from loneliness at the last. For what is there grander than for an old man, who has discharged the high offices and functions of the State, to be able to say as of right, with the great Pythian Apollo in Ennius,[c] that he is the one from

[c] In *Eumenides, ibid.* 270, 271.

unde sibi, si non ' populi et reges,' at omnes sui
cives consilium expetant,

> Suarum rerum incerti ; quos ego mea ope ex
> Incertis certos, compotesque consili
> Dimitto, ut ne res temere tractent turbidas.

200 Est enim sine dubio domus iurisconsulti totius
oraculum civitatis. Testis est huiusce Q. Mucii ianua
et vestibulum, quod in eius infirmissima valetudine,
affectaque iam aetate, maxima quotidie frequentia
civium, ac summorum hominum splendore celebratur.

201 XLVI. Iam vero illa non longam orationem desiderant, quam ob rem existimem publica quoque
iura, quae sunt propria civitatis atque imperii, tum
monumenta rerum gestarum, et vetustatis exempla,
oratori nota esse debere. Nam ut in rerum priva-
tarum causis atque iudiciis depromenda saepe oratio
est ex iure civili, et idcirco, ut ante diximus, oratori
iuris civilis scientia necessaria est : sic in causis publicis iudiciorum, concionum, Senatus, omnis haec et
antiquitatis memoria, et publici iuris auctoritas,
et regendae reipublicae ratio ac scientia, tanquam
aliqua materies, eis oratoribus, qui versantur in republica, subiecta esse debent.

202 Non enim causidicum nescio quem, neque pro-
clamatorem, aut rabulam, hoc sermone nostro con-
quirimus, sed eum virum, qui primum sit eius artis
antistes, cuius cum ipsa natura magnam homini
facultatem daret, tamen dedisse deus putabatur ; ut
et ipsum, quod erat hominis proprium, non partum

140

whom all his fellow-citizens at any rate, if not ' the peoples and the kings,' seek counsel for themselves,

> Men doubtful of their good, whom by my help,
> Their doubts dispelled, confirmed in their designs,
> I send away, no troubled track to thread.

0 For the house of a great lawyer is assuredly the oracular seat of the whole community. This is attested by the gateway and forecourt of our friend here, Quintus Mucius, thronged as they are daily, notwithstanding his very poor health and now advanced age, by a huge concourse of citizens, among whom are personages of the highest distinction.

1 XLVI. " Moreover no long discussion is needed to explain why I think that the orator must also be acquainted with public law, which is exclusively concerned with the State and Empire, and also the records of past events and the precedents of antiquity. For as, in cases and proceedings relating to private interests, his language must often be borrowed from common law, so that, as we have said already, a knowledge of common law is indispensable to the orator ; just so, in public causes, alike in the law-courts, in popular assemblies and in the Senate, all this story of old times, the precedents of public law, and the method and science of State administration should be material, as it were, at the disposal of those orators who occupy themselves with politics. The orator needs learning.

" For in this talk of ours we are not seeking some pettifogger, declaimer or ranter, but that man who, to begin with, is high-priest of that art which, though unaided nature bestowed on mankind a great capacity for it, was yet deemed to have been the gift of a divinity, so that a property peculiar to humanity might seem no offspring of ourselves, but to be

per nos, sed divinitus ad nos delatum videretur ;
deinde, qui possit, non tam caduceo, quam nomine
oratoris ornatus, incolumis, vel inter hostium tela,
versari ; tum, qui scelus fraudemque nocentis possit
dicendo subicere odio civium, supplicioque con-
stringere ; idemque ingenii praesidio innocentiam
iudiciorum poena liberare ; idemque languentem
labentemque populum aut ad decus excitare, aut ab
errore deducere, aut inflammare in improbos, aut
incitatum in bonos, mitigare ; qui denique, quemcumque in animis hominum motum res et causa
postulet, eum dicendo vel excitare possit, vel sedare.

203   Hanc vim si quis existimat, aut ab eis, qui de dicendi
ratione scripserunt, expositam esse, aut a me posse
exponi tam brevi, vehementer errat ; neque solum
inscientiam meam, sed ne rerum quidem magnitudinem perspicit. Equidem vobis, quoniam ita
voluistis, fontes, unde hauriretis, atque itinera ipsa,
ita putavi esse demonstranda, non ut ipse dux essem
—quod et infinitum est, et non necessarium—sed
ut commonstrarem tantum viam, et, ut fieri solet,
digitum ad fontes intenderem.

204   XLVII. Mihi vero, inquit Mucius, satis superque
abs te videtur istorum studiis, si modo sunt studiosi,
esse factum.   Nam, ut Socratem illum solitum aiunt
dicere, perfectum sibi opus esse, si quis satis esset
concitatus cohortatione sua ad studium cognoscendae

sent down upon us from heaven; who secondly can abide unharmed even on the field of battle, through the respect felt for his title of orator rather than any heraldic staff; who furthermore can by his eloquence expose to the indignation of fellow-citizens, and restrain by punishment, the crimes and iniquities of the guilty; who also, by the shield of his talent, can deliver innocence from legal penalties; who again can either inspire a lukewarm and erring nation to a sense of the fitting, or lead them away from their blundering, or kindle their wrath against the wicked, or soothe them when they are excited against good men; who lastly can by his eloquence either arouse or calm, within the souls of men, whatever passion the circumstances and occasion may demand.

203 "If any man imagines that this power has been explained by the writers on the theory of speaking, or that I can explain it in so short a span, he is very greatly mistaken, not even perceiving the vastness of the subject, much less my own ignorance. For myself indeed, as such was your wish, I have thought fit to reveal to you the springs from which to drink, and the approaches to them, not as one seeking to be myself your guide (an endless and superfluous task), but just indicating the road, and, in the usual 204 way, pointing with my finger to the fountains."

XLVII. "To me indeed," observed Mucius, "you seem to have done enough and to spare for the enthusiasms of your friends, if only they are real enthusiasts. For, just as great Socrates is said to have been fond of describing his work as accomplished, once some man had been so far stimulated by his encouragement as to pursue the knowledge and

Acknowledgements; request for further advice.

143

percipiendaeque virtutis—quibus enim id persuasum
esset, ut nihil mallent se esse, quam bonos viros, eis
reliquam facilem esse doctrinam—: sic ego intellego,
si in haec, quae patefecit oratione sua Crassus, intrare volueritis ; facillime vos ad ea, quae cupitis,
perventuros ab hoc aditu, ianuaque patefacta.

205 Nobis vero, inquit Sulpicius, ista sunt pergrata
perque iucunda : sed pauca etiam requirimus, in-
primisque ea, quae valde breviter a te, Crasse, de
ipsa arte percursa sunt, cum illa te et non contemnere, et didicisse confiterere. Ea si paulo latius
dixeris, expleris omnem exspectationem diuturni
desiderii nostri. Nam nunc, quibus studendum rebus
esset, accepimus, quod ipsum est tamen magnum ;
sed vias earum rerum rationemque cupimus cognoscere.

206 Quid si, inquit Crassus, quoniam ego, quo facilius
vos apud me tenerem, vestrae potius obsecutus sum
voluntati, quam aut consuetudini, aut naturae meae,
petimus ab Antonio, ut ea, quae continet, neque
adhuc protulit, ex quibus unum libellum sibi excidisse
iamdudum questus est, explicet nobis, et illa dicendi
mysteria enuntiet ? Ut videtur, inquit Sulpicius.
Nam Antonio dicente, etiam quid tu intellegas, sen-
207 tiemus. Peto igitur, inquit Crassus, a te, quoniam id
nobis, Antoni, hominibus id aetatis, oneris ab horum
adolescentium studiis imponitur, ut exponas, quid eis
de rebus, quas a te quaeri vides, sentias.

apprehension of excellence (since further instruction
came easily to such as had been persuaded to set
the attainment of virtue above all else), so I see that,
if you two will consent to enter upon these courses
revealed by Crassus in what he says, you will most
readily reach the end of your desires by this Way
and through this Door which he has opened."

5 "We," added Sulpicius, "are indeed most grateful
for your statement and highly delighted with it,
but we ask for a little more, and especially for those
particulars concerning the art itself, which you,
Crassus, ran over very briefly, though owning that,
so far from despising, you had even learned them.
If you will state these rather more at large, you will
satisfy every hope of our continual longing. For so
far we have heard what objects we must pursue,
which anyhow is a great thing in itself; but we are
yearning to know the methods and the theory of
these studies."

"Well," said Crassus, "since, to keep you with
me more easily, I have followed your wishes rather
than my own practice or natural bent, what if we
ask Antonius to unfold to us all that he is keeping
to himself and has not yet published abroad, of
which he complained just now that a single little
book had already slipped out of his hands, and
to disclose those secrets of oratory?" "As you
please," replied Sulpicius. "For from the lips of
Antonius we shall be learning your own views also."
"I ask you then, Antonius," went on Crassus, "as
this burden is laid upon people of our years by the
eagerness of these young men, to express your
sentiments upon these matters which you see are
required of you."

XLVIII. Deprehensum equidem me, inquit
Antonius, plane video atque sentio, non solum quod
ea requiruntur a me, quorum sum ignarus atque
insolens, sed quia, quod in causis valde fugere soleo,
ne tibi, Crasse, succedam, id me nunc isti vitare non
208 sinunt. Verum hoc ingrediar ad ea, quae vultis,
audacius, quod idem mihi spero usu esse venturum
in hac disputatione, quod in dicendo solet, ut nulla
exspectetur ornata oratio. Neque enim sum de arte
dicturus, quam nunquam didici, sed de mea consuetudine ; ipsaque illa, quae in commentarium
meum rettuli, sunt eiusmodi, non aliqua mihi doctrina
tradita, sed in rerum usu causisque tractata : quae
si vobis, hominibus eruditissimis, non probabuntur,
vestram iniquitatem accusatote, qui ex me ea quae-
sieritis, quae ego nescirem ; meam facilitatem lauda-
tote, cum vobis, non meo iudicio, sed vestro studio
inductus, non gravate respondero.

209 Tum Crassus : Perge modo, inquit, Antoni. Nullum est enim periculum, ne quid tu eloquare, nisi
ita prudenter, ut neminem nostrum poeniteat ad
hunc te sermonem impulisse.

Ego vero, inquit, pergam : et id faciam, quod in
principio fieri in omnibus disputationibus oportere
censeo : ut, quid illud sit, de quo disputetur, ex-
planetur, ne vagari et errare cogatur oratio, si ei,
qui inter se dissenserint, non idem esse illud, quo
de agitur, intellegant.

146

XLVIII. " For my part," answered Antonius, " I
see and feel myself in evident straits, not only in
being questioned as to things beyond my knowledge
and experience, but also because this time your
friends do not let me shirk a situation from which
in Court I always do my best to run away, I mean
208 that of speaking next after yourself, Crassus. But
I shall the more courageously approach this undertaking of your choice, in that I hope for the same
fortune in this discussion which generally befalls
my speeches, namely, that no elegance of diction
will be expected of me. For I am not going to
speak of an art which I never learned, but of my own
practice ; and those very commonplaces, which I
have set down in my note-book, are no traditions
taught to me by some one or other, but such as have
been used in actual affairs and at the Bar : and if
they do not commend themselves to men of your
consummate accomplishment, pray blame your own
unfairness in seeking to learn of me things I did not
know ; and extol my good nature in answering you
with a good grace, won over by your enthusiasm,
not my own discretion."

09   " Just go on, Antonius," returned Crassus. " For
there is no danger of your delivering yourself without
such practical wisdom that not a man of us will
repent of having urged you on to this discussion."

" Yes, I will go on," said the other : " and I will
do what I think should be the first thing done in
every debate, which is that the subject for discussion
should be clearly ascertained, so that a discourse may
not have to ramble and lose itself, if perhaps the
disputants do not understand the issue in one and
the same sense.

Views of Antonius, gained from his experience.

210   Nam, si forte quaereretur, quae esset ars imperatoris, constituendum putarem principio, quis esset
imperator : qui cum esset constitutus administrator
quidam belli gerendi, tum adiungeremus de exercitu,
de castris, de agminibus, de signorum collationibus,
de oppidorum oppugnationibus, de commeatu, de
insidiis faciendis atque vitandis, de reliquis rebus,
quae essent propriae belli administrandi ; quarum
qui essent animo et scientia compotes, eos esse imperatores dicerem ; utererque exemplis Africanorum
et Maximorum ; Epaminondam atque Hannibalem,
atque eius generis homines nominarem.

211   Sin autem quaereremus quis esset is, qui ad rempublicam moderandam usum, et scientiam, et studium
suum contulisset, definirem hoc modo : Qui, quibus
rebus utilitas reipublicae pararetur augereturque,
teneret, eisque uteretur ; hunc reipublicae rectorem,
et consilii publici auctorem esse habendum ; praedi-
caremque P. Lentulum, principem illum, et Tib.
Gracchum patrem, et Q. Metellum, et P. Africanum,
et C. Laelium, et innumerabiles alios cum ex nostra
212 civitate, tum ex ceteris. Sin autem quaereretur,
quisnam iurisconsultus vere nominaretur ; eum dicerem, qui legum, et consuetudinis eius, qua privati
in civitate uterentur, et ad respondendum, et ad
agendum, et ad cavendum, peritus esset ; et ex eo
genere Sext. Aelium, M'. Manilium, P. Mucium
nominarem.

   XLIX. Atque, ut iam ad leviora artium studia

210　"For, if the question chanced to be as to the nature of the general's art, I should think it proper to settle at the outset, who is a general : and, having defined him as a man in charge of the conduct of war, we should then add some particulars of troops, encampment, marching formation, close fighting, investment of towns, food-supply, laying and avoidance of ambuscades, and all else pertaining to the management of warfare ; and those men who are intellectually and theoretically masters of these subjects I should call generals, citing as examples men like Scipio and Fabius Maximus, and making mention of Epaminondas and Hannibal and persons of that type.

The orator, like the soldier, the statesman and the philosopher, is a specialist.

211　"But if we were inquiring who is he that has devoted his experience, knowledge and enthusiasm to the guidance of the State, I should define him thus : ' Whoever knows and uses everything by which the advantage of a State is secured and developed, is the man to be deemed the helmsman of the State, and the originator of national policy,' and I should tell of Publius Lentulus that illustrious leader, of Tiberius Gracchus the elder, Quintus Metellus, Publius Africanus, Gaius Laelius, and countless others, some from our own community

212　and some from abroad.　If again the question were, who is rightly described as learned in the law, I should say it is the man who is an expert in the statutes, and in the customary law observed by individuals as members of the community, and who is qualified to advise, direct the course of a lawsuit, and safeguard a client, and in this class I should refer to Sextus Aelius, Manius Manilius and Publius Mucius.

XLIX. "And, to come now to the pursuits of the more trivial arts, if the devotee of music, the

veniam, si musicus, si grammaticus, si poeta quaeratur, possim similiter explicare, quid eorum quisque
profiteatur, et quo non amplius ab quoque sit postulandum. Philosophi denique ipsius, qui de sua vi ac
sapientia unus omnia paene profitetur, est tamen
quaedam descriptio, ut is, qui studeat omnium rerum
divinarum atque humanarum vim, naturam causasque
nosse, et omnem bene vivendi rationem tenere et
213 persequi, nomine hoc appelletur. Oratorem autem,
quoniam de eo quaerimus, equidem non facio eumdem, quem Crassus ; qui mihi visus est omnem
omnium rerum atque artium scientiam comprehendere uno oratoris officio ac nomine : atque eum puto
esse, qui verbis ad audiendum iucundis, et sententiis
ad probandum accommodatis uti possit in causis
forensibus atque communibus. Hunc ego appello
oratorem, eumque esse praeterea instructum voce,
et actione, et lepore quodam volo.

214 Crassus vero mihi noster visus est oratoris facultatem non illius artis terminis, sed ingenii sui finibus,
immensis paene, describere. Nam et civitatum regendarum oratori gubernacula sententia sua tradidit :
in quo per mihi mirum visum est, Scaevola, te hoc
illi concedere ; cum saepissime tibi Senatus, breviter impoliteque dicenti, maximis sit de rebus assensus.
M. vero Scaurus, quem non longe, ruri, apud se esse
audio, vir regendae reipublicae scientissimus, si

philologist, or the poet should be under examination, I could explain in like fashion their several claims, and the most that ought to be required of each. Lastly, of the philosopher himself, who by virtue of his special faculty and wisdom stands alone in claiming something like omniscience, there is after all a kind of definition, to the effect that he who strives to know the significance, nature and causes of everything divine or human, and to master and follow out as a whole the theory of right living, 213 is to be thus denominated. But the orator, since it is he whom we are studying, I myself do not picture as Crassus did, who I thought included, under the single vocation and title of orator, omniscience in every topic and every art: in fact I take him to be a man who can use language agreeable to the ear, and arguments suited to convince, in law-court disputes and in debates of public business. Such a man I call an orator, and would have him endowed besides with intonation, delivery and a certain charm.

214 " Now our friend Crassus seemed to me to delimit Crassus's the range of the orator, not by the bounds of the art definition concerned, but by the wellnigh infinite extent of far too wide. his own talent. For by his verdict he even handed over to the orator the helm of statesmanship; and I thought it passing strange, Scaevola, that you should grant him this point, when times without number the Senate has agreed with you on matters of extreme gravity, though your speech has been short and without ornament. Indeed if Marcus Scaurus, who I am told is at his country-house not far away, one of the highest authorities on statesmanship, had happened to hear that the influence

audierit, hanc auctoritatem gravitatis et consilii sui
vindicari a te, Crasse, quod eam oratoris propriam
esse dicas : iam, credo, huc veniat, et hanc loquacitatem nostram vultu ipso aspectuque conterreat :
qui, quanquam est in dicendo minime contemnendus,
prudentia tamen rerum magnarum magis, quam
215 dicendi arte, nititur.   Neque vero, si quis utrumque
potest, aut ille consilii publici auctor, ac senator
bonus, ob eam ipsam causam orator est ; aut hic
disertus atque eloquens, si est idem in procuratione
civitatis egregius, illam scientiam dicendi copia est
consecutus.   Multum inter se distant istae facultates,
longeque sunt diversae atque seiunctae ; neque eadem ratione ac via M. Cato, P. Africanus, Q. Metellus, C. Laelius, qui omnes eloquentes fuerunt,
orationem suam et reipublicae dignitatem exorna-
bant.

216   L. Neque enim est interdictum aut a rerum natura,
aut a lege aliqua atque more, ut singulis hominibus
ne amplius, quam singulas artes, nosse liceat.   Quare
non, etsi eloquentissimus Athenis Pericles, idemque
in ea civitate plurimos annos princeps consilii publici
fuit, idcirco eiusdem hominis atque artis utraque
facultas existimanda est ; nec, si P. Crassus idem fuit
eloquens, et iuris peritus, ob eam causam inest in
217 facultate dicendi iuris civilis scientia.   Nam si quisque, ut in aliqua arte et facultate excellens, aliam
quoque artem sibi assumpserit, ita perficiet, ut, quod
praeterea sciet, id eius, in quo excellet, pars quaedam

natural to his own worth and wisdom was being
claimed by yourself, Crassus, as the right of an
orator, he would, I do believe, instantly proceed
hither and thoroughly frighten us chatterers by the
mere look on his face : for, though no mean speaker,
he yet relies rather on his knowledge of higher
215 politics than on the art of oratory. Then too, if a
man is capable in both ways, such as the originator
of national policy who is also a good senator, he is
not just for that reason an orator ; nor did the
accomplished orator, who happens also to be outstanding in public administration, attain that special
knowledge through his fluency in speaking. There
is a vast difference between these gifts, and far apart
are they sundered ; nor was it by any uniform theory
and method that Marcus Cato, Publius Africanus,
Quintus Metellus and Gaius Laelius, orators all,
gave brilliance to their own style and to the reputation of their community.

6 L. "For neither the nature of things, nor any Wide
statute or custom, requires any one man to refrain culture not
from learning more than one art. And so, although indispens-
Pericles was the most eloquent man at Athens, and able for the
also for very many years the leader of national orator.
policy in that community, it is not therefore to
be supposed that these two accomplishments pertain
to one and the same man or art ; nor, because
Publius Crassus combined eloquence with legal
learning, does it follow that knowledge of common
law is implied in oratorical ability. For if everyone who, while outstanding in some art and capacity,
has embraced another art as well, is thereby to
create the belief that such subsidiary knowledge
is a specific part of that wherein he excels, we may

esse videatur : licet ista ratione dicamus, pila bene,
et Duodecim Scriptis ludere, proprium esse iuris
civilis, quoniam utrumque eorum P. Mucius optime
fecerit ; eademque ratione dicantur, et quos φυσικοὺς
Graeci nominant, eidem poetae, quoniam Empedocles
physicus egregium poema fecerit. At hoc ne philosophi quidem ipsi, qui omnia, sicut propria, sua esse,
atque a se possideri volunt, dicere audent, geo-
metriam, aut musicam, philosophi esse, quia Platonem omnes in illis artibus praestantissimum fuisse
fateantur.

218   Ac, si iam placet omnes artes oratori subiungere,
tolerabilius est, sic potius dicere, ut, quoniam dicendi
facultas non debeat esse ieiuna atque nuda, sed
aspersa atque distincta multarum rerum iucunda
quadam varietate, sit boni oratoris multa auribus
accepisse, multa vidisse, multa animo et cogitatione,
multa etiam legendo percurrisse ; neque ea, ut sua,
possedisse ; sed, ut aliena, libasse. Fateor enim,
callidum quemdam hunc, et nulla in re tironem ac
rudem, nec peregrinum atque hospitem in agendo
esse debere.

219   LI. Neque vero istis tragoediis tuis, quibus uti
philosophi maxime solent, Crasse, perturbor, quod
ita dixisti, neminem posse eorum mentes, qui audirent, aut inflammare dicendo, aut inflammatas restin-
guere, cum eo maxime vis oratoris magnitudoque
cernatur, nisi qui rerum omnium naturam, mores

ᵃ In Cicero's time, and much later, *pila* was no definite
game, but a series of gymnastic exercises for the promotion
of bodily suppleness and health.

Duodecim scripta involved dice-throwing, and the use of
differently coloured counters on a special board, divided into
spaces by 12 slanting lines.

on the same principle assert that to play well at ball or Twelve-Lines*a* is a peculiarity of common lawyers, since Publius Mucius did both things to perfection; and by the same line of argument those also whom the Greeks call 'natural philosophers' may be pronounced to be poets into the bargain, seeing that Empedocles, a natural philosopher, has composed a notable poem. But in reality even the moral philosophers themselves, who would have all things for their own, in right of dominion and in fact of possession as well, do not venture to claim that either geometry or the pursuit of music belongs to the moral philosopher, merely because Plato is admitted on all hands to have been pre-eminent in those arts.

8   " And, if for once we decide to place all the arts in subjection to the orator, our case may more acceptably be stated in this way, that, since ability to speak ought not to starve and go naked, but to be besprinkled and adorned with a kind of charming variety in many details, it is the part of a good orator to have heard and seen much, and to have run over much in thought and reflection, as well as in his reading, not acquiring all this as his own possession, but tasting what belongs to others. For I agree that he ought to be a shrewd sort of man, and nowhere an untrained recruit, and no stranger or sojourner in his sphere of action.

LI. " Nor again, Crassus, am I greatly troubled by those histrionics of yours, the favourite medium of philosophers, setting forth that by the spoken word no man can kindle the feelings of his hearers, or quench them when kindled (though it is in this that the orator's virtue and range are chiefly discerned), unless he has gazed into the depths of the nature of

To influence his audience he needs knowledge of the world;

hominum atque rationes penitus perspexerit : in quo
philosophia sit oratori necessario percipienda ; quo in
studio hominum quoque ingeniosissimorum otiosis-
simorumque totas aetates videmus esse contritas.
Quorum ego copiam magnitudinemque cognitionis
atque artis non modo non contemno, sed etiam vehementer admiror : nobis tamen, qui in hoc populo
foroque versamur, satis est, ea de moribus hominum
et scire, et dicere, quae non abhorrent ab hominum
moribus.

220   Quis enim unquam orator magnus, et gravis, cum
iratum adversario iudicem facere vellet, haesitavit ob
eam causam, quod nesciret, quid esset iracundia,
fervorne mentis, an cupiditas puniendi doloris ? Quis,
cum ceteros animorum motus aut iudicibus, aut
populo dicendo miscere atque agitare vellet, ea dixit,
quae a philosophis dici solent ?   Qui partim omnino
motus negant in animis ullos esse debere, quique eos
in iudicum mentibus concitent, scelus eos nefarium
facere ; partim, qui tolerabiliores volunt esse, et ad
veritatem vitae propius accedere, permediocres ac
potius leves motus debere esse dicunt.

221   Orator autem omnia haec, quae putantur in communi vitae consuetudine, mala, ac molesta, et
fugienda, multo maiora et acerbiora verbis facit ;
itemque ea, quae vulgo expetenda atque optabilia
videntur, dicendo amplificat atque ornat : neque vult
ita sapiens inter stultos videri, uti, qui audiant, aut

ᵃ Wilkins's argument for reading *motibus animorum* for
moribus hominum is unconvincing.
    ᵇ *Cf.* Aristotle, *Rhet.* II. ii. 2 ; and Cicero, *Tusc. Disp.*
iv. 9. 21 and 10. 24.

everything, including human characters and motives : in which connexion the orator must needs make philosophy his own ; and in this pursuit we see that whole lives of most talented and leisured persons have been consumed. The copiousness of their learning and the wide range of their art I am so far from despising that in fact I ardently admire these : yet for ourselves, busied in the public life of this community, it is enough to know and give expression to such things concerning human characters[a] as are not alien to human character.

20 " For what grand and impressive speaker, trying to make an arbitrator angry with his opponent, was ever at a loss merely through not knowing whether wrath is a vehement heat of the mind, or a strong desire to avenge pain ?[b] Who, in seeking by his word to confound and stir up the other feelings in the minds of a tribunal or popular assembly, has uttered the hackneyed sayings of the philosophers ? Of whom some deny to the feelings any rightful place at all within the mind, regarding it as an infamous crime to awaken such in the hearts of a tribunal, while others, pretending to some tolerance and a closer approach to the facts of life, assert that the feelings should be exceedingly temperate, or rather of only trivial force.

" The orator however by his words greatly magnifies and exaggerates the grievousness of such things as in everyday life are thought evils and troubles to be shunned, while he enlarges upon and beautifies by his eloquence whatever is commonly deemed delectable and worthy to be desired : and he does not wish to appear so completely a sage among fools, as to have his hearers either regarding him as a

157

illum ineptum et Graeculum putent ; aut, etiamsi
valde probent ingenium oratoris, sapientiam ad-
222 mirentur, se esse stultos moleste ferant : sed ita
peragrat per animos hominum, ita sensus mentesque
pertractat, ut non desideret philosophorum descrip-
tiones, neque exquirat oratione, summum illud
bonum in animone sit, an in corpore ; virtute an
voluptate definiatur ; an haec inter se iungi copulari-
que possint ; an vero, ut quibusdam visum, nihil
certum sciri, nihil plane cognosci et percipi possit.
Quarum rerum fateor magnam multiplicemque esse
disciplinam, et multas, copiosas variasque rationes ;
sed aliud quiddam, longe aliud, Crasse, quaerimus.
223 Acuto homine nobis opus est, et natura usuque
callido, qui sagaciter pervestiget, quid sui cives, eique
homines, quibus aliquid dicendo persuadere velit,
cogitent, sentiant, opinentur, exspectent.

LII. Teneat oportet venas cuiusque generis, aetatis, ordinis, et eorum, apud quos aliquid aget, aut erit
224 acturus, mentes sensusque degustet ; philosophorum
autem libros reservet sibi ad huiuscemodi Tusculani
requiem atque otium, ne, si quando ei dicendum erit
de iustitia et fide, mutuetur a Platone ; qui, cum
haec exprimenda verbis arbitraretur, novam quamdam finxit in libris civitatem : usque eo illa, quae
dicenda de iustitia putabat, a vitae consuetudine et
225 a civitatum moribus abhorrebant. Quod si ea pro-

clumsy Greekling, or for all their approval of the orator's talent and astonishment at his wisdom, yet
222 taking it ill that they themselves are foolish : but in such way does he range over men's souls, and explore their feelings and thoughts, that he needs no philosophers' definitions, and does not inquire in his discourse whether 'the supreme good' is subjective or objective, whether it is to be defined as virtue or pleasure, or whether these two can be wedded together, or, to be sure, whether, as some have thought, nothing can be known for certain, nothing clearly understood and apprehended. On these questions I admit that the teaching is abundant and manifold, and the theories numerous, copious and varied ; but we, Crassus, are looking for some-
223 thing different, and widely different. We require a man of sharpness, ingenious by nature and experience alike, who with keen scent will track down the thoughts, feelings, beliefs and hopes of his fellow-citizens and of any men whom on any issue he would fain win over by his word.

LII. " He ought to feel the pulses of every class, he does not time of life, and degree, and to taste the thoughts require and feelings of those before whom he is pleading or philosophy.
224 intending to plead any cause ; but his philosophical books he should keep back for a restful holiday, such as this one of ours at Tusculum, so as not to borrow from Plato, if ever he has to speak of justice and righteousness ; for Plato, when he thought fit to put these things into writing, depicted in his pages an unknown sort of republic, so completely in contrast with everyday life and the customs of human communities were his considered statements concerning
225 justice. But if his ideas were approved in real

barentur in populis atque in civitatibus, quis tibi,
Crasse, concessisset, clarissimo viro, et amplissimo
principi civitatis, ut illa diceres in maxima concione
tuorum civium, quae dixisti? 'Eripite nos ex miseriis,
eripite nos ex faucibus eorum, quorum crudelitas
nostro sanguine non potest expleri ; nolite sinere nos
cuiquam servire, nisi vobis universis, quibus et possumus et debemus.' Omitto 'miserias,' in quibus,
ut illi aiunt, vir fortis esse non potest ; omitto
'fauces,' ex quibus te eripi vis, ne iudicio iniquo
exsorbeatur sanguis tuus ; quod sapienti negant
accidere posse ; 'servire' vero non modo te, sed
universum Senatum, cuius tum causam agebas, ausus
es dicere ?

226   Potestne virtus, Crasse, servire, istis auctoribus,
quorum tu praecepta oratoris facultate complecteris ?
Quae et semper, et sola libera est, quaeque, etiamsi
corpora capta sint armis, aut constricta vinculis,
tamen suum ius, atque omnium rerum impunitam
libertatem tenere debeat.   Quae vero addidisti, non
modo Senatum servire 'posse' populo, sed etiam
'debere,' quis hoc philosophus tam mollis, tam
languidus, tam enervatus, tam omnia ad voluptatem
corporis doloremque referens, probare posset, Senatum servire populo, cui populus ipse moderandi et
regendi sui potestatem, quasi quasdam habenas,
tradidisset ?

nations and States, who would have allowed you, Crassus, for all your high reputation, and all your splendour as a political leader, to express yourself as you did before a densely crowded assembly of your fellow-citizens ? 'Deliver us out of our woes, deliver us out of the jaws of those whose ferocity cannot get its fill of our blood ; suffer us not to be in bondage to any, save to yourselves as a nation, whose slaves we can and ought to be.' I pass over 'woes,' in which, according to the philosophers, the brave can never become involved ; I pass over 'jaws,' out of which you desire to be delivered, for fear of your blood being sucked out of you by an unjust judgement, a thing which they say cannot befall the wise ; but 'slavery,' did you dare to say that not yourself only, but the entire Senate, whose interests you were that day upholding, could be slaves ?

"Can Virtue be a slave, Crassus, according to those authorities of yours, whose maxims you include within the range of the orator's knowledge ? She who for ever and alone is free, and who, though the body be made prisoner of war or bound with chains, ought still to hold fast to her own rights and unrestricted freedom in all things ! And as for your further pronouncement, that the Senate not only 'can' but actually 'ought to' be the slaves of the nation, could any philosopher be so unmanly, spiritless and weak, so resolved to make physical pleasure and pain the standard of everything, as to approve of this suggestion that the Senate is in bondage to the nation, when it is to the Senate that the nation itself has committed the power of controlling and guiding it, as some driver might hand over his reins ?

227 LIII. Itaque haec cum a te divinitus ego dicta arbitrarer, P. Rutilius Rufus, homo doctus, et philosophiae deditus, non modo parum commode, sed etiam turpiter et flagitiose dicta esse dicebat. Idemque Servium Galbam, quem hominem probe commeminisse se aiebat, pergraviter reprehendere solebat, quod is, L. Scribonio quaestionem in eum ferente, populi misericordiam concitasset, cum M. Cato, Galbae gravis atque acer inimicus, aspere apud populum Romanum et vehementer esset locutus, quam orationem in Originibus suis exposuit ipse.

228 Reprehendebat igitur Galbam Rutilius, quod is C. Sulpicii Galli, propinqui sui, Quintum pupillum filium ipse paene in humeros suos extulisset, qui patris clarissimi recordatione et memoria fletum populo moveret, et duos filios suos parvos tutelae populi commendasset, ac se, tanquam in procinctu testamentum faceret, sine libra atque tabulis, populum Romanum tutorem instituere dixisset illorum orbitati. Itaque cum et invidia et odio populi tum Galba premeretur, his quoque eum tragoediis liberatum ferebat ; quod item apud Catonem scriptum esse video, ' nisi pueris et lacrimis usus esset, poenas eum daturum fuisse.' Haec Rutilius valde vituperabat, et huic humilitati, dicebat vel exsilium fuisse, 229 vel mortem anteponendam. Neque vero hoc solum

162

227 LIII. "And so, although I personally thought these words of yours inspired, Publius Rutilius Rufus, a man of learning and devoted to philosophy, used to say they were not only wanting in discretion, but positively unseemly and disgraceful. He it was who used also to censure very severely Servius Galba, whom he claimed to remember well, for having worked upon the compassion of the assembly, when Lucius Scribonius was moving for his prosecution, after Marcus Cato, a troublesome and bitter foe to Galba, had harangued the Roman people in a rough and violent strain : this speech Cato himself has recorded in his *Early History*.

Indeed philosophy might disapprove of some effective lines of pleading.

228 "As I was saying, Rutilius used to find fault with Galba, for having almost hoisted on to his shoulders, with his own hands, his ward Quintus, the son of his near relative Gaius Sulpicius Gallus, so that his appearance might set the assembly a-weeping, by recalling the memory of his most illustrious father ; and for having committed two small sons of his own to the guardianship of the nation ; and for having proclaimed, like a soldier making his will under arms, without scales or tablets, that he appointed the Roman people to be their guardians in their father-less plight. The result, according to Rutilius, was that Galba, though at that time weighed down by popular ill-will and hatred, actually secured an acquittal by means of these histrionics, and I also find the incident recorded in Cato's book, with the comment that ' but for his employment of boys and blubbering, the accused would have got his deserts.' These methods Rutilius used roundly to condemn, affirming that banishment or death itself was better

229 than such abjectness. Nor was this mere talk on

dixit, sed ipse et sensit, et fecit. Nam cum esset ille vir exemplum, ut scitis, innocentiae, cumque illo nemo neque integrior esset in civitate, neque sanctior, non modo supplex iudicibus esse noluit, sed ne ornatius quidem, aut liberius causam dici suam, quam simplex ratio veritatis ferebat. Paulum huic Cottae tribuit partium, disertissimo adolescenti, sororis suae filio. Dixit item causam illam quadam ex parte Q. Mucius, more suo, nullo apparatu, pure et dilucide.

230 Quod si tu tunc, Crasse, dixisses, qui subsidium oratori ex illis disputationibus quibus philosophi utuntur, ad dicendi copiam petendum esse paulo ante dicebas ; et, si tibi pro P. Rutilio non philosophorum more, sed tuo licuisset dicere : quamvis scelerati illi fuissent, sicuti fuerunt, pestiferi cives, supplicioque digni ; tamen omnem eorum importunitatem ex intimis mentibus evellisset vis orationis tuae. Nunc talis vir amissus est, dum causa ita dicitur, ut si in illa commentitia Platonis civitate res ageretur. Nemo ingemuit, nemo inclamavit patronorum, nihil cuiquam doluit, nemo est questus, nemo rempublicam imploravit, nemo supplicavit. Quid multa ? pedem nemo in illo iudicio supplosit, credo, ne Stoicis renuntiaretur.

231 LIV. Imitatus est homo Romanus et consularis veterem illum Socratem, qui, cum omnium sapientissimus esset sanctissimeque vixisset, ita in iudicio

his part, but he meant what he said, and acted upon it himself. For though, as you know, that great man was a pattern of righteousness, and there was no more honourable and blameless individual in the community, he declined not only to crave mercy of his judges, but also to be defended more eloquently or elaborately than the plain truth of the matter permitted. To Cotta here, though a highly accomplished young man and his sister's son, he allotted but a fragment of his case. Quintus Mucius too argued a part of it in his own way, with no trappings, his diction simple and crystal-clear.

230 "But had you spoken that day, Crassus,—you who were saying just now that the orator must have recourse to the ordinary debates of the philosophers for the material of his speeches,—and had you been allowed to plead for Publius Rutilius, in no philosophic style but in your own, then, even though those judges had been,—as they were—, accursed and pernicious men deserving of death, the power of your eloquence would none the less have rent away all savagery from the bottom of their hearts. As matters stand, a man of such quality has been lost, through his case being conducted as if the trial had been taking place in that ideal republic of Plato. None of his counsel groaned or shrieked, none was pained at anything, or made any complaint, or invoked the State, or humbled himself. In a word, not one of them stamped a foot during those proceedings, for fear, no doubt, of being reported to the Stoics.

31 LIV. "Thus did a Roman of consular rank follow The instance the example of great Socrates of old who, as he of Socrates. was the wisest of all men, and had lived the most

165

capitis pro se ipse dixit, ut non supplex aut reus, sed
magister, aut dominus videretur esse iudicum. Quin
etiam, cum ei scriptam orationem disertissimus
orator Lysias attulisset, quam, si ei videretur, edis-
ceret, ut ea pro se in iudicio uteretur, non invitus
legit, et commode scriptam esse dixit : ' Sed,' inquit,
' ut, si mihi calceos Sicyonios attulisses, non uterer,
quamvis essent habiles et apti ad pedem, quia non
essent viriles ; sic illam orationem disertam sibi et
oratoriam videri, fortem et virilem non videri.' Ergo
ille quoque damnatus est ; neque solum primis sententiis, quibus tantum statuebant iudices, damnarent,
an absolverent, sed etiam illis, quas iterum legibus
232 ferre debebant. Erat enim Athenis, reo damnato,
si fraus capitalis non esset, quasi poenae aestimatio ;
et sententia cum iudicibus daretur, interrogabatur
reus, quam quasi aestimationem commeruisse se
maxime confiteretur. Quod cum interrogatus Socrates esset, respondit, sese meruisse, ut amplissimis
honoribus et praemiis decoraretur, et ei victus quoti-
dianus in Prytaneo publice praeberetur ; qui honos
233 apud Graecos maximus habetur. Cuius responso
sic iudices exarserunt, ut capitis hominem innocen-
tissimum condemnarent. Qui quidem si absolutus
esset ; quod mehercule, etiamsi nihil ad nos pertinet,
tamen propter eius ingenii magnitudinem vellem :
quonam modo istos philosophos ferre possemus, qui

blameless of lives, defended himself in person, when indicted on a capital charge, in such fashion as to seem no submissive prisoner, but the teacher or domestic superior of his judges. Indeed on Lysias, a most accomplished orator, bringing him a written speech, to be committed to memory, if he thought proper, for use in his defence at his trial, he read it not unwillingly, and said it was aptly phrased: ' But,' quoth he, ' just as, if you had brought me a pair of Sicyonian half-boots, were they never so easy and well-fitting, I should reject them as womanish, even so I think your speech is skilful oratory but not the utterance of a brave man.' And so he too was condemned, not only at the first count, when the tribunal merely determined the issue of conviction or acquittal, but also on the further vote which they were bound by law to give. For at Athens, on a defendant being convicted of an offence carrying no fixed penalty, something like an appraisement of liability was made and, when the judges' vote was being taken, the accused was asked what was the highest assessment, as it were, that he owned to having thoroughly merited. When this question was put to Socrates he replied that he had earned the distinction of the most splendid preferments and rewards, with provision for him, at the public expense, of daily sustenance in the Hall of the Presidents, this being rated among the Greeks as the highest of honours. His answer so incensed the tribunal that they condemned a perfectly blameless man to death. Had he indeed been acquitted, as I devoutly wish he had been,—not that it is any business of ours—but for the sake of his vast genius, how could we ever endure your philosophers, who even as it is, with

167

nunc, cum ille damnatus est, nullam aliam ob culpam, nisi propter dicendi inscientiam, tamen a se
oportere dicunt peti praecepta dicendi ? Quibuscum
ego non pugno, utrum sit melius, aut verius : tantum
dico, et aliud illud esse, atque hoc, et hoc sine illo
summum esse posse.

234   LV. Nam quod ius civile, Crasse, tam vehementer
amplexus es, video, quid egeris. Tum, cum dicebas,
videbam. Primum Scaevolae te dedisti, quem omnes
amare meritissimo pro eius eximia suavitate debemus : cuius artem cum indotatam esse et incom-
ptam videres, verborum eam dote locupletasti et
ornasti. Deinde quod in ea tu plus operae laborisque
consumpseras, cum eius studii tibi et hortator et
magister esset domi, veritus es, nisi istam artem
oratione exaggerasses, ne operam perdidisses.

235   Sed ego ne cum ista quidem arte pugno. Sit sane
tanta, quantam tu illam esse vis. Etenim sine controversia et magna est, et late patet, et ad multos
pertinet, et summo in honore semper fuit, et clarissimi cives ei studio etiam hodie praesunt. Sed vide,
Crasse, ne, dum novo et alieno ornatu velis ornare
iuris civilis scientiam, suo quoque eam concesso et
236 tradito spolies atque denudes. Nam, si ita diceres,
qui iurisconsultus esset, esse eum oratorem, itemque
qui esset orator, iuris eumdem esse consultum : prae-

their Master condemned solely for the offence of
inexperience in oratory, yet tell us that it is from
themselves that the rules of eloquence ought to be
sought ? For my part I have no quarrel with them
as to which of these faculties is the better or more
real ; I simply say that theirs and ours are two
distinct things, and that consummate eloquence can
exist quite apart from philosophy."

234   LV. " For I see now, Crassus, the purpose of your Nor does the
so ardent affection for the common law. Indeed I orator need
saw it as you were speaking. First you did service wide know-
to Scaevola, whom we are all most justly bound to ledge of law.
love for his exceeding great courtesy : seeing his
Art to be portionless and unadorned, you have en-
riched and decorated her with the dower of diction.
Secondly, having squandered upon her too much
work and labour, since you had at home an encourager
and instructor in that pursuit, you were afraid that,
unless you glorified that Art of yours by eloquence,
you would have lost your labour.

35   " But I myself have no quarrel with this art of yours
either. By all means let it be of such consequence
as you would have it be. For indisputably it is a
noble art, extending far and wide and touching
the concerns of many, while it has ever been held
in the highest repute, and even now the most illustrious citizens are the leaders in that field. But see
to it, Crassus, that, in your desire to deck out the
science of common law in new-fangled and foreign
apparel, you do not at the same time despoil and strip
her of what has been confirmed to her and made her
36 own. For if you were to put it in this way, that the
man learned in the law is an orator, and likewise the
orator is one learned in the law, you would be setting

claras duas artes constitueres, atque inter se pares, et
eiusdem socias dignitatis. Nunc vero, iurisconsultum
sine hac eloquentia, de qua quaerimus, fateris esse
posse, fuisseque plurimos ; oratorem negas, nisi illam
scientiam assumpserit, esse posse. Ita est tibi iurisconsultus ipse per se nihil, nisi leguleius quidam
cautus et acutus, praeco actionum, cantor formula-
rum, auceps syllabarum ; sed quia saepe utitur orator
subsidio iuris in causis, idcirco istam iuris scientiam
eloquentiae, tanquam ancillulam pedisequamque,
adiunxisti.

237   LVI. Quod vero impudentiam admiratus es eorum
patronorum, qui aut, cum parva nescirent, magna
profiterentur, aut ea, quae maxima essent in iure
civili, tractare auderent in causis, cum ea nescirent,
nunquamque didicissent ; utriusque rei facilis est et
prompta defensio. Nam neque illud est mirandum,
qui, quibus verbis coemptio fiat, nesciat, eumdem eius
mulieris, quae coemptionem fecerit, causam posse defendere ; nec si parvi navigii et magni eadem est in
gubernando scientia, idcirco qui, quibus verbis erctum
cieri oporteat, nesciat, idem herciscundae familiae
238 causam agere non possit. Nam, quod maximas cen-
tumvirales causas in iure positas protulisti : quae
tandem earum causa fuit, quae ab homine eloquenti,
iuris imperito, non ornatissime potuerit dici ? Quibus

up two glorious arts, on an equality with each other, and partners in one grandeur. But as it is you admit that a man may be learned in the law without possessing this eloquence which we are investigating, and that many such have appeared ; while you deny the possibility of the existence of an orator who has not acquired that legal knowledge as well. So by your account the learned lawyer, in and by himself, is nothing but a circumspect and sharp kind of pettifogger, a crier of legal actions, a chanter of legal formulas, a trapper of syllables ; but, because the orator in Court often employs the aid of the law, you have therefore associated your legal knowledge with Eloquence, as a little maid to follow at her heels.

237 LVI. "But as for your wondering at the shamelessness of those counsel who either made great professions, though ignorant of small details, or dared to handle in Court the highest topics of common law, though they knew nothing about them, and had never studied them, there is a simple and obvious excuse in each case. For there is nothing marvellous in a man, who is ignorant of the formalities of marriage by purchase, being none the less able to conduct the case of a woman married in that manner ; nor, because the same kind of skill is exercised in steering a little craft as a large vessel, does it follow that he, who does not know the technical phrases required for the division of an inheritance, cannot conduct a suit for the partition of an estate. 238 Why ! to take your own citations of most important proceedings before the Hundred Commissioners, which turned upon questions of law, which of those cases, pray, could not have been most handsomely argued by a man of eloquence unversed in law ?

Indeed often the law is uncertain,

quidem in causis omnibus, sicut in ipsa M'. Curii, quae
abs te nuper est dicta, et in C. Hostilii Mancini controversia, atque in eo puero, qui ex altera natus erat
uxore, non remisso nuntio superiori, fuit inter peritis-
239 simos homines summa de iure dissensio. Quaero
igitur, quid adiuverit oratorem in his causis iuris
scientia, cum hic iurisconsultus superior fuerit dis-
cessurus, qui esset non suo artificio, sed alieno, hoc
est, non iuris scientia, sed eloquentia, sustentatus.

Equidem hoc saepe audivi, cum aedilitatem P.
Crassus peteret, eumque maior natu, etiam consularis,
Ser. Galba assectaretur, quod Crassi filiam Gaio filio
suo despondisset, accessisse ad Crassum consulendi
causa quemdam rusticanum : qui cum Crassum sedu-
xisset, atque ad eum rettulisset, responsumque ab eo
verum magis, quam ad suam rem accommodatum abs-
tulisset ; ut eum tristem Galba vidit, nomine appel-
lavit, quaesivitque, qua de re ad Crassum rettulisset.
240 Ex quo ut audivit, commotumque ut vidit hominem,
' Suspenso,' inquit, ' animo et occupato Crassum tibi
respondisse video ' : deinde ipsum Crassum manu pre-
hendit, et, ' Heus tu,' inquit, ' quid tibi in mentem
venit ita respondere ? ' Tum ille fidenter, homo peritissimus, confirmare, ita se rem habere, ut respondisset ;
nec dubium esse posse. Galba autem alludens varie,
et copiose, multas similitudines afferre, multaque pro

172

Indeed in all those suits, as in that very one of
Manius Curius, recently conducted by yourself, and
in the dispute over Gaius Hostilius Mancinus, and
again in the matter of the boy born of the second
wife, before her predecessor had received notice of
divorce, dissent as to the law was complete in the
239 most learned circles. I ask then, of what service and then it
was legal knowledge to an advocate in those cases, is eloquence that wins.
when that learned lawyer was bound to come off
victorious, who had been upheld, not by his own
dexterity but by a stranger's, that is to say, not by
legal knowledge but by eloquence ?

"Often too have I heard how, when Publius Crassus
was a candidate for the aedileship, and Servius Galba,
his senior and a past consul, was in attendance upon
him, having arranged a marriage between his son
Gaius and the daughter of Crassus, a certain country-
man approached Crassus to obtain his opinion : he
took Crassus apart and laid the facts before him, but
brought away from him advice that was more correct
than conformable to his interest ; whereupon Galba,
noting his chagrin, accosted him by name, inquiring
what the question was on which he had consulted
240 Crassus. Having heard the client's tale and observing his agitation, ' I see,' said he, ' that Crassus
was preoccupied and distracted when he advised
you ' : he then seized Crassus himself by the hand
and asked, ' How now, what ever entered your
head to suggest such an opinion ? ' Upon this the
other, with the assurance of profound knowledge,
repeated that the position was as he had advised
and the point unarguable. Galba however, sportively
and with varied and manifold illustrations, brought
forward a number of analogies, and urged many

173

aequitate contra ius dicere ; atque illum, cum dis-
serendo par esse non posset—quanquam fuit Crassus
in numero disertorum, sed par Galbae nullo modo—,
ad auctores confugisse, et id, quod ipse diceret, et in
P. Mucii, fratris sui, libris, et in Sext. Aelii commentariis scriptum protulisse, ac tamen concessisse,
Galbae disputationem sibi probabilem et prope veram
videri.

241   LVII. Attamen, quae causae sunt eiusmodi, ut de
earum iure dubium esse non possit, omnino in iudicium vocari non solent.   Num quis eo testamento,
quod paterfamilias ante fecit, quam ei filius natus
esset, hereditatem petit ?   Nemo ; quia constat, ag-
nascendo rumpi testamentum.   Ergo in hoc genere
iuris iudicia nulla sunt.   Licet igitur impune oratori
omnem hanc partem iuris incontroversi ignorare,
242 quae pars sine dubio multo maxima est : in eo autem
iure, quod ambigitur inter peritissimos, non est difficile oratori, eius partis, quamcumque defendat,
auctorem aliquem invenire ; a quo cum amentatas
hastas acceperit, ipse eas oratoris lacertis viribusque
torquebit.   Nisi vero—bona venia huius optimi viri
dixerim, Scaevolae—tu libellis aut praeceptis soceri
tui, causam M'. Curii defendisti.   Nonne arripuisti
patrocinium aequitatis et defensionem testamentorum, ac voluntatis mortuorum ?

243   Ac mea quidem sententia—frequens enim te audivi,
atque adfui—multo maiorem partem sententiarum sale

ᵃ These were javelins with a slinging-strap to help the
thrower.

considerations in favour of equity as against rigid law, and it is related that Crassus, being no match for him in discussion—though ranked among the accomplished, Crassus came nowhere near Galba—, took refuge in authorities, and pointed out his own statement both in the works of his brother Publius Mucius, and in the text-book of Sextus Aelius, yet after all admitted that Galba's argument seemed to him persuasive, and very near the truth.

241 LVII. "And yet those cases which are such that the law involved in them is beyond dispute, do not as a rule come to a hearing at all. Does anyone claim an inheritance under a will made by the head of a household before the birth of a son of his? No one; since it is settled law that the will is revoked by such subsequent birth. Thus there are no judicial decisions on this branch of the law. And so the orator may safely disregard all this region of un-questionable law, being as it certainly is by far the 242 larger portion of the science: while, as for the law which is unsettled in the most learned circles, it is easy enough for him to find some authority in favour of whichever side he is supporting, and, having obtained a supply of thonged shafts [a] from him, he himself will hurl these with all the might of an orator's arm. Unless indeed (let me say this by the kind indulgence of our excellent friend here Scaevola) it was by means of the works and maxims of your father-in-law that you argued the case for Manius Curius? Did you not rather snatch at the chance of protecting righteousness and upholding last wills and the intentions of dead men?

243 "And in my opinion, at any rate,—for I often heard you and was at your elbow—, it was by your wit and

175

tuo, et lepore, et politissimis facetiis pellexisti, cum
et illud nimium acumen illuderes, et admirarere ingenium Scaevolae, qui excogitasset, nasci prius oportere, quam emori ; cumque multa colligeres, et ex
legibus et ex senatusconsultis, et ex vita ac sermone
communi, non modo acute, sed etiam ridicule ac
facete, ubi si verba, non rem sequeremur, confici nil
posset. Itaque hilaritatis plenum iudicium ac laetitiae fuit : in quo quid tibi iuris civilis exercitatio
profuerit, non intellego ; dicendi vis egregia, summa
festivitate et venustate coniuncta, profuit.

244　Ipse ille Mucius, paterni iuris defensor, et q̅ı̅asi
patrimonii propugnator sui, quid in illa causa, cum
contra te diceret, attulit, quod de iure civili deprom-
ptum videretur ? quam legem recitavit ? quid patefecit dicendo, quod fuisset imperitis occultius ?
Nempe eius omnis oratio versata est in eo, ut scriptum
plurimum valere oportere defenderet. At in hoc
genere pueri apud magistros exercentur omnes,
cum in eiusmodi causis alias scriptum, alias aequi-
tatem defendere docentur.

245　Et, credo, in illa militis causa, si tu aut heredem,
aut militem defendisses, ad Hostilianas te actiones,
non ad tuam vim et oratoriam facultatem contulisses !

---

a See § 175, *supra.*
b A work otherwise unknown.

charm and highly refined pleasantries that you won
the vast majority of your verdicts, while you were
mocking at that over-subtlety of Scaevola's, and
marvelling at his cleverness in having thought out
the proposition that a man must be born before he
can die; and while, amusingly and with a sense of
humour, as well as shrewdly, you were adducing
numerous examples, gathered from statutes and
senatorial ordinances, and also from everyday life
and conversation, in which our pursuit of the letter
instead of the spirit would lead to no result.   And
so the Court was filled with gaiety and delight: but
of what avail your practice in the common law was to
you in these proceedings I cannot see; it was your
surpassing power of eloquence, in union with consummate cheerfulness and grace, that proved of service.

44   "That very Mucius, upholder of his ancestral
science, and champion, as it were, of his hereditary
rights,—what argument did he introduce in that
case wherein he was opposed to you, which sounded
like a borrowing from common law?   What statute
did he read over?   What did he reveal in his speech
that would have been too obscure for the uninitiated?
Surely his entire address was concerned with the one
contention that the written word ought to prevail to
the uttermost.   Yet it is in this kind of thing that
all students are trained in the schools, when in mock
trials of this kind they are taught to uphold in turn
the written word and true equity.

5   "I presume too that, in *The Soldier's Case*,[a] if you
had been counsel for the heir or for the soldier,
you would have betaken yourself to *Precedents in
Pleading* [b] by Hostilius, and not to the force of your
own ability in oratory!   On the contrary, if you

177

Tu vero, vel si testamentum defenderes, sic ageres, ut omne omnium testamentorum ius in eo iudicio positum videretur ; vel si causam ageres militis, patrem eius, ut soles, dicendo a mortuis excitasses ; statuisses ante oculos ; complexus esset filium, flensque eum centumviris commendasset ; lapides mehercule omnes flere ac lamentari coegisset : ut totum illud, UTI LINGUA NUNCUPASSIT, non in Duodecim Tabulis, quas tu omnibus bibliothecis anteponis, sed in magistri carmine scriptum videretur.

246   LVIII. Nam quod inertiam accusas adolescentium, qui istam artem, primum facillimam, non ediscant ; quae quam sit facilis, illi viderint, qui eius artis arrogantia, quasi difficillima sit, ita subnixi ambulant, deinde etiam tu ipse videris, qui eam artem facilem esse dicis, quam concedis adhuc artem omnino non esse, sed aliquando, si quis aliam artem didicerit, ut hanc artem efficere possit, tum esse illam artem futuram : deinde, quod sit plena delectationis ; in quo tibi remittunt omnes istam voluptatem, et ea se carere patiuntur ; nec quisquam est eorum, qui, si iam sit ediscendum sibi aliquid, non Teucrum Pacuvii malit quam Manilianas venalium vendendorum leges

247 ediscere.   Tum autem, quod amore patriae censes

---

^a See *Remains of Old Latin* (L.C.L.), iii. pp. 456-457.
^b *Ibid.* ii. pp. 286 303.

had been propounding the will, you would have so managed matters that the entire security of every will would have seemed to be staked on the issue of those proceedings ; and, if you had been appearing for the soldier, you would by your eloquence, in your usual way, have called up his father from the shades ; you would have set him in sight of all ; he would have embraced his son and tearfully committed him to the care of the Hundred Commissioners ; I pledge my word he would have made every stone weep and wail, with the result that the whole section beginning ' As the tongue hath proclaimed it ' would have seemed no part of the Twelve Tables,[a] which you rate higher than all the libraries, but just a piece of moralizing doggerel by some professor.

46   LVIII. " For as to your indictment of the young for their laziness, in that they do not commit to memory that art of yours, its exceeding simplicity being your first point, I leave the question of its simplicity to those who parade about in the haughty assurance imparted by this art, just as though it were extremely difficult, and do you yourself see to this, who describe an art as simple which by your own admission is not yet an art at all, but some day, should somebody have learned another art, and so be able to make an art of this one, will then become an art : secondly you urge its copious delights, in which respect they all resign in your favour this pleasure of yours, and are content themselves to go without it, nor is there a man among them who, if ever he had to learn some work by heart, would not choose for that purpose the *Teucer* [b] of Pacuvius rather than Manilius's *Conditions of Sale.* Taking next your opinion that love of country obliges us

Given a general knowledge of law, special points can be looked up.

nos nostrorum maiorum inventa nosse debere : non
vides, veteres leges aut ipsa sua vetustate consenuisse,
aut novis legibus esse sublatas ? Quod vero viros
bonos iure civili fieri putas, quia legibus et praemia
proposita sint virtutibus, et supplicia vitiis : equidem
putabam, virtutem hominibus—si modo tradi ratione
possit—instituendo et persuadendo, non minis, et vi,
ac metu tradi. Nam ipsum quidem illud, etiam sine
cognitione iuris, quam sit bellum, cavere malum,
scire possumus.

248 De me autem ipso, cui uni tu concedis, ut, sine ulla
iuris scientia, tamen causis satisfacere possim, tibi
hoc, Crasse, respondeo, neque me unquam ius civile
didicisse, neque tamen in eis causis, quas in iure possem defendere, unquam istam scientiam desiderasse.
Aliud est enim, esse artificem cuiusdam generis atque
artis, aliud in communi vita et vulgari hominum con-
249 suetudine nec hebetem, nec rudem. Cui nostrum
non licet fundos nostros obire, aut res rusticas, vel
fructus causa, vel delectationis, invisere ? Tamen
nemo tam sine oculis, tam sine mente vivit, ut,
quid sit sementis ac messis, quid arborum putatio
ac vitium, quo tempore anni, aut quo modo ea
fiant, omnino nesciat. Num igitur, si cui fundus
inspiciendus, aut si mandandum aliquid procuratori
de agricultura, aut imperandum villico sit, Magonis
Carthaginiensis sunt libri perdiscendi ? An hac communi intellegentia contenti esse possumus ? Cur ergo

to get a knowledge of the devices of our ancestors, do you not observe that the ancient statutes have either sunk into the decrepitude of their old age, or been repealed by modern legislation ? And as for your belief that men are made good by the common law, since by its rules prizes are offered to virtue and punishments appointed for vice, I certainly used to regard virtue as being taught to mankind (assuming it to be methodically teachable at all) by training and persuasion, not by threats, and force and even terror. For thus much, at any rate, we can learn even without legal study, namely, how lovely a thing it is to eschew evil.

248 " Now as to myself, to whom alone you allow the faculty of doing justice to my cases without any legal knowledge, I give you this answer, Crassus, that I never learned the common law, and yet never felt the want of that knowledge in the suits I was able to argue before the Praetor. For it is one thing to be a craftsman in a specific subject and art, and another to be no dullard or raw hand in social life 249 and the general practices of mankind. Which of us may not survey his estate or go to see his rural concerns, whether in quest of profit or of amusement ? Yet no one passes his days so bereft of sight and sense as to be wholly ignorant of the nature of sowing and reaping, or of the lopping of trees and pruning of vines, or of the times of year for doing these things, or of how they are done. If then some one of us has occasion to look over his estate, or give some commission to his agent, or order to his bailiff, on details of husbandry, need he get by heart the volumes of Mago of Carthage ? Or may we be satisfied with our own mother-wit ? If so then, especially as we

non eidem in iure civili, praesertim cum in causis, et
in negotiis, et in foro conteramur, satis instructi esse
possumus ad hoc duntaxat, ne in nostra patria pere-
250 grini atque advenae esse videamur ? Ac si iam sit
causa aliqua ad nos delata obscurior, difficile, credo,
sit cum hoc Scaevola communicare ; quanquam ipsi
omnia, quorum negotium est, consulta ad nos et
exquisita deferunt. An vero si de re ipsa, si de
finibus, cum in rem praesentem non venimus, si de
tabulis, et perscriptionibus controversia est, contortas
res et saepe difficiles necessario perdiscimus : si leges
nobis, aut si hominum peritorum responsa cognoscenda sunt, veremur ne ea, si ab adolescentia iuri
civili minus studuerimus, non queamus cognoscere ?

LIX. Nihilne igitur prodest oratori iuris civilis
scientia ? Non possum negare prodesse ullam scientiam, ei praesertim, cuius eloquentia copia rerum
debeat esse ornata ; sed multa, et magna, et difficilia
sunt ea, quae sunt oratori necessaria, ut eius indu-
striam in plura studia distrahere nolim.

251 Quis neget, opus esse oratori, in hoc oratorio motu
statuque, Roscii gestum et venustatem? Tamen nemo
suaserit studiosis dicendi adolescentibus, in gestu di-
scendo histrionum more elaborare. Quid est oratori
tam necessarium, quam vox ? Tamen, me auctore,
nemo dicendi studiosus, Graecorum more tragoe-

are worn out with legal and other business and with public affairs, why may we not likewise be well enough equipped in common law, to the extent at any rate of not seeming to be sojourners and strangers 250 in our own country? And if some day an exceptionally doubtful case were submitted to us, it would be quite easy, I suppose, to take counsel with Scaevola here; although in fact the parties themselves, whose affair it is, furnish us with all the professional opinions and researches. If again the dispute relates to a question of fact, or to boundaries, without our having a view of the very spot, or to account-books and entries, we are obliged to get up complicated and often troublesome matters: if we have to master statutes, or the opinions of the learned in the law, are we afraid of not being able to do so, just because, from our youth upwards, our study of the common law has been inadequate?

LIX. "Is a knowledge of the common law, then, useless to an orator? I cannot assert that any knowledge is useless, least of all to one whose eloquence ought to be furnished with material in plenty; but the essential needs of an orator are many and weighty and hard to come by, so that I would not dissipate his energy over too wide a field of study.

51 "Who would deny that in his movements and carriage the orator must have the bearing and elegance of Roscius? Yet no one will urge young devotees of eloquence to toil like actors at the study of gesture. What is so essential to an orator as intonation? Yet no devotee of eloquence will become, by my advice, a slave to his voice, after the manner of the Greek tragedians, who both

Similarly delivery does not require special study.

dorum, voci serviet, qui et annos complures sedentes declamitant, et quotidie, antequam pronuntient,
vocem cubantes sensim excitant, eamdemque, cum
egerunt, sedentes ab acutissimo sono usque ad gravissimum sonum recipiunt, et quasi quodam modo
colligunt. Hoc nos si facere velimus, ante condem-
nentur ei, quorum causas receperimus, quam, toties,
quoties perscribitur, paeanem, aut nomionem[1]
citarimus.

252 Quod si in gestu, qui multum oratorem adiuvat, et
in voce, quae una maxime eloquentiam vel commendat, vel sustinet, elaborare nobis non licet ; ac
tantum in utroque assequi possumus, quantum in hac
acie quotidiani muneris, spatii nobis datur : quanto
minus est ad iuris civilis perdiscendi occupationem
descendendum, quod et summatim percipi sine doctrina potest, et hanc habet ab illis rebus dissimilitu-
dinem, quod vox et gestus subito sumi et aliunde
arripi non potest ; iuris utilitas ad quamque causam,
quamvis repente, vel a peritis, vel de libris depromi
potest !

253 Itaque illi disertissimi homines ministros habent in
causis iuris peritos, cum ipsi sint peritissimi, et qui,
ut abs te paulo ante dictum est, pragmatici vocantur.
In quo nostri omnino melius multo, quod clarissimo-
rum hominum auctoritate leges et iura tecta esse
voluerunt. Sed tamen non fugisset hoc Graecos
homines, si ita necesse esse arbitrati essent, oratorem

---

[1] nomionem (*an invocation of* 'Απόλλων Νόμιος) *is the conjectural emendation adopted by Kayser, Piderit, and others
for the various corruptions of the* MSS.

---

[a] The most eloquent Greek orators.

for many a year practise declamation from their
chairs, and every day, before their performance on
the stage, lie down and gradually raise the voice,
and later, after playing their parts, take their seats,
and bring it back again from the highest treble
to the lowest bass, and in a way regain control of it.
If we had a fancy to do this, the parties whose cases
we had undertaken would lose their cases, before we
had recited our hymn or chant the regulation number
of times.

52 "But if we are not to work hard either at gesture,
a great help to an orator, or at intonation, that
singular and unrivalled recommendation and prop
of eloquence; and if in each of these matters we
can attain only such proficiency as corresponds to
the leisure allowed us amid this array of daily duties;
how much the less must we sink into becoming
engrossed with getting by heart the common law,
of which a general knowledge may be gained even
without instruction, and which bears this unlikeness
to those other things, that intonation and gesture
cannot be acquired all at once and caught up from
external sources, while anything in the law that is
of use for a particular case, may be fetched, as
hurriedly as you please, from experts or text-books!

53 "This is why those most accomplished speakers,[a]
for all their own profound skill, have with them in
Court assistants learned in the law, and these, as you
said a little while ago, are called attorneys. In this
respect our own folk have done infinitely better, by
requiring the statutes and rules of law to be safe-
guarded by the influence of most illustrious men.
But after all, had they thought it necessary, this
idea of training the orator himself in the common

185

ipsum erudire in iure civili, non ei pragmaticum
adiutorem dare.

254   LX. Nam quod dicis senectutem a solitudine vindicari iuris civilis scientia : fortasse etiam pecuniae
magnitudine.   Sed nos, non quid nobis utile, verum
quid oratori necessarium sit, quaerimus.   Quanquam,
quoniam multa ad oratoris similitudinem ab uno
artifice sumimus, solet idem Roscius dicere, se, quo
plus sibi aetatis accederet, eo tardiores tibicinis
modos, et cantus remissiores esse facturum.   Quod
si ille, astrictus certa quadam numerorum moderatione et pedum, tamen aliquid ad requiem senectutis
excogitat, quanto facilius nos non laxare modos, sed
255 totos mutare possumus !   Neque enim hoc te, Crasse,
fallit, quam multa sint, et quam varia genera dicendi,
et quod haud sciam, an tu primus ostenderis, qui
iamdiu multo dicis remissius et lenius, quam solebas ;
neque minus haec tamen tua gravissimi sermonis
lenitas, quam illa summa vis et contentio probatur :
multique oratores fuerunt, ut illum Scipionem audi-
mus, et Laelium, qui omnia sermone conficerent paulo
intentiore, nunquam, ut Ser. Galba, lateribus, aut
clamore contenderent.   Quod si iam hoc facere non
poteris, aut noles : vereris, ne tua domus, talis et viri,
et civis, si a litigiosis hominibus non colatur, a ceteris
deseratur ?   Equidem tantum absum ab ista sen-

law, instead of giving him an attorney to help him,
would not have failed to occur to the Greeks.

254   LX. " As for your theory that old age is redeemed
from loneliness by a knowledge of the common law,
possibly a large fortune will do as much. However
we are not investigating our own advantage, but the
essential needs of the orator. And yet, as we are
taking from a single artist a number of details for
our likeness of an orator, that same Roscius is fond
of saying, that, the older he grows, the slower he will
make the flute-player's rhythms and the lighter the
music. Now if he, fettered as he is by a definite
system of measures and metres, is none the less
thinking out some relief for his old age, how much
more easily can we not merely slacken our methods,
255 but change them altogether ! For you cannot fail
to see, Crassus, how many and diverse are the styles
of oratory, a fact which I should almost think you
have been the first to make plain, who for a long time
have been speaking in a far lighter and calmer
fashion than was your wont ; though the present
serenity of your very dignified discourse finds as
ready acceptance as did your extreme energy and
passion of old : and there have been many orators
including, we are told, the famous Scipio and Laelius,
who obtained all their results by discourse little
more emphatic than the ordinary, and never strained
their lungs or shouted, as Servius Galba did. But
if some day you should be unable or unwilling to do
even this, are you afraid that the house of such a
man and citizen as yourself will be left desolate by
the rest of the community, just because it may no
longer be the shrine of the litigious ? Truly I am
so far from agreeing with that view of yours, that I

Old age does not require knowledge of the law to give it occupation.

tentia, ut non modo non arbitrer subsidium senectutis
in eorum, qui consultum veniant, multitudine esse
ponendum, sed tanquam portum aliquem, exspectem
istam, quam tu times, solitudinem.   Subsidium enim
bellissimum existimo esse senectuti, otium.

256   Reliqua vero etiamsi adiuvant, historiam dico, et
prudentiam iuris publici, et antiquitatis iter,[1] et exemplorum copiam, si quando opus erit, a viro optimo,
et istis rebus instructissimo, familiari meo, Congo [2]
mutuabor.   Neque repugnabo, quominus—id quod
modo hortatus es—omnia legant, omnia audiant, in
omni recto studio atque humanitate versentur : sed
mehercule non ita multum spatii mihi habere videntur, si modo ea facere et persequi volent, quae a te,
Crasse, praecepta sunt ; qui mihi prope etiam nimis
duras leges imponere visus es huic aetati, sed tamen
ad id, quod cupiunt, adipiscendum prope necessarias.

257 Nam et subitae ad propositas causas exercitationes, et
accuratae, et meditatae commentationes, ac stylus ille
tuus, quem tu vere dixisti perfectorem dicendi esse ac
magistrum, multi sudoris est ; et illa orationis suae
cum scriptis alienis comparatio, et de alieno scripto
subita, vel laudandi, vel vituperandi, vel comprobandi,
vel refellendi causa, disputatio, non mediocris contentionis est, vel ad memoriam, vel ad imitandum.

258   LXI. Illud vero fuit horribile, quod mehercule
vereor, ne maiorem vim ad deterrendum habuerit,
quam ad cohortandum.   Voluisti enim in suo genere

---

[1] scita *Reid*, memoriam *Koch*.
[2] *Roth ;* Longo (Longino *edd.*).

not only do not think the prop of old age is to be found in the multitude of those who come to seek its counsel, but I look for that loneliness which you dread, as I might for a haven. For I hold that the finest prop of old age is its leisure.

56 " But the remaining acquirements,—useful as they are,—I am speaking of history, and a knowledge of public law, and the ways of the ancients, and a store of precedents,—I shall borrow, if ever I need them, from my friend Congus, an excellent man who is thoroughly versed in these things. And I shall not object to these young men reading and listening to everything, and busying themselves with every fitting pursuit and with general culture—as you advised just now—: but, I vow, they do not seem to me to have so very much time to spare, provided that they hope to accomplish and follow out all your bidding, Crassus ; for I thought that the conditions you imposed were rather too rigorous for their time of life, though possibly necessary for the attainment
7 of the end of their desire. Indeed the impromptu exercises on problems set, the elaborate and considered reflections, and your practice of written composition, which you justly called the finishing schoolmaster of eloquence, all demand much toil ; and that comparison of the student's own dissertation with the writings of others, and the unprepared estimate of another's work, by way of praise or disparagement, approval or refutation, involve exceptional efforts of memory and of the imitative faculty as well.

LXI. " Then that further claim of yours was terrifying, and upon my word I am afraid that its effect will be to deter rather than encourage. For you

General culture is sufficient.

189

unumquemque nostrum quasi quemdam esse Roscium; dixistique, non tam ea, quae recta essent,
probari, quam quae prava sunt fastidiis adhaerescere:
quod ego non tam fastidiose in nobis, quam in hi-
259 strionibus, spectari puto. Itaque nos raucos saepe
attentissime audiri video : tenet enim res ipsa atque
causa : at Aesopum, si paulum irrauserit, explodi. A
quibus enim nihil praeter voluptatem aurium quaeritur, in eis offenditur, simul atque imminuitur aliquid
de voluptate. In eloquentia autem multa sunt, quae
teneant; quae si omnia summa non sunt—et pleraque
tamen magna sunt—necesse est, ea ipsa quae sunt,
mirabilia videri.

260 Ergo, ut ad primum illud revertar, sit orator nobis
is, qui, ut Crassus descripsit, accommodate ad persuadendum possit dicere. Is autem concludatur in
ea, quae sunt in usu civitatum vulgari ac forensi ;
remotisque ceteris studiis, quamvis ea sint ampla
atque praeclara, in hoc uno opere, ut ita dicam, noctes
et dies urgeatur ; imiteturque illum, cui sine dubio
summa vis dicendi conceditur, Atheniensem Demosthenem, in quo tantum studium fuisse, tantusque
labor dicitur, ut primum impedimenta naturae diligentia industriaque superaret : cumque ita balbus
esset, ut eius ipsius artis, cui studeret, primam litteram non posset dicere, perfecit meditando, ut nemo

---

^a For the great orator's ways of conquering his natural
handicaps see Schaefer's *Demosthenes*, vol. i. pp. 299-301;
Cicero, *De Finibus* v. 2. 5; Plutarch's *Life of Demosthenes*
(c. 11); and Quintilian x. 3. 30.
^b Rhetorica.

would have every man of us be a kind of Roscius in his own line ; and you said that the approbation accorded to the good points of a speech is short-lived in comparison with the enduring aversion inspired by its shortcomings, whereas I hold that the criticism of our oratory is less squeamish than
259 that directed upon actors. This explains why I see that, even when hoarse, we are often listened to with rapt attention, since the very fact of our hoarseness and our case grip the audience : while Aesopus, should he be a little husky, is hissed off the stage. For, in those arts of which nothing is expected save the gratification of the ear, offence is given directly that gratification is at all weakened. But of oratory the fascinating features are many, and even if all are not there in perfection—still, most of them are highly developed—, such as are actually present must needs be thought marvellous.

30 " And so, to return to our starting-point, let us take the orator to be, as Crassus defined him, a man who can speak in a way calculated to convince. But let him be shut up within the sphere of the daily inter-course and public life of bodies politic ; and forsaking all other pursuits, be they as noble and glorious as you please, let him press forward night and day (so to speak) in this single vocation, and do as the famous Athenian Demosthenes [a] did, whose pre-eminence in oratory is unhesitatingly admitted, and whose zeal and exertions are said to have been such that at the very outset he surmounted natural drawbacks by diligent perseverance : and though at first stuttering so badly as to be unable to pro-nounce the initial R. of the name of the art of his devotion,[b] by practice he made himself accounted as

The important thing is practice.

191

261 planius eo locutus putaretur ; deinde, cum spiritus eius esset angustior, tantum continenda anima in dicendo est assecutus, ut una continuatione verborum —id quod eius scripta declarant—binae ei contentiones vocis et remissiones continerentur ; qui etiam —ut memoriae proditum est—, coniectis in os calculis, summa voce versus multos uno spiritu pronuntiare consuescebat ; neque is consistens in loco, sed inambulans, atque ascensu ingrediens arduo.

262 Hisce ego cohortationibus, Crasse, ad studium et ad laborem incitandos iuvenes vehementer assentior : cetera, quae collegisti ex variis et diversis studiis et artibus, tametsi ipse es omnia consecutus, tamen ab oratoris proprio officio atque munere seiuncta esse arbitror.

LXII. Haec cum Antonius dixisset, sane dubitare visus est Sulpicius, et Cotta, utrius oratio propius ad 263 veritatem videretur accedere. Tum Crassus : Operarium nobis quemdam, Antoni, oratorem facis ; atque haud scio, an aliter sentias, et utare tua illa mirifica ad refellendum consuetudine, qua tibi nemo unquam praestitit ; cuius quidem ipsius facultatis exercitatio oratorum propria est, sed iam in philosophorum consuetudine versatur, maximeque eorum, qui de omni re proposita in utramque partem solent copiosissime 264 dicere. Verum ego non solum arbitrabar, his praesertim audientibus, a me informari oportere, qualis esse posset is, qui habitaret in subselliis, neque quid-

61 distinct a speaker as anyone ; later on, though his breath was rather short, he succeeded so far in making his breath hold during a speech, that a single oratorical period—as his writings prove—covered two risings and two fallings of tone ; moreover—as the tale goes—it was his habit to slip pebbles into his mouth, and then declaim a number of verses at the top of his voice and without drawing breath, and this not only as he stood still, but while walking about, or going up a steep slope.

2   " By encouragements of this sort, Crassus, I thoroughly agree with you that the young should be spurred on to severe application : all else that you have brought together from various and dissimilar pursuits and arts, though you yourself have attained everything, I nevertheless regard as lying outside the strict business and function of an orator."

LXII. At the conclusion of these observations of Antonius, Sulpicius, and Cotta too, appeared to be in grave doubt as to which of the two speakers' discourses bore the closer resemblance to the truth. Presently Crassus replied : " Antonius, you are making our orator something of a mechanic ; and I rather suspect you are really of a different opinion, and are gratifying that singular liking of yours for contradiction, in which no one has ever outdone you ; the exercise of this power belongs peculiarly to orators, though nowadays it is in regular use among philosophers, and chiefly those who make a practice of arguing at extreme length either for or against any proposition whatever laid before them. Now I did not think it my duty, especially before my present audience, to delineate only the possible quality of such a speaker as would live in Court, and

Adjourn-ment of the debate.

193

quam amplius afferret, quam quod causarum necessitas postularet; sed maius quiddam videbam, cum
censebam, oratorem, praesertim in nostra republica,
nullius ornamenti expertem esse oportere. Tu autem,
quoniam exiguis quibusdam finibus totum oratoris
munus circumdedisti, hoc facilius nobis expones ea,
quae abs te de officiis praeceptisque oratoris quaesita
sunt: sed, opinor, secundum hunc diem. Satis enim
265 multa a nobis hodie dicta sunt. Nunc et Scaevola,
quoniam in Tusculanum ire constituit, paulum re-
quiescet, dum se calor frangat; et nos ipsi, quoniam
id temporis est, valetudini demus operam.

Placuit sic omnibus. Tum Scaevola: Sane, inquit,
vellem non constituissem, in Tusculanum me hodie
venturum esse, Laelio; libenter audirem Antonium.
Et, cum exsurgeret, simul arridens: Neque enim,
inquit, tam mihi molestus fuit, quod ius nostrum civile
pervellit, quam iucundus, quod se id nescire con-
fessus est.

bring thither nothing more than the needs of his cases demanded ; but I was envisaging a loftier ideal when I stated my view that the orator, especially in our own community, ought to lack nothing in the way of equipment. You on the other hand, having enclosed within certain narrow confines the whole function of an orator, will the more easily expound to us the result of your investigations into his duties and rules : but that, I think, must be another time. For our talk to-day has been long enough. Now too Scaevola, as he has arranged to go to his Tusculan villa, will rest awhile, until the heat has abated ; and let us ourselves, considering the time of day, take care of our health."

This suggestion pleased everybody. Then Scaevola observed : " I devoutly wish that I had not arranged with Laelius to arrive at my Tusculan villa to-day ; I should like to hear Antonius." And, as he got up, he added with a smile : " For I was not so much vexed by his tearing our common law to tatters, as delighted by his admission that he knew nothing about it."

DE ORATORE

DIALOGUS SEU LIBER SECUNDUS

1   I. Magna nobis pueris, Quinte frater, si memoria
tenes, opinio fuit, L. Crassum non plus attigisse doctrinae, quam quantum prima illa puerili institutione
potuisset; M. autem Antonium omnino omnis erudi-
tionis expertem atque ignarum fuisse. Erantque
multi qui, quanquam non ita sese rem habere arbitrarentur, tamen, quo facilius nos incensos studio
dicendi a doctrina deterrerent, libenter id quod dixi,
de illis oratoribus praedicarent, ut, si homines non
eruditi summam essent prudentiam atque incredibilem eloquentiam consecuti, inanis omnis noster esse
labor, et stultum in nobis erudiendis, patris nostri,
2   optimi ac prudentissimi viri, studium videretur. Quos
tum, ut pueri, refutare domesticis testibus patre et
C. Aculeone propinquo nostro et L. Cicerone patruo
solebamus, quod de Crasso pater, et Aculeo (quocum
erat nostra matertera), quem Crassus dilexit ex

196

THE MAKING OF AN ORATOR

BOOK THE SECOND

1 I. When we were boys, brother Quintus, there was, if you remember, a widespread belief that Lucius Crassus had dabbled no further in learning than the early training of a lad of his day allowed, and that Marcus Antonius was absolutely without any education and ignorant. And there were many who, while they did not hold this to be the truth of the matter, none the less hoped the more readily to deter us eager students in search of eloquence from the pursuit of learning, and so they did not scruple to make such statements about those eminent orators; to the intent that we ourselves, on seeing that men who were no scholars had attained the highest degree of practical wisdom, and a standard of eloquence passing belief, might come to look upon all our own labour as being but in vain, and to think mere folly the care bestowed upon our education by a man so excellent and widely experienced as our father. Such sophists we used at that time to confound, in boyish fashion, by calling witnesses from home, namely our father, our near kinsman Gaius Aculeo, and our paternal uncle Lucius Cicero, inasmuch as our father, and Aculeo, who married our mother's sister, and was esteemed by Crassus above all other

Introduction: eloquence of Crassus and Antonius based on erudition.

197

omnibus plurimum, et patruus, qui cum Antonio in
Ciciliam profectus una decesserat, multa nobis de
eius studio doctrinaque saepe narravit. Cumque nos
cum consobrinis nostris, Aculeonis filiis, et ea disce-
remus, quae Crasso placerent, et ab his doctoribus,
quibus ille uteretur, erudiremur, etiam illud saepe
intelleximus cum essemus eius domi,[1] quod vel pueri
sentire poteramus, illum et Graece sic loqui, nullam
ut nosse aliam linguam videretur, et doctoribus nostris ea ponere in percontando, eaque ipsum omni in
sermone tractare, ut nihil esse ei novum, nihil inau-
3 ditum videretur.   De Antonio vero, quanquam saepe
ex humanissimo homine, patruo nostro, acceperamus,
quemadmodum ille vel Athenis vel Rhodi se doctis-
simorum hominum sermonibus dedisset, tamen ipse
adolescentulus, quantum illius ineuntis aetatis meae
patiebatur pudor, multa ex eo saepe quaesivi.   Non
erit profecto tibi, quod scribo, hoc novum nam iam
tum ex me audiebas, mihi illum, ex multis variisque
sermonibus, nullius rei, quae quidem esset in his
artibus, de quibus aliquid existimare possem, rudem
aut ignarum esse visum.

4   Sed fuit hoc in utroque eorum, ut Crassus non tam
existimari vellet non didicisse, quam illa despicere,

---

[1] eius domi. *The correction of Piderit and Sorof for the
indefensible* eius modi *of the* MSS.

men, and our paternal uncle, who went out to Cilicia
with Antonius, and was with him when he left his
province for home, all severally and often related to
us a great deal about Crassus, his application to
study, and his intellectual attainments.   And since,
in the company of our cousins, the sons of Aculeo
and our mother's sister, we were not only studying
such subjects as attracted Crassus, but were also
being instructed by those very teachers whom he
made his friends, we, being as we were at his
home, often perceived,—as even we boys could perceive,—that, besides speaking Greek so perfectly as
to suggest that it was the only tongue he knew,
he propounded such topics to our masters in the
way of inquiry and himself so handled matters in
his discourse, that nothing seemed strange to him,
nothing beyond his range of knowledge.   But as for
Antonius, although we had frequently understood
from our highly accomplished paternal uncle how, at
Athens and at Rhodes alike, that orator had devoted
himself to conversation with the most learned men,
yet I myself, in early life, went as far as the modesty
natural to my youth permitted, in questioning him
time and again on many subjects.   What I am writing will assuredly be no news to you, for I used to tell
you even then that the result of many conversa-
tions with him on various subjects was to convey to
me the impression that there was nothing—at least in
any studies about which I could form an opinion—
about which he was inexperienced or ignorant.

   There was nevertheless this point of difference
between the two men, that Crassus did not so much
wish to be thought to have learned nothing, as to
have the reputation of looking down upon learning,

et nostrorum hominum in omni genere prudentiam Graecis anteferre ; Antonius autem probabiliorem hoc populo orationem fore censebat suam, si omnino didicisse nunquam putaretur. Atque ita se uterque graviorem fore, si alter contemnere, alter ne nosse 5 quidem Graecos videretur. Quorum consilium quale fuerit, nihil sane ad hoc tempus ; illud autem est huius institutae scriptionis ac temporis, neminem eloquentia, non modo sine dicendi doctrina, sed ne sine omni quidem sapientia, florere unquam et praestare potuisse.

II. Etenim ceterae fere artes se ipsae per se tuentur singulae ; bene dicere autem, quod est scienter, et perite, et ornate dicere, non habet definitam aliquam regionem, cuius terminis septa teneatur. Omnia, quaecumque in hominum disceptationem cadere possunt, bene sunt ei dicenda, qui hoc se posse profitetur, aut eloquentiae nomen relinquendum 6 est. Quare equidem et in nostra civitate, et in ipsa Graecia, quae semper haec summa duxit, multos et ingeniis, et magna laude dicendi sine summa rerum omnium scientia fuisse fateor ; talem vero exsistere eloquentiam, qualis fuerit in Crasso et Antonio, non cognitis rebus omnibus, quae ad tantam prudentiam pertinerent, tantamque dicendi copiam, quanta in illis 7 fuit, non potuisse confirmo. Quo etiam feci libentius, ut eum sermonem, quem illi quondam inter se

and of placing the wisdom of our own fellow-country-men above that of the Greeks in all departments; while Antonius held that his speeches would be the more acceptable to a nation like ours, if it were thought that he had never engaged in study at all. Thus the one expected to grow in influence by being thought to hold a poor opinion of the Greeks, and the other by seeming never even to have heard of them.

5 What the value of these opinions was, would clearly not matter now, but it does belong to this treatise which I have in hand, and to this occasion, to insist that no man has ever succeeded in achieving splendour and excellence in oratory, I will not say merely without training in speaking, but without taking all knowledge for his province as well.

II. For, while nearly all the other arts can look after themselves, the art of speaking well, that is to say, of speaking with knowledge, skill and elegance, has no delimited territory, within whose borders it is enclosed and confined. All things whatsoever, that can fall under the discussion of human beings, must be aptly dealt with by him who professes to have this power, or he must abandon the name of eloquent. *Oratory must be backed by learning.*

6 And so on my own part, I admit that, both in our own country and in Greece itself, which has ever held these pursuits in the highest esteem, there have appeared many men of natural parts and great reputation in oratory, without the fullest universal knowledge; yet I maintain that such eloquence as Crassus and Antonius attained could never have been realized without a knowledge of every matter that went to produce that wisdom and that power of

7 oratory which were manifest in those two. And so I was the readier to commit to writing a conversation

de his rebus habuissent, mandarem litteris, vel ut illa opinio, quae semper fuisset, tolleretur, alterum non doctissimum, alterum plane indoctum fuisse ; vel ut ea, quae existimarem a summis oratoribus de eloquentia divinitus esse dicta, custodirem litteris, si ullo modo assequi complectique potuissem ; vel mehercule etiam, ut laudem eorum, iam prope senescentem, quantum ego possem, ab oblivione hominum

8 atque a silentio vindicarem. Nam si ex scriptis cognosci ipsi suis potuissent, minus hoc fortasse mihi esse putassem laborandum : sed cum alter non multum quod quidem exstaret, et id ipsum adolescens, alter nihil admodum scripti reliquisset, deberi hoc a me tantis hominum ingeniis putavi, ut, cum etiam nunc vivam illorum memoriam teneremus, hanc

9 immortalem redderem, si possem. Quod hoc etiam spe aggredior maiore ad probandum, quia non de Ser. Galbae, aut C. Carbonis eloquentia scribo aliquid, in quo liceat mihi fingere, si quid velim, nullius memoria iam me refellente : sed edo haec eis cognoscenda, qui eos ipsos, de quibus loquor, saepe audierunt ; ut duos summos viros eis, qui neutrum illorum viderint, eorum, quibus ambo illi oratores cogniti sint, vivorum et praesentium memoria teste, commendemus.

they once had on the subject, my purpose being, in the first place, to dispel that notion, which had always prevailed, that one of them had no great learning and the other none at all; secondly, to preserve in literary form the sentiments concerning eloquence which to my thinking were expressed to perfection by those consummate orators, if in any way I should have succeeded in recapturing and representing their pronouncements; and lastly, I protest, to rescue, as far as possible, from disuse and from silence, the reputation of these men which was 8 already beginning to wane. For could their own writings have made those orators known, perhaps I should have seen smaller need for this work that I have undertaken, but as one of them had written little (at all events little that survived), and had written that little in early life, while the other had left nothing whatever in writing, I thought that it was a tribute due from me to those great intellects, that while all still held them in living memory I should render that memory immortal, if I could. 9 And my hope is so much the greater that I shall establish the case which I am approaching, because I am not treating of the eloquence of Servius Galba or Gaius Carbo, in which case I should be able to invent at pleasure, no one now surviving to contradict me with his reminiscences, but I am publishing what will be criticized by those who have often actually listened to the men of whom I am speaking, in order that I may recommend an illustrious pair to those who have never seen either of them, on the testimony of the recollections of men to whom both those famous orators were personally known, and who themselves are living and still among us.

10   III. Nec vero te, carissime frater atque optime,
rhetoricis nunc quibusdam libris, quos tu agrestes
putas, insequor ut erudiam : quid enim tua potest
oratione aut subtilius, aut ornatius esse ? Sed, sive
iudicio, ut soles dicere, sive, ut ille pater eloquentiae
de se Isocrates scripsit ipse, pudore a dicendo et
timiditate ingenua quadam refugisti, sive, ut ipse
iocari soleo, unum putasti satis esse non modo in una
familia rhetorem, sed paene in tota civitate, non
tamen arbitror tibi hos libros in eo fore genere, quod
merito, propter eorum, qui de dicendi ratione dis-
putarunt, ieiunitatem bonarum artium, possit illudi.

11 Nihil enim mihi quidem videtur in Crassi et Antonii
sermone esse praeteritum, quod quisquam summis
ingeniis, acerrimis studiis, optima doctrina, maximo
usu cognosci ac percipi potuisse arbitraretur, quod
tu facillime poteris iudicare, qui prudentiam rationemque dicendi per te ipsum, usum autem per nos
percipere voluisti. Sed, quo citius hoc, quod susce-
pimus, non mediocre munus conficere possimus, omis-
sa nostra adhortatione, ad eorum, quos proposuimus,
sermonem disputationemque veniamus.

12   Postero igitur die, quam illa erant acta, hora fere
secunda, cum etiam tum in lecto Crassus esset et
apud eum Sulpicius sederet, Antonius autem in-
ambularet cum Cotta in porticu, repente eo Q.

10   III. But you are the last man, my dear and The topic
excellent brother, that I should try to instruct by commended.
means of a lot of books which you think only crude ;
for what can be more exact or graceful than your
own diction ? But whether it be on principle, as you
generally affirm, or from modesty and what I may
call the diffidence of the well-bred, that you have
shrunk from public speaking (as that eminent father
of eloquence, Isocrates, has declared to have been
the case with himself), or whether, as I myself am
wont to say in jesting mood, you thought one
declaimer enough in a family, and wellnigh enough
in an entire community, still I think that you will not
place this essay among that class of writings which
may be a fitting object of ridicule, because of the
sheer want of good learning in those who have
11 therein discussed the art of speaking. For to my mind
nothing has been passed over, in the dialogue between Crassus and Antonius, that anyone would have
thought possible to be known and understood by men
of the highest ability, the most eager application, the
profoundest learning, and the most complete experience,—a point which you will have no trouble in deciding, since you have chosen to master the lore and
principles of oratory by your own study, its practice
by my assistance. But in order the sooner to discharge this important duty that we have undertaken,
let us proceed, without any preamble of mine, to the
discourse and arguments of those orators whom we
have set before us.

On the morrow, then, of that former debate, at The second
about eight in the morning, while Crassus was still in day's
debate.
bed and Sulpicius sitting by his side, and Antonius Arrival of
strolling with Cotta in the colonnade, Quintus Catulus Catulus
and Caesar.

205

Catulus senex cum C. Iulio fratre venit. Quod ubi
audivit, commotus Crassus surrexit omnesque ad-
mirati maiorem aliquam esse causam eorum adven-
13 tus suspicati sunt. Qui cum inter se, ut ipsorum
usus ferebat, amicissime consalutassent : Quid vos
tandem ? Crassus, num quidnam, inquit, novi ? Nihil
sane, inquit Catulus : etenim vides esse ludos.
Sed (vel tu nos ineptos licet, inquit, vel moles-
tos putes) cum ad me in Tusculanum heri vesperi
venisset Caesar de Tusculano suo, dixit mihi, a se
Scaevolam hinc euntem esse conventum, ex quo
mira quaedam se audisse dicebat ; te, quem ego,
toties omni ratione tentans, ad disputandum elicere
non potuissem, permulta de eloquentia cum Antonio
disseruisse, et tanquam in schola, prope ad Grae-
14 corum consuetudinem, disputasse. Ita me frater ex-
oravit, ne ipsum quidem a studio audiendi nimis ab-
horrentem, sed mehercule verentem, ne molesti vobis
interveniremus, ut huc secum venirem ; Scaevolam
etenim ita dicere aiebat, bonam partem sermonis in
hunc diem esse dilatam. Hoc si tu cupidius factum
existimas, Caesari attribues ; si familiarius, utrique
nostrum : nos quidem, nisi forte molesti intervenimus,
venisse delectat.
15   IV. Tum Crassus : Equidem, quaecumque causa
vos huc attulisset, laetarer, cum apud me viderem

the elder suddenly arrived at the house, accompanied by his brother Gaius Julius. On being informed of this, Crassus rose in a state of excitement, and general astonishment prevailed, everyone surmising that the reason for this visit must be something out of the

13 ordinary. After exchanging very cordial greetings with one another, as their practice was, Crassus inquired, "What in the world brings you here? Have you any news?" "None whatever," replied Catulus; "you see the Games are on. Think us impertinent or troublesome, as you please, but the fact is, that on arriving yesterday evening at my Tusculan villa from his own, Caesar told me that he had met Scaevola, who was on his way from this place, and who related to him a marvellous tale, the purport of which was that you, whom all my inducements, so often employed, could never draw into a discussion, had been stating your views on oratory at large, in debate with Antonius, and reasoning as if in the schools, and very much in the Greek mode.

14 And this was how my brother's entreaties prevailed upon me to accompany him hither,—not indeed that I have any particular aversion to playing the part of a listener, but I vow I was afraid that our pushing in might be troublesome to you—; for he explained that, according to Scaevola, a good part of the discourse stood adjourned until to-day. If you think this action of ours impertinent curiosity, you will blame Caesar, if it seems an abuse of friendship, you will blame the pair of us; for our part we are charmed to be here, provided always that our coming in does not happen to be a nuisance."

15 IV. To which Crassus made answer, "Whatever occasion had brought you here, I should be delighted

General conversation.

homines mihi carissimos et amicissimos ; sed tamen,
vere dicam, quaevis mallem fuisset, quam ista, quam
dicis. Ego enim ut, quemadmodum sentiam, loquar,
nunquam mihi minus, quam hesterno die, placui ;
magis adeo id facilitate, quam alia ulla culpa mea
contigit, qui, dum obsequor adolescentibus, me senem
esse sum oblitus, fecique id, quod ne adolescens quidem feceram, ut eis de rebus, quae doctrina aliqua
continerentur, disputarem. Sed hoc tamen cecidit
mihi peropportune, quod, transactis iam meis partibus, ad Antonium audiendum venistis.

16 Tum Caesar : Equidem, inquit, Crasse, ita sum
cupidus te in illa longiore ac perpetua disputatione
audiendi, ut, si id mihi minus contingat, vel hoc sim
quotidiano tuo sermone contentus. Itaque experiar
equidem illud, ut ne Sulpicius, familiaris meus, aut
Cotta, plus quam ego apud te valere videantur ; et
te exorabo profecto, ut mihi quoque et Catulo tuae
suavitatis aliquid impertias. Sin tibi id minus libebit,
non te urgebo, neque committam, ut, dum vereare, tu
ne sis ineptus, me esse iudices.

17 Tum ille : Ego mehercule, inquit, Caesar, ex
omnibus Latinis verbis huius verbi vim vel maximam
semper putavi. Quem enim nos ' ineptum ' vocamus,
is mihi videtur ab hoc nomen habere ductum, quod
non sit aptus ; idque in sermonis nostri consuetudine
perlate patet ; nam qui aut, tempus quid postulet,

to see at my home men who are among my dearest
and best friends; yet, to tell the truth, I had rather
it had been any other object than the one you mention. For, to speak my mind, I personally have never
been so dissatisfied with myself as I was yesterday;
indeed it was just good-nature rather than any fault
of mine when, in humouring the young, I forgot that
I was old, and did a thing which even as a youth I
had never done, in discussing subjects that involved
a certain degree of learning. One circumstance
however has turned out most happily for me, in that
my part is already played out, so Antonius is the
one you have come to hear."

3 "For my part, Crassus," returned Caesar, "while
I am longing to hear you in that fuller and uninter-
rupted style of debate, yet, if that is not to be had,
I could even make shift with your everyday talk.
One thing therefore I shall certainly attempt, which
is to prevent people from supposing that either my
friend Sulpicius or Cotta has more influence with
you than I have, and assuredly I shall implore you
to spare a little of your amiability even for Catulus
and myself. If however that suggestion does not
commend itself to you, I shall not press you, nor give
you occasion to deem me tactless, while dreading
any tactlessness on your own part."

"Truly, Caesar," rejoined the other, "I have always thought that, of all the words in the Latin language, none has so wide a signification as this word
that you have just used. Of course the man whom we
call 'tactless' seems to me to bear a title derived
from his want of tact, and this is most amply illustrated in our ordinary conversation, inasmuch as
whosoever fails to realize the demands of the occa-

209

non videt, aut plura loquitur, aut se ostentat, aut eorum, quibuscum est, vel dignitatis, vel commodi rationem non habet, aut denique in aliquo genere aut
18 inconcinnus, aut multus est, is ineptus dicitur. Hoc vitio cumulata est eruditissima illa Graecorum natio : itaque quod vim huius mali Graeci non vident, ne nomen quidem ei vitio imposuerunt ; ut enim quaeras omnia, quomodo Graeci ineptum appellent, non reperies. Omnium autem ineptiarum, quae sunt innumerabiles, haud scio, an nulla sit maior, quam, ut illi solent, quocumque in loco, quoscumque inter homines visum est, de rebus aut difficillimis, aut non necessariis, argutissime disputare. Hoc nos ab istis adolescentibus facere inviti et recusantes heri coacti sumus.
19 V. Tum Catulus : Ne Graeci quidem, inquit, Crasse, qui in civitatibus suis clari et magni fuerunt, sicuti tu es, nosque omnes in nostra republica volumus esse, horum Graecorum, qui se inculcant auribus nostris, similes fuerunt, nec in otio sermones
20 huiusmodi, disputationesque fugiebant. Ac si tibi videntur, qui temporis, qui loci, qui hominum rationem non habent, inepti, sicut debent videri, num tandem aut locus hic non idoneus videtur, in quo porticus haec ipsa, ubi ambulamus, et palaestra, et tot locis sessiones, gymnasiorum, et Graecorum disputationum memoriam quodam modo commovent ? Aut num importunum tempus in tanto otio, quod et

---

[a] Originally designed for physical exercise, the *gymnasia* had become the scene of lectures on philosophy.

sion, or talks too much, or advertises himself, or
ignores the prestige or convenience of those with
whom he has to deal, or, in short, is in any way awk-
18 ward or tedious, is described as 'tactless.' The
Greek nation, with all its learning, abounds in this
fault, and so, as the Greeks do not perceive the
significance of this plague, they have not even
bestowed a name upon the fault in question, for,
search where you may, you will not find out how the
Greeks designate the 'tactless' man. But, of all the
countless forms assumed by want of tact, I rather
think that the grossest is the Greeks' habit, in any
place and any company they like, of plunging into the
most subtle dialectic concerning subjects that present
extreme difficulty, or at any rate do not call for
discussion. This is what we were obliged to do
yesterday by our young friends here, albeit we
yielded but reluctantly and under protest."

9   V. Thereupon Catulus observed, "But even among
the Greeks, Crassus, those who were famous and
great men in their respective communities, as in our
own republic you are, and we all hope to be, were
wholly unlike these Greeks, who obtrude themselves
upon our hearing; and yet in their hours of ease they
were not averse to discussion and debate of this kind.
And, although you are justified in deeming those
people tactless, who take no heed of seasons, places
or persons, yet do you really think this scene ill-fitting,
where this very colonnade, in which we are now walking, this exercise-ground, and these benches placed
at so many points, in some degree awaken memories
of the gymnastic schools [a] and the discussions of the
Greeks ? Or can it be the season that is ill-chosen,
occurring as it does during a holiday of a length such

Philo-
sophical
discussion
and the
employment
of leisure.

raro datur, et nunc peroptato nobis datum est ? Aut homines ab hoc genere disputationis alieni, qui omnes ei sumus, ut sine his studiis vitam nullam esse ducamus ?

21 Omnia ista, inquit Crassus, ego alio modo interpretor, qui primum palaestram, et sedes, et porticus etiam ipsos, Catule, Graecos exercitationis et delectationis causa non disputationis invenisse arbitror. Nam et saeculis multis ante gymnasia inventa sunt, quam in eis philosophi garrire coeperunt, et hoc ipso tempore, cum omnia gymnasia philosophi teneant, tamen eorum auditores discum audire quam philosophum malunt : qui simul ut increpuit, in media oratione de maximis rebus et gravissimis disputantem philosophum omnes unctionis causa relinquunt : ita levissimam delectationem gravissimae, ut 22 ipsi ferunt, utilitati anteponunt. Otium autem quod dicis esse, assentior ; verum otii fructus est, non contentio animi, sed relaxatio.

VI. Saepe ex socero meo audivi, cum is diceret socerum suum Laelium semper fere cum Scipione solitum rusticari eosque incredibiliter repuerascere esse solitos, cum rus ex urbe, tanquam e vinculis, evolavissent. Non audeo dicere de talibus viris, sed tamen ita solet narrare Scaevola, conchas eos et umbilicos ad Caietam et ad Laurentum legere consuesse, et ad omnem animi remissionem ludumque

---

ᵃ *Vitam nullam* corresponds to the Platonic βίον οὐ βιωτόν (*Apol.* 38 A).
ᵇ *Unctionis causa* refers to the wrestler's use of suppling-oil in preparation for the *palaestra*.

as we seldom enjoy and find especially welcome at the present time? Or are we new to debate of this kind, we being all of us men of such sort as to hold that life *a* without these exercises is worth nothing?"

21 " Everything that you urge," said Crassus, " I look at in a different light, since in the first place, Catulus, it is my belief that even the Greeks themselves devised their exercise-ground, benches and colonnades, for purposes of physical training and enjoyment, not for dialectic. For not only were their gymnastic schools introduced ages before the philosophers began to chatter therein, but even in the present day, although the sages may be in occupation of all the gymnastic schools, yet their audiences would rather listen to the discus than to the Master, and the moment its clink is heard, they all desert the lecturer, in the middle of an oration upon the most sublime and weighty topics, in order to anoint *b* themselves for athletic exercise; so definitely do they place the most trifling amusement before that which the philosophers describe as the most solid advantage.

22 And, as to your saying that it is a holiday, I agree with you; but the enjoyment of a holiday is not mental effort, but relaxation.

VI. " Often have I heard my father-in-law say that his own father-in-law Laelius almost invariably had Scipio with him upon his country excursions, and that the pair of them used to become boys again, in an astonishing degree, as soon as ever they had flitted from the prison of town to rural scenes. I am afraid to say it of personages so august, but Scaevola is fond of relating how at Caieta and Laurentum it was their wont to collect mussels and top-shells, and to condescend to every form of mental recreation and

23 descendere. Sic enim se res habet : ut, quemadmodum volucres videmus, procreationis atque utilitatis suae causa, fingere et construere nidos, easdem
autem, cum aliquid effecerint, levandi laboris sui
causa, passim ac libere, solutas opere, volitare ; sic
nostri animi, forensibus negotiis atque urbano opere
defessi, gestiant ac volitare cupiant, vacui cura ac
24 labore. Itaque illud, quod ego in causa Curiana
Scaevolae dixi, non dixi secus ac sentiebam, ' Nam si,'
inquam, ' Scaevola, nullum erit testamentum recte
factum, nisi quod tu scripseris, omnes ad te cives
cum tabulis veniemus, omnium testamenta tu scribes
unus : quid igitur ? ' inquam : ' quando ages negotium
publicum ? quando amicorum ? quando tuum ? quando denique nihil ages ? ' Tum illud addidi : ' Mihi
enim liber esse non videtur, qui non aliquando nihil
agit.' In qua permaneo, Catule, sententia ; meque,
cum huc veni, hoc ipsum nihil agere et plane cessare
delectat.

25 Nam quod addidisti tertium, vos eos esse, qui vitam
insuavem sine his studiis putaretis, id me non modo
non hortatur ad disputandum, sed etiam deterret.
Nam ut C. Lucilius, homo doctus et perurbanus,
dicere solebat ea quae scriberet neque ab indoctis-
simis se, neque a doctissimis legi velle ; quod alteri
nihil intellegerent, alteri plus fortasse, quam ipse ;

23 pastime. For nature is so ordered, that even as we see the birds fashioning and building their nests, with a view to raising families and to their own comfort, but yet, as soon as any part of their task is done, seeking some relief from their toil by flying about at random in full freedom from work, so in like manner our human minds, when worn out by the business of the Courts and the work of the City, grow restless and yearn to go a-roving, in freedom from worry and

24 exertion. And so, in those observations that I addressed to Scaevola, in the course of my defence of Curius, I said no more than I thought, when I declared, ' Well, Scaevola, if no will is to be duly made, unless it be of your drafting, all we citizens will come to you with our tablets, and you alone shall draw the wills of us all, but in that event,' I went on, ' when will you conduct affairs of State? when those of your friends? when your own? when, in one word, will you do nothing?' And I added also the proposition, ' For to my mind he is no free man, who is not sometimes doing nothing.' To that view, Catulus, I still adhere, and it is just this inaction and utter idleness that charm me on my comings to this place.

25 " As for the third argument, which you threw in, that you are men so constituted that you would find life insipid without these pursuits, this consideration, so far from encouraging me to debate, positively frightens me away from it. For just as Gaius Lucilius, himself a learned and highly accomplished man, was wont to say that he wished his writings to be read neither by the most ignorant nor the most learned, since the former class understood nothing, and the latter possibly more than he himself did, in which

de quo etiam scripsit, 'Persium non curo legere'
(hic enim fuit, ut noramus, omnium fere nostrorum
hominum doctissimus), 'Laelium Decumum volo'
(quem cognovimus virum bonum, et non illiteratum,
sed nihil ad Persium): sic ego, si iam mihi disputandum sit de his nostris studiis, nolim equidem apud
rusticos, sed multo minus apud vos ; malo enim non
intellegi orationem meam, quam reprehendi.

26 VII. Tum Caesar: Equidem, inquit, Catule, iam
mihi videor navasse operam, quod huc venerim, nam
haec ipsa recusatio disputationis disputatio quaedam
fuit mihi quidem periucunda. Sed cur impedimus
Antonium, cuius audio esse partes, ut de tota eloquentia disserat, quemque iamdudum Cotta et Sul-
27 picius exspectant ? Ego vero, inquit Crassus, neque
Antonium verbum facere patiar, et ipse obmutescam,
nisi prius a vobis impetraro — Quidnam? inquit
Catulus. Ut hic sitis hodie. Tum, cum ille dubi-
taret, quod ad fratrem promiserat, Ego, inquit Iulius,
pro utroque respondeo. Sic faciemus ; atque ista
quidem conditione, vel ut verbum nullum faceres,
me teneres.

28 Hic Catulus arrisit ; et simul : Praecisa, inquit, mihi
quidem dubitatio est, quoniam neque domi impera-
ram, et hic, apud quem eram futurus, sine mea
sententia tam facile promisit. Tum omnes oculos

ª *Remains of Old Latin* (L.C.L.), iii. pp. 202-203.

connexion he also wrote [a] :—' I don't want Persius to
read me ' (Persius, as we knew him, being about the
most erudite of all our fellow-citizens), and he continued :—' Laelius Decumus for me ' (which Laelius
we also knew for an excellent man of some learning,
but nothing to Persius) : so too I, if I should now
have to discuss these pursuits of ours, should of
course be sorry to speak before an audience of
clowns, but far more reluctant to do so in this present
company, for I had rather have my discourse misunderstood than disapproved."

26   VII. " Truly, Catulus," answered Caesar, " I think
already that I have bestowed my pains to advantage
in coming hither, for to myself at any rate this very
protest against discussion has been in itself a discussion of a most agreeable character. But why are we
delaying Antonius, whose function, I hear, is to treat
of eloquence at large, and for whom Cotta has been
27 a long time waiting, and so has Sulpicius ? "   " Nay,"
interposed Crassus, " I will not have Antonius utter
a syllable, and I will myself be dumb, until I have
first obtained a boon from you."   " Name it," said
Catulus.   " That you spend the day here."   Then,
as the other hesitated, because he had promised to go
to his brother's, Julius observed, " I answer for both
of us.   We will do as you ask, and on the terms you
offer, you would keep me here, even though you
should not contribute a word to the debate."

28   Here Catulus smiled on him and said, " There's an
end of my hesitation anyhow, since I had given no
orders at home, and my brother here, at whose
house I was to have been, has so readily engaged
me, without my having any say in the matter."
At this point all eyes were turned on Antonius,

Resumption of yester-day's discussion. Antonius states his own position.

217

in Antonium coniecerunt ; et ille : Audite vero,
audite, inquit. Hominem enim audietis de schola,
atque a magistro et Graecis litteris eruditum ; et eo
quidem loquar confidentius, quod Catulus auditor
accessit, cui non solum nos Latini sermonis, sed etiam
Graeci ipsi solent suae linguae subtilitatem elegan-
29 tiamque concedere. Sed quia tamen hoc totum,
quidquid est, sive artificium, sive studium dicendi,
nisi accessit os, nullum potest esse, docebo vos, dis-
cipuli, quod ipse non didici, quid de omni genere
dicendi sentiam.

30   Hic posteaquam arriserunt, Res mihi videtur esse,
inquit, facultate praeclara, arte mediocris. Ars enim
earum rerum est, quae sciuntur ; oratoris autem
omnis actio opinionibus, non scientia continetur.
Nam et apud eos dicimus, qui nesciunt, et ea dicimus,
quae nescimus ipsi : itaque et illi alias aliud eisdem de
rebus et sentiunt et iudicant et nos contrarias saepe
causas dicimus, non modo ut Crassus contra me dicat
aliquando, aut ego contra Crassum, cum alterutri
necesse sit falsum dicere, sed etiam ut uterque nostrum eadem de re alias aliud defendat, cum plus uno
verum esse non possit. Ut igitur in eiusmodi re,
quae mendacio nixa sit, quae ad scientiam non saepe
perveniat, quae opiniones hominum, et saepe errores

---

a *Facultate.* Similarly Aristotle describes rhetoric as a
δύναμις, not a τέχνη (*Rhet.* I. ii. 1).

who exclaimed, "Attention, pray! Attention! For you will be listening to a man from the schools, polished by professorial instruction and the study of Greek literature ; and I shall speak with all the fuller assurance, in that Catulus has joined my audience, he whose possession of accuracy and taste in the Greek language is ever acknowledged, not only by us men of Latin speech, but by the Greeks themselves as

29 well. Seeing however that all this art or vocation of speaking, whichever it may be, can avail nothing without the addition of 'cheek,' I will teach you, my disciples, something that I have not learned myself, to wit, my theory of oratory in all its branches."

30   When their laughter had subsided, he continued, *Oratory not* "Oratory, it seems to me, derives distinction from *a science;* ability,[a] but owes little to art. For, while art is concerned with the things that are known, the activity of the orator has to do with opinion, not knowledge. For we both address ourselves to the ignorant, and speak of matters unknown to ourselves, with the result, that while our hearers form different conceptions and judgements at different times, concerning the selfsame subjects, we on our part often take opposite sides, not merely in the sense that Crassus sometimes argues against me, or I against him, when one or the other of us must of necessity be urging what is false, but also because we both maintain different opinions at different times on an identical issue, in which case only one of such opinions can possibly be right. I shall therefore speak as one who is dealing with a subject which is founded upon falsehood, which seldom attains to demonstration, which sets its snares to entrap the fancies and often the

219

aucupetur, ita dicam, si causam putatis esse, cur
audiatis.

31 VIII. Nos vero et valde quidem, Catulus inquit,
putamus, atque eo magis, quod nulla mihi ostenta-
tione videris esse usurus. Exorsus es enim non
gloriose ; magis a veritate, ut tu putas, quam a nescio
32 qua dignitate. Ut igitur de ipso genere sum con-
fessus, inquit Antonius, artem esse non maximam, sic
illud affirmo, praecepta posse quaedam dari peracuta
ad pertractandos animos hominum et ad excipiendas
eorum voluntates. Huius rei scientiam si quis volet
magnam quamdam artem esse dicere, non repugnabo. Etenim cum plerique temere ac nulla ratione
causas in foro dicant, nonnulli autem propter exercitationem, aut propter consuetudinem aliquam, cal-
lidius id faciant, non est dubium quin, si quis
animadverterit, quid sit, quare alii melius quam alii
33 dicant, id possit notare. Ergo id qui toto in genere
fecerit, is si non plane artem, at quasi artem quamdam
invenerit.

Atque utinam, ut mihi illa videre videor in foro
atque in causis, item nunc, quemadmodum ea reperi-
rentur, possem vobis exquirere ! Sed de me videro :
nunc hoc propono, quod mihi persuasi, quamvis ars

delusions of mankind, provided of course that you think there is any reason for listening to me."

31 VIII. "Assuredly we think so most decidedly," said Catulus, "and all the more in that you do not seem to me to intend the use of any self-advertisement. For you have opened in no vaunting fashion, starting, as you think, from the actual facts of the case, rather than from any supposed grandeur of

32 your theme." "Well then," resumed Antonius, "while I have admitted, on the general question, that oratory is not the highest form of art, I yet make this assertion—that some very clever rules may be laid down for playing upon men's feelings and making prize of their goodwill. If anyone is for claiming that the knowledge of such devices is an art of real significance, I am not going to quarrel with him. For, inasmuch as very many advocates argue their cases in Court carelessly and without method, while some others, thanks to training or to a certain amount of experience, do such work more skilfully, it is indisputable that any man who applies his mind to finding out the reason why some speak better than others,

33 may succeed in discerning it. Whence it follows, that he who extends his survey over the whole province of rhetoric, will discover that which, though not absolutely an art, yet wears the likeness of an art.

"And I would that, even as I think I see, with the mind's eye, the course of proceedings in the Courts, and at the hearing of actions, so I could now go on to bring these before you as they really are! But of myself hereafter : for the time being I enunciate this proposition, which I have proved to my own satisfaction,—that, although oratory may not be

Marginal note: but rules for effective speaking may be drawn from experiences

non sit, tamen nihil esse perfecto oratore praeclarius. Nam, ut usum dicendi omittam, qui in omni pacata et libera civitate dominatur, tanta oblectatio est in ipsa facultate dicendi, ut nihil hominum aut auribus, aut

34 mentibus iucundius percipi possit. Qui enim cantus moderata oratione dulcior inveniri potest? Quod carmen artificiosa verborum conclusione aptius? Qui actor imitanda, quam orator suscipienda veritate iucundior? Quid autem subtilius, quam acutae crebraeque sententiae? Quid admirabilius, quam res splendore illustrata verborum? quid plenius, quam omni rerum genere cumulata oratio? Neque ulla non propria oratoris est res, quae quidem ornate dici graviterque debet.

35 IX. Huius est in dando consilio de maximis rebus cum dignitate explicata sententia; eiusdem et languentis populi incitatio, et effrenati moderatio. Eadem facultate et fraus hominum ad perniciem, et integritas ad salutem vocatur. Quis cohortari ad virtutem ardentius, quis a vitiis acrius revocare? Quis vituperare improbos asperius, quis laudare bonos ornatius? Quis cupiditatem vehementius frangere accusando potest? Quis maerorem levare mitius consolando?

one of the arts, still there is nothing more splendid than a complete orator. For to pass over the actual practice of eloquence—that governing force in every tranquil and free community—, there is such a charm about the mere power to deliver a set speech, that no impression more delightful than this can be received by the ear or the intelligence of man.

34 Can any music be composed that is sweeter than a well-balanced speech ? Is any poem better rounded than an artistic period in prose ? What actor gives keener pleasure by his imitation of real life than your orator affords in his conduct of some real case ? Does anything display more exact precision than a rapid succession of pointed reflections ? Is there aught more wonderful than the lighting-up of a topic by verbal brilliance, or aught richer than a discourse furnished forth with material of every sort ? And there is not a subject that is not the orator's own, provided only that it is one which deserves elegant and impressive treatment.

35 IX. " It is the part of the orator, when advising on affairs of supreme importance, to unfold his opinion as a man having authority : his duty too it is to arouse a listless nation, and to curb its unbridled impetuosity. By one and the same power of eloquence the deceitful among mankind are brought to destruction, and the righteous to deliverance. Who more passionately than the orator can encourage to virtuous conduct, or more zealously than he reclaim from vicious courses ? Who can more austerely censure the wicked, or more gracefully praise men of worth ? Whose invective can more forcibly subdue the power of lawless desire ? Whose comfortable words can soothe grief more tenderly ?

Importance of oratory: all subjects require exposition.

223

36 Historia vero testis temporum, lux veritatis, vita memoriae, magistra vitae, nuntia vetustatis, qua voce alia, nisi oratoris, immortalitati commendatur ? Nam si qua est ars alia, quae verborum aut faciendorum aut legendorum scientiam profiteatur ; aut si quisquam dicitur nisi orator formare orationem eamque variare et distinguere quasi quibusdam verborum sententiarumque insignibus ; aut si via ulla, nisi ab hac una arte, traditur, aut argumentorum, aut sententiarum, aut denique discriptionis atque ordinis, fateamur aut hoc, quod haec ars profiteatur, alienum 37 esse aut cum aliqua alia arte esse commune. Sed si in hac una est ea ratio atque doctrina, non, si qui aliarum artium bene locuti sunt, eo minus id est huius unius proprium ; sed, ut orator de eis rebus, quae ceterarum artium sunt, si modo eas cognovit (ut heri Crassus dicebat), optime potest dicere, sic ceterarum artium homines ornatius illa sua dicunt, si 38 quid ab hac arte didicerunt. Neque enim si de rusticis rebus agricola quispiam, aut etiam, id quod multi, medicus de morbis, aut de pingendo pictor aliquis diserte dixerit aut scripserit, idcirco illius artis putanda est eloquentia : in qua quia vis magna est in

---

ᵃ *Insignia* are the ' purple patches ' of Horace, *A.P.* 15-16.
224

36 "And as History, which bears witness to the passing of the ages, sheds light upon reality, gives life to recollection and guidance to human existence, and brings tidings of ancient days, whose voice, but the orator's, can entrust her to immortality? For if there be any other art, which pretends to skill in the coinage and choice of language, or if it be claimed for anyone but the orator that he gives shape and variety to a speech, and marks it out with ª high lights of thought and phrase, or if any method be taught, except by this single art, for producing proofs or reflections, or even in the distribution and arrangement of subject-matter, then let us admit that the skill professed by this art of ours either belongs really to some other art, or is shared in common with some 7 other. Whereas, if all reasoning and all teaching really belong to this one art alone, then, even though professors of other arts have expressed themselves with success, it does not therefore follow that such instruction is not the monopoly of this single art; but (as Crassus was saying yesterday) just as the orator is best qualified to discuss the subjects pertaining to the other arts, assuming always that he has acquainted himself with them, so the masters of the other arts expound their own topics with the better grace, if they have learned something 8 from the art with which we are dealing. For even though some farmer may have written or spoken with address upon country matters or perhaps a medical man upon pathology, as many have done, or a painter upon painting, it does not therefore follow that eloquence belongs to the particular art, the truth being that in the art of speaking, by reason of the vast energy inherent in human intelli-

hominum ingeniis, eo multi etiam sine doctrina aliquid omnium generum atque artium consequuntur.
Sed, quid cuiusque sit proprium, etsi ex eo iudicari
potest, cum videris, quid quaeque doceat, tamen hoc
certius nihil esse potest, quam quod omnes artes aliae
sine eloquentia suum munus praestare possunt, orator
sine ea nomen obtinere suum non potest : ut ceteri,
si diserti sint, aliquid ab hoc habeant, hic nisi domesticis se instruxerit copiis, aliunde dicendi copiam
petere non possit.

39 X. Tum Catulus : Etsi, inquit, Antoni, minime
impediendus est interpellatione iste cursus orationis
tuae, patiere tamen, mihique ignosces. ' Non enim
possum quin exclamem,' ut ait ille in Trinummo : ita
mihi vim oratoris cum exprimere subtiliter visus es,
tum laudare copiosissime. Quod quidem eloquentem
vel optime facere oportet, ut eloquentiam laudet ;
debet enim ad eam laudandam ipsam illam adhibere,
quam laudat. Sed perge porro : tibi enim assentior,
vestrum esse hoc totum, diserte dicere, idque si quis
in alia arte faciat, eum assumpto aliunde uti bono,
40 non proprio, nec suo. Et Crassus : Nox te, inquit,
nobis, Antoni, expolivit, hominemque reddidit : nam
hesterno sermone, unius cuiusdam operis, ut ait Caecilius, remigem aliquem, aut baiulum, nobis oratorem

---

^a Plautus, *Trinummus* iii. 2. 79.

gence, many a man, whatever his class or his calling, attains some degree of proficiency even without any regular training. But, although the peculiar property of each art may be determined by noting what it is which each teaches, there can be nothing more certain than this, that while all other arts are able to discharge their functions unaided by eloquence, the orator cannot even earn his distinctive title without being eloquent; so that the rest of the world, if they be fluent speakers, gain something from him, while he, unless he has equipped himself from his own private store, cannot seek his supplies as a speaker from any other source."

39 X. At this point Catulus interposed, saying, "Antonius, although that flowing discourse of yours should never be checked by interruption, still you will bear with me and forgive me. For, as the man says in *The Threepenny Piece*, 'I cannot help applauding'[a]: so exquisitely, as I think, have you described the power of the orator, and with such wealth of diction have you extolled it. And yet, to be sure, a man of eloquence must needs sing the praises of eloquence better than all others, since he is bound to bring, to the performance of his task, that very gift which he is praising. But pray proceed, for I agree with you that you have this skill in speaking wholly for your own, and that any man discoursing with ability upon any other art does but use an accomplishment borrowed from elsewhere, and one that is not peculiar to himself, or even his own." And Crassus added,

40 "A night's rest has smoothed and humanized you, Antonius, from our point of view, for in the course of yesterday's discussion you sketched the orator as a one-talent man, 'Just a galley-slave or porter,' to

descripseras, inopem quemdam humanitatis atque inurbanum.

Tum Antonius : Heri enim, inquit, hoc mihi proposueram, ut, si te refellissem, hos a te discipulos abducerem : nunc, Catulo audiente et Caesare, videor debere non tam pugnare tecum, quam, quid ipse

41 sentiam, dicere. Sequitur igitur, quoniam nobis est hic, de quo loquimur, in foro atque in oculis civium constituendus, ut videamus, quid ei negotii demus, cuique eum muneri velimus esse praepositum. Nam Crassus heri, cum vos, Catule et Caesar, non adessetis, posuit breviter in artis distributione idem, quod Graeci plerique posuerunt, neque sane quid ipse sentiret, sed quid ab illis diceretur, ostendit : duo prima genera quaestionum esse, in quibus eloquentia

42 versaretur, unum infinitum, alterum certum. Infinitum mihi videbatur id dicere, in quo aliquid generatim quaereretur, hoc modo : ' Expetendane esset eloquentia, expetendine honores ? ' Certum autem, in quo quid in personis, et in constituta re et definita quaereretur : cuius modi sunt, quae in foro atque in civium causis disceptationibusque versantur.

43 Ea mihi videntur aut in lite oranda, aut in consilio dando esse posita, nam illud tertium, quod et a Crasso tactum est, et, ut audio, ille ipse Aristoteles, qui haec

---

[a] *Remains of Old Latin* (L.C.L.), i. pp. 558-559.
[b] *Rhet.* I. iii. 1.

quote Caecilius[a]; in fact as a fellow destitute of breeding and a mere boor."

"I did," returned Antonius, "for yesterday it was my design, if I should have succeeded in refuting your arguments, to steal these pupils from you; but to-day, with Catulus and Caesar among my hearers, I think it my duty not so much to fight with you as 41 to enunciate my own personal views. And so, now that we are to have this orator, whom we are discussing, brought into Court and exposed to public scrutiny, our next task is to consider what business we shall assign to him, and what function we would suggest that he has been appointed to discharge. For yesterday, Catulus and Caesar, when you were not here, Crassus made in concise terms, with regard to the classification of this art, the identical statement that most of the Greeks have made, and of course expressed no opinion of his own, but just their affirmations: his proposition being that there are two main divisions of the questions wherewith eloquence is con- 42 cerned, the one abstract, the other concrete. By abstract problems I thought he meant those wherein questions are propounded in general terms, as for instance, 'Is eloquence to be desired?' 'Should public office be sought?' The concrete class, by contrast, was composed of such as raise investigations dealing with individual persons and settled and defined points, to which kind belong the issues discussed in Court, and in the judicial proceedings and 43 the disputes between private citizens. The sphere of such oratory is limited, in my view, to the conduct of litigation and to advising, for that third category, just barely noticed by Crassus, and included, as I am told, by Aristotle[b] himself, who has elucidated these

The proper sphere of rhetoric.

maxime illustravit, adiunxit, etiamsi opus est, tamen minus est necessarium. Quidnam? inquit Catulus; an laudationes? id enim video poni genus tertium.

44 XI. Ita, inquit Antonius, et in eo quidem genere scio et me, et omnes qui adfuerunt, delectatos esse vehementer, cum abs te est Popilia, mater vestra, laudata, cui primum mulieri hunc honorem in nostra civitate tributum puto. Sed non omnia, quaecumque loquimur, mihi videntur ad artem et ad praecepta 45 esse revocanda. Ex eis enim fontibus, unde omnia praecepta dicendi sumuntur, licebit etiam laudationem ornare, neque illa elementa desiderare, quae ut nemo tradat, quis est, qui nesciat, quae sint in homine laudanda? Positis enim eis rebus, quas Crassus in illius orationis suae, quam contra collegam censor habuit, principio dixit, 'Quae natura aut fortuna darentur hominibus, in eis rebus se vinci posse animo aequo pati; quae ipsi sibi homines parare possent, in eis rebus se pati non posse vinci': qui laudabit quempiam, intelleget, exponenda sibi esse 46 fortunae bona. Ea sunt, generis, pecuniae, propinquorum, amicorum, opum, valetudinis, formae, virium, ingenii, ceterarumque rerum, quae sunt aut corporis, aut extraneae: si habuerit, bene rebus eis usum; si

---

a Laudatio here has its wider sense of any encomiastic speech delivered in public, not necessarily a funeral oration.

matters as clearly as possible, is serviceable enough, but not essential in the same degree." "What kind is that?" said Catulus. "Do you refer to panegyrics?[a] for I notice that these are set down as a third variety."

4 XI. "Precisely so," replied Antonius, "and, with regard to this type of oratory, I know that I myself, and all who were present, were highly delighted when your mother Popilia was eulogized in this fashion by yourself; she being, I think, the first woman to whom such honour was ever rendered in our own community. But to my mind not everything that we say need be reduced to theory and rule.
5 For from those same sources, whence the rules of speaking are all derived, we shall also be able to set off a funeral oration without feeling the want of those scholastic rudiments, since, even though no one were to teach these, is there a man who would not know the good points of a human being? In fact, if he has laid down those axioms enunciated by Crassus in the opening of that famous speech of his, which he delivered when censor in opposition to his colleague in office, when he declared, that while he could cheerfully endure inferiority in respect of the gifts bestowed on mankind by nature or by chance, he could not consent to be surpassed in such credit as men may win for themselves, he who proposes to be the panegyrist of anyone will understand that he has in the first place to deal fully with the favours of fortune. These are the advantages of race, wealth, connexions, friendships, power, good health, beauty, vigour, talent, and the rest of the attributes that are either physical or externally imposed : it must be explained that the person commended made a right use of these benefits if he possessed them, managed sensibly

Panegyric oratory needs no special rules;

231

non habuerit, sapienter caruisse ; si amiserit, moderate tulisse ; deinde, quid sapienter is, quem laudet,
quid liberaliter, quid fortiter, quid iuste, quid magni-
fice, quid pie, quid grate, quid humaniter, quid
denique cum aliqua virtute aut fecerit, aut tulerit.
Haec, et quae sunt eius generis, facile videbit, qui
volet laudare ; et qui vituperare, contraria.

47 Cur igitur dubitas, inquit Catulus, facere hoc
tertium genus, quoniam est in ratione rerum ? Non
enim, si est facilius, eo de numero quoque est excer-
pendum. Quia nolo, inquit, omnia, quae cadunt
aliquando in oratorem, quamvis exigua sint, ea sic
tractare, quasi nihil possit dici sine praeceptis suis.

48 Nam et testimonium saepe dicendum est, ac nonnunquam etiam accuratius, ut mihi etiam necesse fuit
in Sex. Titium, seditiosum civem et turbulentum.
Explicavi in eo testimonio dicendo, omnia consilia
consulatus mei, quibus illi tribuno plebis pro republica restitissem, quaeque ab eo contra rempublicam
facta arbitrarer, exposui. Diu retentus sum, multa
audivi, multa respondi. Num igitur placet, cum de
eloquentia praecipias, aliquid etiam de testimoniis

without them, if they were denied to him, and bore
the loss with resignation, if they were taken away
from him; and after that the speaker will marshal
instances of conduct, either active or passive, on the
part of the subject of his praises; whereby he manifested wisdom, generosity, valour, righteousness,
greatness of soul, sense of duty, gratitude, kindliness
or, in short, any moral excellence you please. These
and similar indications of character the would-be
panegyrist will readily discern, and he who seeks to
disparage will as readily find evidence in rebuttal."

47   "Why then hesitate," interposed Catulus, " to
regard this as a third kind, since its existence is
inherent in the nature of the case? For the fact of
its being easier of accomplishment is no reason for
eliminating it from the classification." " My reason,"
replied the other, " is that I do not wish to handle all
matters, however petty, that at one time or another
fall under oratorical treatment, upon the footing that
nothing can be mentioned without reference to its
48 own special rules. For instance, evidence has often
to be given, and, upon occasions, with precision even
closer than usual, as I myself was compelled to give
it against Sextus Titius, a factious and troublesome
member of the community. In the course of such
evidence I revealed all the measures whereby, in
defence of the State, I as consul had withstood him in
his character of tribune of the commons, and I laid
bare every proceeding of his that I considered inimical
to the public benefit. I was long obstructed, had to
listen to a great deal, and replied to many objections.
But do you on that account think it fitting, when
laying down rules of rhetoric, to add any teaching on
how to give evidence, as though this came within the

dicendis, quasi in arte tradere? Nihil sane, inquit
Catulus, necesse est.

49 XII. Quid? si quod saepe summis viris accidit
mandata sint exponenda, aut in senatu ab imperatore, aut ad imperatorem, aut ad regem, aut ad
populum aliquem a senatu, num quia genere orationis in eiusmodi causis accuratiore est utendum,
idcirco pars etiam haec causarum numeranda videtur,
aut propriis praeceptis instruenda? Minime vero,
inquit Catulus : non enim deerit homini diserto in
eiusmodi rebus facultas, ex ceteris rebus et causis
comparata.

50 Ergo item, inquit, illa, quae saepe diserte agenda
sunt, et quae ego paulo ante cum eloquentiam
laudarem dixi oratoris esse, neque habent suum
locum ullum in divisione partium, neque certum
praeceptorum genus, et agenda sunt non minus
diserte, quam quae in lite dicuntur, obiurgatio, co-
hortatio, consolatio : quorum nihil est, quod non
summa dicendi ornamenta desideret ; sed ex artificio
res istae praecepta non quaerunt. Plane, inquit
Catulus, assentior.

51 Age vero, inquit Antonius, qualis oratoris, et
quanti hominis in dicendo, putas esse, historiam
scribere? Si, ut Graeci scripserunt, summi, inquit
Catulus ; si, ut nostri, nihil opus est oratore : satis

sphere of the art?" Catulus answered, "There is no need whatever to do so."

49 XII. "And what if (as often happens to the most exalted personages) messages have to be communicated from a general at a meeting of the Senate, or conveyed from the Senate to a general or to any prince or nation? Because, on occasions of this sort, a style of diction more elaborate than the ordinary has to be employed, does it therefore seem to follow that this type of speaking should be accounted a distinct department of oratorical activity, or should be fitted out with its own peculiar rules?" "Why of course not," returned Catulus, "since the ability acquired by a ready speaker, from the treatment of his other subjects and topics, will not fail him in situations of that description." *nor do official dispatches,*

50 "And so," continued Antonius, "those matters which often demand fluent expression, and which just now, in my praise of eloquence, I asserted to be within the part of the orator, have no special place in the formal classification of the branches of rhetoric, nor any particular code of rules, and yet they must be handled quite as skilfully as arguments at the Bar: I am speaking of rebuke, encouragement, and the giving of comfort, each of which topics calls for the finest graces of diction, while such subjects ask no directions from theory." "I am in complete agreement with you," said Catulus.

51 "Now further," proceeded Antonius, "what class of orator, and how great a master of language is qualified, in your opinion, to write history?" "If he is to write as the Greeks have written," answered Catulus, "a man of supreme ability is required: if the standard is to be that of our own fellow-country- *nor history.*

est, non esse mendacem. Atqui, ne nostros con-
temnas, inquit Antonius, Graeci quoque sic initio
52 scriptitarunt, ut noster Cato, ut Pictor, ut Piso. Erat
enim historia nihil aliud nisi annalium confectio, cuius
rei, memoriaeque publicae retinendae causa, ab
initio rerum Romanarum usque ad P. Mucium ponti-
ficem maximum, res omnes singulorum annorum
mandabat litteris pontifex maximus, referebatque in
album, et proponebat tabulam domi, potestas ut
esset populo cognoscendi, hique etiam nunc Annales
53 Maximi nominantur. Hanc similitudinem scribendi
multi secuti sunt, qui sine ullis ornamentis monumenta solum temporum, hominum, locorum ges-
tarumque rerum reliquerunt. Itaque qualis apud
Graecos Pherecydes, Hellanicus, Acusilas fuit, aliique
permulti, talis noster Cato, et Pictor, et Piso, qui
neque tenent, quibus rebus ornetur oratio—modo
enim huc ista sunt importata,—et, dum intellegatur,
quid dicant, unam dicendi laudem putant esse
54 brevitatem. Paulum se erexit, et addidit historiae
maiorem sonum vocis vir optimus, Crassi familiaris,
Antipater : ceteri non exornatores rerum, sed
tantummodo narratores fuerunt.

XIII. Est, inquit Catulus, ut dicis. Sed iste ipse
Coelius neque distinxit historiam varietate locorum,
neque verborum collocatione et tractu orationis leni

men, no orator at all is needed ; it is enough that the man should not be a liar." "But nevertheless," rejoined Antonius, "(and I say this, that you may not think lightly of our own folk) the Greeks themselves also used to write, in the beginning, just like 52 our Cato, Pictor and Piso. For history began as a mere compilation of annals, on which account, and in order to preserve the general traditions, from the earliest period of the City down to the pontificate of Publius Mucius, each High Priest used to commit to writing all the events of his year of office, and record them on a white surface, and post up the tablet at his house, that all men might have liberty to acquaint themselves therewith, and to this day those records 53 are known as the Pontifical Chronicles. A similar style of writing has been adopted by many who, without any rhetorical ornament, have left behind them bare records of dates, personalities, places and events. In this sense Pherecydes, Hellanicus, Acusilas, and very many others among the Greeks, correspond to our own Cato, Pictor and Piso, who do not understand the adornment of composition—since it is only of late that decoration of that sort has been brought into this country—and, so long as their narrative is understood, regard conciseness as the historian's 4 single merit. Antipater, an admirable man and a close friend of Crassus, raised his crest a little higher, and imparted to history a richer tone : the rest did not embellish their facts, but were chroniclers and nothing more."

XIII. " It is as you say," rejoined Catulus. "But even your friend Coelius did not set off his narrative with any diversity of reflections, or give finish to his famous work by his marshalling of words and a

et aequabili perpolivit illud opus ; sed ut homo neque
doctus, neque maxime aptus ad dicendum, sicut
potuit, dolavit : vicit tamen, ut dicis, superiores.

55   Minime mirum, inquit Antonius, si ista res adhuc nostra lingua illustrata non est. Nemo enim
studet eloquentiae nostrorum hominum, nisi ut in
causis atque in foro eluceat ; apud Graecos autem
eloquentissimi homines, remoti a causis forensibus,
cum ad ceteras res illustres, tum ad scribendam
historiam maxime se applicaverunt. Namque et
Herodotum illum, qui princeps genus hoc ornavit, in
causis nihil omnino versatum esse accepimus : atqui
tanta est eloquentia, ut me quidem, quantum ego
Graece scripta intellegere possum, magnopere de-
56   lectet. Et post illum Thucydides omnes dicendi
artificio, mea sententia, facile vicit : qui ita creber
est rerum frequentia, ut verborum prope numerum
sententiarum numero consequatur, ita porro verbis
est aptus et pressus, ut nescias, utrum res oratione,
an verba sententiis illustrentur. Atqui ne hunc quidem, quanquam est in republica versatus, ex numero
accepimus eorum, qui causas dictitarunt : et hos
ipsos libros tum scripsisse dicitur, cum a republica
remotus, atque, id quod optimo cuique Athenis ac-
57   cidere solitum est, in exsilium pulsus esset. Hunc
consecutus est Syracusius Philistus, qui, cum
Dionysii tyranni familiarissimus esset, otium suum
consumpsit in historia scribenda, maximeque Thucy-

smooth and unvarying flow of style, but he rough-hewed it as best he could, like a man who was no scholar and had no special turn for rhetoric : nevertheless, as you observe, he excelled his forerunners."

55 " No wonder," returned Antonius, " if this subject has never yet been brilliantly treated in our language. For not one of our own folk seeks after eloquence, save with an eye to its display at the Bar and in public speaking, whereas in Greece the most eloquent were strangers to forensic advocacy, and applied themselves chiefly to reputable studies in general, and particularly to writing history. Indeed even of renowned Herodotus, who first imparted distinction to such work, we have heard that he was in no way concerned with lawsuits, and yet his eloquence is of such quality as to afford intense pleasure, to myself at any rate, so far as I can comprehend what 56 is written in Greek. After his day Thucydides, in my judgement, easily surpassed all others in dexterity of composition : so abounding is he in fullness of material that in the number of his ideas he well-nigh equals the number of his words, and furthermore he is so exact and clear in expression that you cannot tell whether it be the narrative that gains illumination from the style, or the diction from the thought. Yet even of him, though a man of public affairs, we are not told that he was numbered among forensic speakers ; and it is related that when writing the volumes in question, he was far away from civic life, having in fact been driven into exile, as generally 7 happened at Athens to anyone of excellence. He was succeeded by Philistus of Syracuse, who, living in the closest intimacy with the tyrant Dionysius, spent his leisure in writing history and, to my

The great Greek historians. reviewed.

239

didem est, sicut mihi videtur, imitatus. Postea vero,
rhetorum ex clarissima quasi officina, duo praestantes
ingenio, Theopompus et Ephorus, ab Isocrate magistro impulsi, se ad historiam contulerunt; causas
omnino nunquam attigerunt.

58   XIV. Denique etiam a philosophia profectus princeps Xenophon, Socraticus ille, post ab Aristotele
Callisthenes, comes Alexandri, scripsit historiam, et
is quidem rhetorico paene more; ille autem superior
leniore quodam sono est usus, et qui illum impetum
oratoris non habeat, vehemens fortasse minus, sed
aliquanto tamen est, ut mihi quidem videtur, dulcior.
Minimus natu horum omnium Timaeus, quantum
autem iudicare possum, longe eruditissimus, et rerum
copia et sententiarum varietate abundantissimus, et
ipsa compositione verborum non impolitus, magnam
eloquentiam ad scribendum attulit, sed nullum usum
forensem.

59   Haec cum ille dixisset : Quid est, inquit, Catule?
Caesar; ubi sunt, qui Antonium Graece[a] negant
scire? Quot historicos nominavit! Quam scienter!
quam proprie de unoquoque dixit! Id mehercule,
inquit Catulus, admirans, illud iam mirari desino,
quod multo magis ante mirabar, hunc, cum haec
nesciret, in dicendo posse tantum. Atqui, Catule,
inquit Antonius, non ego utilitatem aliquam ad di-

---

[a] *i.e.* Greece.

thinking, was above all else an imitator of Thucydides. Afterwards, however, from what I may call that most famous factory of rhetoricians,[a] there issued a pair of outstanding talent in Theopompus and Ephorus, who betook themselves to history at the instance of their teacher Isocrates : lawsuits they never handled at all.

58   XIV. " And at length historians appeared who had begun as philosophers, first Xenophon, that notable follower of Socrates, afterwards Callisthenes, Aristotle's disciple and Alexander's familiar friend ; the latter approaching the rhetorical in method, while his predecessor adopted a gentler kind of tone, lacking the characteristic vigour of oratory and possibly less animated but, in my view at any rate, somewhat more pleasing. Timaeus, the latest-born of all these, but as well as I can judge, by far the best informed, the most amply endowed in wealth of material and range of thought, and a man whose very style had some polish, brought to authorship abounding eloquence but no experience of public speaking."

59   When Antonius had finished Caesar exclaimed, " What now, Catulus ? Where are those who say Antonius does not know the Greek tongue ? What a number of historians he has mentioned ! With what insight and discrimination he has described every one ! " " Upon my word," returned Catulus, " in my astonishment at this I marvel no longer at something which hitherto surprised me far more, I mean that our friend here, being all unversed in these matters, could speak so effectively." " And yet, Catulus," rejoined Antonius," it is not because I am on the look-out for aids to oratory, but just for

cendum aucupans, horum libros et nonnullos alios, sed delectationis causa, cum est otium, legere soleo.

60 Quid ergo ? Est, fatebor, aliquid tamen : ut, cum in sole ambulem, etiamsi aliam ob causam ambulem, fieri natura tamen, ut colorer : sic, cum istos libros ad Misenum (nam Romae vix licet) studiosius legerim, sentio illorum tactu orationem meam quasi colorari. Sed ne latius hoc vobis patere videatur, haec duntaxat in Graecis intellego, quae ipsi, qui

61 scripserunt, voluerunt vulgo intellegi. In philosophos vestros si quando incidi, deceptus indicibus librorum, quod sunt fere inscripti de rebus notis et illustribus, de virtute, de iustitia, de honestate, de voluptate, verbum prorsus nullum intellego : ita sunt angustis et concisis disputationibus illigati. Poetas omnino, quasi alia quadam lingua locutos, non conor attingere : cum his me (ut dixi) oblecto, qui res gestas, aut qui orationes scripserunt suas, aut qui ita loquuntur, ut videantur voluisse nobis, qui non sumus eruditissimi, esse familiares. Sed illuc redeo.

62 XV. Videtisne, quantum munus sit oratoris historia ? Haud scio, an flumine orationis et varietate maximum. Neque tamen eam reperio usquam separatim instructam rhetorum praeceptis : sita sunt enim ante oculos. Nam quis nescit, primam esse

pleasure, that I make a habit, when I have time, of reading the works of these authors and a few more.

60 To what purpose then? Well, I will own to some benefit : just as, when walking in the sunshine, though perhaps taking the stroll for a different reason, the natural result is that I get sunburnt, even so, after perusing those books rather closely at Misenum (having little chance in Rome), I find that under their influence my discourse takes on what I may call a new complexion. However,—not to let you think this claim too extravagant—I understand no more of Greek literature than its authors themselves intended to be understood by the multi-

61 tude. Whenever I light upon your philosophers, cheated by the titles of their books, which commonly bear headings descriptive of well-known and obvious subjects, such as virtue, justice, integrity or pleasure, I do not comprehend a single word, so inextricably are they entangled in closely reasoned and condensed dialectic. Your poets, speaking as they do an altogether different tongue, I do not attempt to handle at all : I divert myself (as I said) in the company of those who have written the story of events, or speeches delivered by themselves, or whose style suggests their wish to be accessible to us men of no very profound learning. But I return to my argument.

62 XV. "Do you see how great a responsibility the orator has in historical writing ? I rather think that for fluency and diversity of diction it comes first. Yet nowhere do I find this art supplied with any independent directions from the rhetoricians ; indeed its rules lie open to the view. For who does not know history's first law to be that an author must

The systems of rhetoric contain no rules of style for history,

historiae legem, ne quid falsi dicere audeat ? Deinde
ne quid veri non audeat ? Ne qua suspicio gratiae
63 sit in scribendo ? Ne qua simultâtis ? Haec scilicet
fundamenta nota sunt omnibus ; ipsa autem exaedi-
ficatio posita est in rebus et verbis. Rerum ratio
ordinem temporum desiderat, regionum descrip-
tionem ; vult etiam, quoniam in rebus magnis me-
moriaque dignis consilia primum, deinde acta, postea
eventus expectentur, et de consiliis significari quid
scriptor probet, et in rebus gestis declarari, non solum
quid actum aut dictum sit, sed etiam quomodo ; et
cum de eventu dicatur, ut causae explicentur omnes,
vel casus, vel sapientiae, vel temeritatis, hominumque
ipsorum non solum res gestae, sed etiam, qui fama
ac nomine excellant, de cuiusque vita atque natura.
64 Verborum autem ratio et genus orationis fusum atque
tractum, et cum lenitate quadam aequabili profluens,
sine hac iudiciali asperitate, et sine sententiarum
forensium aculeis persequendum est. Harum tot
tantarumque rerum videtisne ulla esse praecepta,
quae in artibus rhetorum reperiantur ?

In eodem silentio multa alia oratorum officia iacue-
runt, cohortationes, consolationes, praecepta, ad-
monita : quae tractanda sunt omnia disertissime ;
sed locum suum in his artibus, quae traditae sunt,
65 habent nullum. Atque in hoc genere illa quoque est

not dare to tell anything but the truth ? And its second that he must make bold to tell the whole truth ? That there must be no suggestion of partiality anywhere in his writings ? Nor of malice ?

63 This groundwork of course is familiar to every one ; the completed structure however rests upon the story and the diction. The nature of the subject needs chronological arrangement and geographical representation : and since, in reading of important affairs worth recording, the plans of campaign, the executive actions and the results are successively looked for, it calls also, as regards such plans, for some intimation of what the writer approves, and, in the narrative of achievement, not only for a statement of what was done or said, but also of the manner of doing or saying it ; and, in the estimate of consequences, for an exposition of all contributory causes, whether originating in accident, discretion or foolhardiness ; and, as for the individual actors, besides an account of their exploits, it demands particulars of the lives and characters of such as are outstanding

64 in renown and dignity. Then again the kind of language and type of style to be followed are the easy and the flowing, which run their course with unvarying current and a certain placidity, avoiding alike the rough speech we use in Court and the advocate's stinging epigrams. Upon all these numerous and important points, do you observe that any directions are to be found in the rhetoricians' systems ?

"In a like silence have languished many other duties of the orator, those of encouraging, comforting, teaching and warning, all worthy of most eloquent treatment, yet having no place of their own in those

65 systems hitherto propounded. In this region also

nor for handling abstract topics.

infinita silva, quod oratori plerique, ut etiam Crassus
ostendit, duo genera ad dicendum dederunt : unum,
de certa definitaque causa, quales sunt, quae in
litibus, quae in deliberationibus versantur, addat, si
quis volet, etiam laudationes : alterum, quod appellant omnes fere scriptores, explicat nemo, infinitam
generis, sine tempore, et sine persona, quaestionem.
66 Hoc quid et quantum sit, cum dicunt, intellegere
mihi non videntur. Si enim est oratoris, quaecumque
res infinite posita sit, de ea posse dicere, dicendum
erit ei, quanta sit solis magnitudo, quae forma terrae :
de mathematicis, de musicis rebus non poterit, quin
dicat, hoc onere suscepto, recusare. Denique ei, qui
profitetur esse suum, non solum de eis controversiis,
quae temporibus et personis notatae sunt, hoc est, de
omnibus forensibus, sed etiam de generum infinitis
quaestionibus dicere, nullum potest esse genus
orationis, quod sit exceptum.

67   XVI. Sed si illam quoque partem quaestionum
oratori volumus adiungere vagam, et liberam, et
late patentem, ut de rebus bonis aut malis, expeten-
dis aut fugiendis, honestis aut turpibus, utilibus aut
inutilibus, de virtute, de iustitia, de continentia, de
prudentia, de magnitudine animi, de liberalitate, de
pietate, de amicitia, de fide, de officio, de ceteris
virtutibus contrariisque vitiis, dicendum oratori pute-
mus ; itemque de republica, de imperio, de re militari, de disciplina civitatis, de hominum moribus :
assumamus eam quoque partem, sed ita, ut sit cir-

there lies a boundless forest of topics : because (as Crassus too has shown) most writers have assigned to the orator two kinds of subject to talk upon, the one concerned with what is specific and determinate, such as the matters handled in lawsuits and consultations,—to which he who will may add panegyrics—; the other spoken of by nearly every writer,—though explained by none—, as the abstract sort of inquiry, 66 unrelated to times or persons. When discussing this kind they do not seem to me to grasp its nature and range. For if it be an orator's part to be able to speak on any subject whatever that is laid before him in general terms, he will have to discuss the size of the sun and the contour of the earth ; and after undertaking this duty he will not be able to refuse to handle mathematics or the cult of the Muses. In a word, for the man who claims the right to speak, not only on problems identified with specific times and persons (that is, on all judicial issues), but also on propositions of an abstract character, there can be no sort of debate which he can decline.

67 XVI. " But if we would connect with the orator that indeterminate, unrestricted and far-extending sort of investigation, and so think it his duty to discuss good and evil, things to be preferred and things to be shunned, fair repute and infamy, the useful and the unuseful, besides moral perfection, righteousness, self-control, discretion, greatness of soul, generosity, loyalty, friendship, good faith, sense of duty and the rest of the virtues and their corresponding vices, as well as the State, sovereignty, warlike operations, political science and the ways of mankind—then let us take up that kind of inquiry also, but only on condition that it be confined within

Treatment of these can be left to tact.

68 cumscripta modicis regionibus. Equidem omnia,
quae pertinent ad usum civium, morem hominum,
quae versantur in consuetudine vitae, in ratione
reipublicae, in hac societate civili, in sensu hominum
communi, in natura, in moribus, comprehendenda
esse oratori puto ; si minus, ut separatim de his rebus
philosophorum more respondeat, at certe, ut in causa
prudenter possit intexere : hisce autem ipsis de rebus
ut ita loquatur, ut ei, qui iura, qui leges, qui civitates
constituerunt, locuti sunt, simpliciter et splendide,
sine ulla serie disputationum, et sine ieiuna con-
certatione verborum.

69   Hoc loco, ne qua sit admiratio, si tot tantarumque
rerum nulla a me praecepta ponentur, sic statuo : Ut
in ceteris artibus, cum tradita sint cuiusque artis
difficillima, reliqua, quia aut faciliora, aut similia sint,
tradi non necesse esse ; ut in pictura, qui hominis
speciem pingere perdidicerit, posse eum cuiusvis vel
formae, vel aetatis, etiamsi non didicerit, pingere
neque esse periculum, qui leonem aut taurum pingat
egregie, ne idem in multis aliis quadrupedibus facere
non possit (neque est omnino ars ulla, in qua omnia,
quae illa arte effici possunt, a doctore tradantur, sed
qui primarum et certarum rerum genera ipsa didicerunt, reliqua non incommode per se asse-
70 quuntur) : similiter arbitror in hac sive ratione, sive
exercitatione dicendi, qui illam vim adeptus sit, ut
eorum mentes, qui aut de republica, aut de ipsis

68 reasonable limits. Of course I hold that all things relating to the intercourse of fellow-citizens and the ways of mankind, or concerned with everyday life, the political system, our own corporate society, the common sentiments of humanity, natural inclinations and morals must be mastered by the orator; if not in the sense that he is to advise on these matters one by one, as the philosophers do, yet so far at least as to enable him to weave them skilfully into his discourse, and moreover to speak of these very things in the same way as the founders of rules of law, statutes and civil communities spoke, frankly and lucidly, with no formal train of argument or barren verbal controversy.

69 "And here, to prevent any surprise at my omitting to lay down any regulations on so many highly important subjects, I make this declaration : ' Just as in the other arts, when the hardest portions of each have been taught, the rest, through being either easier or just like the former, call for no teaching ; as in painting, for instance, he who has thoroughly learned how to paint the semblance of a man, can without further lessons paint one of any figure or time of life, nor is there any danger that he, who would paint to admiration a lion or bull, will be unable to do the like with many other four-footed animals (there being no art whatever wherein all its possibilities require professorial teaching, since those who have rightly learned the general principles of fundamental and established things attain the rest without difficulty and unaided) ; even so I hold that in this oratory, be it an art or the outcome of practice, he who has acquired such power as to be able to sway at his pleasure the minds of hearers

249

rebus, aut de eis, contra quos aut pro quibus dicat,
cum aliqua statuendi potestate audiant, ad suum
arbitrium movere possit, illum de toto illo genere
reliquarum orationum non plus quaesiturum esse,
quid dicat, quam Polyclitum illum cum Herculem
fingebat, quemadmodum pellem aut hydram fingeret,
etiamsi haec nunquam separatim facere didicisset.

71 XVII. Tum Catulus : Praeclare mihi videris,
Antoni, posuisse, inquit, ante oculos, quid discere
oporteret eum, qui orator esset futurus, quid etiam,
si non didicisset, ex eo, quod didicisset, assumeret :
deduxisti enim totum hominem in duo genera solum
causarum ; cetera innumerabilia exercitationi et
similitudini reliquisti. Sed videto, ne in istis duobus
generibus hydra tibi sit et pellis, Hercules autem, et
alia opera maiora, in illis rebus, quas praetermittis,
relinquantur. Non enim mihi minus operis videtur
de universis generibus rerum, quam de singulorum
causis, ac multo etiam maius de natura deorum, quam
72 de hominum litibus dicere. Non est ita, inquit
Antonius. Dicam enim tibi, Catule, non tam doctus,
quam, id quod est maius, expertus. Omnium ceterarum rerum oratio, mihi crede, ludus est homini non
hebeti, neque inexercitato, neque communium litterarum et politioris humanitatis experti. In causarum contentionibus magnum est quoddam opus,
atque haud sciam, an de humanis operibus longe
maximum : in quibus vis oratoris plerumque ab im-

---

a i.e. concrete and abstract problems.

invested with authority to determine some issue concerning the State, or questions of fact, or the parties whom he may be attacking or defending, will on any other oratorical topic whatever be no more at a loss for words than famous Polyclitus, when modelling his "Hercules," was at a loss how to model the wild beast's skin or the water-serpent, even though he had never been taught to fashion these subjects in isolation.' "

71 XVII. Here Catulus interposed : " Antonius, I think you have admirably set before us what the would-be orator ought to learn, as well as what he would absorb from his learning even without independent study : for you have restricted the whole man to just two kinds of subject,[a] leaving the countless other matters to practice and analogy. But please see that you do not include the water-serpent and wild beast's skin in your two kinds, and leave the ' Hercules ' and other more important work among the things you pass over. For it seems to me just as difficult to discuss the abstract types of things as the concerns of individuals, and even far more difficult to discuss the nature of the gods than the legal squabbles 72 of men." " Not so," answered Antonius. " For to you, Catulus, I will speak as one having less learning than experience, which is the bigger thing. To discourse on any other topic, take my word for it, is but pastime to a man who is no dullard and has had some training and is not unacquainted with general literature and a tolerably polite education. But the battles of the law-courts involve really great difficulty and, I rather think, by far the most arduous of human enterprises ; for here ignorant people commonly judge an orator's power by the test of a

Forensic oratory the most difficult.

peritis exitu et victoria iudicatur; ubi adest arma-
tus adversarius, qui sit et feriendus et repellendus;
ubi saepe is, qui rei dominus futurus est, alienus atque
iratus, aut etiam amicus adversario et inimicus tibi
est; cum aut docendus is est, aut dedocendus, aut
reprimendus, aut incitandus, aut omni ratione ad
tempus, ad causam oratione moderandus; in quo saepe
benevolentia ad odium, odium autem ad benevolentiam deducendum est; aut tanquam machinatione
aliqua, tum ad severitatem, tum ad remissionem
animi, tum ad tristitiam, tum ad laetitiam est contor-
quendus. Omnium sententiarum gravitate, omnium
73 verborum ponderibus est utendum. Accedat oportet
actio varia, vehemens, plena animi, plena spiritus,
plena doloris, plena veritatis. In his operibus si quis
illam artem comprehenderit, ut tanquam Phidias
Minervae signum efficere possit, non sane, quemadmodum ut in clipeo idem artifex minora illa opera
facere discat, laborabit.

74 XVIII. Tum Catulus: Quo ista maiora ac mira-
biliora fecisti, eo me maior exspectatio tenet qui-
busnam rationibus quibusque praeceptis ea tanta vis
comparetur: non quo mea quidem iam intersit—neque
enim aetas id mea desiderat et aliud quoddam genus
dicendi nos secuti sumus, qui nunquam sententias de
manibus iudicum vi quadam orationis extorsimus, ac
potius placatis eorum animis, tantum, quantum ipsi
patiebantur, accepimus—, sed tamen ista tua nullum

triumphant result, and a panoplied antagonist confronts you who must be smitten as well as countered, and often he who is to adjudge the victory is ill-disposed and angry or even friendly to the other side while hostile to yourself, when he has to be convinced or undeceived, or reined back or spurred on, or managed by eloquent suggestion of every consideration befitting the occasion or the circumstances (in which process goodwill has often to be transmuted into hatred and hatred into goodwill), or he must be alternately swung round, as though by some machinery, to hardness and to gentleness of heart, to melancholy and to gaiety. Every impressive reflec-

73 tion, every weighty word must be employed. There must be added a delivery that is free from monotony and forceful and rich in energy, animation, pathos and reality. In such labours, if any man shall have so firmly grasped this art as to be able to produce a statue of Minerva, in the manner of Phidias, assuredly he will have no trouble in learning how to carry out the lesser details, as that same Master did, upon the shield."

74 XVIII. To this Catulus rejoined : "The greater and more marvellous you make out these achievements to be, the greater longing possesses me to know the methods or instructions whereby so mighty a power is to be acquired : not indeed that I am now personally affected,—for a man of my years is in no want of it, and my generation pursued a rather different style of oratory, in that we never wrested our verdicts from the grasp of the tribunals by any special force of eloquence, but rather had them presented to us, after conciliating the feelings of the members just so far as they themselves would permit,—but none

Theory not based on experience unless in practice.

ad usum meum, tantum cognoscendi studio adductus,
75 requiro. Nec mihi opus est Graeco aliquo doctore, qui
mihi pervulgata praecepta decantet, cum ipse nunquam forum, nunquam ullum iudicium aspexerit :
ut Peripateticus ille dicitur Phormio, cum Hannibal
Carthagine expulsus Ephesum ad Antiochum venisset
exsul, proque eo, quod eius nomen erat magna apud
omnes gloria, invitatus esset ab hospitibus suis, ut eum,
quem dixi, si vellet, audiret ; cumque is se non nolle
dixisset, locutus esse dicitur homo copiosus aliquot
horas de imperatoris officio, et de omni re militari.
Tum, cum ceteri, qui illum audierant, vehementer
essent delectati, quaerebant ab Hannibale, quidnam
ipse de illo philosopho iudicaret ; hic Poenus non
optime Graece, sed tamen libere respondisse fertur,
multos se deliros senes saepe vidisse, sed qui magis
76 quam Phormio deliraret, vidisse neminem. Neque
mehercule iniuria ; quid enim aut arrogantius, aut
loquacius fieri potuit, quam Hannibali, qui tot annis
de imperio cum populo Romano, omnium gentium
victore, certasset, Graecum hominem, qui nunquam
hostem, nunquam castra vidisset, nunquam denique
minimam partem ullius publici muneris attigisset,
praecepta de re militari dare ? Hoc mihi facere
omnes isti, qui de arte dicendi praecipiunt, videntur : quod enim ipsi experti non sunt, id docent ceteros. Sed hoc minus fortasse errant, quod non
te, ut Hannibalem, sed pueros, aut adolescentulos
docere conantur.

the less I am asking for these secrets of yours, not for my own use but prompted solely by love of knowledge. 75 Nor do I need any Greek professor to chant at me a series of hackneyed axioms, when he himself never had a glimpse of a law-court or judicial proceeding, as the tale goes of Phormio the well-known Peripatetic; for when Hannibal, banished from Carthage, had come in exile to Antiochus at Ephesus and, inasmuch as his name was highly honoured all the world over, had been invited by his hosts to hear the philosopher in question, if he so pleased, and he had intimated his willingness to do so, that wordy individual is said to have held forth for several hours upon the functions of a commander-in-chief and military matters in general. Then, when the other listeners, vastly delighted, asked Hannibal for his opinion of the eminent teacher, the Carthaginian is reported to have thereupon replied, in no very good Greek, but at any rate candidly, that time and again he had seen many old madmen but never one madder 76 than Phormio. And upon my word he was right, for what better example of prating insolence could there be than for a Greek, who had never seen a foeman or a camp, or even had the slightest connexion with any public employment, to lecture on military matters to Hannibal, who all those years had been disputing empire with the Roman people, the conquerors of the world? Just so do all those seem to me to behave who lay down rules for the art of speaking, for they are for teaching others a thing with which they themselves are unacquainted. But possibly their blunder is the less serious, in that they do not try to instruct yourself, as Phormio did Hannibal, but only boys or very young men."

77 XIX. Erras, Catule, inquit Antonius : nam egomet
in multos iam Phormiones incidi. Quis enim est
istorum Graecorum, qui quemquam nostrum quidquam intellegere arbitretur ? Ac mihi quidem non
ita molesti sunt ; facile omnes perpetior et perfero.
Nam aut aliquid afferunt, quod mihi non displiceat,
aut efficiunt, ut me non didicisse minus poeniteat.
Dimitto autem eos non tam contumeliose quam
philosophum illum Hannibal, et eo fortasse plus
habeo etiam negotii ; sed tamen est eorum doctrina,
78 quantum ego iudicare possum, perridicula. Dividunt
enim totam rem in duas partes, in causae controversiam, et in quaestionis. Causam appellant, rem
positam in disceptatione reorum et controversia ;
quaestionem autem, rem positam in infinita dubitatione. De causa praecepta dant ; de altera parte
79 dicendi mirum silentium est. Denique quinque
faciunt quasi membra eloquentiae, invenire quid
dicas, inventa disponere, deinde ornare verbis, post
memoriae mandare, tum ad extremum agere ac pronuntiare : rem sane non reconditam. Quis enim hoc
non sua sponte viderit, neminem posse dicere, nisi et
quid diceret, et quibus verbis, et quo ordine diceret,
haberet, et ea meminisset ? Atque haec ego non
reprehendo, sed ante oculos posita esse dico, ut eas
item quatuor, quinque, sexve partes, vel etiam sep-
tem, quoniam aliter ab aliis digeruntur, in quas est
80 ab his omnis oratio distributa. Iubent enim exordiri
ita, ut eum, qui audiat, benevolum nobis faciamus, et

256

77 XIX. "You are mistaken, Catulus," answered Some rules of rhetoric superfluous or misleading. Antonius, "for I myself ere now have fallen in with many a Phormio. Is there in fact a man among those Greeks who would credit one of us with understanding anything? Not that they worry me so much; I gladly suffer and bear with them all. For they either contribute to my amusement, or contrive to soften my regret at not having been a student. And I send them on their ways less contemptuously than Hannibal sent his philosopher, and for that reason perhaps I have even more trouble with them; their theory however, so far as I can judge, is utterly

78 ludicrous. For they divide the whole subject into two branches—the discussion of concrete and of abstract problems. By the concrete they mean a question in debate and dispute between litigants, by the abstract something involved in boundless uncertainty. For the treatment of the concrete they lay down rules; as to the other branch of

79 oratory their silence is remarkable. After that they set forth a sort of fivefold division of rhetoric, to choose what to say, to marshal the chosen material, next to express it elegantly, then to commit it to memory, and in the end actually to deliver it— assuredly no mysterious progress. For who would not instinctively realize that no one can make a speech without having settled what to say, and in what terms and sequence, and without remembering all this? And without complaining of this classification I say it is one that is obvious, as also are those four, five, six or even seven subdivisions (for different authorities adopt different analyses) into which these people

80 distribute every speech. For they bid us open in such a way as to win the goodwill of the listener and

257

docilem et attentum, deinde rem narrare et ita, ut
verisimilis narratio sit, ut aperta, ut brevis ; post
autem dividere causam, aut proponere ; nostra confirmare argumentis ac rationibus ; deinde contraria
refutare : tum autem alii conclusionem orationis, et
quasi perorationem collocant, alii iubent, antequam
peroretur, ornandi aut augendi causa, digredi deinde
81 concludere ac perorare. Ne haec quidem reprehendo : sunt enim concinne distributa ; sed tamen,
id quod necesse fuit hominibus expertibus veritatis,
non perite. Quae enim praecepta principiorum et
narrationum esse voluerunt, ea in totis orationibus
82 sunt conservanda. Nam ego mihi benevolum iudicem
facilius facere possum cum sum in cursu orationis, quam
cum omnia sunt inaudita ; docilem autem, non cum
polliceor me demonstraturum, sed tum, cum doceo
et explano : attentum vero, tota actione, non prima de-
83 nuntiatione efficere possumus. Iam vero narrationem
quod iubent verisimilem esse et apertam, et brevem,
recte nos admonent ; quod haec narrationis magis
putant esse propria quam totius orationis, valde mihi
videntur errare : omninoque in hoc omnis est error,
quod existimant, artificium esse hoc quoddam non
dissimile ceterorum, cuiusmodi de ipso iure civili
hesterno die Crassus componi posse dicebat : ut
genera rerum primum exponerentur, in quo vitium
est, si genus ullum praetermittatur ; deinde singulorum partes generum, in quo et deesse aliquam

make him receptive and attentive ; then in stating
the case to make our statement plausible, lucid and
brief ; after that to dissect or define the matter in
hand, establishing our own propositions by evidence
and reasonings before disproving those of the other
side : some masters place next the summing-up of
the address and the so-called peroration, while others
require, before such peroration, a digression for the
sake of effect or amplification, to be followed by
81 the summing-up and the close. I find no fault
with even this distribution, for it is neat, though
unscientific, as was sure to happen with teachers
unversed in practical advocacy. For the rules which
they have sought to restrict to the openings and
the statements of cases ought to be observed in all
82 speeches. Thus I can more readily win an arbitrator's goodwill as my address proceeds than before
a word of it has been heard, and I make him receptive, not when I am promising proof, but when I
am instructing him and making all plain ; moreover
we can secure his attention by our argument as a
83 whole, not by our opening allegations. Then again,
in requiring the statement of the case to be plausible,
lucid and brief, they advise us well ; but, in deeming
these qualities more appropriate to such statement
than to the address as a whole, I think they are
greatly mistaken ; and undoubtedly their blunder
arises solely from their idea that this oratory is a
kind of art, just like the other arts, such as Crassus
said yesterday could be constructed on the model of
the common law itself, so that the general kinds of
subject-matter must first be set out, the omission of
any kind being an error, next the particular species
of each kind, wherein too little or too much of any

partem, et superare, mendosum est ; tum verborum
omnium definitiones, in quibus neque abesse quidquam decet neque redundare.

84 XX. Sed hoc si in iure civili, si etiam in parvis aut
mediocribus rebus doctiores assequi possunt, non
idem sentio tanta hac in re, tamque immensa, posse
fieri. Sin autem qui arbitrantur, deducendi sunt ad
eos, qui haec docent ; omnia iam explicata et per-
polita assequentur : sunt enim innumerabiles de
his rebus libri, neque abditi neque obscuri. Sed
videant, quid velint : ad ludendumne, an ad pugnan-
dum arma sint sumpturi ; aliud enim pugna et acies,
aliud ludus campusque noster desiderat. Attamen
ars ipsa ludicra armorum et gladiatori et militi prodest
aliquid ; sed animus acer, et praesens, et acutus idem
atque versutus, invictos viros efficit [non difficilius
arte coniuncta].[1]

85 Quare ego tibi oratorem sic iam instituam, si
potuero, ut, quid efficere possit, ante perspiciam. Sit
enim mihi tinctus litteris ; audierit aliquid, legerit,
ista ipsa praecepta acceperit : tentabo quid deceat,
quid voce, quid viribus, quid spiritu, quid lingua
efficere possit. Si intellegam posse ad summos pervenire, non solum hortabor, ut elaboret, sed etiam,
si vir quoque bonus mihi videbitur esse, obsecrabo :

[1] *Ellendt, Sorof and others reject the words in brackets as
a copyist's addition.*

species is a fault, and finally the definitions of all
terms, in which nothing ought to be missing and
nothing redundant.

84   XX. "But, granting that the more learned can It is natural
attain such orderliness in common law and also in ${}^{\text{capacity}}_{\text{that}}$
matters of slight or no great importance, I do not matters.
think the same is possible in this subject, with its
vast significance and range. If however some hold
otherwise, they must be brought to the teachers of
these studies; they will find everything already displayed and highly finished; for there are countless
books on these topics, neither recondite nor hard
to understand. But let them consider what they
want; whether it be for sport or warfare that they
mean to arm; for the requirements of a pitched
battle are not those of a sham fight or our own
training-ground. For all that, the management of
arms in mere sport has its value for gladiator and
soldier alike, though it is the keen and ready intelligence, endowed with sharpness and resource-
fulness, that secures men against defeat, and no less
easily when allied with art.

85   "And so I shall now begin making an orator for
you, if I can, by first discovering the extent of his
capacity. I would have him be a man of some
learning, who has done some listening and some
reading, and received those very teachings we have
mentioned; I will make trial of what suits him, and
of his powers of intonation, physique, energy and
fluency. If I find him capable of reaching the
highest class, I will not merely encourage him to
work out his purpose but will positively implore him
so to do, provided that I also think his character
sound—so much glory to the whole community do

tantum ego in excellenti oratore, et eodem viro
bono, pono esse ornamenti universae civitati. Sin
videbitur, cum omnia summa fecerit, tamen ad
mediocres oratores esse venturus, permittam ipsi,
quid velit ; molestus magnopere non ero ; sin plane
abhorrebit, et erit absurdus, ut se contineat, aut ad
86 aliud studium transferat, admonebo. Nam neque is,
qui optime potest, deserendus ullo modo est a cohortatione nostra, neque is, qui aliquid potest, deter-
rendus : quod alterum divinitatis mihi cuiusdam
videtur, alterum, vel non facere, quod non optime
possis, vel facere, quod non pessime facias, humanitatis. Tertium vero illud, clamare contra quam deceat, et quam possit, hominis est, ut tu, Catule, de
quodam clamatore dixisti, stultitiae suae quam
87 plurimos testes domestico praeconio colligentis. De
hoc igitur, qui erit talis, ut cohortandus adiuvandus-
que sit, ita loquamur, ut ei tradamus ea duntaxat,
quae nos usus docuit, ut nobis ducibus veniat eo, quo
sine duce ipsi pervenimus, quoniam meliora docere
non possumus.

88 XXI. Atque, ut a familiari nostro exordiar, hunc
ego, Catule, Sulpicium, primum in causa parvula
adolescentulum audivi : voce et forma, et motu corporis, et reliquis rebus aptis ad hoc munus, de quo
quaerimus ; oratione autem celeri et concitata, quod
erat ingenii, et verbis effervescentibus, et paulo
nimium redundantibus, quod erat aetatis. Non sum

I see in an outstanding orator who is also a man of
worth. But if he seems likely, after doing his utmost
in every way, to attain only the level of the ordinary
speaker, I will leave him to his own choice and not
worry him much, while, if he prove wholly unsuitable and out of his element, I will recommend
either self-repression or recourse to some other
86 vocation. For by no means must a man of the
highest capacity be left without our encouragement,
or one of any ability scared away, since to my mind
the state of the former partakes in a sense of the
godlike, while the other course, that of refraining
from doing what you cannot do perfectly, or doing
what you can do without complete discredit, is
natural to a gentleman. But that third alternative
of bawling, in defiance of propriety and of the
speaker's own limitations, marks the man who, as
you, Catulus, observed of a certain bawler, assembles
as many witnesses of his folly as he can, by acting as
87 his own crier. Of him then, who shall be found
deserving of our encouragement and help, let us so
speak as to impart to him merely what practice has
taught us, so that under our leadership he may
reach that stage at which we ourselves have arrived
without a leader, since better teaching we cannot
give.

88 XXI. "And so, Catulus, to begin with our friend
here, I first heard Sulpicius, when he was almost a
boy, in a petty case : as to intonation, presence,
bearing and the other essentials he was well fitted
for this function we are investigating, but his delivery
was rapid and impetuous—the result of his genius—,
his diction agitated and a little too exuberant, as
was natural at his age. I did not underrate him,

Instance of
capacity
appropri-
ately
cultivated.

263

aspernatus ; volo enim se efferat in adolescente
fecunditas : nam sicut facilius, in vitibus, revocantur
ea, quae sese nimium profuderunt, quam, si nihil valet
materies, nova sarmenta cultura excitantur : ita volo
esse in adolescente, unde aliquid amputem ; non
enim potest in eo sucus esse diuturnus, quod nimis
89 celeriter est maturitatem assecutum. Vidi statim
indolem, neque dimisi tempus, et eum sum cohor-
tatus, ut forum sibi ludum putaret esse ad discendum ;
magistrum autem, quem vellet, eligeret ; me quidem
si audiret, L. Crassum ; quod iste arripuit, et ita sese
facturum confirmavit, atque etiam addidit, gratiae
scilicet causa, me quoque sibi magistrum futurum.
Vix annus intercesserat ab hoc sermone cohortationis
meae, cum iste accusavit C. Norbanum, defendente
me. Non est credibile, quid interesse mihi sit visum
inter eum qui tum erat, et qui anno ante fuerat.
Omnino in illud genus eum Crassi magnificum atque
praeclarum natura ipsa ducebat : sed ea non satis
proficere potuisset, nisi eodem studio atque imitatione
intendisset, atque ita dicere consuesset, ut tota mente
Crassum atque omni animo intueretur.

90   XXII. Ergo hoc sit primum in praeceptis meis, ut
demonstremus, quem imitetur atque ita ut, quae
maxime excellant in eo, quem imitabitur, ea diligentissime persequatur. Tum accedat exercitatio,
qua illum, quem delegerit, imitando effingat, atque
ita exprimat, non ut multos imitatores saepe cognovi,
qui aut ea, quae facilia sunt, aut etiam illa, quae
insignia ac paene vitiosa, consectantur imitando.

---

a See § 197 **n.**

being well content that luxuriance should exalt itself in the youthful, for, as with vines it is easier to cut back the branches which have shot out too riotously than to produce new growths by cultivation from a feeble stock, even so in a young man I want something to prune, because the sap can never live 89 long in anything which has ripened too early. I instantly perceived his quality and did not miss the opportunity, but urged him to regard the law-courts as his school of instruction, choosing what master he pleased, but Lucius Crassus if he would take my advice; he caught at this suggestion and assured me that he would follow it, adding, out of politeness of course, that I too should be his teacher. Scarcely a year had elapsed, after this advisory talk with me, when our friend prosecuted Gaius Norbanus,[a] whom I was defending. Incredible was the difference I saw between the Sulpicius of that day and of a year earlier. Assuredly Nature herself was leading him into the grand and glorious style of Crassus, but could never have made him proficient enough, had he not pressed forward on that same way by careful imitation, and formed the habit of speaking with every thought and all his soul fixed in contemplation of Crassus.

90 XXII. " Let this then be my first counsel, that we show the student whom to copy, and to copy in such a way as to strive with all possible care to attain the most excellent qualities of his model. Next let practice be added, whereby in copying he may reproduce the pattern of his choice and not portray him as time and again I have known many copyists do, who in copying hunt after such characteristics as are easily copied or even abnormal and possibly

Rules for practice.

CICERO

91 Nihil est facilius quam amictum imitari alicuius, aut
statum, aut motum. Si vero etiam vitiosi aliquid est,
id sumere et in eo ambitiosum esse non magnum est,
ut ille, qui nunc etiam, amissa voce, furit in republica,
Fufius, nervos in dicendo C. Fimbriae, quos tamen
habuit ille, non assequitur, oris pravitatem et verborum latitudinem imitatur. Sed tamen ille nec
deligere scivit, cuius potissimum similis esset, et in
eo ipso, quem delegerat, imitari etiam vitia voluit.

92 Qui autem ita faciet, ut oportet, primum vigilet
necesse est in deligendo ; deinde, quem probarit, in
eo, quae maxime excellent, ea diligentissime persequatur.

Quid enim causae censetis esse, cur aetates ex-
tulerint singulae singula prope genera dicendi ? Quod
non tam facile in nostris oratoribus possumus iudicare, quia scripta, ex quibus iudicium fieri posset, non
multa sane reliquerunt, quam in Graecis ; ex quorum
scriptis, cuiusque aetatis quae dicendi ratio voluntas-

93 que fuerit, intellegi potest. Antiquissimi fere sunt,
quorum quidem scripta constent, Pericles atque
Alcibiades, et eadem aetate Thucydides, subtiles,
acuti, breves, sententiis magis quam verbis abundantes. Consecuti sunt hos Critias, Theramenes,
Lysias : multa Lysiae scripta sunt ; nonnulla Critiae ;
de Theramene audivimus. Non potuisset accidere
ut unum esset omnium genus, nisi aliquem sibi pro-
ponerent ad imitandum[1] : omnes etiam tum re-
tinebant illum Periclis sucum ; sed erant paulo

---

[1] non . . . imitandum *hic Warmington : ante* Consecuti.

266

91 faulty. For nothing is easier than to imitate a man's style of dress, pose or gait. Moreover, if there is a fault, it is not much trouble to appropriate that and to copy it ostentatiously, just as that Fufius, who even now is raving in the political world, though his voice has gone, fails to attain the energy in speaking which Gaius Fimbria certainly possessed, though hitting off his uncouth mouthings and broad pronunciation. For all that, however, he did not know how to choose the model whom he would most willingly resemble, and it was positively the faults

92 in his chosen pattern that he elected to copy. But he who is to proceed aright must first be watchful in making his choice, and afterwards extremely careful in striving to attain the most excellent qualities of the model he has approved.

"Why now is it, do you suppose, that nearly every age has produced its own distinctive style of oratory ? Of this truth we can judge less easily in the case of our own orators, since they have left but very few writings on which a judgement could be based, than as regards the Greeks, from whose works the method and tendency of the oratory of every genera-

93 tion may be understood. Quite the earliest, of whom we have any authentic remains, are Pericles and Alcibiades, with Thucydides of the same generation, all of them accurate, pointed, terse and wealthier in ideas than diction. These were followed by Critias, Theramenes and Lysias : we possess many writings of Lysias, of Critias a few ; Theramenes is but a name to us. Their uniformity of style could never have come about, had they not kept before them some single model for imitation : they all still retained the peculiar vigour of Pericles, but their

The various schools of oratory.

267

CICERO

94 uberiore filo. Ecce tibi exortus est Isocrates, magister rhetorum[1] omnium, cuius e ludo, tanquam ex equo
Troiano, meri principes exierunt ; sed eorum partim
in pompa, partim in acie illustres esse voluerunt.

XXIII. Atque[2] et illi, Theopompi, Ephori, Philisti,
Naucratae, multique alii naturis differunt, voluntate
autem similes sunt et inter sese et magistri, et ei,
qui se ad causas contulerunt, ut Demosthenes, Hyperides, Lycurgus, Aeschines, Dinarchus, aliique complures, etsi inter se pares non fuerunt, tamen omnes
sunt in eodem veritatis imitandae genere versati,
quorum quamdiu mansit imitatio, tamdiu genus illud
95 dicendi studiumque vixit. Posteaquam, exstinctis
his, omnis eorum memoria sensim obscurata est et
evanuit, alia quaedam dicendi molliora ac remissiora
genera viguerunt. Inde Demochares, quem aiunt
sororis filium fuisse Demosthenis ; tum Phalereus ille
Demetrius, omnium istorum, mea sententia, politis-
simus, aliique horum similes exstiterunt. Quae si
volemus usque ad hoc tempus persequi, intellegemus,
ut hodie Alabandensem illum Meneclem, et eius
fratrem Hieroclem, quos ego audivi, tota imitetur
Asia : sic semper fuisse aliquem, cuius se similes
96 plerique esse vellent. Hanc igitur similitudinem qui
imitatione assequi volet, cum exercitationibus crebris
atque magnis, tum scribendo maxime persequatur :
quod si hic noster Sulpicius faceret, multo eius oratio
esset pressior ; in qua nunc interdum, ut in herbis

---

[1] rhetorum *Reid :* istorum. [2] Atque *Wilkins*,: Itaque.

94 texture was a little more luxuriant. Then behold! there arose Isocrates, the Master of all rhetoricians, from whose school, as from the Horse of Troy, none but leaders emerged, but some of them sought glory in ceremonial, others in action.

XXIII. "And indeed the former sort, men like Theopompus, Ephorus, Philistus, Naucrates and many more, while differing in natural gifts, yet in spirit resemble one another and their Master too; and those who betook themselves to lawsuits, as did Demosthenes, Hyperides, Lycurgus, Aeschines, Dinarchus and several others, although of varying degrees of ability, were none the less all busy with the same type of imitation of real life, and as long as the imitation of these persisted, so long did their **95** kind of oratory and course of training endure. Afterwards, when these men were dead and all remembrance of them gradually grew dim and then vanished away, certain other less spirited and lazier styles of speaking flourished. Then came Demochares, said to have been the son of Demosthenes' sister, and after him the distinguished Demetrius of Phalerum, the most elegant, to my thinking, of all that school, and others like them. And, if we please to trace this subject down to our own times, we shall find, that just as to-day all Asia is copying the great Menecles of Alabanda and his brother Hierocles, both of whom I have heard, so there has always been some speaker **96** whom the majority would fain resemble. Let him then, who hopes by imitation to attain this likeness, carry out his purpose by frequent and large practice, and if possible, by written composition: if our friend Sulpicius here were to do so, his diction would be far more condensed; at present, as countrymen are

rustici solent dicere in summa ubertate, inest luxuries quaedam, quae stylo depascenda est.

97 Hic Sulpicius : Me quidem, inquit, recte mones, idque mihi gratum est : sed ne te quidem, Antoni, multum scriptitasse arbitror.

Tum ille: Quasi vero, inquit, non ea praecipiam aliis, quae mihi ipsi desint : sed tamen ne tabulas quidem conficere existimor. Verum et in hoc, ex re familiari mea, et in illo, ex eo, quod dico, quantulum 98 id cumque est, quid faciam, iudicari potest. Atque esse tamen multos videmus, qui neminem imitentur et suapte natura, quod velint, sine cuiusquam similitudine consequantur. . Quod et in vobis animadverti recte potest, Caesar et Cotta ; quorum alter inusitatum nostris quidem oratoribus leporem quemdam et salem, alter acutissimum et subtilissimum dicendi genus est consecutus. Neque vero vester aequalis Curio, patre, mea sententia, vel eloquentissimo temporibus illis, quemquam mihi magnopere videtur imitari ; qui tamen verborum gravitate et elegantia et copia suam quamdam expressit quasi formam, figuramque dicendi : quod ego maxime potui iudicare in ea causa, quam ille contra me apud centumviros pro fratribus Cossis dixit ; in qua nihil illi defuit, quod non modo copiosus, sed etiam sapiens orator habere deberet.

99 XXIV. Verum, ut aliquando ad causas deducamus illum, quem constituimus, et eas quidem, in quibus plusculum negotii est, iudiciorum atque litium—

wont to say of grass in times of extreme productiveness, it occasionally has a certain luxuriance about it, which should be grazed off by the pen."

97 Here Sulpicius interposed, "Truly you give me good counsel and I thank you for it, but I fancy that even you, Antonius, have done but little scribbling."

To which Antonius made answer, "As though I could not teach others what I lack myself; though certainly I am credited with not even keeping accounts! But what little I can do in this direction *But gifted* can be judged from my financial situation, and in *individuals* *can dispense* 98 the other from what I say. And indeed we see *with models.* that there are many who copy no man, but gain their objects by natural aptitude, without resembling any model. And the truth of this may be observed in you two, Caesar and Cotta, for one of you has acquired a degree of humour and wit unusual in orators, at any rate in our own, and the other a thoroughly keen and subtle type of oratory. Curio too, your contemporary, whose father I consider quite the most eloquent of his day, seems to me to copy no one in particular, though in the dignity, refinement and copiousness of his language he has given expression to what may be called his own peculiar pattern and type of oratory, of which I could judge to perfection in that action which he conducted against me before the Hundred Commissioners, on behalf of the brothers Cossi; on that occasion he lacked no qualification which an orator of insight, not of copiousness alone, should possess.

9 XXIV. "However, to introduce at last this man *First master* we are portraying to the business of trials and law- *facts of case.* suits, especially such cases as involve rather more

271

riserit aliquis fortasse hoc praeceptum; est enim non
tam acutum, quam necessarium, magisque monitoris
non fatui, quam eruditi magistri—hoc ei primum
praecipiemus, quascumque causas erit tractaturus, ut
100 eas diligenter penitusque cognoscat. Hoc in ludo
non praecipitur: faciles enim causae ad pueros
deferuntur. 'Lex peregrinum vetat in murum
ascendere; ascendit; hostes repulit; accusatur.'
Nihil est negotii eiusmodi causam cognoscere; recte
igitur nihil de causa discenda praecipiunt: haec
est enim in ludo causarum fere formula. At vero
in foro, tabulae, testimonia, pacta conventa, stipula-
tiones, cognationes, affinitates, decreta, responsa, vita
denique eorum qui in causa versantur, tota cognoscenda est: quarum rerum neglegentia plerasque
causas, et maxime privatas (sunt enim multo saepe
101 obscuriores) videmus amitti. Ita nonnulli, dum
operam suam multam existimari volunt, ut toto foro
volitare et a causa ad causam ire videantur, causas
dicunt incognitas. In quo est illa quidem magna
offensio, vel neglegentiae, susceptis rebus; vel per-
fidiae, receptis; sed etiam illa maior opinione, quod
nemo potest de ea re, quam non novit, non turpissime
dicere. Ita dum inertiae vituperationem, quae maior
est, contemnunt, assequuntur etiam illam, quam
magis ipsi fugiunt, tarditatis.

102   Equidem soleo dare operam, ut de sua quisque re

trouble,—someone will perhaps laugh at this axiom, for it is not so much shrewd as necessary, and comes from an adviser who is no fool, rather than from a learned Master—, we shall first instruct 100 him to get up carefully and thoroughly whatever cases he proposes to conduct. This is no canon of the schools, for the cases set to the boys are simple. ' Statute forbids a foreigner to mount the wall ; a foreigner mounts ; he has driven off the enemy ; he is prosecuted.' It is no trouble to get up a case like that, and so they are right in giving no directions for mastering the case, for this is just about the type of wording in cases set in the schools. But in the law-courts documents, evidence, informal agreements, formal contracts, relationship by blood or marriage, magisterial orders, opinions of counsel, and finally the life-history of the parties to the proceedings, must all be examined ; and we see that it is generally through neglect of these matters that cases are lost, particularly such as concern private rights, for these are often of peculiar difficulty. 01 Thus some practitioners, wishing their business to be thought large, and themselves to be seen flitting from lawsuit to lawsuit all round the courts, argue cases which they have not got up. Herein they incur very grave reproach, either of carelessness, if their services are volunteered, or of bad faith, if they are retained ; but that reproach is deemed all the greater, in that no man can speak, without the direst disgrace, on a subject which he has not mastered. And so, while scorning the accusation of laziness, in reality the more serious, they encounter as well that of dullness, which they themselves more sedulously avoid.

" It is my own practice to take care that every client

me ipse doceat et ut ne quis alius adsit, quo liberius
loquatur, et agere adversarii causam, ut ille agat
suam et, quidquid de sua re cogitarit, in medium
proferat. Itaque cum ille discessit, tres personas unus
sustineo summa animi aequitate, meam, adversarii,
iudicis. Qui locus est talis, ut plus habeat adiumenti
quam incommodi, hunc iudico esse dicendum ; ubi
plus mali quam boni reperio, id totum abiudico atque
103 eicio. Ita assequor, ut alio tempore cogitem, quid
dicam, et alio dicam : quae duo plerique ingenio freti
simul faciunt ; sed certe eidem illi melius aliquanto
dicerent, si aliud sumendum sibi tempus ad cogitandum, aliud ad dicendum putarent.

104 Cum rem penitus causamque cognovi, statim
occurrit animo, quae sit causa ambigendi. Nihil est
enim, quod inter homines ambigatur (sive ex crimine
causa constat, ut facinoris, sive ex controversia, ut
hereditatis, sive ex deliberatione, ut belli, sive ex
persona, ut laudis, sive ex disputatione, ut de ratione
vivendi) in quo non, aut quid factum sit, aut fiat,
futurumve sit, quaeratur, aut quale sit, aut quid
vocetur.

105 XXV. Ac nostrae fere causae, quae quidem sunt
criminum, plerumque infitiatione defenduntur. Nam
et de pecuniis repetundis, quae maximae sunt, ne-
ganda fere sunt omnia, et de ambitu raro illud datur,
ut possis liberalitatem atque benignitatem ab ambitu

personally instructs me on his affairs, and that no one else shall be present, so that he may speak the more freely ; and to argue his opponent's case to him, so that he may argue his own and openly declare whatever he has thought of his position. Then, when he has departed, in my own person and with perfect impartiality I play three characters, myself, my opponent and the arbitrator. Whatever consideration is likely to prove more helpful than embarrassing I decide to discuss ; wherever I find more harm than good I entirely reject and discard the topic concerned.

103 In this way I gain the advantage of reflecting first on what to say and saying it later, two things which most people, trusting in their talent, do simultaneously, though those same individuals would certainly speak rather more successfully, if they thought fit to take one occasion for reflection and another for speaking.

104 "When I have thoroughly mastered the circum- The issue stances of a case the issue in doubt comes instantly to then manifest, under my mind. For of all the issues disputed among men, one of three whether the matter is criminal, as a charge of outrage, heads : or a civil proceeding, as one relating to an inheritance, or a discussion of policy, as one touching a war, or of a personal kind, as a panegyric, or a philosophical debate, as on the way to live, there is not one of which the point is not either what has been done, or what is being done, or going to be done, or as to the nature or description of something.

05 XXV. "In almost all our cases, in prosecutions at (1) fact of any rate, the usual defence is a plea of not guilty. alleged act, For, in trials for extortion, the most important class, nearly every allegation must be denied, and, on a charge of corrupt practices, lavish generosity can seldom be distinguished from profuse bribery ; in

atque largitione seiungere ; de sicariis, de veneficiis, de peculatu infitiari necesse est. Id est igitur genus primum causarum in iudiciis ex controversia facti ; in deliberationibus plerumque ex futuri, raro ex 106 instantis aut acti. Saepe etiam res non sit necne, sed qualis sit quaeritur ; ut cum L. Opimii causam defendebat apud populum, audiente me, C. Carbo consul, nihil de C. Gracchi nece negabat, sed id iure pro salute patriae factum esse dicebat ; ut eidem Carboni tribuno plebis alia tum mente rem publicam capessenti P. Africanus de Ti. Graccho interroganti responderat iure caesum videri. Iure autem omnia defenduntur, quae sunt eius generis, ut aut oportuerit aut licuerit aut necesse fuerit aut impru- 107 dentia aut casu facta esse videantur. Iam quid vocetur, quaeritur, cum quo verbo quid appellandum sit, contenditur ; ut mihi ipsi cum hoc Sulpicio fuit in Norbani causa summa contentio. Pleraque enim de eis, quae ab isto obiciebantur, cum confiterer, tamen ab illo maiestatem minutam negabam, ex quo verbo lege Appuleia tota illa causa 108 pendebat. Atque in hoc genere causarum non nulli praecipiunt ut verbum illud, quod causam facit, breviter uterque definiat, quod mihi quidem perquam puerile videri solet. Alia est enim, cum inter doctos homines de eis ipsis rebus quae versantur in artibus disputatur, verborum definitio, ut cum

---

[a] See § 197 n.
[b] In 100 B.C., appointing a commission to investigate treasons committed during the Cimbrian war, 113—101 B.C.

cases of assassination, poisoning or misappropriation
a denial is the inevitable plea. Thus in Court the
first class of cases is that of disputed facts ; debate
generally proceeds from something still to come,
106 seldom from anything present or past. Often too (2) its
the question is not whether something be the nature,
fact or not, but what is its nature ; as, when I
heard Gaius Carbo, in his consulship, defending
Lucius Opimius before the people, he denied no detail of the killing of Gaius Gracchus, but urged that
it was justifiable and for the public safety ; or as
when Publius Africanus made answer to that very
Carbo (by then a tribune of the commons with
changed political views and putting a question as to
Tiberius Gracchus), that ' his death appeared to be
justifiable.' Now all acts may be defended as justifi- (3) its defi-
able which are such that the doing thereof was a nition.
duty, or permissible, or necessary, or which are shown
to have been done inadvertently or by accident.
107 Again the question is one of definition, when the
terms in which an act should be described are in dispute, as in the main contention between myself and
our friend Sulpicius at the trial of Norbanus.[a] For,
while admitting most of our friend's indictment, I
still maintained that the defendant was not guilty of
' treason,' since the whole case depended on the construction of this word, by virtue of the Statute of
108 Appuleius.[b] And in such proceedings some lay down
a rule that each side shall concisely define the de-
batable term, a proposition which I myself always
think thoroughly childish. For definition of terms is
another thing when controversy arises among special-
ists touching the intimate concerns of the arts, for
instance when inquiry is made as to the essential

quaeritur, quid sit ars, quid sit lex, quid sit civitas, in
quibus hoc praecipit ratio atque doctrina, ut vis eius
rei quam definias sic exprimatur ut neque absit
109 quicquam neque supersit. Quod quidem in illa causa
neque Sulpicius fecit neque ego facere conatus sum ;
nam quantum uterque nostrum potuit, omni copia
dicendi dilatavit, quid esset maiestatem minuere.
Etenim definitio primum reprehenso verbo uno aut
addito aut dempto saepe extorquetur e manibus ;
deinde genere ipso doctrinam redolet exercitatio-
nemque paene puerilem ; tum et in sensum et in
mentem iudicis intrare non potest, ante enim prae-
terlabitur, quam percepta est.

110   XXVI. Sed in eo genere, in quo quale sit quid,
ambigitur, exsistit etiam ex scripti interpretatione
saepe contentio, in quo nulla potest esse nisi ex
ambiguo controversia. Nam illud ipsum, quod scriptum a sententia discrepat, genus quoddam habet
ambigui ; quod tum explicatur, cum ea verba, quae
desunt, suggesta sunt, quibus additis defenditur
sententiam scripti perspicuam fuisse. Ex contrariisque scriptis si quid ambigitur, non novum genus
nascitur, sed superioris generis causa duplicatur.
Idque aut numquam diiudicari poterit aut ita diiudi-
cabitur, ut referendis praeteritis verbis id scriptum,
quodcumque defendemus, suppleatur. Ita fit, ut
unum genus in eis causis, quae propter scriptum
ambiguntur, relinquatur, si est scriptum aliquid
ambigue.

111   Ambiguorum autem cum plura genera sunt, quae

nature of an art, a statute or a community, in which circumstances scientific method ordains that the significance of whatever you are defining shall be
109 made plain, with no omission or redundance. But in that case of ours Sulpicius did no such thing nor did I attempt it, since we both, to the utmost of our power, enlarged with all our fluency upon the meaning of 'act of treason.' For, in the first place, if the addition or substraction of a word be seized on, a definition is often wrung from our grasp, and then too the very suggestion savours of the schools and a training little better than elementary, and lastly the definition cannot reach the understanding and reason of the arbitrator, as it slips by him before he has taken it in.

110   XXVI. "But in that kind of cases, wherein the nature of something is in issue, a further contest often arises out of the construction of a document, when the only possible dispute comes from an equivocation. For the mere fact that letter and spirit are at variance involves something of an equivocation ; and this is solved directly the missing words are supplied, and, when these are inserted, it is contended that the sense of the writing has become plain. And, if uncertainty arises from passages which contradict one another, there emerges no new sort of problem, but a double example of the former kind. And this will either prove insoluble, or will be so solved, that by the restoration of the words omitted, whichever version we are upholding will be completed. It follows that only one class is left of problems turning on the writer's language, these arising where something has been equivocally expressed.

These three issues explained.

111   "Now, although there are several kinds of equivo-

mihi videntur ei melius nosse, qui dialectici appellantur, hi autem nostri ignorare, qui non minus nosse debeant, tum illud est frequentissimum in omni consuetudine vel sermonis vel scripti, cum idcirco aliquid ambigitur, quod aut verbum aut verba sint
112 praetermissa. Iterum autem peccant, cum genus hoc causarum, quod in scripti interpretatione versatur, ab illis causis, in quibus, qualis quaeque res sit, disceptatur, seiungunt ; nusquam enim tam quaeritur, quale sit genus ipsum rei quam in scripto, quod totum a facti controversia separatum est.

113 Ita tria sunt omnino genera, quae in disceptationem et controversiam cadere possunt : quid fiat factum futurumve sit, aut quale sit, aut quo modo nominetur. Nam illud quidem, quod quidam Graeci adiungunt, ʻrectene factum sit,ʼ totum in eo est, ʻquale sit.ʼ

114 XXVII. Sed iam ad institutum revertar meum. Cum igitur accepta causa et genere cognito rem tractare coepi, nihil prius constituo, quam quid sit illud, quo mihi sit referenda omnis illa oratio, quae sit propria quaestionis et iudicii. Deinde illa duo diligentissime considero, quorum alterum commendationem habet nostram aut eorum, quos defendimus, alterum est accommodatum ad eorum animos, apud quos dicimus, ad id, quod volumus, commovendos. Ita omnis ratio dicendi tribus ad persuadendum rebus est nixa : ut probemus vera esse, quae defendimus ; ut conciliemus eos nobis, qui audiunt ; ut animos eorum, ad quemcumque causa postulabit motum, vocemus.
116 Ad probandum autem duplex est oratori subiecta

ª *i.e.* the rhetoricians.

cation (better understood, I think, by the so-called
logicians, and unknown to these *a* friends of ours,
who should understand them just as well), yet the
most common, in the whole range of verbal or written
intercourse, is the equivocation due to the omission
12 of a word or words. And they are wrong again in
distinguishing between this sort of cases, concerned with documentary construction, and those
where the nature of something is in debate ; for
never is the precise character of anything so closely
investigated as in the construction of a document,
which has nothing in common with questions of fact.

13 "Then questions of three kinds in all may fall under
debate and dispute—, what is being done, or has been
done or is going to be done, or what is the nature of
something, or what is its right designation ? For
that further question, added by sundry Greeks,
whether something was lawfully done, is completely
covered by the question of its nature.

14 XXVII. "But to return at length to my own plan. Three
As soon then as I have received my instructions and objects in
view.
classed the case and taken the matter in hand, the
very first thing I determine is that point to which I
must devote all such part of my speech as belongs
peculiarly to the issue and the verdict. Next I contemplate with the utmost care those other two
essentials, the one involving the recommendation of
myself or my clients, the other designed to sway the
15 feelings of the tribunal in the desired direction. Thus
for purposes of persuasion the art of speaking relies
wholly upon three things : the proof of our allegations,
the winning of our hearers' favour, and the rousing of
their feelings to whatever impulse our case may
16 require. For purposes of proof, however, the material

materies : una rerum earum, quae non excogitantur
ab oratore, sed in re positae ratione tractantur, ut
tabulae, testimonia, pacta conventa, quaestiones,
leges, senatus consulta, res iudicatae, decreta, responsa, reliqua, si quae sunt, quae non ab oratore
pariuntur, sed ad oratorem a causa atque a reis
deferuntur ; altera est, quae tota in disputatione et

117 in argumentatione oratoris collocata est. Ita in
superiore genere de tractandis argumentis, in hoc
autem etiam de inveniendis cogitandum est. Atque
isti quidem, qui docent, cum causas in plura genera
secuerunt, singulis generibus argumentorum copiam
suggerunt. Quod etiamsi ad instituendos adolescentulos magis aptum est, ut, simul ac posita causa sit,
habeant quo se referant, unde statim expedita
possint argumenta depromere, tamen et tardi ingenii
est rivulos consectari, fontis rerum non videre, et
iam aetatis est ususque nostri a capite quod velimus
arcessere et unde omnia manent videre.

118 Et primum genus illud earum rerum, quae ad
oratorem deferuntur, meditatum nobis in perpetuum
ad omnem usum similium rerum esse debebit ; nam et
pro tabulis et contra tabulas et pro testibus et contra
testes et pro quaestionibus et contra quaestiones
et item de ceteris rebus eiusdem generis vel separatim dicere solemus de genere universo vel definite de
singulis temporibus, hominibus, causis ; quos quidem
locos—vobis hoc, Cotta et Sulpici, dico—multa com-
mentatione atque meditatione paratos atque expe-

at the orator's disposal is twofold, one kind made up of the things which are not thought out by himself, but depend upon the circumstances and are dealt with by rule, for example documents, oral evidence, informal agreements, examinations, statutes, decrees of the Senate, judicial precedents, magisterial orders, opinions of counsel, and whatever else is not produced by the orator, but is supplied to him by the case itself or by the parties : the other kind is founded

17 entirely on the orator's reasoned argument. And so, with the former sort, he need only consider the handling of his proofs, but with the latter, the discovery of them as well. And indeed those professors, after distinguishing a larger number of types of cases, suggest proofs in plenty for each type. But, even if this plan is better fitted for training the young, to the end that, directly a case is propounded, they may have authorities from which they can forthwith borrow ready-made proofs, yet it is a symptom of congenital dullness to follow up the tiny rills, but fail to discern the sources of things : and by this time it is the privilege of men of our years and experience to call up what we want from the water's head, and to discern the springs of every stream.

18 "And, to begin with, that class of things supplied to the orator we shall have to study constantly, with a view to the general use of similar instances ; for in attacking or defending documents, witnesses or examinations by torture, and also in dealing with all other such subjects, it is our habit to discuss either the whole class in the abstract, or individual occasions, persons or circumstances in the concrete : these commonplaces (I am speaking to you, Cotta and Sulpicius) you ought, by dint of large study and practice, to

Facts must be established by evidence or argument.

Methods of handling these acquired by study.

119 ditos habere debetis. Longum est enim nunc me explicare, qua ratione aut confirmare aut infirmare testes, tabulas, quaestiones oporteat. Haec sunt omnia ingenii vel mediocris, exercitationis autem maximae; artem quidem et praecepta dumtaxat hactenus requi-
120 runt, ut certis dicendi luminibus ornentur. Itemque illa, quae sunt alterius generis, quae tota ab oratore pariuntur, excogitationem non habent difficilem; explicationem magis illustrem perpolitamque desiderant. Itaque cum haec duo nobis quaerenda sint in causis, primum quid, deinde quo modo dicamus, alterum, quod totum arte tinctum videtur, tametsi artem requirit, tamen prudentiae est paene mediocris quid dicendum sit videre ; alterum est, in quo oratoris vis illa divina virtusque cernitur, ea, quae dicenda sunt, ornate, copiose varieque dicere.

121 XXVIII. Qua re illam partem superiorem, quoniam semel ita vobis placuit, non recusabo quo minus perpoliam atque conficiam—quantum consequar, vos iudicabitis—quibus ex locis ad eas tres res, quae ad fidem faciendam solae valent, ducatur oratio, ut et concilientur animi et doceantur et moveantur. Haec sunt enim tria. Ea vero quem ad modum illustrentur, praesto est, qui omnes docere possit, qui hoc primus in nostros mores induxit, qui maxime auxit,
122 qui solus effecit. Namque ego, Catule,—dicam enim non reverens assentandi suspicionem—neminem esse oratorem paulo illustriorem arbitror, neque Graecum neque Latinum, quem aetas nostra tulerit, quem non et saepe et diligenter audierim. Itaque si quid est in me—quod iam sperare videor, quoniam quidem vos,

---

a i.e. inventio, or the discovery of what to say.

119 have ready at hand. It would be a long story for me
to unfold just now the right way to corroborate or
weaken witnesses, documents or examinations. All
this demands no great talent but vast practice, and
Art and her maxims only to this extent—that it be
120 illuminated by good and effective diction. So too
those subjects of the other class, produced entirely
by the orator, are easy enough to think out, but call
for clearer and highly finished exposition. Thus,
while in our cases we have these two objectives, first
what to say, and secondly how to say it, the former,
which seems to be art pure and simple, cannot indeed
dispense with art, though it needs but ordinary skill
to discover what ought to be said ; but it is in the
latter that the orator's godlike power and excellence
are discerned, that is, his delivery of what he has to
say in a style elegant, copious and diversified.

21 XXVIII. " Accordingly, as you have once for all so
resolved, I shall not object to working out completely
(you will judge of the measure of my success) that
former *a* portion, dealing with those commonplaces
from which may be drawn a speech such as to attain
those three things which alone can carry conviction ;
I mean the winning over, the instructing and the
stirring of men's minds. For these are the three.
But how to embellish these arguments we have at
hand him who could teach the world, the man who
first made this accomplishment habitual among us,
did most to improve it, and alone has mastered it.
22 For I think, Catulus (and I shall say so without fear
of being suspected of flattery), that I have listened
often and attentively to every one of the rather more
brilliant speakers of our day, Greek and Roman alike.
And so, if there be anything in me (as I think I may

Mode of stating arguments effectively left to Crassus.

his ingeniis homines, tantum operae mihi ad audiendum datis—ex eo est, quod nihil quisquam umquam me audiente egit orator, quod non in memoria mea penitus insederit. Atque ego is, qui sum, quantuscumque sum ad iudicandum, omnibus auditis oratoribus, sine ulla dubitatione sic statuo et iudico, neminem omnium tot et tanta, quanta sunt in Crasso,

123 habuisse ornamenta dicendi. Quam ob rem, si vos quoque hoc idem existimatis, non erit, ut opinor, iniqua partitio, si, cum ego hunc oratorem, quem nunc fingo, ut institui, crearo, aluero, confirmaro, tradam eum Crasso et vestiendum et ornandum.

124 Tum Crassus : Tu vero, inquit, Antoni, perge, ut instituisti. Neque enim est boni neque liberalis parentis, quem procrearis et eduxeris, eum non et vestire et ornare, praesertim cum te locupletem esse negare non possis. Quod enim ornamentum, quae vis, qui animus, quae dignitas illi oratori defuit, qui in causa peroranda non dubitavit excitare reum consularem et eius diloricare tunicam et iudicibus cicatrices adversas senis imperatoris ostendere ? Qui idem, hoc accusante Sulpicio, cum hominem seditiosum furiosumque defenderet, non dubitavit seditiones ipsas ornare, ac demonstrare gravissimis verbis multos saepe impetus populi non iniustos esse, quos praestare nemo possit ; multas etiam e re publica seditiones saepe esse factas, ut cum reges essent exacti, ut cum tribunicia potestas constituta ; illam Norbani seditionem ex luctu civium et ex

---

[a] M'. Aquilius, see § 194 n
[b] See § 197 n.

hope there is, now that men of your talents take so much trouble to hear me), it is because no orator ever delivered a speech in my hearing which did not settle deep within my memory. And I, being what I am, and so far as I am competent to judge, after hearing all the orators, do unhesitatingly decree and pronounce as follows, that not one of them all possessed so many and excellent resources of diction

123 as appear in Crassus. Therefore, if you share this estimate of mine, it will, I think, be no unfair division of labour if, having begotten, nurtured and made strong this orator, whom I am now moulding as I planned, I hand him over to Crassus, to be clothed and fitted out."

124   Here Crassus observed : " Nay, Antonius, you go on with your plan. For it ill becomes a good and generous father to refuse clothing and equipment to the child you have begotten and reared, especially as you cannot plead poverty. For what did that advocate lack, in the way of resource, passion, energy or greatness, who in closing his case did not hesitate to call forward the defendant[a] of consular rank, and tear open his tunic, and display to the tribunal the scars on the old general's breast ? Who again, in his defence of a factious and frenzied client, prosecuted by Sulpicius here, did not hesitate to glorify civil discord in itself, and to show, in most convincing terms, that many popular movements are justifiable, and no one by any possibility answerable for them ; that moreover civil discord has often been aroused in the interest of the community, witness the expulsion of the kings and the establishment of the authority of tribunes ; that the outbreak of Norbanus,[b] arising as it did from public mourning and indignation against

Crassus urges Antonius to explain his own method.

Caepionis odio, qui exercitum amiserat, neque re-
125 primi potuisse et iure esse conflatam ? Potuit hic
locus tam anceps, tam inauditus, tam lubricus, tam
novus sine quadam incredibili vi ac facultate dicendi
tractari ? Quid ego de Cn. Mallii, quid de Q. Regis
commiseratione dicam ? Quid de aliis innumerabilibus ? in quibus non hoc maxime enituit, quod tibi
omnes dant, acumen quoddam singulare, sed haec
ipsa, quae nunc ad me delegare vis, ea semper in
te eximia et praestantia fuerunt.

126 XXIX. Tum Catulus : Ego vero, inquit, in vobis
hoc maxime admirari soleo, quod, cum inter vos in
dicendo dissimillimi sitis, ita tamen uterque vestrum
dicat, ut ei nihil neque a natura denegatum neque a
doctrina non delatum esse videatur. Qua re, Crasse,
neque tu tua suavitate nos prívabis, ut, si quid ab
Antonio aut praetermissum aut relictum sit, non
explices ; neque te, Antoni, si quid non dixeris,
existimabimus non potuisse potius quam a Crasso
dici maluisse.

127 Hic Crassus : Quin tu, inquit, Antoni, omittis
ista, quae proposuisti, quae nemo horum desiderat :
quibus ex locis ea, quae dicenda sunt in causis, reperiantur ; quae quamquam a te novo quodam modo
praeclareque dicuntur, sunt tamen et re faciliora
et praeceptis pervagata. Illa deprome nobis unde
afferas, quae saepissime tractas semperque divinitus. Depromam equidem, inquit, et quo facilius

Caepio, who had lost his army, could not have been
125 restrained and was justifiably kindled. Could this
line of argument, so hazardous, startling, treacherous
and unfamiliar, be handled otherwise than by
oratorical power and readiness truly marvellous?
What shall I say of the lamentation over Gnaeus
Mallius, or of that over Quintus Rex? What of
countless other cases, wherein the really unequalled
acuteness, universally recognized as yours, was not
the most brilliant feature, but those very qualifications, which you would now delegate to me, were
consistently displayed in outstanding excellence by
yourself?"

26 XXIX. "For my part," interposed Catulus, "the
thing about you two which most persistently excites
my wonder is, that while you are utterly different in
style, yet each speaks as though nothing had been
denied him by nature or withheld from him by training. And so, Crassus, you will not stint us of your
charm to the extent of declining to expound anything
passed over or left out by Antonius, nor shall we
suppose, Antonius, that you could have a speaker
more welcome to you than Crassus, to say what you
may have omitted to say."

27 "Not so, Antonius," continued Crassus, "rather
please omit that part of your programme which none
of our friends here wants, touching the commonplaces
which supply us with what we have to say in our
cases: although you discuss these things with brilliant
originality, they are for all that really rather easy
and widely current in maxims. Produce for us the
sources of what you so often handle and always in
inspired fashion." "I will certainly produce them,"
replied the other, "and, the more readily to exact

289

id a te exigam, quod petam, nihil tibi a me
128 postulanti recusabo. Meae totius orationis et
istius ipsius in dicendo facultatis, quam modo
Crassus in caelum verbis extulit, tres sunt rationes,
ut ante dixi : una conciliandorum hominum, altera
129 docendorum, tertia concitandorum. Harum trium
partium prima lenitatem orationis, secunda acumen, tertia vim desiderat. Nam hoc necesse est, ut
is, qui nobis causam adiudicaturus sit, aut inclina-
tione voluntatis propendeat in nos, aut defensionis
argumentis adducatur, aut animi permotione cogatur.
Sed quoniam illa pars, in qua rerum ipsarum explicatio ac defensio posita est, videtur omnem huius
generis quasi doctrinam continere, de ea primum
loquemur et pauca dicemus. Pauca enim sunt, quae
usu iam tractata et animo quasi notata habere
videamur.

130 XXX. Ac tibi sapienter monenti, Crasse, libenter
assentiemur, ut singularum causarum defensiones
quas solent magistri pueris tradere, relinquamus,
aperiamus autem capita ea, unde omnis ad omnem et
causam et orationem disputatio ducitur. Neque
enim, quotiens verbum aliquod est scribendum nobis,
totiens eius verbi litterae sunt cogitatione conqui-
rendae ; nec quotiens causa dicenda est, totiens ad
eius causae seposita argumenta revolvi nos oportet,
sed habere certos locos, qui, ut litterae ad verbum
scribendum, sic illi ad causam explicandam statim
131 occurrant. Sed hi loci ei demum oratori prodesse
possunt, qui est versatus in rerum vel usu, quem aetas

what I want from you, I will refuse nothing that you
128 demand of me. Under my whole oratorical system
and that very readiness in speaking which Crassus
just now lauded to the skies, lie three principles, as I
said before, first the winning of men's favour, secondly
129 their enlightenment, thirdly their excitement. Of
these three the first calls for gentleness of style, the
second for acuteness, the third for energy. For, of
necessity, the arbitrator who is to decide in our
favour must either lean to our side by natural inclination, or be won over by the arguments for the defence,
or constrained by stirring his feelings. But as the
portion including the exposition of the actual facts
and the line of defence seems to include the whole
doctrine on this subject, we will speak of that first
and briefly. For there are a few points which I have
perhaps already handled in practice and noted in
my memory.

30 XXX. "And I shall gladly follow your good Employ-
counsel, Crassus, ignoring the lines of defence 'common-
proper to particular types of cases, as taught places.'
regularly by the professors to the boys, while I
open up the sources from which the whole argument
for every case and speech is derived. For just as,
whenever we have some word to write, we need not
search out its component letters by hard thinking,
so, whenever we have some case to argue, our right
course is not to fall back upon proofs laid away for
that particular type of cases, but to have in readiness
sundry commonplaces which will instantly present
themselves for setting forth the case, as the letters
31 do for writing the word. But these commonplaces
can be useful only to a speaker who is a man of
affairs, qualified by experience, which age assuredly

denique affert, vel auditione et cogitatione, quae
studio et diligentia praecurrit aetatem. Nam si tu
mihi quamvis eruditum hominem adduxeris, quamvis
acrem et acutum in cogitando, quamvis ad pro-
nuntiandum expeditum, si erit idem in consuetudine
civitatis, in exemplis, in institutis, in moribus ac
voluntatibus civium suorum hospes, non multum ei
loci proderunt illi, ex quibus argumenta promuntur.
Subacto mihi ingenio opus est, ut agro non semel
arato, sed et[1] novato et iterato, quo meliores fetus
possit et grandiores edere. Subactio autem est usus,
auditio, lectio, litterae.

132   Ac primum naturam causae videat, quae numquam
latet, factumne sit quaeratur, an quale sit, an quod
nomen habeat; quo perspecto statim occurrit
naturali quadam prudentia, non his subductionibus,
quas isti docent, quid faciat causam, id est, quo
sublato controversia stare non possit; deinde quid
veniat in iudicium, quod isti sic iubent quaerere.
'Interfecit Opimius Gracchum. Quid facit causam?
Quod rei publicae causa, cum ex senatus consulto ad
arma vocasset. Hoc tolle, causa non erit. At id
ipsum negat contra leges licuisse Decius. Veniet
igitur in iudicium licueritne ex senatus consulto
servandae rei publicae causa.' Perspicua sunt haec
quidem et in volgari prudentia sita; sed illa quae-

----

[1] et *add. Reid;* [novato et] *alii.*

brings, or by listening and reflection, which through
careful study outruns age. For bring me a man
as accomplished, as clear and acute in thinking,
and as ready in delivery as you please ; if, for
all that, he is a stranger to social intercourse,
precedent, tradition, and the manners and disposition of his fellow-countrymen, those commonplaces from which proofs are derived will avail
him but little. I must have talent which has been
cultivated, soil, as it were, not of a single ploughing,
but both broken and given a second ploughing so as
to be capable of bearing better and more abundant
produce. And the cultivation is practice, listening,
reading and written composition.

32   "And let the pupil first discern the nature of a Some
case, never an obscure thing, whether the question 'commonplace'
relate to the doing of an act, or to its character or always
right designation : this once ascertained, the sub- available.
stance of the case, or that without which the discussion must collapse, leaps instantly to the mind,
through what I may call native intuition, not through
the reckonings taught by those people ; next he
must determine the issue to be decided, which they
would have him investigate as follows. ' Opimius
killed Gracchus. What is the substance of the
case ? That he did so in the interest of the community, after proclaiming a state of war in obedience
to the Senate's decree. Strike out this plea, and
there will be no case. Decius however denies the
legality of the decree itself, as being contrary to
statute. So the issue will be whether the Senate's
decree and the salvation of the community justified
the act.' These points are quite clear and within
the compass of ordinary knowledge, but a search is

renda, quae et ab accusatore et a defensore argumenta ad id, quod in iudicium venit, spectantia debent afferri.

133   XXXI. Atque hic illud videndum est, in quo summus est error istorum magistrorum, ad quos liberos nostros mittimus, non quo hoc quidem ad dicendum magno opere pertineat, sed tamen ut videatis quam[1] sit genus hoc eorum qui sibi eruditi videntur hebes atque impolitum.[2] Constituunt enim in partiendis orationum modis duo genera causarum : unum appellant, in quo sine personis atque temporibus de universo genere quaeratur ; alterum, quod personis certis et temporibus definiatur ; ignari omnes controversias ad universi generis vim et naturam referri.

134 Nam in ea ipsa causa, de qua ante dixi, nihil pertinet ad oratoris locos Opimii persona, nihil Decii. De ipso universo genere infinita quaestio est, num poena videatur esse afficiendus, qui civem ex senatus consulto patriae conservandae causa interemerit, cum id per leges non liceret. Nulla denique est causa, in qua id, quod in iudicium venit, reorum personis ac non generum ipsorum universa dubitatione

135 quaeratur. Quin etiam in eis ipsis, ubi de facto ambigitur, ceperitne pecunias contra leges P. Decius, argumenta et criminum et defensionis revocentur oportet ad genus et ad naturam universam : quod sumptuosus, de luxurie, quod alieni appetens, de avaritia, quod seditiosus, de turbulentis et malis

---

[1] quam *Piderit :* quale.
[2] [hebes atque impolitum] *Kayser.*

necessary to discover the proofs, bearing upon the issue, which are proper to be adduced by the prosecution and the defence respectively.

133   XXXI. "And here we must notice the very great mistake made by those professors, to whom we send our sons; not indeed that this has much to do with speaking, but just to let you see how dull and inelegant is this class of the people who fancy themselves accomplished. For in their division of the different kinds of speeches they set up two sorts of cases : one they describe as raising general questions, not related to individuals or occasions ; and the other as depending upon specific individuals and occasions ; not knowing that any debate whatsoever can be brought under the notion and quality 34 of the general kind. For, in the very case I mentioned just now, the personality of Opimius or of Decius has nothing to do with the orator's commonplaces. There is an abstract question of a purely general kind, ' Is a defendant to be deemed deserving of punishment, who has slain a fellow-countryman in obedience to a decree of the Senate, and for the salvation of his native land, though by statute such act was unlawful ? ' There is in fact no case wherein the issue for decision turns on the personalities of the parties, and not on the abstract 5 discussion of general conceptions. Indeed, even where the question is one of pure fact, such as ' Did Publius Decius take moneys unlawfully ? ' the evidence for prosecution and defence alike must have reference to general terms and essential qualities : to convict of extravagance you must refer to profusion ; of covetousness, to greed ; of sedition, to turbulent and wicked members of

Error of separating 'commonplaces' from instances.

295

civibus, quod a multis arguitur, de genere testium, contraque, quae pro reo dicentur, omnia necessario a tempore atque homine ad communes rerum et gene-

136 rum summas revolventur. Atque haec forsitan homini non omnia, quae sunt in natura rerum, celeriter animo comprehendenti permulta videantur, quae veniant in iudicium tum, cum de facto quaeratur; sed tamen criminum multitudo est et defensionum, non locorum infinita.

137 XXXII. Quae vero, cum de facto non ambigitur, quaeruntur, qualia sint, ea si ex reis numeres, et innumerabilia sunt et obscura; si ex rebus, valde et modica et illustria. Nam si Mancini causam in uno Mancino ponimus, quotienscumque is, quem pater patratus dediderit, receptus non erit, totiens causa nova nascetur. Sin illa controversia causam facit, videaturne ei, quem pater patratus dediderit, si is non sit receptus, postliminium esse, nihil ad artem dicendi nec ad argumenta defensionis Mancini

138 nomen pertinet. Ac, si quid affert praeterea hominis aut dignitas aut indignitas, extra quaestionem est et ea tamen ipsa oratio ad universi generis disputationem referatur necesse est. Haec ego non eo consilio disputo, ut homines eruditos redarguam; quamquam reprehendendi sunt qui in genere definiendo istas causas describunt in personis et in

139 temporibus positas esse. Nam etsi incurrunt tempora

***

a See Book I, xl.

the community; to prove that the defendant's accusers are many, you must deal with witnesses in the mass: and conversely all the evidence for the defence will have to turn away from the particular occasion and individual to general con-

136 ceptions of circumstances and kinds. And, to a man who is slow in his intellectual apprehension of all that there is in life, the issues arising for decision on questions of fact may perhaps seem very numerous, but in reality it is the charges and the lines of defence, not the commonplaces, which are endless in their variety.

137 XXXII. But the cases wherein there is no ques- *The great* tion of fact, and only the character of an act is in *variety of cases can be* doubt, are innumerable and intricate if reckoned *brought* up by the actors, but very few and clear if reckoned *under few heads.* up by the acts. For, if we confine the decision in the *Case of Mancinus* ᵃ to Mancinus alone, then every time the surrender of anyone delivered up by the Priestly Envoy has been rejected, a fresh debate will begin. But, if the substance of that case is the problem 'Whether a man delivered up by the Priestly Envoy has the right of re-entry if his surrender is rejected,' then the person of Mancinus has nothing to do with the art of speaking or the

38 evidence for the defence. Moreover whatever help a man's worth or his want of it affords is irrelevant to the inquiry, and yet that part of the speech also must be classed as discussion of a general proposition. I treat these matters not in order to contradict accomplished people, though they are to be censured who, in determining their classification, define such cases as depending upon specific individuals and

9 occasions. For occasions and individuals do indeed

et personae, tamen intellegendum est, non ex eis, sed
ex genere quaestionis pendere causas. Sed hoc
nihil ad me ; nullum enim nobis certamen cum istis
esse debet. Tantum satis est intellegi ne hoc quidem
eos consecutos, quod in tanto otio, etiam sine hac
forensi exercitatione, efficere potuerunt, ut genera
rerum discernerent eaque paulo subtilius explicarent.

140 Verum hoc, ut dixi, nihil ad me. Illud ad me ac
multo etiam magis ad vos, Cotta noster et Sulpici :
quo modo nunc se istorum artes habent, pertimes-
cenda est multitudo causarum ; est enim infinita, si
in personis ponitur ; quot homines, tot causae ; sin ad
generum universas quaestiones referuntur, ita modicae
et paucae sunt, ut eas omnes diligentes et memores
et sobrii oratores percursas animo et prope dicam
decantatas habere debeant ; nisi forte existimatis
a M'. Curio causam didicisse L. Crassum et ea re
multa attulisse, quam ob rem postumo non nato
Curium tamen heredem Coponii esse oporteret.

141 Nihil ad copiam argumentorum neque ad causae vim
ac naturam nomen Coponii aut Curii pertinuit. In
genere erat universo rei negotiique, non in tempore
ac nominibus, omnis quaestio : cum scriptum ita sit
Si mihi filius genitur, isque prius moritur, et cetera,
tum mihi ille sit heres, si natus filius non sit,
videaturne is, qui filio mortuo institutus heres sit,

---

^a See Book I, § 180.

298

enter into the inquiry, but it must be understood
that the cases do not depend upon these, but upon
general questions. This however is nothing to me,
for we are not obliged to quarrel with those people.
It is quite enough to make it known that they have
not even succeeded in distinguishing different classes
of things, and in describing them a little more
accurately, as with their unbounded leisure they
could have done, even though they lacked our own
10 public practice. But this, as I said, is nothing to
me. What is important to me, and far more so
to you, friends Cotta and Sulpicius, is that, in
the present stage of those men's attainments, a
multiplicity of cases is greatly to be feared; for their
variety is endless if they are identified with individuals; every man then has his case; but, if they
are brought under general heads of inquiry, they are
so ordinary and so few that careful and thoughtful
speakers with good memories should be able to
handle them all, after mentally running through
them and all but sing-songing them; unless you
happen to think that Lucius Crassus got up his brief
from Manius Curius,[a] and for that reason adduced
all those grounds for holding Curius entitled to
succeed as heir to Coponius, though no posthumous
son had been born. The identity of Coponius or of
Curius had nothing to do with the wealth of argument or with the essential character of the case.
The whole inquiry turned upon an abstract question,
founded in the facts of the matter, not in any occasion
or personalities: the words in the will being ' *If a
son is born to me, and such son dies before, etc., then let
So-and-so be my heir,*' and no son having in fact been
born, ought that party to inherit who was nominated

heres esse. Perpetui iuris et universi generis quaestio
non hominum nomina, sed rationem dicendi et argumentorum fontes desiderat.

142   XXXIII. In quo etiam isti nos iuris consulti im-
pediunt a discendoque deterrent. Video enim in
Catonis et in Bruti libris nominatim fere referri quid
alicui de iure viro aut mulieri responderit : credo, ut
putaremus in hominibus, non in re, consultationis aut
dubitationis causam aliquam fuisse ; ut, quod homines innumerabiles essent, debilitati a iure cognoscendo voluntatem discendi simul cum spe perdiscendi abiceremus. Sed haec Crassus aliquando
nobis expediet et exponet discripta generatim ; est
enim, ne forte nescias, heri nobis ille hoc, Catule,
pollicitus se ius civile, quod nunc diffusum et dissipatum esset, in certa genera coacturum et ad artem
facilem redacturum.

143   Et quidem, inquit Catulus, haudquaquam id est
difficile Crasso, qui et, quod disci potuit de iure,
didicit et, quod eis, qui eum docuerunt, defuit, ipse
afferet, ut, quae sint in iure, vel apte discribere vel
ornate illustrare possit. Ergo ista, inquit Antonius,
tum a Crasso discemus, cum se de turba et a subselliis
144 in otium, ut cogitat, soliumque contulerit. Iam id
quidem saepe, inquit Catulus, ex eo audivi, cum
diceret sibi certum esse a iudiciis causisque discedere ;

heir in substitution for a deceased son ? An inquiry depending upon a fixed and general rule of law needs no men's names, but methodical presentation and the sources of arguments.

42   XXXIII. "And here again those learned lawyers embarrass us and frighten us away from more learning. For I observe that in the treatises of Cato and Brutus the advice given by counsel to clients of either sex is generally set down with the parties named : I suppose, to make us think that some reason for seeking advice or for the discussion originated in the parties and not in the circumstances ; to the end that, seeing the parties to be innumerable, we might be discouraged from studying the law, and might cast away our inclination to learn at the same moment as our hope of mastery. But these matters Crassus will one day disentangle for us and set forth arranged under heads ; for you must know, Catulus, that yesterday he promised us that he would collect under definite heads the common law, at present dispersed in disorder, and would reduce it to an easy system."

3   "To be sure," answered Catulus, " that is easy enough for Crassus, who has learned all there is to be learned about law, and will personally supply the deficiencies of his teachers, to make it possible for him to arrange fittingly and elucidate elegantly the contents of the law." "Well then," said Antonius, "we shall learn those things from Crassus, when as he is thinking of doing, he has withdrawn from the hubbub of the Courts to the peace of his armchair." "I have often heard him say so," rejoined Catulus, "when he has been announcing his resolve to retire from practice at the Bar, but, as I

sed, ut ipsi soleo dicere, non licebit; neque enim ipse
auxilium suum saepe a viris bonis frustra implorari
patietur neque id aequo animo feret civitas, quae si
voce L. Crassi carebit, ornamento quodam sese
spoliatam putabit. Nam hercle, inquit Antonius,
si haec vere a Catulo dicta sunt, tibi mecum in eodem
est pistrino, Crasse, vivendum; et istam oscitantem
et dormitantem sapientiam Scaevolarum et cete-
145 rorum beatorum otio concedamus. Arrisit hic
Crassus leniter et: Pertexe modo, inquit, Antoni,
quod exorsus es; me tamen ista oscitans sapientia,
simul atque ad eam confugero, in libertatem vin-
dicabit.

XXXIV. Huius quidem loci, quem modo sum
exorsus, hic est finis, inquit Antonius; quoniam
intellegitur non in hominum innumerabilibus personis neque in infinita temporum varietate, sed in
generum causis atque naturis omnia sita esse, quae in
dubium vocarentur, genera autem esse definita non
solum numero, sed etiam paucitate, ut eam materiem
orationis, quae cuiusque esset generis, studiosi qui
essent dicendi, omnibus locis discriptam, instructam
ornatamque comprehenderent rebus dico et senten-
146 tiis. Ea vi sua verba parient, quae semper satis
ornata mihi quidem videri solent, si eius modi sunt, ut
ea res ipsa peperisse videatur. Ac si verum quaeritis,
quod mihi quidem videatur—nihil enim aliud affir-
mare possum nisi sententiam et opinionem meam—
hoc instrumentum causarum et generum universorum
in forum deferre debemus neque, ut quaeque res
delata ad nos erit, tum denique scrutari locos, ex

always tell him, he will not get the chance : for he himself will seldom suffer his aid to be begged in vain by men of worth, nor will the community bear it, but will think itself robbed of its jewel, as it were, if it miss the tones of Lucius Crassus." "Upon my word, Crassus," interposed Antonius, "if Catulus has been telling the truth, you and I will have to pass our lives together in the same pounding-mill ; and we shall let leisure have (—and welcome too) that yawning and drowsy philosophizing of men like 145 Scaevola and the others who are lucky." Crassus laughed quietly at this, observing, " Just weave out the warp you have begun, Antonius, but that yawning Philosophy of yours, when once I have found sanctuary with her, will claim my freedom."

XXXIV. " This then," resumed Antonius, " is the aim of the topic whose warp I opened just now : it being understood that all the possible subjects of debate are not founded on a countless host of human beings or an endless diversity of occasions, but on typical cases and characters, and that the types are not merely limited in number but positively few, I wished the devotees of eloquence to contemplate the fabric of speeches of the several kinds, in distribution under all the headings, and in good order and well 46 furnished, with facts, I mean, and reflections. These things, by their own natural force, will beget the words, which I, at any rate, always think well enough found, if they are such as seem to grow out of the inherent circumstances. And if you want the truth, at any rate as I see it (for I can assert only my own verdict and belief), we ought to bring this stock of cases and types down to Court with us, and not wait until we have accepted a brief, before we search the

[margin note:] Necessity of being equipped in advance with arguments—especially by study.

quibus argumenta eruamus; quae quidem omnibus,
qui ea mediocriter modo considerarint, studio adhibito
et usu pertractata esse possunt; sed tamen animus
referendus est ad ea capita et ad illos, quos saepe
iam appellavi, locos, ex quibus omnia ad omnem
147 orationem inventa ducuntur. Atque hoc totum est
sive artis sive animadversionis sive consuetudinis
nosse regiones, intra quas venere et pervestiges,
quod quaeras. Ubi eum locum omnem cogitatione
saepseris, si modo usu rerum percallueris, nihil te
effugiet atque omne, quod erit in re, occurret atque
incidet.

XXXV. Et sic, cum ad inveniendum in dicendo
tria sint: acumen, deinde ratio, quam licet, si volumus, appellemus artem, tertium diligentia, non
possum equidem non ingenio primas concedere, sed
tamen ipsum ingenium diligentia etiam ex tarditate
148 incitat; diligentia, inquam, quae cum omnibus in
rebus tum in causis defendendis plurimum valet.
Haec praecipue colenda est nobis; haec semper
adhibenda; haec nihil est quod non assequatur.
Causa ut penitus, quod initio dixi, nota sit, diligentia
est; ut adversarium attente audiamus atque ut eius
non solum sententias, sed etiam verba omnia ex-
cipiamus, voltus denique perspiciamus omnes, qui
149 sensus animi plerumque indicant, diligentia est. Id
tamen dissimulanter facere, ne sibi ille aliquid proficere videatur, prudentia est. Deinde ut in eis locis,
quos proponam paulo post, pervolvatur animus, ut
penitus insinuet in causam, ut sit cura et cogitatione

commonplaces, from which to dig out our proofs; which indeed can be handled, after no very deep consideration, by anyone who is helped by study and practice, but for all that the mind must needs return to those headings and those commonplaces which I have often mentioned as such already, from which every device for every speech whatever is derived. 147 Again, in art, in observation and in practice alike, it is everything to be familiar with the ground over which you are to chase and track down your quarry. When you have mentally encompassed all that area, if only you are quite hardened to practical dealings, nothing will escape you, but every detail of an affair will come up with a rush and fall into your net.

XXXV. "And so, since in oratory three things are necessary to discovery of arguments, first acuteness, secondly theory, or art, as we may call it if we like, and thirdly painstaking, I must needs grant pride of place to talent, though talent itself is roused from lethargy by painstaking, painstaking, I repeat, which is always valuable, and most of all in fighting a case. This virtue we must especially cultivate and ever be calling it to our aid; there is nothing that this cannot attain. By painstaking comes that intimate knowledge of a case, to which I alluded at first; it is painstaking to listen with close attention to our opponent, and so as to catch not only his periods, but his every word as well, and finally to read all his changes of countenance, which generally gives the clue to his frame of mind. But to do this unobtrusively, so that he may not think he has scored a point, is discretion. Then that the mind should dwell upon those commonplaces which I shall set forth presently, that it should worm itself into the roots of a matter, with its powers

intentus, diligentia est ; ut his rebus adhibeat tamquam lumen aliquod memoriam, ut vocem, ut vires,
150 diligentia est.   Inter ingenium quidem et diligentiam
perpaulum loci reliquum est arti.   Ars demonstrat
tantum, ubi quaeras, atque ubi sit illud, quod studeas
invenire ; reliqua sunt in cura, attentione animi,
cogitatione, vigilantia, assiduitate, labore ; complectar uno verbo, quo saepe iam usi sumus, diligentia ; qua una virtute omnes virtutes reliquae
151 continentur.   Nam orationis quidem copia videmus
ut abundent philosophi, qui, ut opinor—sed tu haec,
Catule, melius—nulla dant praecepta dicendi nec
idcirco minus, quaecumque res proposita est, suscipiunt, de qua copiose et abundanter loquantur.
152   XXXVI. Tum Catulus : Est, inquit, ut dicis,
Antoni, ut plerique philosophi nulla tradant praecepta
dicendi et habeant paratum tamen quid de quaque
re dicant.   Sed Aristoteles, is, quem ego maxime
admiror, proposuit quosdam locos, ex quibus omnis
argumenti via non modo ad philosophorum disputationem, sed etiam ad hanc, qua in causis
utimur, inveniretur ; a quo quidem homine iam
dudum, Antoni, non aberrat oratio tua, sive tu
similitudine illius divini ingenii in eadem incurris
vestigia sive etiam illa ipsa legisti atque didicisti,
quod quidem magis veri simile videtur.   Plus enim
te operae Graecis dedisse rebus video, quam
153 putaramus.   Tum ille : Verum, inquit, ex me

<hr>

_a_ In _Topica._

of attention and thought at full stretch, is still pains-taking ; to supplement all this with the torch of memory, with intonation and with energy, is pains-taking once more. Indeed between talent and painstaking there is very little room left for art. Art merely points out where to search, and the locality of what you are anxious to find : all else depends on carefulness, mental concentration, reflection, watch-fulness, persistence and hard work ; I shall sum up these in the single word I have often used already, painstaking to wit, on which single virtue all other virtues are dependent. For we notice the over-flowing copiousness of the diction of the philosophers who, I think (though you, Catulus, are better in-formed on these points), prescribe no rules for speak-ing, but none the less undertake to discuss with overflowing copiousness, whatever subject is laid before them."

XXXVI. Thereupon Catulus remarked, " You are right, Antonius, in saying that most philosophers prescribe no rules for speaking, and yet have some-thing ready to say about everything. Aristotle, however, my own most particular admiration, set forth[a] certain commonplaces, among which every line of argument might be found, not merely for philo-sophical debate, but also for our own contentions in the Courts : it is certainly long, Antonius, since your own style deviated from his principles, whether it be that through likeness to that godlike genius you fall into the same track, or, as seems far more probable, you too have perused and learned those very maxims. For I perceive that you have bestowed more pains on Greek literature than we had supposed." And the other answered, " Catulus, I will tell you the

audies, Catule : semper ego existimavi iucundiorem
et probabiliorem huic populo oratorem fore, qui
primum quam minimam artificii alicuius, deinde
nullam Graecarum rerum significationem daret.   Atque ego idem existimavi pecudis esse, non hominis,
cum tantas res Graeci susciperent, profiterentur,
agerent seseque et videndi res obscurissimas et
bene vivendi et copiose dicendi rationem daturos
hominibus pollicerentur, non admovere aurem et,
si palam audire eos non auderes, ne minueres apud
tuos cives auctoritatem tuam, subauscultando tamen
excipere voces eorum et procul quid narrarent attendere.   Itaque feci, Catule, et istorum omnium
summatim causas et genera ipsa gustavi.

154   XXXVII. Valde hercule, inquit Catulus, timide
tamquam ad aliquem libidinis scopulum sic tuam
mentem ad philosophiam appulisti, quam haec civitas
aspernata numquam est.   Nam et referta quondam
Italia Pythagoreorum fuit tum, cum erat in hac
gente magna illa Graecia ; ex quo etiam quidam
Numam Pompilium, regem nostrum, fuisse Pytha-
goreum ferunt ; qui annis ante permultis fuit quam
ipse Pythagoras ; quo etiam maior vir habendus est,
quod illam sapientiam constituendae civitatis duobus
prope saeculis ante cognovit, quam eam Graeci natam
esse senserunt.   Et certe non tulit ullos haec civitas
aut gloria clariores aut auctoritate graviores aut
humanitate politiores P. Africano, C. Laelio, L.
Furio, qui secum eruditissimos homines ex Graecia

truth: I always considered that a speaker would be more pleasing and acceptable to a nation like ours if he were to show, first, as little trace as possible of any artifice, and secondly none whatever of things Greek. And at the same time I considered that, with the Greeks undertaking, professing and achieving such marvels, and promising to reveal to mankind the way to understand the profoundest mysteries, to live rightly and to speak copiously, it would be brutish and inhuman not to lend an ear, and, though perhaps not venturing to listen to them openly, for fear of lessening your influence with your fellow-citizens, yet to pick up their sayings by eavesdropping, and keep a look-out from afar for their talk. Accordingly I did so, Catulus, and took a little taste of the cases and actual types of all those friends of yours."

154 XXXVII. "Upon my word," said Catulus, "you are like a pilot cautiously steering towards a dangerous reef, some Sirens' isle, when you direct your mind to Philosophy, which this country has never disdained! For even of old Italy was crowded with Pythagoreans, in the days when a part of this land was Great Greece as they called it; so that some even claim our King Numa Pompilius as a Pythagorean, though he lived very many years earlier than Pythagoras himself, for which reason he must be accounted an even greater man, in that he mastered the famous science of community-building nearly two centuries before the Greeks perceived its existence. And surely this community has produced no men of more splendid fame, more weighty influence or more polished manners, than Publius Africanus, Gaius Laelius and Lucius Furius, who at all times and in public had about them most accomplished

Roman attitude towards philosophy.

309

155 palam semper habuerunt. Atque ego hoc ex eis
saepe audivi, cum dicerent pergratum Athenienses
et sibi fecisse et multis principibus civitatis, quod,
cum ad senatum legatos de suis maximis rebus
mitterent, tres illius aetatis nobilissimos philosophos
misissent, Carneadem et Critolaum et Diogenem ;
itaque eos, dum Romae essent, et a se et ab aliis fre-
quenter auditos ; quos tu cum haberes auctores,
Antoni, miror cur philosophiae sicut Zethus ille
156 Pacuvianus prope bellum indixeris.   Minime, inquit
Antonius, ac sic decrevi philosophari potius, ut Neoptolemus apud Ennium ' Paucis : nam omnino haud
placet.'   Sed tamen haec est mea sententia, quam
videbar exposuisse : ego ista studia non improbo,
moderata modo sint : opinionem istorum studiorum
et suspicionem artificii apud eos, qui res iudicent,
oratori adversariam esse arbitror, imminuit enim
et oratoris auctoritatem et orationis fidem.

157   XXXVIII. Sed, ut eo revocetur, unde huc de-
clinavit oratio, ex tribus istis clarissimis philosophis,
quos Romam venisse dixisti, videsne Diogenem eum
fuisse, qui diceret artem se tradere bene disserendi
et vera ac falsa diiudicandi, quam verbo Graeco
διαλεκτικήν appellaret ?   In hac arte, si modo est
haec ars, nullum est praeceptum, quo modo verum
158 inveniatur, sed tantum est, quo modo iudicetur.   Nam
et omne, quod eloquimur sic, ut id aut esse dicamus
aut non esse, et, si simpliciter dictum sit, suscipiunt

---

^a In 155 b.c. The Athenians had pillaged Oropus, on
the Boeotian frontier, and had bəen sentenced by umpires
appointed by the Romans to a fine of 500 talents, reduced
to 100 after this embassy.

^b See *Remains of Old Latin* (L.C.L.), ii. pp. 162-163.

^c *Ibid.* i. pp. 368-369, and Aulus Gellius v. 15. 9 and 16. 5.

155 personages from Greece. Moreover I have often heard those notables speak of the vast pleasure afforded to themselves and many leaders of the State by the Athenians, in having sent,[a] as envoys to the Senate on business of supreme importance to Athens, the three most illustrious philosophers of that day, Carneades, Critolaus and Diogenes, who accordingly, during their stay in Rome, frequently had my informants and others for an audience : with these witnesses before you, Antonius, I marvel why, like that Zethus described by Pacuvius,[b] you have all but

156 declared war against Philosophy." "Not at all," replied Antonius, " but rather I have determined to philosophize, as Neoptolemus says in Ennius, ' In a few things, for I don't want to do so in all ways.'[c] For all that, however, my verdict, as I thought I had made plain, is this : I do not disapprove of such pursuits, if kept within limits, though I hold that a reputation for such pursuits, or any suggestion of artifice, is likely to prejudice an orator with the judiciary : for it weakens at once the credibility of the orator and the cogency of his oratory.

157 XXXVIII. "But, to recall Oratory to the point at which this digression started, do you observe that, of those three most illustrious philosophers, who visited Rome as you told us, it was Diogenes who claimed to be teaching an art of speaking well, and of distinguishing truth from error, which art he called by the Greek name of dialectic ? This art, if indeed it be an art, contains no directions for discovering truth, but only for testing it. For as to every proposition that we enunciate with an affirmation of its truth or falsity, if it be affirmed without qualification, the dialecticians undertake to decide

Stoic doctrine useless for the orator.

311

dialectici, ut iudicent, verumne sit an falsum, et, si
coniuncte sit elatum, et adiuncta sint alia, iudicant,
rectene adiuncta sint et verane summa sit unius
cuiusque rationis, et ad extremum ipsi se compungunt
suis acuminibus et multa quaerendo reperiunt non
modo ea, quae iam non possint ipsi dissolvere, sed
etiam quibus ante exorsa, et potius detexta, prope
159 retexantur. Hic nos igitur Stoicus iste nihil adiuvat,
quoniam, quem ad modum inveniam quid dicam, non
docet ; atque idem etiam impedit, quod et multa
reperit, quae negat ullo modo posse dissolvi, et genus
sermonis affert non liquidum, non fusum ac profluens,
sed exile, aridum, concisum ac minutum, quod si
quis probabit, ita probabit, ut oratori tamen aptum
non esse fateatur. Haec enim nostra oratio multitudinis est auribus accommodanda, ad oblectandos
animos, ad impellendos, ad ea probanda, quae non
aurificis statera, sed populari quadam trutina ex-
aminantur.

160   Qua re istam artem totam dimittamus, quae in ex-
cogitandis argumentis muta nimium est, in iudicandis
nimium loquax. Critolaum istum, quem cum Diogene
venisse commemoras, puto plus huic nostro studio prodesse potuisse. Erat enim ab isto Aristotele, a cuius
inventis tibi ego videor non longe aberrare. Atque
inter hunc Aristotelem, cuius et illum legi librum, in
quo exposuit dicendi artes omnium superiorum, et
illos, in quibus ipse sua quaedam de eadem arte dixit,

whether it be true or false ; and, if again it be stated
hypothetically, with collateral propositions annexed,
then they decide whether these others are properly
annexed, and whether the conclusion drawn from
each and every reasoning is correct : and in the end
they prick themselves with their own barbs, and by
wide investigation discover not only difficulties such
as they themselves can no longer solve, but also
others by which webs already attacked, or rather well-
159 nigh unwound, are tangled up again. In this connexion then that eminent Stoic is of no help to us,
since he does not teach me how to discover what to
say ; and he actually hinders me, by finding many
difficulties which he pronounces quite insoluble, and
by introducing a kind of diction that is not lucid,
copious and flowing, but meagre, spiritless, cramped
and paltry ; and, if any man commends this style, it
will only be with the qualification that it is unsuitable
to an orator. For this oratory of ours must be adapted
to the ears of the multitude, for charming or urging
their minds to approve of proposals, which are weighed
in no goldsmith's balance, but in what I may call
common scales.

160 " Let us therefore renounce entirely that art which *Insight of*
has too little to say when proofs are being thought *Aristotle
and ability*
out, and too much when they are being assessed. *in argument of*
That Critolaus, whose visit in company with Diogenes *Carneades.*
you recall, might have been more useful, I think, in this
pursuit of ours. For he was a follower of your Aristotle, from whose doctrines you think my own differ
but little. And between this Aristotle (I read also
that book of his, setting forth the rhetorical theories
of all his forerunners, and those other works containing sundry observations of his own on the same art),

313

et hos germanos huius artis magistros hoc mihi visum
est interesse, quod ille eadem acie mentis, qua rerum
omnium vim naturamque viderat, haec quoque
aspexit, quae ad dicendi artem, quam ille despicie-
bat, pertinebant ; illi autem, qui hoc solum colendum
ducebant, habitarunt in hac una ratione tractanda
non eadem prudentia, qua ille, sed usu in hoc uno
161 genere studioque maiore. Carneadi vero vis incredibilis illa dicendi et varietas perquam esset optanda
nobis, qui nullam umquam in illis suis disputationibus
rem defendit, quam non probarit, nullam oppugnavit,
quam non everterit. Sed hoc maius est quiddam,
quam ab eis, qui haec tradunt et docent, postulandum
sit.

162   XXXIX. Ego autem, si quem nunc rudem plane
institui ad dicendum velim, his potius tradam assiduis
uno opere eandem incudem diem noctemque tun-
dentibus, qui omnes tenuissimas particulas atque
omnia minima mansa ut nutrices infantibus pueris in
os inserant. Sin sit is, qui et doctrina mihi liberaliter
institutus et aliquo iam imbutus usu et satis acri
ingenio esse videatur, illuc eum rapiam, ubi non
seclusa aliqua acula teneatur, sed unde universum
flumen erumpat ; qui illi sedes et quasi domicilia
omnium argumentorum commonstret et ea breviter
163 illustret verbisque definiat. Quid enim est, in quo
haereat, qui viderit omne, quod sumatur in oratione

and these true professors of this art, there seemed
to me to be this difference,—that he surveyed these
concerns of the art of rhetoric, which he disdained,
with that same keen insight, by which he had discerned the essential nature of all things ; whereas
those others, considering this the only thing worth
cultivating, have dwelt upon the treatment of this
single subject, without his sagacity, but, in this one
instance, with larger practice and closer application.
161 As for Carneades, however, the extraordinary power
and diversity of his oratory would be extremely to
our liking ; since, in those debates of his he supported
no contention without proving it, and attacked none
which he did not overthrow.   But this is rather more
than should be asked of the authors and teachers of
these maxims.

162   XXXIX. " For my part, if just now I were to want
a complete novice trained up to oratory, I should
rather entrust him to these untiring people, who
hammer day and night on the same anvil at their one
and only task, for them to put into his mouth none
but the most delicate morsels—everything chewed
exceedingly small—in the manner of wet nurses
feeding baby-boys.   But should he, whom I have
had liberally educated in theory, and who by this
time has some tincture of practice, show also signs
of sufficient natural acuteness, I will hurry him off
to that source where no sequestered pool is land-
locked, but from it bursts forth a general flood ;
to that teacher who will point out to him the very
homes of all proofs, so to speak, illustrating these
163 briefly and defining them in terms.   For in what
respect could a speaker be at a loss, who has con-
templated everything to be employed in a speech,

The
doctrine of
'topics,'
which are
derived
either from
the case
itself or
from
without.

315

aut ad probandum aut ad refellendum aut ex sua
sumi vi atque natura aut assumi foris? Ex sua vi,
cum aut res quae sit tota quaeratur, aut pars eius
aut vocabulum quod habeat aut quippiam, rem illam
quod attingat; extrinsecus autem, cum ea, quae
sunt foris neque inhaerent in rei natura, colliguntur.

164 Si res tota quaeritur, definitione universa vis ex-
plicanda est, sic: 'si maiestas est amplitudo ac
dignitas civitatis, is eam minuit, qui exercitum hosti-
bus populi Romani tradidit, non qui eum, qui id

165 fecisset, populi Romani potestati tradidit.' Sin pars,
partitione, hoc modo: 'aut senatui parendum de
salute rei publicae fuit aut aliud consilium insti-
tuendum aut sua sponte faciendum; aliud consilium, superbum; suum, arrogans; utendum igitur
fuit consilio senatus.' Si ex vocabulo, ut Carbo:
'si consul est, qui consulit patriae, quid aliud fecit

166 Opimius?' Sin ab eo, quod rem attingat, plures
sunt argumentorum sedes ac loci, nam et coniuncta
quaeremus et genera et partes generibus subiectas
et similitudines et dissimilitudines et contraria et
consequentia et consentanea et quasi praecurrentia
et repugnantia et causas rerum vestigabimus et ea,

for purposes of either proof or disproof, or to be derived from the essential nature of the case, or adopted from without ? Intrinsic arguments, when the problem concerns the character of the subject as a whole, or of part of it, or the name it is to bear, or anything whatever relating to the subject ; extrinsic arguments, on the other hand, when topics are assembled from without and are not inherent in the nature of the case.

64 " If the problem concerns the whole subject, the general idea of it has to be made plain by definition ; for example : ' If sovereignty be the grandeur and glory of the State, it was violated by the man who delivered up to the enemy an army of the Roman People, not by him who delivered the man that did it into the power of the Roman People.' But if only a part is being dealt with, its nature must be explained by distribution, as follows : ' The right course, in a situation affecting the welfare of the State, was to obey the Senate, or to set up another advisory body, or to act on his own initiative : to set up another body would have been insolence, to follow his own counsel, arrogance ; therefore he should have taken the advice of the Senate.' If the argument turns on a word, remember Carbo's ' If a consul's duty is to consult the interests of his native land, what else has Opimius done ? ' If it turns on something correlated with the subject, the proofs come from several sources or common-places ; for we shall investigate connected terms, and general heads with their sub-divisions, and resemblances and differences, and opposites, and corresponding and concurrent circumstances, and so-called antecedents, and contradictories, and we shall track down the causes of

317

quae ex causis orta sunt, et maiora, paria, minora quaeremus.

167 XL. Ex coniunctis sic argumenta ducuntur : ' si pietati summa tribuenda laus est, debetis moveri, cum Q. Metellum tam pie lugere videatis.' Ex genere autem : ' si magistratus in populi Romani potestate esse debent, quid Norbanum accusas, cuius tribunatus voluntati paruit civitatis ? '

168 Ex parte autem ea, quae est subiecta generi : ' si omnes, qui rei publicae consulunt, cari nobis esse debent, certe in primis imperatores, quorum consiliis, virtute, periculis, retinemus et nostram salutem et imperii dignitatem.' Ex similitudine autem : ' si ferae partus suos diligunt, qua nos in liberos nostros 169 indulgentia esse debemus ! ' At ex dissimilitudine : ' si barbarorum est in diem vivere, nostra consilia sempiternum tempus spectare debent.' Atque utroque in genere et similitudinis et dissimilitudinis exempla sunt ex aliorum factis aut dictis aut eventis, et fictae narrationes saepe ponendae. Iam ex contrario : ' si Gracchus nefarie, praeclare Opimius.'

170 Ex consequentibus : ' si et ferro interfectus ille et tu inimicus eius cum gladio cruento comprehensus es in illo ipso loco et nemo praeter te ibi visus est et causa nemini et tu semper audax, quid est quod de facinore dubitare possimus ? ' Ex consentaneis et

things, and the effects proceeding from causes, and investigate things of relatively greater, equal or lesser significance.

167   XL. "An instance of proof deduced from connected terms is : ' If the highest praise is due to loyalty, you should be stirred at the sight of Quintus Metellus mourning so loyally.' One of deduction from a general term is : ' If the magistracies ought to be under the control of the Roman People, why impeach Norbanus, whose conduct as tribune was subservient to the will of the community ? '

168   "As a deduction from a subdivision of a general head take: ' If we are bound to esteem all who make the interests of the State their care, surely our commanders-in-chief stand foremost, by whose strategy, valour and hazards we preserve both our own security and the grandeur of our sovereignty.' Then, as a deduction from resemblance, we have : ' If the wild beasts cherish their young, what tenderness ought

169 we to bear to our children ! ' One from difference, on the other hand, is : ' If it be the mark of uncivilized folk to live but for the day, our own purposes should contemplate all time.' And, in cases involving both resemblance and difference, analogies are found in the deeds or the words or the fate of other people, and feigned tales must often be cited. Again, as a deduction from an opposite, take : ' If Gracchus did

170 wickedly, Opimius did nobly.' And, as one from corresponding circumstances : ' If he was killed by a sword, and you, his enemy, were caught on the very spot with a bloody blade, and none other than yourself was seen there or had any motive, and you were ever a man of violence, what doubt could we feel as to the crime ? ' And, to illustrate deduction

praecurrentibus et repugnantibus, ut olim Crassus adolescens : 'non si Opimium defendisti, Carbo, idcirco te isti bonum civem putabunt ; simulasse te et aliud quid quaesisse perspicuum est, quod Ti. Gracchi mortem saepe in contionibus deplorasti, quod P. Africani necis socius fuisti, quod eam legem in tribunatu tulisti, quod semper a bonis dissedisti.'

171 Ex causis autem rerum sic : 'avaritiam si tollere vultis, mater eius est tollenda, luxuries.' Ex eis autem, quae sunt orta de causis : 'si aerarii copiis et ad belli adiumenta et ad ornamenta pacis utimur,

172 vectigalibus serviamus.' Maiora autem et minora et paria comparabimus sic : ex maiore : 'si bona existimatio divitiis praestat et pecunia tantopere expetitur, quanto gloria magis est expetenda ?' ex minore :

> Hic parvae consuetudinis
> Causa huius mortem tam fert familiariter :
> Quid si ipse amasset ? quid hic mihi faciet patri ?

ex pari : 'est eiusdem et eripere et contra rem publicam largiri pecunias.'

173 Foris autem assumuntur ea, quae non sua vi, sed extranea sublevantur, ut haec : 'hoc verum est ; dixit enim Q. Lutatius.' 'Hoc falsum est ; habita enim quaestio est.' 'Hoc sequi necesse est ; recito

---

ᵃ P. Cornelius Scipio Africanus Minor, who captured Carthage 146 B.C., died in 129, probably from a stroke, but the Gracchans were suspected of assassination.

ᵇ Apparently extending the use of the ballot.

ᶜ From Terence, *Andria* 110-112.

from concurrent circumstances, antecedents and contradictories, we remember Crassus arguing in his youth : ' This tribunal, Carbo, is not going to deem you a patriotic citizen just because you defended Opimius : clearly you were only pretending, and had some other end in view, inasmuch as in your harangues you frequently lamented the death of Tiberius Gracchus, and you were a party to the murder of Publius Africanus,[a] and you brought in that statute[b] during your tribuneship, and always disagreed with the patriotic.' And a deduction from the causes of things is : ' If you would abolish covetousness, you must abolish its mother, profusion.' And one from the effects of causes is : ' If we are using the funds of the Treasury to aid war and beautify peace, let us become the slaves of taxation.' And, to show how we shall compare things of relatively greater, lesser and equal significance, a deduction from the greater is : ' If good repute is above riches, and money is so keenly desired, how far more keenly should fame be desired ? ' For one from the lesser take :

> Just for a slender acquaintance !
> So heartfelt his grief at her death !
> What had he loved her ? What sorrow
> Will he show for his father—for me ?[c]

For one from the equal we have : ' It is one and the same man's part to snatch the State's money and lavish it to her detriment.'

Finally, proofs adopted from outside are such as rest upon no intrinsic force of their own but upon external authority, instances being : ' This is true, for Quintus Lutatius said so ' : ' This evidence is false, for torture has been employed ' : ' This must

enim tabulas.' De quo genere toto paulo ante dixi.

174 XLI. Haec, ut brevissime dici potuerunt, ita a me dicta sunt. Ut enim si aurum cui, quod esset multifariam defossum, commonstrare vellem, satis esse deberet, si signa et notas ostenderem locorum, quibus cognitis ipse sibi foderet et id, quod vellet, parvulo labore, nullo errore, inveniret : sic has ego argumentorum novi notas, quae illa mihi quaerenti demonstrant, ubi sint; reliqua cura et cogitatione eruuntur.

175 Quod autem argumentorum genus cuique causarum generi maxime conveniat, non est artis exquisitae praescribere, sed est mediocris ingenii iudicare. Neque enim nunc id agimus, ut artem aliquam dicendi explicemus, sed ut doctissimis hominibus usus nostri quasi quaedam monita tradamus. His igitur locis in mente et cogitatione defixis et in omni re ad dicendum posita excitatis, nihil erit quod oratorem effugere possit, non modo in forensibus disceptationibus, sed omnino in ullo genere dicendi.

176 Si vero assequetur, ut talis videatur, qualem se videri velit, et animos eorum ita afficiat, apud quos aget, ut eos, quocumque velit, vel trahere vel rapere possit, nihil profecto praeterea ad dicendum requiret.

Iam illud videmus nequaquam satis esse, reperire
177 quid dicas, nisi id inventum tractare possis. Tractatio autem varia esse debet, ne aut cognoscat artem qui audiat aut defatigetur similitudinis satietate. Proponi

inevitably follow, for I am reading from the documents.' Of all this kind of thing I spoke just now.

174   XLI. "I have sketched these topics as shortly as possible. For if I wished to reveal to somebody gold that was hidden here and there in the earth, it should be enough for me to point out to him some marks and indications of its positions, with which knowledge he could do his own digging, and find what he wanted, with very little trouble and no chance of mistake: so I know these indications of proofs, which reveal to me their whereabouts when I am looking for them; all the rest is dug out by dint of careful consideration.

A brief treatment is enough, as attention and acumen will do more than theory.

175 But what type of proofs best befits each type of case needs not consummate art to dictate, but only ordinary talent to decide. For our immediate task is not to display any system of speaking, but to hand on to highly educated men certain lessons, as I may call them, learned from our own practice. Accordingly, with these commonplaces firmly established in his mind and memory, and roused into activity with every topic proposed for discussion, nothing will be able to elude the orator, either in our own contentions at the Bar, or in any department whatever of speaking. If however he shall succeed in appearing, to those before whom he is to plead, to be such a man as he would desire to seem, and in touching their hearts in such fashion as to be able to lead or drag them whithersoever he pleases, he will assuredly be completely furnished for oratory.

176

"Again, we see that the discovery of what to say is wholly insufficient, unless you can handle it when found. But the handling should be diversified, so that your hearer may neither perceive the art of it, nor be worn out by too much monotony. You ought

Variety of treatment essential.

77

oportet quid afferas et id qua re ita sit ostendere ; et
ex eisdem illis locis interdum concludere, relinquere
alias alioque transire; saepe non proponere ac ratione
ipsa afferenda quid proponendum fuerit, declarare ;
si cui quid simile dicas, prius ut simile confirmes,
deinde quod agitur, adiungas ; interpuncta argumentorum plerumque occulas, ne quis ea numerare possit, ut re distinguantur, verbis confusa esse
videantur.

178   XLII. Haec properans ut et apud doctos et semi-
doctus ipse percurro, ut aliquando ad illa maiora
veniamus.   Nihil est enim in dicendo, Catule, maius,
quam ut faveat oratori is, qui audiet, utque ipse sic
moveatur, ut impetu quodam animi et perturbatione,
magis quam iudicio aut consilio regatur.   Plura
enim multo homines iudicant odio aut amore aut
cupiditate aut iracundia aut dolore aut laetitia aut
spe aut timore aut errore aut aliqua permotione
mentis, quam veritate aut praescripto aut iuris norma
179 aliqua aut iudicii formula aut legibus.   Qua re,
nisi quid vobis aliud placet, ad illa pergamus.

    Paulum, inquit Catulus, etiam nunc deesse vi-
detur eis rebus, Antoni, quas exposuisti, quod sit
tibi ante explicandum, quam illuc proficiscare, quo
te dicis intendere. Quidnam ? inquit. Qui ordo
tibi placeat, inquit Catulus, et quae dispositio

to formulate your proposition, and give the reasons
for its being what it is; and from those same
commonplaces you should sometimes draw your conclusion, and sometimes abandon them to pass elsewhere; often it is better not to formulate expressly,
but to make it plain, by affirming the underlying
principle, what the formulation would have been;
if you are putting a parallel case to something, you
should first show how it is like, and then annex the
matter in hand; as a rule you should conceal the
intervals between successive proofs, to prevent them
from being counted, so that, though separate in fact,
they may seem blended in statement.

178   XLII. "I am running over these things in a hurry,
and like a half-trained man who is facing experts, in
order that we may come at last to those more essential
matters. Now nothing in oratory, Catulus, is more
important than to win for the orator the favour of his
hearer, and to have the latter so affected as to be
swayed by something resembling a mental impulse
or emotion, rather than by judgement or deliberation.
For men decide far more problems by hate, or love,
or lust, or rage, or sorrow, or joy, or hope, or fear, or
illusion, or some other inward emotion, than by
reality, or authority, or any legal standard, or judicial
179 precedent, or statute. And so, unless you think
differently, let us proceed to the things I spoke of."

    "Even now," returned Catulus, "there seems
to be a little something missing, Antonius, from
your exposition, which you should clear up, before
setting out for that region whither you say you
are bound." "Pray what is that?" asked the
other. "Your view as to the right arrangement
and distribution of proofs," said Catulus, "in which

Favour of audience must be secured.

Arrangement to be discussed later.

325

argumentorum, in qua tu mihi semper deus videri soles."

180 Vide quam sim, inquit, deus in isto genere, Catule: non hercule mihi, nisi admonito, venisset in mentem; ut possis existimare me in ea, in quibus nonnunquam aliquid efficere videor, usu solere in dicendo, vel casu potius incurrere. Ac res quidem ista, quam ego, quia non noram, sic tanquam ignotum hominem praeteribam, tantum potest in dicendo, ut

181 ad vincendum nulla plus possit; sed tamen mihi videris ante tempus a me rationem ordinis et disponendarum rerum requisisse. Nam si ego omnem vim oratoris in argumentis et in re ipsa per se comprobanda posuissem, tempus esset iam de ordine argumentorum, et de collocatione aliquid dicere. Sed cum tria sint a me proposita, de uno dictum, cum de duobus reliquis dixero, tum erit denique de disponenda tota oratione quaerendum.

182 XLIII. Valet igitur multum ad vincendum probari mores et instituta et facta et vitam eorum, qui agent causas, et eorum, pro quibus, et item improbari adversariorum, animosque eorum, apud quos agetur, conciliari quam maxime ad benevolentiam, cum erga oratorem tum erga illum pro quo dicet orator. Conciliantur autem animi dignitate hominis, rebus gestis, existimatione vitae; quae facilius ornari possunt, si modo sunt, quam fingi, si nulla sunt. Sed haec adiuvant in oratore: lenitas vocis, vultus pudoris

---

a See the opening of chapter xxxv., *supra.*

connexion your practice always strikes me as ideal."

"Observe, Catulus," came the answer, "how far I am ideal in that kind of thing : upon my word, but for your suggestion, the notion would never have entered my head : so that you may look upon me as generally running into those ways, in which now and then I seem effective, just in the course of speaking, or rather by accident. And indeed that factor which, through failure to recognize it, I was passing by unnoticed, as I might a human stranger, is second to none in the making of oratorical success, but, for all that, I think you have been premature in asking me for my theory of the arrangement and distribution of topics. For had I based the orator's essential power solely upon his proofs, and upon his establishing personally his actual case, it would now be the time to say a word as to the arrangement and marshalling of proofs. But since I have assumed three [a] elements in discovery and discussed only one of them, it will be time to conclude by investigating the arrangement of a speech as a whole, when I have first discussed the two elements that remain.

XLIII. "A potent factor in success, then, is for the characters, principles, conduct and course of life, both of those who are to plead cases and of their clients, to be approved, and conversely those of their opponents condemned ; and for the feelings of the tribunal to be won over, as far as possible, to goodwill towards the advocate and the advocate's client as well. Now feelings are won over by a man's merit, achievements or reputable life, qualifications easier to embellish, if only they are real, than to fabricate where nonexistent. But attributes useful in an advocate are a mild tone, a countenance expressive of modesty,

Means of securing favour of audience.

327

significatio,[1] verborum comitas ; si quid persequare
acrius, ut invitus et coactus facere videare. Facili-
tatis, liberalitatis, mansuetudinis, pietatis, grati animi,
non appetentis, non avidi, signa proferri perutile est ;
eaque omnia, quae proborum, demissorum, non acrium,
non pertinacium, non litigiosorum, non acerborum
sunt, valde benevolentiam conciliant abalienantque
ab eis, in quibus haec non sunt ; itaque eadem sunt in
183 adversarios ex contrario conferenda. Sed genus hoc
totum orationis in eis causis excellet, in quibus minus
potest inflammari animus iudicis acri et vehementi
quadam incitatione. Non enim semper fortis oratio
quaeritur, sed saepe placida, summissa, lenis, quae
maxime commendat reos. Reos autem appello non
eos modo, qui arguuntur, sed omnes, quorum de re
184 disceptatur ; sic enim olim loquebantur. Horum igitur
exprimere mores oratione, iustos, integros, religiosos,
timidos, perferentes iniuriarum, mirum quiddam valet ;
et hoc vel in principiis vel in re narranda vel in peroranda tantam habet vim, si est suaviter et cum sensu
tractatum, ut saepe plus quam causa valeat. Tantum
autem efficitur sensu quodam ac ratione dicendi, ut
quasi mores oratoris effingat oratio. Genere enim
quodam sententiarum et genere verborum, adhibita
etiam actione leni facilitatemque significante efficitur, ut probi, ut bene morati, ut boni viri esse
videantur.

[1] pudor[is significatio] *Bakius*.

gentle language, and the faculty of seeming to be dealing reluctantly and under compulsion with something you are really anxious to prove. It is very helpful to display the tokens of good-nature, kindness, calmness, loyalty and a disposition that is pleasing and not grasping or covetous, and all the qualities belonging to men who are upright, unassuming and not given to haste, stubbornness, strife or harshness, are powerful in winning goodwill, while the want of them estranges it from such as do not possess them; accordingly the very opposites of these qualities 33 must be ascribed to our opponents. But all this kind of advocacy will be best in those cases wherein the arbitrator's feelings are not likely to be kindled by what I may call the ardent and impassioned onset. For vigorous language is not always wanted, but often such as is calm, gentle, mild : this is the kind that most commends the parties. By ' parties ' I mean not only persons impeached, but all whose interests are being determined, for that was how people used the term 4 in the old days. And so to paint their characters in words, as being upright, stainless, conscientious, modest and long-suffering under injustice, has a really wonderful effect ; and this topic, whether in opening, or in stating the case, or in winding-up, is so compelling, when agreeably and feelingly handled, as often to be worth more than the merits of the case. Moreover so much is done by good taste and style in speaking, that the speech seems to depict the speaker's character. For by means of particular types of thought and diction, and the employment besides of a delivery that is unruffled and eloquent of good-nature, the speakers are made to appear upright, well-bred and virtuous men.

185 XLIV. Huic autem est illa dispar adiuncta ratio
orationis, quae alio quodam genere mentes iudicum
permovet, impellitque, ut aut oderint aut diligant
aut invideant aut salvum velint aut metuant aut
sperent aut cupiant aut abhorreant aut laetentur
aut maereant aut misereantur aut punire velint, aut
ad eos motus adducantur, si qui finitimi sunt et propinqui his[1] ac talibus animi perturbationibus.

Atque illud optandum est oratori, ut aliquam permo-
tionem animorum sua sponte ipsi afferant ad causam
iudices, ad id, quod utilitas oratoris feret, accommo-
186 datam. Facilius est enim currentem, ut aiunt, incitare
quam commovere languentem. Sin id aut non erit
aut erit obscurius, sicut medico diligenti, priusquam
conetur aegro adhibere medicinam, non solum morbus
eius, cui mederi volet, sed etiam consuetudo valentis
et natura corporis cognoscenda est.

Sic equidem cum aggredior ancipitem causam et
gravem, ad animos iudicum pertractandos, omni mente
in ea cogitatione curaque versor, ut odorer, quam
sagacissime possim, quid sentiant, quid existiment,
quid exspectent, quid velint, quo deduci oratione
187 facillime posse videantur. Si se dant et, ut ante dixi,
sua sponte, quo impellimus, inclinant atque propen-
dent, accipio quod datur et ad id, unde aliquis
flatus ostenditur, vela do. Sin est integer quietusque
iudex, plus est operis; sunt enim omnia dicendo

[1] sunt et propinqui his *Ellendt :* sunt de propinquis.

185 XLIV. "But closely associated with this is that dissimilar style of speaking which, in quite another way, excites and urges the feelings of the tribunal towards hatred or love, ill-will or well-wishing, fear or hope, desire or aversion, joy or sorrow, compassion or the wish to punish, or by it they are prompted to whatever emotions are nearly allied and similar to these passions of the soul, and to such as these.

"Another desirable thing for the advocate is that the members of the tribunal, of their own accord, should carry within them to Court some mental emotion that is in harmony with what the advocate's interest will suggest. For, as the saying goes, it is 186 easier to spur the willing horse than to start the lazy one. But if no such emotion be present, or recognizable, he will be like a careful physician who, before he attempts to administer a remedy to his patient, must investigate not only the malady of the man he wishes to cure, but also his habits when in health, and his physical constitution.

"This indeed is the reason why, when setting about a hazardous and important case, in order to explore the feelings of the tribunal, I engage wholeheartedly in a consideration so careful, that I scent out with all possible keenness their thoughts, judgements, anticipations and wishes, and the direction in which they seem likely to be led away most easily by eloquence. If they surrender to me, and as I said before, of their own accord lean towards and are prone to take the course in which I am urging them on, I accept their bounty and set sail for that quarter which promises something of a breeze. If however an arbitrator is neutral and free from predisposition, my task is harder, since everything has to be called

CICERO

excitanda, nihil adiuvante natura. Sed tantam vim
habet illa, quae recte a bono poeta dicta est ' flex-
anima atque omnium regina rerum,' oratio, ut non
modo inclinantem excipere aut stantem inclinare,
sed etiam adversantem ac repugnantem ut imperator bonus ac fortis capere possit.

188   XLV. Haec sunt illa, quae me ludens Crassus modo
flagitabat, cum a me divinitus tractari solere diceret
et in causa M'. Aquilii, Gaiique Norbani, non nullis-
que aliis quasi praeclare acta laudaret. Quae mehercule ego, Crasse, cum a te tractantur in causis,
horrere soleo : tanta vis animi, tantus impetus, tantus
dolor, oculis, vultu, gestu, digito denique isto tuo
significari solet ; tantum est flumen gravissimorum
optimorumque verborum, tam integrae sententiae,
tam verae, tam novae, tam sine pigmentis fucoque
puerili, ut mihi non solum tu incendere iudicem, sed
ipse ardere videaris.

189   Neque fieri potest, ut doleat is, qui audit, ut oderit,
ut invideat, ut pertimescat aliquid, ut ad fletum
misericordiamque deducatur, nisi omnes illi motus,
quos orator adhibere volet iudici, in ipso oratore
impressi esse atque inusti videbuntur. Quodsi
fictus aliquis dolor suscipiendus esset et si in eius
modi genere orationis nihil esset nisi falsum atque
imitatione simulatum, maior ars aliqua forsitan esset
requirenda. Nunc ego, quid tibi, Crasse, quid ceteris
accidat, nescio ; de me autem causa nulla est, cur

ᵃ *i.e.* Pacuvius, in his tragedy *Hermione.* See *Remains of Old Latin*, ii. pp. 232-233 (L.C.L.).

forth by my speech, with no help from the listener's character. But so potent is that Eloquence, rightly styled, by an excellent poet,[a] 'soulbending sovereign of all things,' that she can not only support the sinking and bend the upstanding, but, like a good and brave commander, can even make prisoner a resisting antagonist.

XLV. "These are the details for which Crassus was playfully importuning me just now, when he said that I always handled them ideally, and he praised what he called the brilliant treatment of them in the cases of Manius Aquilius, Gaius Norbanus and sundry others. Now I give you my word, Crassus, that I always tremble when these things are handled by yourself in Court : such is the mental power, such the passion, so profound the indignation, ever manifest in your glance, features, gesture, even in that wagging finger of yours ; so mighty is the flow of your most impressive and happy diction, so sound, true and original your sentiments, and so innocent of colouring-matter or paltry dye, that to me you seem to be not merely inflaming the arbitrator, but actually on fire yourself.

"Moreover it is impossible for the listener to feel indignation, hatred or ill-will, to be terrified of anything, or reduced to tears of compassion, unless all those emotions, which the advocate would inspire in the arbitrator, are visibly stamped or rather branded on the advocate himself. Now if some feigned indignation had to be depicted, and that same kind of oratory afforded only what was counterfeit and produced by mimicry, some loftier art would perhaps be called for. As things stand, Crassus, I do not know how it may be with yourself or the rest, but in my

success of Crassus in this.

The speaker must himself feel the emotions he wishes to excite;

apud homines prudentissimos atque amicissimos mentiar : non mehercule unquam apud iudices, aut
dolorem, aut misericordiam aut invidiam aut odium
dicendo excitare volui, quin ipse in commovendis
iudicibus eis ipsis sensibus, ad quos illos adducere
190 vellem, permoverer. Neque est enim facile perficere,
ut irascatur cui tu velis, iudex, si tu ipse id lente ferre
videare ; neque ut oderit eum, quem tu velis, nisi te
ipsum flagrantem odio ante viderit ; neque ad misericordiam adducetur, nisi tu ei signa doloris tui verbis,
sententiis, voce, vultu, collacrimatione denique ostenderis. Ut enim nulla materies tam facilis ad
exardescendum est, quae nisi admoto igni ignem
concipere possit, sic nulla mens est tam ad compre-
hendendam vim oratoris parata, quae possit incendi,
nisi ipse inflammatus ad eam et ardens accesserit.

191 XLVI. Ac, ne hoc forte magnum ac mirabile esse
videatur hominem toties irasci, toties dolere, toties
omni motu animi concitari, praesertim in rebus alienis,
magna vis est earum sententiarum atque eorum
locorum, quos agas tractesque dicendo, nihil ut opus
sit simulatione et fallaciis ; ipsa enim natura orationis eius, quae suscipitur ad aliorum animos per-
movendos, oratorem ipsum magis etiam quam quem-
192 quam eorum, qui audiunt, permovet. Et ne hoc in
causis, in iudiciis, in amicorum periculis, in concursu
hominum, in civitate, in foro accidere miremur, cum

own case there is no reason why I should lie to men of consummate experience, who are also my best friends : I give you my word that I never tried, by means of a speech, to arouse either indignation or compassion, either ill-will or hatred, in the minds of a tribunal, without being really stirred myself, as I worked upon their minds, by the very feelings to which I was seeking to prompt them. For it is not easy to succeed in making an arbitrator angry with the right party, if you yourself seem to treat the affair with indifference ; or in making him hate the right party, unless he first sees you on fire with hatred yourself ; nor will he be prompted to compassion, unless you have shown him the tokens of your own grief by word, sentiment, tone of voice, look and even by loud lamentation. For just as there is no substance so ready to take fire, as to be capable of generating flame without the application of a spark, so also there is no mind so ready to absorb an orator's influence, as to be inflammable when the assailing speaker is not himself aglow with passion.

XLVI. "Again, lest haply it should seem a mighty miracle, for a man so often to be roused to wrath, indignation and every inward emotion—and that too about other people's business—the power of those reflections and commonplaces, discussed and handled in a speech, is great enough to dispense with all make-believe and trickery : for the very quality of the diction, employed to stir the feelings of others, stirs the speaker himself even more deeply than any of his hearers. And, not to have us astonished at this happening in litigation, or before arbitrators, or in the impeachments of our friends, or among a crowd of people, or in political life, or

as he naturally will, considering his themes : examples.

agitur non solum ingenii nostri existimatio, (nam id
esset levius ;—quanquam, cum professus sis te id
posse facere, quod pauci, ne id quidem neglegendum
est) ; sed alia sunt maiora multo, fides, officium, diligentia, quibus rebus adducti, etiam cum alienis-
193 simos defendimus, tamen eos alienos, si ipsi viri boni
volumus haberi, existimare non possumus. Sed, ut
dixi, ne hoc in nobis mirum esse videatur, quid potest
esse tam fictum quam versus, quam scaena, quam
fabulae ? Tamen in hoc genere saepe ipse vidi, ut
ex persona mihi ardere oculi hominis histrionis vide-
rentur spondalia illa dicentis :

> segregare abs te ausu's aut sine illo Salamina ingredi,
> neque paternum aspectum es veritus?

Nunquam illum ' aspectum ' dicebat, quin mihi
Telamon iratus furere luctu filii videretur.   Ut idem
inflexa ad miserabilem sonum voce,

> quem aetate exacta indigem
> liberum lacerasti, orbasti, exstinxti ; neque fratris nccis,
> neque eius gnati parvi, qui tibi in tutelam est traditus?

flens ac lugens dicere videbatur.   Quae si ille
histrio, cotidie cum ageret, tamen agere sine
dolore non poterat, quid Pacuvium putatis in
scribendo leni animo ac remisso fuisse ? Fieri nullo
194 modo potuit. Saepe enim audivi poetam bonum
neminem—id quod a Democrito et Platone in scriptis

ᵃ These lines are from the *Teucer*, a tragedy of Pacuvius.
See *Remains of Old Latin*, ii. pp. 292-293 (L.C.L.).

public debate, when not only our talent is under criticism (no great matter, though even this should not be overlooked, when you have claimed a proficiency attained by few), but other and far more important attributes are on trial, I mean our loyalty, sense of duty and carefulness, under whose influence, even when defending complete strangers, we still cannot regard them as strangers, if we would be 93 accounted good men ourselves. However, as I said, not to have this seem a marvel among us, what can be so unreal as poetry, the theatre or stage-plays ? And yet, in that sort of things, I myself have often been a spectator when the actor-man's eyes seemed to me to be blazing behind his mask, as he spoke those solemn lines,[a]

Darest thou part from thy brother, or Salamis enter without him,
Dreading the mien of thy sire not at all ?

Never did he utter that word ' mien,' without my beholding an infuriated Telamon maddened by grief for his son. Whenever too he lowered his voice to a plaintive tone, in the passage,[a]

Aged and childless,
Didst tear and bereave and didst quench me, forgetting the death of thy brother,
Forgetting his tiny son, though entrusted to thee as a guardian ?

I thought I heard sobs of mourning in his voice. Now if that player, though acting it daily, could never act that scene without emotion, do you really think that Pacuvius, when he wrote it, was in a calm and careless frame of mind ? That could never be. For I have often heard that—as they say Democritus

relictum esse dicunt—sine inflammatione animorum
exsistere posse, et sine quodam afflatu quasi furoris.

XLVII. Qua re nolite existimare me ipsum, qui non
heroum veteres casus fictosque luctus vellem imitari
atque adumbrare dicendo, neque actor essem alienae
personae, sed auctor meae, cum mihi M'. Aquilius
in civitate retinendus esset, quae in illa causa pero-
195 randa fecerim, sine magno dolore fecisse. Quem
enim ego consulem fuisse, imperatorem, ornatum a
Senatu, ovantem in Capitolium ascendisse meminis-
sem, hunc cum afflictum, debilitatum, maerentem, in
summum discrimen adductum viderem, non prius
sum conatus misericordiam aliis commovere, quam
misericordia sum ipse captus. Sensi equidem tum
magnopere moveri iudices, cum excitavi maestum
ac sordidatum senem et cum ista feci, quae tu,
Crasse, laudas, non arte, de qua quid loquar nescio,
sed motu magno animi ac dolore, ut discinderem
196 tunicam, ut cicatrices ostenderem. Cum C. Marius
maerorem orationis meae praesens ac sedens multum
lacrimis suis adiuvaret, cumque ego illum crebro
appellans collegam ei suum commendarem atque
ipsum advocatum ad communem imperatorum for-
tunam defendendam invocarem, non fuit haec sine
meis lacrimis, non sine dolore magno miseratio,
omniumque deorum et hominum et civium et
sociorum imploratıo ; quibus omnibus verbis, quae a

---

a Aquilius was consul in 101 B.C. After suppressing the
Servile War in Sicily, he was prosecuted in 98 B.C. for extortion, but successfully defended by Antonius (*cf.* § 188).
  b Marius was consul for the fifth time in 101 B.C.

and Plato have left on record—no man can be a good poet who is not on fire with passion, and inspired by something very like frenzy.

XLVII. "Do not suppose then that I myself, though not concerned to portray and reproduce in language the bygone misfortunes and legendary griefs of heroes, and though presenting my own personality and not representing another's, did without profound emotion the things I did when closing that famous case,[a] in which my task was to 195 maintain Manius Aquilius in his civic rights. For here was a man whom I remembered as having been consul, commander-in-chief, honoured by the Senate, and mounting in procession to the Capitol ; on seeing him cast down, crippled, sorrowing and brought to the risk of all he held dear, I was myself overcome by compassion before I tried to excite it in others. Assuredly I felt that the Court was deeply affected when I called forward my unhappy old client, in his garb of woe, and when I did those things approved by yourself, Crassus—not by way of technique, as to which I know not what to say, but under stress of deep emotion and indignation—I mean my tear- 196 ing open his tunic and exposing his scars. While Gaius Marius, from his seat in court, was strongly reinforcing, by his weeping, the pathos of my appeal, and I, repeatedly naming him, was committing his colleague [b] to his care, and calling upon him to speak himself in support of the common interests of com- manders-in-chief, all this lamentation, as well as my invocation of every god and man, every citizen and ally, was accompanied by tears and vast in- dignation on my own part ; had my personal in- dignation been missing from all the talking I did

CICERO

me tum sunt habita, si dolor afuisset meus, non
modo non miserabilis, sed etiam irridenda fuisset
oratio mea. Quam ob rem hoc vos doceo, Sulpici,
bonus ego videlicet atque eruditus magister, ut in
dicendo irasci, ut dolere, ut flere possitis.

197 Quanquam te quidem quid hoc doceam, qui in
accusando sodali et quaestore meo tantum incendium
non oratione solum, sed etiam multo magis vi et dolore
et ardore animi concitaras, ut ego ad id restinguen-
dum vix conarer accedere? Habueras enim tum
omnia in causa superiora : vim, fugam, lapida-
tionem, crudelitatem tribuniciam in Caepionis gravi
miserabilique casu, in iudicium vocabas ; deinde
principem et senatus et civitatis, M. Aemilium, lapide
percussum esse constabat ; vi pulsum ex templo
L. Cottam, et T. Didium, cum intercedere vellent
rogationi, nemo poterat negare.

198 XLVIII. Accedebat, ut haec tu adolescens pro
re publica queri summa cum dignitate existimarere ;
ego, homo censorius, vix satis honeste viderer seditiosum civem et in hominis consularis calamitate
crudelem posse defendere. Erant optimi cives
iudices, bonorum virorum plenum forum, vix ut mihi
tenuis quaedam venia daretur excusationis, quod
tamen eum defenderem, qui mihi quaestor fuisset.
Hic ego quid dicam me artem aliquam adhibuisse ?

---

a i.e. Gaius Norbanus, who had been Antonius's quaestor
in 103 b.c. (*cf.* Book II, §§ 89, 107, 124). Q. Servilius
Caepio, as proconsul in Gaul, had been the main cause of
the crushing defeat inflicted upon the Roman army by the
Cimbri at Arausio. Being subsequently prosecuted and
condemned for his treason and embezzlement in Gaul, he
was exiled. Norbanus had been active in the proceedings
against him, and this led to the prosecution of Norbanus

340

on that occasion, my address, so far from inspiring compassion, would positively have deserved ridicule. And so I am telling you this, Sulpicius, as naturally such a kindly and accomplished teacher would do, in order to help you to be wrathful, indignant and tearful in your speech-making.

197 "But why indeed should I teach this to you, who, in prosecuting my comrade and quaestor,[a] had kindled such a blaze, not by eloquence only, but far more by vehemence, indignation and fiery enthusiasm, that I hardly ventured to draw near and put it out? For all the advantages in that case had been yours: you were citing to the Court the violence, the flight, the stone-throwing and the tribunes' ruthlessness that marked the disastrous and lamentable affair of Caepio; then too it was established that Marcus Aemilius, chief of Senate and chief of State, had been struck by a stone, while it was undeniable that Lucius Cotta and Titus Didius, on trying to veto a resolution, had been forcibly driven from sanctuary.

198 XLVIII. "In the result, while you, only a stripling, were thought to be conducting this public prosecution with consummate distinction, I, a past censor, was thought to be acting not quite honourably in bearing to defend a factious citizen, who moreover had been merciless to a past consul in distress. Citizens of the best repute formed the tribunal; men of respectability crowded the Court; so that I had difficulty in winning a grudging sort of acceptance of my plea that at any rate my client was my old quaestor. In these circumstances how can I say

himself by the aristocrats in 95 B.C., when Antonius conducted his defence, as here described.

Quid fecerim, narrabo ; si placuerit, vos meam defensionem in aliquo artis loco reponetis.

199 Omnium seditionum genera, vitia, pericula collegi, eamque orationem ex omni rei publicae nostrae temporum varietate repetivi, conclusique ita, ut dicerem, etsi omnes semper molestae seditiones fuissent, iustas tamen fuisse non nullas et prope necessarias. Tum illa, quae modo Crassus commemorabat, egi : neque reges ex hac civitate exigi, neque tribunos plebis creari, neque plebiscitis toties consularem potestatem minui, neque provocationem, patronam illam civitatis ac vindicem libertatis, populo Romano dari sine nobilium dissensione potuisse ; ac, si illae seditiones saluti huic civitati fuissent, non continuo, si quis motus populi factus esset, id C. Norbano in nefario crimine atque in fraude capitali esse ponendum. Quodsi unquam populo Romano concessum esset, ut iure concitatus videretur, id quod docebam saepe esse concessum, nullam illa causam iustiorem fuisse. Tum omnem orationem traduxi et converti in increpandam Caepionis fugam, in deplorandum interitum exercitus : sic et eorum dolorem, qui lugebant suos, oratione refricabam, et animos equitum Romanorum, apud quos tum iudices causa agebatur, ad

I used any particular technique ? What I did I will relate, if you think fit, you will give my line of defence some place or other in your system.

199   "I classified all the types of civil discord, their weaknesses and dangers, and that part of my speech I derived from all the vicissitudes in the history of our own community, winding up with the assertion that civil discords, though always troublesome, had yet sometimes been justifiable and well-nigh unavoidable. Next I discussed the considerations lately recalled by Crassus ; how that neither the expulsion of kings from this State, nor the establishment of tribunes of the commons, nor the frequent restriction of the consuls' power by decrees of the commons, nor the bestowal upon the Roman People of the right of appeal, that famous buttress of the State and defence of freedom, could any of them have been effected without aristocratic opposition ; and that, if those particular civil discords had been beneficial to our community, the mere fact of a popular movement having been caused must not instantly be counted against Gaius Norbanus for heinous wickedness and indeed a capital offence. That if rightfulness had ever been conceded to an incitement of the Roman People to sedition,—a concession which I was showing to have been frequent—, there had never been a juster cause than this one. After that I altered my course and turned my entire speech into a denunciation of the running-away of Caepio and a lament for the destruction of his army : in this way, besides chafing anew by my words the sores of people mourning for their own folk, I was kindling the feelings of the Roman Knights, who constituted the Court I was addressing, into fresh

Q. Caepionis odium, a quo erant ipsi propter iudicia abalienati, renovabam.

200   XLIX. Quod ubi sensi me in possessione iudicii ac defensionis meae constitisse, quod et populi benevolentiam mihi conciliaram, cuius ius etiam cum seditionis coniunctione defenderam, et iudicum animos totos vel calamitate civitatis vel luctu ac desiderio propinquorum vel odio proprio in Caepionem ad causam nostram converteram, tum admiscere huic generi orationis vehementi atque atroci genus illud alterum, de quo ante disputavi, lenitatis et mansuetudinis coepi : me pro meo sodali, qui mihi in liberum loco more maiorum esse deberet, et pro mea omni fama prope fortunisque decernere ; nihil mihi ad existimationem turpius, nihil ad dolorem acerbius accidere posse, quam si is, qui saepe alienissimis a me, sed meis tamen civibus, saluti existimarer fuisse,

201 sodali meo auxilium ferre non potuissem. Petebam a iudicibus, ut illud aetati meae, ut honoribus, ut rebus gestis, si iusto, si pio dolore me esse affectum viderent, concederent ; praesertim si in aliis causis intellexissent omnia me semper pro amicorum periculis, nihil unquam pro me ipso deprecatum. Sic in illa omni defensione atque causa, quod esse in arte positum videbatur, ut de lege Appuleia dicerem, ut quid esset minuere maiestatem explicarem, perquam breviter perstrinxi atque attigi. His duabus partibus orationis,

---

a Caepio in 106 B.C. had proposed to deprive the *equites* of their monopoly of the jury functions, and to have the tribunals composed of senators and *equites* in equal proportions.   *b* See Book II, § 107 n. *b*.

hatred of Quintus Caepio, from whom they had been estranged already over the composition of the criminal Courts.[a]

200   XLIX. " But when I felt I had a firm hold on the Court and on my line of defence, and I had won the goodwill of the public, whose claims I had upheld even when involved with civil discord, and I had turned all hearts on the tribunal in favour of my cause, by reason either of the national disaster, or of yearning grief for kindred, or of private hatred of Caepio, then I began to blend with this impetuous and violent type of oratory that other mild and gentle type, which I have already discussed, pleading that I was fighting for my comrade, who by ancestral tradition should stand in a filial relation to myself, and also (I might say) for my own fair fame and general welfare ; no happening could more deeply disgrace my reputation, or cause me more bitter sorrow, than for it to be thought that I, so often the saviour of complete strangers to myself, provided only they were my fellow-citizens, had been unable

201 to aid my own comrade.   I begged the Court, should they see me affected by justifiable and loyal grief, to excuse this in consideration of my years, official career and achievements, particularly if, in the course of other trials, they had observed that I always made my petitions on behalf of friends in jeopardy, never for myself.   Thus all through that speech for the defence, and indeed the trial itself, it was in the fewest possible words that I glanced over and lightly touched the matters which seemed dependent upon scientific treatment, I mean my discussion of the Statute of Appuleius,[b] and my exposition of the nature of treason.   By means of these two modes

quarum altera concitationem habet, altera commendationem, quae minime praeceptis artium sunt per-
politae, omnis est a me illa causa tractata, ut et
acerrimus in Caepionis invidia renovanda et in meis
moribus erga meos necessarios declarandis man-
suetissimus viderer. Ita magis affectis animis iudicum quam doctis, tua, Sulpici, est a nobis tum
accusatio victa.

202   L. Hic Sulpicius : Vere hercle, inquit, Antoni,
ista commemoras ; nam ego nihil unquam vidi, quod
tam e manibus elaberetur, quam mihi tum est elapsa
illa causa. Cum enim, quem ad modum dixisti, tibi
ego non iudicium, sed incendium tradidissem, quod
tuum principium, di immortales, fuit! Qui timor !
Quae dubitatio ! Quanta haesitatio tractusque verborum ! Ut illud initio, quod tibi unum ad ignoscendum homines dabant, tenuisti, te pro homine per-
necessario, quaestore tuo, dicere ! Quam tibi primum
203 munisti ad te audiendum viam ! Ecce autem, cum
te nihil aliud profecisse arbitrarer, nisi ut homines
tibi civem improbum defendenti ignoscendum propter necessitudinem arbitrarentur, serpere occulte
coepisti, nihildum aliis suspicantibus, me vero iam
pertimescente, ut illam non Norbani seditionem, sed
Populi Romani iracundiam neque eam iniustam, sed
meritam ac debitam fuisse defenderes. Deinde qui
locus a te praetermissus est in Caepionem ? Ut tu
illa omnia odio, invidia, misericordia miscuisti ! Neque
haec solum in defensione, sed etiam in Scauro ce-

of speech, the one inflammatory, the other eulogistic,
and neither of them much elaborated by rules of art,
I so managed the whole of that case as to seem most
passionate when reviving hatred of Caepio, and
mildest when describing my conduct towards my
own connexions. So, Sulpicius, it was rather by
working upon, than by informing, the minds of the
tribunal, that I beat your prosecution on that
occasion."

202   L. Here Sulpicius observed, " Upon my word, Sulpicius
Antonius, your account of those matters is true, for testifies to
never did I see anything slip through the fingers in success in
the way that verdict slipped that day through mine. the latter
For when (as you told us) I had left you with a con- case.
flagration rather than a case to dispose of,—ye Gods !
—what an opening you made ! How nervous, how
irresolute you seemed ! How stammering and halt-
ing was your delivery ! How you clung at the outset
to the solitary excuse everyone was making for you
—that you were defending your own familiar friend
and quaestor ! So, in the first place, did you prepare
203 the way towards getting a hearing ! Then, just as
I was deciding that you had merely succeeded in
making people think intimate relationship a possible
excuse for your defending a wicked citizen,—lo and
behold !—so far unsuspected by other people, but
already to my own serious alarm, you began to
wriggle imperceptibly into your famous defence, of
no factious Norbanus, but of an incensed Roman
People, whose wrath, you urged, was not wrongful,
but just and well-deserved. After that what point
against Caepio did you miss ? How you leavened
every word with hatred, malice and pathos ! And
all this not only in your speech for the defence, but

terisque meis testibus, quorum testimonia non refellendo, sed ad eundem impetum populi confugiendo
refutasti. Quae cum abs te modo commemora-
204 rentur, equidem nulla praecepta desiderabam; ipsam
tamen istam demonstrationem defensionum tuarum
abs te ipso commemoratam doctrinam esse non
mediocrem puto.

Atqui, si ita placet, inquit Antonius, trademus
etiam, quae nos sequi in dicendo quaeque maxime
spectare solemus; docuit enim iam nos longa vita
ususque rerum maximarum, ut quibus rebus animi
hominum moverentur teneremus.

205 LI. Equidem primum considerare soleo, postuletne
causa; nam neque parvis in rebus adhibendae sunt
hae dicendi faces neque ita animatis hominibus, ut
nihil ad eorum mentes oratione flectendas proficere
possimus, ne aut irrisione aut odio digni putemur, si
aut tragoedias agamus in nugis aut convellere adoria-
206 mur ea, quae non possint commoveri. Iam[1] quoniam
haec fere maxime sunt in iudicum animis, aut qui-
cumque illi erunt, apud quos agemus, oratione mo-
lienda, amor, odium, iracundia, invidia, misericordia,
spes, laetitia, timor, molestia, sentimus amorem conciliari, si id videare, quod sit utile ipsis, apud quos
agas, defendere, aut si pro bonis viris aut certe pro
eis, qui illis boni atque utiles sint, laborare. Namque
haec res amorem magis conciliat, illa virtutis defensio caritatem; plusque proficit, si proponitur spes
utilitatis futurae quam praeteriti beneficii com-
207 memoratio. Enitendum est, ut ostendas in ea re,

[1] Iam. *Madvig's correction for the inappropriate* Nam *of
the* MSS.

---

[a] Reading *aut si* for the *si aut* of the MSS.

also in your handling of Scaurus and the rest of my witnesses, whose evidence you rebutted by no disproof, but by fleeing for refuge to that same national 204 outbreak. When just now you were reminding us of these things, I certainly felt no need of any maxims, for that actual reproduction, in your own words, of your methods of defence is to my mind the most instructive of teaching."

" For all that," answered Antonius, " we will, if you please, go on to set forth the principles we generally adopt in speaking, and the points we chiefly keep in view : for a long career and experience in the most weighty affairs have taught us, by this time, to hold fast to the ways of stirring the feelings of mankind.

Rules and cautions for emotional oratory.

205 LI. " My own practice is to begin by reflecting whether the case calls for such treatment ; for these rhetorical fireworks should not be used in petty matters, or with men of such temper that our eloquence can achieve nothing in the way of influencing their minds, unless we would be deemed fit objects of ridicule, or even of disgust, as indulging in heroics over trifles, or setting out to uproot the immovable. 206 Now, since the emotions which eloquence has to excite in the minds of the tribunal, or whatever other audience we may be addressing, are most commonly love, hate, wrath, jealousy, compassion, hope, joy, fear or vexation, we observe that love is won if you are thought to be upholding the interests of your audience, or [a] to be working for good men, or at any rate for such as that audience deems good and useful. For this last impression more readily wins love, and the protection of the righteous esteem ; and the holding-out of a hope of advantage to come is more 207 effective than the recital of past benefit. You must

349

quam defendas, aut dignitatem inesse aut utilitatem,
eumque, cui concilies hunc amorem, significes nihil
ad utilitatem suam rettulisse ac nihil omnino fecisse
causa sua. Invidetur enim commodis hominum ipsorum, studiis autem eorum ceteris commodandi
favetur.

208   Videndumque hoc loco est, ne, quos ob benefacta
diligi volemus, eorum laudem atque gloriam, cui
maxime invideri solet, nimis efferre videamur. Atque
eisdem his ex locis et in alios odium struere discemus
et a nobis ac nostris demovere ; eademque haec
genera tractanda sunt in iracundia vel excitanda vel
sedanda. Nam si, quod ipsis, qui audiunt, perniciosum
aut inutile sit, id factum augeas, odium creatur ;
sin, quod aut in bonos viros aut in eos, in quos minime
quisque debuerit, aut in rem publicam, tum excitatur,
si non tam acerbum odium, tamen aut invidiae aut
209 odii non dissimilis offensio. Item timor incutitur aut
ex ipsorum periculis aut ex communibus : interior
est ille proprius, sed hic quoque communis ad eandem similitudinem est perducendus.

LII. Par atque una ratio est spei, laetitiae, moles-
tiae ; sed haud sciam an acerrimus longe sit omnium
motus invidiae nec minus virium opus sit in ea
comprimenda quam in excitanda. Invident autem
homines maxime paribus aut inferioribus, cum se
relictos sentiunt, illos autem dolent evolasse ; sed

struggle to reveal the presence, in the cause you are upholding, of some merit or usefulness, and to make it plain that the man, for whom you are to win this love, in no respect consulted his own interests and did nothing at all from personal motives. For men's private gains breed jealousy, while their zeal for others' service is applauded.

208 "And here we must be watchful, not to seem to extol unduly the merits and renown—jealousy's favourite target—of those whom we would have beloved for their good works. Then too, from these same commonplaces, we shall learn as well to instigate hatred of others as to turn it away from ourselves and our clients: and these same general heads are to be employed in kindling and also in assuaging wrath. For, if you glorify the doing of something ruinous or unprofitable to your particular audience, hate is engendered: while, if it be something done against good men in general, or those to whom the particular doer should never have done it, or against the State, no such bitter hate is excited, but a disgust 209 closely resembling ill-will or hate. Fear again is struck from either the perils of individuals or those shared by all: that of private origin goes deeper, but universal fear also is to be traced to a similar source.

LII. "The treatment of hope, joy and vexation Prevalence of jealousy is similar to this, and identical in each case, but I rather think that the emotion of jealousy is by far the fiercest of all, and needs as much energy for its repression as for its stimulation. Now people are especially jealous of their equals, or of those once beneath them, when they feel themselves left behind and fret at the others' upward flight; but jealousy

351

etiam superioribus invidetur saepe vehementer et
eo magis, si intolerantius se iactant et aequa-
bilitatem iuris praestantia dignitatis aut fortunae
suae transeunt; quae si inflammanda sunt, maxime
dicendum est non esse virtute parta, deinde etiam
vitiis atque peccatis, tum, si erunt honestiora atque
graviora, tamen non esse tanta illa merita, quanta
210 insolentia hominis quantumque fastidium.   Ad
sedandum autem, magno illa labore, magnis periculis
esse parta nec ad suum commodum, sed ad aliorum
esse collata; eumque si quam[1] gloriam peperisse
videatur, tamenetsi ea non sit iniqua merces periculi,
tamen ea non delectari totamque abicere atque
deponere; omninoque perficiendum est, quoniam
plerique sunt invidi maximeque hoc est commune
vitium et pervagatum, invidetur autem praestanti
florentique fortunae, ut haec opinio minuatur et
illa excellens opinione fortuna cum laboribus et
211 miseriis permixta esse videatur. Iam misericordia
movetur, si is, qui audit, adduci potest, ut illa,
quae de altero deplorentur, ad suas res revocet,
quas aut tulerit acerbas aut timeat, aut intuens alium crebro ad se ipsum revertatur.   Ita
cum singuli casus humanarum miseriarum graviter
accipiuntur, si dicuntur dolenter, tum afflicta et
prostrata virtus maxime luctuosa est.   Et, ut illa
altera pars orationis, quae probitatis commendatione

---

[1] *Piderit :* collataque suam.

of their betters also is often furious, and all the more
so if these conduct themselves insufferably, and
overstep their rightful claims on the strength of
pre-eminent rank or prosperity ; if these advantages
are to be made fuel for jealousy, it should before all
be pointed out that they were not the fruit of merit ;
next that they even came by vice and wrongdoing,
finally that the man's deserts, though creditable and
impressive enough, are still exceeded by his arro-
210 gance and disdain. To quench jealousy, on the other
hand, it is proper to emphasize the points that those
advantages were the fruit of great exertion and great
risks, and were not turned to his own profit but to
that of other people ; and that, as for any renown
he himself may seem to have won, though no unfair
recompense for his risk, he nevertheless finds no
pleasure therein, but casts it aside and disclaims
it altogether : and we must by all means make sure
(since most people are jealous, and this failing is
remarkably general and widespread, while jealousy
is attracted by surpassingly brilliant prosperity) that
the belief in such prosperity shall be weakened, and
that what was supposed to be outstanding prosperity
shall be seen to be thoroughly blended with labour
211 and sorrow. Lastly compassion is awakened if the Appeals to
hearer can be brought to apply to his own adversities, compassion.
whether endured or only apprehended, the lamenta-
tions uttered over someone else, or if, in his contemplation of another's case, he many a time goes
back to his own experience. Thus, while particular
occasions of human distress are deeply felt, if described in moving terms, the dejection and ruin of
the righteous are especially lamentable. And, just
as that other kind of style, which by bearing witness

boni viri debet speciem tueri, lenis, ut saepe iam
dixi, atque summissa, sic haec, quae suscipitur ab
oratore ad commutandos animos atque omni ratione
flectendos, intenta ac vehemens esse debet.

212 LIII. Sed est quaedam in his duobus generibus,
quorum alterum lene, alterum vehemens esse volumus, difficilis ad distinguendum similitudo. Nam et
ex illa lenitate, qua conciliamur eis, qui audiunt,
ad hanc vim acerrimam, qua eosdem excitamus,
influat oportet aliquid, et ex hac vi nonnunquam
animi aliquid inflammandum est illi lenitati; neque
est ulla temperatior oratio quam illa, in qua asperitas
contentionis oratoris ipsius humanitate conditur,
remissio autem lenitatis quadam gravitate et contentione firmatur.

213 In utroque autem genere dicendi, et illo, in quo vis
atque contentio quaeritur, et hoc, quod ad vitam et
mores accommodatur, et principia tarda sunt et
exitus tamen spissi et producti esse debent. Nam
neque assiliendum statim est ad genus illud orationis;
abest enim totum a causa, et homines prius ipsum
illud, quod proprium sui iudicii est, audire desiderant;
nec cum in eam rationem ingressus sis, celeriter
214 discedendum est. Non enim, sicut argumentum, simul
atque positum est, arripitur, alterumque et tertium
poscitur, ita misericordiam aut invidiam aut iracundiam, simul atque intuleris, possis commovere. Argumentum enim ratio ipsa confirmat, idque, simul atque

to the speaker's integrity is to preserve the semblance
of a man of worth, should be mild and gentle (as
I have repeatedly said already), so this kind, assumed
by the speaker in order to transform men's feelings
or influence them in any desired way, should be
spirited and emotional.

212   LIII. "But these two styles, which we require to Conciliatory style and unhurried treatment of emotional passages.
be respectively mild and emotional, have something
in common, making them hard to keep apart. For
from that mildness, which wins us the goodwill of
our hearers, some inflow must reach this fiercest of
passions, wherewith we inflame the same people,
and again, out of this passion some little energy
must often be kindled within that mildness : nor
is any style better blended than that wherein the
harshness of strife is tempered by the personal
urbanity of the advocate, while his easy-going mildness is fortified by some admixture of serious strife.

213   "Now in both styles of speaking, the one demanding passion and strife, and the other adapted to recommendation of the speaker's life and manners, the
opening of a speech is unhurried, and none the less
its closing should also be lingering and long drawn-
out. For you must not bound all of a sudden into
that emotional style, since it is wholly alien to the
merits of the case, and people long to hear first just
what is peculiarly within their own cognizance,
while, once you have assumed that style, you must
214 not be in a hurry to change it. For you could not
awaken compassion, jealousy or wrath at the very
instant of your onset, in the way that a proof is
seized upon as soon as propounded, and a second
and third called for. This is because the hearer's
mentality corroborates the proof, and no sooner is

emissum est, adhaerescit ; illud autem genus orationis non cognitionem iudicis, sed magis perturbationem requirit, quam consequi nisi multa et varia
et copiosa oratione, et simili contentione actionis,
215 nemo potest.   Quare qui aut breviter aut summisse
dicunt, docere iudicem possunt, commovere non
possunt ; in quo sunt omnia.

   Iam illud perspicuum est, omnium rerum in contrarias partes facultatem ex eisdem suppeditari locis.
Sed argumento resistendum est aut eis, quae comprobandi eius causa sumuntur, reprehendendis, aut
demonstrando, id, quod concludere illi velint, non
effici ex propositis nec esse consequens ; aut, si ita non
refellas, afferendum est in contrariam partem, quod
216 sit aut gravius aut aeque grave.   Illa autem, quae aut
conciliationis causa leniter, aut permotionis vehementer aguntur, contrariis commotionibus auferenda
sunt, ut odio benevolentia, misericordia invidia
tollatur.

   LIV. Suavis autem est et vehementer saepe utilis
iocus et facetiae ; quae, etiamsi alia omnia tradi
arte possunt, naturae sunt propria certe neque ullam
artem desiderant.   In quibus tu longe aliis mea
sententia, Caesar, excellis, quo magis mihi etiam
aut testis esse potes nullam esse artem salis aut,
si qua est, eam tu potissimum nos docebis.
217 Ego vero, inquit Caesar, omni de re facetius
puto posse ab homine non inurbano, quam de ipsis
facetiis disputari.   Itaque cum quosdam Graecos
inscriptos libros esse vidissem DE RIDICULIS, non-

it uttered than it is sticking in his memory, whereas
that passionate style searches out an arbitrator's
emotional side rather than his understanding, and
that side can only be reached by diction that is rich,
diversified and copious, with animated delivery to
215 match. Thus concise or quiet speakers may inform
an arbitrator, but cannot excite him, on which
excitement everything depends.

"By this time it is plain that the power to argue
both sides of every question is abundantly furnished
from the same commonplaces. But your opponents'
proof must be countered, either by contradicting the
arguments chosen to establish it, or by showing that
their desired conclusion is not supported by their
premisses and does not follow therefrom ; or, if you
do not so rebut it, you must adduce on the opposite
216 side some proof of greater or equal cogency. Lastly
appeals, whether mild or passionate, and whether
for winning favour or stirring the feelings, must be
swept aside by exciting the opposite impressions,
so that goodwill may be done away with by hate,
and compassion by jealousy.

Argument to be met by argument, appeal to emotion by exciting the contrary.

LIV. "Jesting too and shafts of wit are agreeable
and often highly effective : but these, even if all else
can be taught by art, are assuredly the endowment
of nature and in no need of art. To my mind, Caesar,
you far surpass all others in this field, so that you are
also the better able to bear me witness that no art
of pleasantry exists, or, if any such there be, you will
17 best teach it to us." "For my part," returned
Caesar, "I hold that a man with any tincture of
humour in him can discuss anything in the world
more wittily than actual witticisms. Thus, on seeing
sundry Greek books entitled *Concerning the Laughable,*

Employment of wit.

Wit a natural gift; its two kinds.

357

nullam in spem veneram posse me ex eis aliquid discere ; inveni autem ridicula et salsa multa Graecorum ; nam et Siculi in eo genere et Rhodii et Byzantii et praeter ceteros Attici excellunt ; sed qui eius rei rationem quandam conati sunt artemque tradere, sic insulsi exstiterunt, ut nihil aliud eorum 218 nisi ipsa insulsitas rideatur. Quare mihi quidem nullo modo videtur doctrina ista res posse tradi. Etenim cum duo genera sint facetiarum, alterum aequabiliter in omni sermone fusum, alterum peracutum et breve, illa a veteribus superior cavillatio, haec altera dicacitas nominata est. Leve nomen 219 habet utraque res ! quippe leve enim est totum hoc risum movere. Verum tamen, ut dicis, Antoni, multum in causis persaepe lepore et facetiis profici vidi. Sed cum illo in genere perpetuae festivitatis ars non desideretur (natura enim fingit homines et creat imitatores et narratores facetos, adiuvante et voltu et voce et ipso genere sermonis), tum vero in hoc altero dicacitatis quid habet ars loci, cum ante illud facete dictum emissum haerere debeat, quam cogitari 220 potuisse videatur ? Quid enim hic meus frater ab arte adiuvari potuit, cum a Philippo interrogatus quid latraret, furem se videre respondit ? Quid in omni oratione Crassus vel apud centumviros contra Scaevolam vel contra accusatorem Brutum, cum pro Cn. Planco diceret ? Nam id, quod tu mihi tribuis, Antoni, Crasso est omnium sententia concedendum. Non enim fere quisquam reperietur

---

a For Philippus see Index and Book I, § 24, *supra.* 'Catulus' of course is Latin for a little dog.

I entertained the hope of being able to learn something from them, and did indeed find much in Greek
life that was laughable and pungent, the inhabitants
of Sicily, Rhodes, Byzantium, and particularly Athens
having distinguished themselves in this kind of thing;
all however who tried to teach anything like a theory
or art of this matter proved themselves so conspicuously silly that their very silliness is the only laugh-
218 able thing about them. That is why I think that
this accomplishment cannot possibly be imparted by
teaching. For, there being two sorts of wit, one
running with even flow all through a speech, while the
other, though incisive, is intermittent, the ancients
called the former ' irony ' and the latter ' raillery.'
219 Each of these has a trivial name, but then of course
all this business of laughter-raising is trivial. For all
that, Antonius, as you remind me, I have very often
seen much done in Court by humour and flashes of
wit. But, while Art is not wanted in that continuous
sort of jocularity (since Nature moulds mankind, and
produces mimics and witty story-tellers, helped by
their features, intonation and individual style of
speaking), what room, pray, is there for Art in raillery,
that other sort, wherein the shaft of wit has to be
sped and hit its mark, with no palpable pause for
220 thought? For what help could my brother here Illustra-
have got from Art, when Philippus [a] inquired of him, tions of wit.
' What are you barking at, Master Puppy,' and he
answered, ' I see a thief ' ? Or what help could
Crassus have so got, all through his reply to Scaevola
before the Hundred Commissioners, or his defence of
Gnaeus Plancus, when prosecuted by Brutus ? In
fact, Antonius, the tribute you pay me ought, by
unanimous verdict, to be yielded to Crassus. For

praeter hunc in utroque genere leporis excellens,
et illo quod in perpetuitate sermonis, et hoc quod in
221 celeritate atque dicto est. Nam haec perpetua
contra Scaevolam Curiana defensio tota redundavit
hilaritate quadam et ioco ; dicta illa brevia non
habuit. Parcebat enim adversarii dignitati, in quo
ipse conservabat suam ; quod est hominibus facetis
et dicacibus difficillimum, habere hominum rationem
et temporum et ea, quae occurrant, cum salsissime
222 dici possint, tenere. Itaque nonnulli ridiculi homines
hoc ipsum non insulse interpretantur dicere [1] Ennium,
flammam a sapiente facilius ore in ardente opprimi,
quam bona dicta teneat ; haec scilicet bona dicta,
quae salsa sint ; nam ea dicta appellantur proprio
iam nomine.

LV. Sed ut in Scaevolam continuit ea Crassus
atque in illo altero genere, in quo nulli aculei con-
tumeliarum inerant, causam illam disputationemque
lusit, sic in Bruto, quem oderat et quem dignum
contumelia iudicabat, utroque genere pugnavit.
223 Quam multa de balneis, quas nuper ille vendiderat,
quam multa de amisso patrimonio dixit ! Atque
illa brevia, cum ille diceret se sine causa sudare,
'minime mirum,' inquit, 'modo enim existi de
balneis.' Innumerabilia talia fuerunt, sed non minus
iucunda illa perpetua. Cum enim Brutus duo lectores

---

[1] *Piderit :* dicere enim aiunt.

---

scarcely a single other speaker is to be found, who is outstanding in both kinds of humour, the one displayed all through a continuous discourse, the other
221 in instantaneous bons-mots. For that continuous speech, on behalf of Curius [a] and in reply to Scaevola, overflowed throughout with unmistakable mirth and jocularity ; of those sudden shafts it contained none. For the speaker was sparing his opponent's reputation, and in so doing was maintaining his own, because it is a most difficult thing for men given to wit and raillery to have regard to personages and occasions, and to refrain from making observations which suggest themselves, when these could be brought out
222 with most pungent effect. So true is this that sundry jesters explain it (shrewdly enough) as being exactly what Ennius speaks of, when he says that ' it is easier for a wise man to stifle a flame within his burning mouth than to keep words of worth to himself,' ' worth ' in this passage of course meaning ' pungency,' for such sayings are now known by a name of their own.

LV. " But although against Scaevola Crassus suppressed those shafts, and in fact romped through his argument and the whole of the trial in that other mode, which involved no stinging invective, yet when encountering Brutus, whom he detested and deemed deserving of invective, he fought in both modes.
223 How much he had to say about the baths then recently sold by his adversary, and about his wasted heritage ! Those repartees too ! as when Brutus declared himself to be sweating all for nothing and the other retorted ' Likely enough, for you are just ousted from your sweating-room ! ' Such shots were countless, but his continuous vein was just as pleasing. For

Skilful use of wit by Crassus.

excitasset et alteri de colonia Narbonensi Crassi orationem legendam dedisset, alteri de lege Servilia, et cum contraria inter sese de re publica capita contulisset, noster hic facetissime tres patris Bruti de 224 iure civili libellos tribus legendos dedit. Ex libro primo : 'FORTE EVENIT, UT IN PRIVERNATI ESSEMUS.' 'Brute, testificatur pater se tibi Privernatem fundum reliquisse.' Deinde ex libro secundo : 'IN ALBANO ERAMUS EGO ET MARCUS FILIUS.' 'Sapiens videlicet homo cum primis nostrae civitatis norat hunc gurgitem ; metuebat, ne, cum is nihil haberet, nihil esse ei relictum putaretur.' Tum ex libro tertio, in quo finem scribendi fecit—tot enim, ut audivi Scaevolam dicere, sunt veri Bruti libri—'IN TIBURTI FORTE ASSEDIMUS EGO ET MARCUS FILIUS.' 'Ubi sunt hi fundi, Brute, quos tibi pater publicis commentariis consignatos reliquit ? Quod nisi puberem te, inquit, iam haberet, quartum librum composuisset et se etiam in balneis lotum cum filio scriptum reliquisset.'

225 Quis est igitur, qui non fateatur, hoc lepore atque his facetiis non minus refutatum esse Brutum quam illis tragoediis, quas egit idem, cum casu in eadem causa funere efferretur anus Iunia ? Pro di

---

a For a boy of fourteen or more to bathe in his father's company was considered indecorous.

after Brutus had summoned a couple of readers, and
handed them a speech of Crassus apiece to recite,
one on the Narbonian settlement and the other on
the Statute of Servilius, and had himself noted some
inconsistencies in their accounts of affairs of State,
our friend here most humorously delivered to three
of these people for recital three pamphlets on the
224 common law by Brutus the elder. On an extract
from the first book, ' It chanced that we were in the
Privernian district,' his comment was, ' Brutus, your
father bears witness that he has bequeathed you an
estate at Privernum.' Next, at the citation from the
second book, ' I and my son Marcus were on the
Alban Hills,' he observed, ' See how a man as shrewd
as any in our community had discerned the nature of
this devouring gulf ; he was afraid that, when he had
nothing left, it might be thought that nothing had
been bequeathed to him.' Finally, on the words ' I
and my son Marcus happened to sit down together
on Tiburtine land ' being read out from the third and
concluding book (for I have heard Scaevola say that
the authentic volumes of Brutus are three in number), Crassus exclaimed, ' Where are these estates,
Brutus, which your father registered in his public
memoirs as bequeathed to you ? Why,' he went
on, ' had you not already turned fourteen, he would
have put together a fourth book, leaving it on record
that he had also washed in his son's company at
those baths ! ' [a]

25   "Who then would deny that this pleasantry and
these witticisms had as much to do with the repulse
of Brutus as those histrionics gone through by our
same friend when, during the same trial, it happened
that the aged Junia was carried forth in funeral pro-

immortales, quae fuit illa, quanta vis! quam inex-
spectata! quam repentina! cum coniectis oculis,
gestu omni ei imminenti, summa gravitate et celeritate verborum 'Brute, quid sedes? Quid illam
anum patri nuntiare vis tuo? quid illis omnibus,
quorum imagines duci vides? quid maioribus tuis?
quid L. Bruto, qui hunc populum dominatu regio
liberavit? Quid te agere? Cui rei, cui gloriae, cui
virtuti studere? Patrimonione augendo? At id non
est nobilitatis, sed fac esse, nihil superest; libi-
226 dines totum dissipaverunt. An iuri civili? est paternum. Sed dicet te, cum aedes venderes, ne in rutis
quidem et caesis solium tibi paternum recepisse. An
rei militari? Qui nunquam castra videris! An eloquentiae? quae nulla est in te, et, quicquid est vocis
ac linguae, omne in istum turpissimum calumniae
quaestum contulisti! Tu lucem aspicere audes? tu
hos intueri? tu in foro, tu in urbe, tu in civium esse
conspectu? Tu illam mortuam, tu imagines ipsas non
perhorrescis? quibus non modo imitandis, sed ne
collocandis quidem tibi locum ullum reliquisti.'

227 LVI. Sed haec tragica atque divina; faceta autem
et urbana innumerabilia ex una contione meministis.

ᵃ In Roman Law minerals already quarried and timber
already felled were deemed to be excepted from the sale of a
farm, unless expressly included.

cession? Ha! ye deathless gods! what boundless vigour he displayed! and how sudden and unlooked-for it was! when, with piercing gaze, with menace in his every motion, in the severest tones, and in a torrent of words he declaimed: 'Brutus, why seated? What news would you have that venerable dame carry to your sire? to all those whose busts you behold borne along? to your ancestors? to Lucius Brutus, who freed this community from the tyranny of the kings? What shall she tell them you are doing? What affairs, what glorious deeds, what worthy ends are you busied with? Is it increasing your heritage? That is no occupation for the nobly-born, but—assuming it were so—you have nothing left to increase; sensuality has squandered every shilling. Are you cultivating the common law, your father's field? Why, Junia will report that, on selling-up your home, you did not even reserve his arm-chair for yourself, along with the quarried minerals and felled timber! [a] Are you following a military career? You, who will never set eyes on a camp? Are you a devotee of eloquence? There is no spark of it about you, and any power you had of intonation or language you applied to making money by the foulest perversion of justice! Dare you behold the light of day? Or look upon this assembly? Or show yourself in Court, or within the City, or before the eyes of your fellow-citizens? Do not you tremble exceedingly at the spectacle of that dead lady? and of those same busts, you who have left yourself no room even for setting them up, much less for emulating their originals?'

LVI. "All this however was in the grand and inspired style, but you also recall a host of sparkling

365

Nec enim contentio maior unquam fuit, nec apud populum gravior oratio, quam huius contra collegam in censura nuper, neque lepore et festivitate conditior.

Quare tibi, Antoni, utrumque assentior, et multum facetias in dicendo prodesse saepe, et eas arte nullo modo posse tradi. Illud quidem admiror, te nobis in eo genere tribuisse tantum, et non huius rei quoque palmam, ut ceterarum, Crasso detulisse.

228 Tum Antonius : Ego vero ita fecissem, inquit, nisi interdum in hoc Crasso paulum inviderem : nam esse quamvis facetum atque salsum, non nimis est per se ipsum invidendum ; sed, cum omnium sit venustissimus et urbanissimus, omnium gravissimum et severissimum et esse, et videri, quod isti contigit uni, id mihi vix ferendum videbatur.

229 Hic cum arrisisset ipse Crassus, Attamen, inquit Antonius, cum artem esse facetiarum, Iuli, ullam negares, aperuisti quiddam, quod praecipiendum videretur. Haberi enim dixisti rationem oportere hominum, rei, temporis, ne quid iocus de gravitate decerperet ; quod quidem in primis a Crasso observari solet. Sed hoc praeceptum praetermittendarum est facetiarum, cum eis nihil opus sit ; nos autem quomodo utamur, cum opus sit, quaerimus, ut in adversarium, et maxime, si eius stultitia poterit agitari, in testem stultum, cupidum, levem, si facile

---

[a] *i.e.* Gnaeus Domitius Ahenobarbus.

witticisms from a single harangue. For never was there a more spirited effort, or a speech more effective with the public, than that of our friend here, not long since, against his colleague *a* in the censorship, or one better tempered with charm and gaiety.

"And so, Antonius, I grant both your points, first the great and frequent utility of witticisms in oratory, secondly the absolute impossibility of learning these from art. One thing certainly surprises me, and that is your ascribing so much success in this sphere to myself, instead of awarding the prize for this, as for all else, to Crassus."

228 "I should certainly have done so," answered Antonius, "were I not now and then a little envious of Crassus in this connexion; for merely to be as witty and shrewd as you please need not excite unmeasured envy, but that the most attractive and polished of all speakers should at the same time be obviously the most impressive and austere, as has been the lot of our friend alone,—this did seem rather more than I could bear."

229 Even Crassus smiled at this, and Antonius went on, "However, Julius, though you denied the existence of any art of pleasantry, you did just start something that seemed worth teaching. For you said that regard ought to be paid to personages, topics and occasions, so that the jest should not detract from dignity; Crassus of course always observes this principle as strictly as anyone. But it is a rule for the omission of uncalled-for witticisms, whereas we seek to know how to employ witticisms when wanted, —against an enemy, for instance, and most of all, if his stupidity can be ruffled, against a stupid, biased or unreliable witness, when people seem inclined to

230 homines audituri videbuntur. Omnino probabiliora
sunt, quae lacessiti dicimus, quam quae priores, nam
et ingenii celeritas maior est, quae apparet in respon-
dendo, et humanitatis est responsio. Videmur enim
quieturi fuisse, nisi essemus lacessiti, ut in ista ipsa
contione nihil fere dictum est ab hoc, quod quidem
facetius dictum videretur, quod non provocatus
responderit. Erat autem tanta gravitas in Domitio,
tanta auctoritas, ut, quod esset ab eo obiectum,
lepore magis elevandum, quam contentione frangen-
dum videretur.

231   LVII. Tum Sulpicius: Quid igitur? inquit, pa-
tiemur Caesarem, qui, quanquam Crasso facetias
concedit, tamen multo in eo studio magis ipse ela-
borat, non explicare nobis totum genus hoc iocandi,
quale sit, et unde ducatur; praesertim cum tantam
vim et utilitatem salis et urbanitatis esse fateatur?
Quid si, inquit Iulius, assentior Antonio dicenti,
232 nullam esse artem salis? Hic cum Sulpicius re-
ticuisset: Quasi vero, inquit Crassus, horum ipsorum, de quibus Antonius iamdiu loquitur, ars ulla
sit: observatio quaedam est, ut ipse dixit, earum
rerum, quae in dicendo valent; quae si eloquentes
facere posset, quis esset non eloquens? Quis enim
haec non vel facile, vel certe aliquo modo posset
ediscere? Sed ego in his praeceptis hanc vim et hanc
utilitatem esse arbitror, non ut ad reperiendum, quid
dicamus, arte ducamur, sed ut ea quae natura, quae
studio, quae exercitatione consequimur, aut recta esse
confidamus aut prava intellegamus, cum, quo re-

230 give him a ready hearing. The things we say when exasperated are altogether more persuasive than those we say in our first attack, as greater quickness of device is shown in retort, and to retort is human. For we give the impression that we should have remained quiet, had we not been exasperated, just as, in that identical harangue, our friend here said scarcely anything we thought particularly witty, which was not said by way of retort to a challenge. Yet there was such an air of worth and distinction about Domitius, that it seemed more fitting to make light of his charges by pleasantry than to shatter them by force."

231 LVII. "How now?" interposed Sulpicius, "shall we permit Caesar, who, though yielding precedence in wit to Crassus, yet toils far harder in that field himself, to deny us a complete exposition of this type of jesting, its nature and its sources, particularly as he recognizes such power and value in pleasantry and humour?" "But suppose," said Julius, "I agree with Antonius that no art of pleasantry exists?"

Practical rules for judging witticisms.

232 Sulpicius remaining silent, Crassus observed, "An art of these things which Antonius has been discussing all this time! a practice indeed there is, as he himself told us, of observing sundry conventions serviceable to speakers, but, if this practice could impart eloquence, who would fail to be eloquent? For who could not master these conventions, either readily or at any rate in some measure? However I hold the virtue and benefit of these maxims to lie in this : we do not discover what to say by artificial devices, but, after we have learned a true standard of comparison, they assure us of the soundness, or reveal to us the weakness, of whatever resources we

233 ferenda sint, didicerimus. Quare, Caesar, ego quoque a te hoc peto, ut, si tibi videtur, disputes de hoc
toto iocandi genere, quid sentias, ne qua forte dicendi
pars, quoniam ita voluistis, in hoc tali coetu, atque in
tam accurato sermone praeterita esse videatur. Ego
vero, inquit ille, quoniam collectam a conviva, Crasse,
exigis, non committam, ut, si defugerim, tibi causam
aliquam dem recusandi, quanquam soleo saepe mirari
eorum impudentiam, qui agunt in scena gestum,
spectante Roscio ; quis enim sese commovere potest,
cuius ille vitia non videat ? Sic ego nunc, Crasso
audiente, primum loquar de facetiis, et docebo sus,
ut aiunt, oratorem eum, quem cum Catulus nuper
234 audisset, ' foenum alios aiebat esse oportere.' Tum
ille : Iocabatur, inquit, Catulus, praesertim cum
ita dicat ipse, ut ambrosia alendus esse videatur.
Verum te, Caesar, audiamus, ut ad Antonii reliqua
redeamus. Et Antonius : Perpauca quidem mihi
restant, inquit ; sed tamen, defessus iam labore
atque itinere disputationis meae, requiescam in
Caesaris sermone quasi in aliquo peropportuno deversorio.

LVIII. Atqui, inquit Iulius, non nimis liberale
hospitium meum dices : nam te in viam, simul ac
235 perpaulum gustaris, extrudam et eiciam. Ac, ne
diutius vos demorer, de omni isto genere, quid sentiam, perbreviter exponam. De risu quinque sunt,

---

[a] Caesar refers to his forthcoming talk as if it were his
contribution to a feast.

[b] See Book I, lix.-lxi.

[c] Said to have tendered advice to the Goddess of Wisdom.
Compare the English proverb as to a grandchild giving its
ancestress hints on egg-sucking.

[d] As seeming but brute beasts in comparison with Crassus.

233 attain by native talent, study or practice. And so, Caesar, I too beg you, if you think proper, to discuss fully this type of jesting, and to state your views, lest haply one branch of oratory should be thought to have been passed over, with your approval, in such a company as this, and in a conversation so carefully elaborated." "Assuredly, Crassus," replied Caesar, "seeing that you are collecting a boon companion's 'shot,'[a] I will not run away and so give you any occasion for complaint, although I am generally amazed at the shamelessness of those who strut the stage under the very eye of Roscius[b]; for what man can so much as stir without that artist noticing his weak points? Just so I, with Crassus in my audience, am now going to discuss witticisms for the first time and, in emulation of the proverbial hog,[c] to instruct that orator of whom, after recently hearing him, Catulus declared that 'all
234 others ought to be fed on hay.'"[d] "Catulus was speaking in jest," returned Crassus, "and the more plainly so in that his own style seems to entitle him to heavenly sustenance. But let us hear you, Caesar, and come back afterwards to what Antonius has still in hand." "In fact I have very few things left to say," observed Antonius, "but in any case I am already worn-out by my long and toilsome debate, and shall repose, while Caesar is talking, as though in a most convenient roadside inn."

LVIII. "Well then," said Julius, "you will not call my hospitality unduly generous, for I shall thrust you forth and cast you out upon the road, directly
5 you have taken the tiniest taste of it. And now, to delay you no longer, I will very concisely state my views on that subject of yours in general. As

The laughable:

quae quaerantur : unum, quid sit ; alterum, unde
sit ; tertium sitne oratoris, velle risum movere ;
quartum, quatenus ; quintum, quae sint genera
ridiculi.

Atque illud primum, quid sit ipse risus, quo pacto
concitetur, ubi sit, quomodo exsistat, atque ita repente erumpat, ut eum cupientes tenere nequeamus,
et quomodo simul latera, os, venas, vultum, oculos
occupet, viderit Democritus : neque enim ad hunc
sermonem hoc pertinet ; et, si pertineret, nescire me
tamen id non puderet quod ne illi quidem scirent, qui
pollicerentur.

236 Locus autem, et regio quasi ridiculi (nam id pro-
xime quaeritur) turpitudine et deformitate quadam
continetur : haec enim ridentur vel sola, vel maxime,
quae notant et designant turpitudinem aliquam non
turpiter.

Est autem, ut ad illud tertium veniam, est plane
oratoris movere risum ; vel quod ipsa hilaritas benevolentiam conciliat ei, per quem excitata est ; vel
quod admirantur omnes acumen uno saepe in verbo
positum maxime respondentis, nonnunquam etiam
lacessentis ; vel quod frangit adversarium, quod
impedit, quod elevat, quod deterret, quod refutat :
vel quod ipsum oratorem politum esse hominem
significat, quod eruditum, quod urbanum, maximeque
quod tristitiam ac severitatem mitigat et relaxat,

---

a An eminent Greek physicist of the 5th century B.C.:
known as ' the laughing philosopher.'

regards laughter there are five matters for consideration : first, its nature ; second, its source ; third, whether willingness to produce it becomes an orator ; fourth, the limits of his licence ; fifth, the classification of things laughable.

" Now the first of these topics, the essential nature of laughter, the way it is occasioned, where it is seated, and how it comes into being, and bursts out so unexpectedly that, strive as we may, we cannot restrain it, and how at the same instant it takes possession of the lungs, voice, pulse, countenance and eyes,—all this I leave to Democritus [a] : for it does not concern the present conversation, and, even if it did, I should still not be ashamed to show ignorance of something which even its professed expositors do not understand. (1) its nature;

" Then the field or province, so to speak, of the laughable (this being our next problem), is restricted to that which may be described as unseemly or ugly ; for the chief, if not the only, objects of laughter are those sayings which remark upon and point out something unseemly in no unseemly manner. (2) its province;

" And again, to come to our third topic, it clearly becomes an orator to raise laughter, and this on various grounds ; for instance, merriment naturally wins goodwill for its author ; and everyone admires acuteness, which is often concentrated in a single word, uttered generally in repelling, though sometimes in delivering an attack ; and it shatters or obstructs or makes light of an opponent, or alarms or repulses him ; and it shows the orator himself to be a man of finish, accomplishment and taste ; and, best of all, it relieves dullness and tones down austerity, and, by a jest or a laugh, often dispels dis- (3) its rhetorical appropriateness;

236

odiosasque res saepe, quas argumentis dilui non
facile est, ioco risuque dissolvit.

237   Quatenus autem sint ridicula tractanda oratori,
perquam diligenter videndum est, id quod in quarto
loco quaerendi posueramus. Nam nec insignis im-
probitas, et scelere iuncta, nec rursus miseria insignis
agitata ridetur : facinorosos enim maiore quadam vi
quam ridiculi vulnerari volunt ; miseros illudi nolunt
nisi se forte iactant. Parcendum est autem maxime
caritati hominum, ne temere in eos dicas qui
diliguntur.

238   LIX. Haec igitur adhibenda est primum in iocando
moderatio. Itaque ea facillime luduntur, quae neque
odio magno, neque misericordia maxima digna sunt.
Quam ob rem materies omnis ridiculorum est in istis
vitiis quae sunt in vita hominum neque carorum
neque calamitosorum, neque eorum qui ob facinus
ad supplicium rapiendi videntur ; eaque belle agi-
239 tata ridentur. Est etiam deformitatis et corporis
vitiorum satis bella materies ad iocandum ; sed
quaerimus idem, quod in ceteris rebus maxime quaerendum est, quatenus. In quo non modo illud praecipitur, ne quid insulse, sed etiam, si quid perridicule
possis, vitandum est oratori utrumque, ne aut scurrilis
iocus sit, aut mimicus. Quae cuiusmodi sint, facilius
iam intellegemus, cum ad ipsa ridiculorum genera
venerimus.

tasteful suggestions not easily weakened by reasonings.

237   "But the limits within which things laughable are to be handled by the orator, that fourth question we put to ourselves, is one calling for most careful consideration. For neither outstanding wickedness, such as involves crime, nor, on the other hand, outstanding wretchedness is assailed by ridicule, for the public would have the villainous hurt by a weapon rather more formidable than ridicule; while they dislike mockery of the wretched, except perhaps if these bear themselves arrogantly. And you must be especially tender of popular esteem, so that you do not inconsiderately speak ill of the well-beloved. (4) limits of its use;

238   LIX. "Such then is the restraint that, above all else, must be practised in jesting. Thus the things most easily ridiculed are those which call for neither strong disgust nor the deepest sympathy. This is why all laughing-matters are found among those blemishes noticeable in the conduct of people who are neither objects of general esteem nor yet full of misery, and not apparently merely fit to be hurried off to execution for their crimes; and these blemishes, 239 if deftly handled, raise laughter. In ugliness too and in physical blemishes there is good enough matter for jesting, but here as elsewhere the limits of licence are the main question. As to this, not only is there a rule excluding remarks made in bad taste, but also, even though you could say something with highly comical effect, an orator must avoid each of two dangers: he must not let his jesting become buffoonery or mere mimicking. We shall more readily understand examples of each kind when we come to the actual classification of things laughable. (5) its objects classified

Duo enim sunt genera facetiarum, quorum alterum
240 re tractatur, alterum dicto. Re, si quando quid, tanquam aliqua fabella narratur ; ut olim tu, Crasse, in
Memmium, ' comedisse eum lacertum Largi,' cum
esset cum eo Tarracinae de amicula rixatus : salsa,
at tamen a te ipso ficta tota narratio. Addidisti clau-
sulam, tota Tarracina tum omnibus in parietibus
inscriptas fuisse litteras, LLL, MM ; cum quaereres
id quid esset, senem tibi quendam oppidanum dixisse
' Lacerat Lacertum Largi Mordax Memmius.'
241 Perspicitis, hoc genus quam sit facetum, quam ele-
gans, quam oratorium, sive habeas vere, quod narrare
possis, quod tamen est mendaciunculis aspergen-
dum, sive fingas. Est autem haec huius generis
virtus, ut ita facta demonstres, ut mores eius, de quo
narres, ut sermo, ut vultus omnes exprimantur, ut eis
242 qui audiunt, tum geri illa fierique videantur. In re
est item ridiculum, quod ex quadam depravata imitatione sumi solet ; ut idem Crassus : ' Per tuam
nobilitatem, per vestram familiam.' Quid aliud fuit,
in quo contio rideret, nisi illa vultus et vocis imitatio ? ' Per tuas statuas ' vero cum dixit, et extento
bracchio paululum etiam de gestu addidit, vehementius risimus. Ex hoc genere est illa Rosciana imitatio
senis : ' Tibi ego, Antipho, has sero,' inquit. Senium

---

[a] Gaius Memmius, a turbulent tribune of 111 B.C., against
whose ferocious character this jest of Crassus seems to be
levelled.

[b] This merriment may have been excited by an attack of
Crassus upon Domitius Ahenobarbus, who was possibly
disliked for his excessive family pride.

376

"For there are two types of wit, one employed upon
240 facts, the other upon words. Upon facts, whenever
any tale is told, some anecdote for instance, just as
you, Crassus, alleged one day, in a speech against
Memmius,[a] that Memmius 'had made a mouthful
of Largus's arm,' when brawling with him at Tarracina over a lady-love ; it was a spicy story, but every
word of your own fabrication. You wound up by
relating that the letters M.M.L.L.L. were inscribed
on every wall in Tarracina, and that some ancient in-
habitant answered, when you asked what they meant,
241 'Mordacious Memmius lacerates Largus's limb.' You
see plainly how graceful, choice and well befitting an
orator is a jest of this sort, whether you have some
truth you can relate,—which for all that may be
sprinkled with fibs,—or whether you are only fabri-
cating. Now the beauty of such jesting is, that you
state your incidents in such a way, that the character,
the manner of speaking and all the facial expressions
of the hero of your tale, are so presented that those
incidents seem to your audience to take place and
to be transacted concurrently with your description
242 of them. Another sort of jest depending on facts,
is that which is generally derived from what may be
called vulgarized mimicry, as when on another occasion, Crassus was adjuring an adversary in the words,
'By your rank, by your lineage!' What else had the
assembly to laugh at in this than that mimicry of
facial expression and intonation ? But when he went
on to say, 'By your statuary,' and lent a touch of
action to the word by stretching out his arm, we
laughed quite consumedly.[b] To this class belongs
Roscius's famous representation of an old man, when
he quavers out, 'For you, son Antipho, I'm planting

est, cum audio. Atqui ita est totum hoc ipso genere ridiculum, ut cautissime tractandum sit. Mimorum est enim ethologorum, si nimia est imitatio, sicut obscenitas. Orator surripiat oportet imitationem ut is qui audiet, cogitet plura, quam videat; praestet idem ingenuitatem et ruborem suum, verborum turpitudine et rerum obscenitate vitanda.

243 LX. Ergo haec duo genera sunt eius ridiculi, quod in re positum est; quae sunt propria perpetuarum facetiarum, in quibus describuntur hominum mores, et ita effinguntur, ut aut re narrata aliqua, quales sint, intellegantur, aut, imitatione brevi iniecta, in aliquo insigni ad irridendum vitio reperiantur.

244 In dicto autem ridiculum est id, quod verbi, aut sententiae quodam acumine movetur. Sed ut in illo superiore genere vel narrationis, vel imitationis, vitanda est mimorum ethologorum similitudo, sic in hoc scurrilis oratori dicacitas magnopere fugienda est. Qui igitur distinguemus a Crasso, a Catulo, a ceteris familiarem vestrum, Granium, aut Vargulam, amicum meum? Non mehercule in mentem mihi quidem venit: sunt enim dicaces; Granio quidem nemo dicacior. Hoc, opinor, primum, ne, quotienscumque 245 potuerit dictum dici, necesse habeamus dicere. Pusillus testis processit. ' Licet,' inquit, ' rogare ? '

ᵃ From a lost play.

these.' [a] I think I am listening to testy Eld personi-
fied. However this particular kind of laughing-
matter is all such as to need extreme circumspection
in the handling of it. For if the caricature is too
extravagant, it becomes the work of buffoons in
pantomime, as also does grossness. It behoves the
orator to borrow merely a suspicion of mimicry, so
that his hearer may imagine more than meets his
eye ; he must also testify to his own well-bred
modesty, by avoiding all unseemly language and
offensive gestures.

243   LX. "These then are the two kinds of the jesting
that is founded on facts ; and they are appropriate
to continuous irony, wherein the characters of individuals are sketched and so portrayed, that either
through the relation of some anecdote their real
natures are understood, or, by the infusion of a trifle
of mimicry, they are found out in some fault sufficiently marked to be laughed at.

The latter, wit of form, to be used sparingly.

244   "As regards words, however, the laughter is
awakened by something pointed in a phrase or reflection. But just as, with the former kind, both in
narrative and in mimicry, all likeness to buffoons in
pantomime is to be avoided, so in this latter case the
orator must scrupulously shun all buffoonish raillery.
How then shall we distinguish from Crassus, from
Catulus, and from the others, your familiar acquaintance Granius, or my own friend Vargula ? Upon my
word, I have never considered this matter, for all of
them are witty, none indeed more so than Granius.
The first point to make, I think, is that we should
not feel bound to utter a witticism every time an
245 occasion offers. A very small witness once came
forward. ' May I examine him ? ' said Philippus.

Philippus. Tum quaesitor properans: 'Modo breviter.' Hic ille: 'Non accusabis; perpusillum
rogabo.' Ridicule. Sed sedebat iudex L. Aurifex,
brevior ipse, quam testis etiam: omnis est risus in
iudicem conversus: visum est totum scurrile ridiculum. Ergo haec quae cadere possunt in quos nolis,
quamvis sint bella, sunt tamen ipso genere scurrilia.

246 Ut iste, qui se vult dicacem, et mehercule est, Appius,
sed nonnunquam in hoc vitium scurrile delabitur.
'Cenabo,' inquit, 'apud te,' huic lusco, familiari
meo, C. Sextio; 'uni enim locum esse video.' Est
hoc scurrile, et quod sine causa lacessivit; et tamen
id dixit quod in omnis luscos conveniret; ea, quia
meditata putantur esse, minus ridentur. Illud
egregium Sextii, et ex tempore: 'Manus lava,'
inquit, 'et cena.'

247   Temporis igitur ratio, et ipsius dicacitatis moderatio et temperantia et raritas dictorum distinguet
oratorem a scurra, et quod nos cum causa dicimus,
non ut ridiculi videamur, sed ut proficiamus aliquid,
illi totum diem et sine causa. Quid enim est Vargula
assecutus, cum eum candidatus A. Sempronius cum
Marco suo fratre complexus esset: 'Puer, abige
muscas?' Risum quaesivit, qui est, mea sententia,
vel tenuissimus ingenii fructus. Tempus igitur di-

    ͣ Apparently a reflection upon the self-invited guest's
probity. Compare the English legal maxim: 'He that
cometh to Equity must come with clean hands.'
    ᵇ Musca was a cognomen of the gens Sempronia, and is
also Latin for various winged insects. Vargula seems to
have intended a subtle comparison between humming and
biting insects and chattering and irritating canvassers.

The president of the Court, who was in a hurry, answered, ' Only if you are short.' ' You will not complain,' returned Philippus, ' for I shall be just as short as that man is.' Quite comical ; but there on the tribunal sat Lucius Aurifex, and he was even tinier than the witness : all the laughter was directed against Lucius, and the joke seemed merely buffoonish. And so those shafts which may light upon unintended victims, however featly they may be winged, are none the less essentially those of a 246 buffoon. For instance, that Appius, who tries to be witty, and egad ! succeeds, though occasionally slipping into this failing of buffoonery, said to my one-eyed friend here, Gaius Sextius, ' I will sup with you, for I see you have room for another one.' This is the joke of a buffoon, for he attacked unprovoked, and even so only said what would apply to every one-eyed individual. Jokes of that sort, as they seem to be thought out in advance, win but little laughter. The retort of Sextius was brilliant and spontaneous : ' Wash your hands,' says he, ' before supper.'[a]

247 "Regard then to occasions, control and restraint of our actual raillery, and economy in bon-mots, will distinguish an orator from a buffoon, as also will the fact that we people speak with good reason, not just to be thought funny, but to gain some benefit, while those others are jesting from morning to night, and without any reason at all. Thus, when Aulus Sempronius was on canvassing bent, along with Marcus his brother, and embraced Vargula, what good did it do Vargula to shout ' Boy, drive away these buzzers ? '[b] His object was to get a laugh—to my mind the very poorest return for cleverness. The

cendi prudentia et gravitate moderabimur : quarum
utinam artem aliquam haberemus ! sed domina natura est.

248   LXI. Nunc exponamus genera ipsa summatim,
quae risum maxime moveant. Haec igitur sit prima
partitio, quod facete dicatur, id alias in re habere
alias in verbo facetias : maxime autem homines
delectari, si quando risus coniuncte re verboque
moveatur. Sed hoc mementote, quoscumque locos
attingam, unde ridicula ducantur, ex eisdem locis fere
etiam graves sententias posse duci. Tantum interest,
quod gravitas honestis in rebus severe, iocus in tur-
piculis et quasi deformibus ponitur, velut eisdem
verbis et laudare frugi servum possumus, et, si est
nequam, iocari. Ridiculum est illud Neronianum
vetus in furaci servo, ' Solum esse, cui domi nihil sit
nec obsignatum, nec occlusum ' : quod idem in bono
249 servo dici solet, sed hoc eisdem etiam verbis. Ex
eisdem autem locis nascuntur omnia. Nam quod Sp.
Carvilio graviter claudicanti ex vulnere ob rempublicam accepto, et ob eam causam verecundanti in
publicum prodire, mater dixit, ' Quin prodis, mi
Spuri ? quotienscumque gradum facies, totiens tibi
tuarum virtutum veniet in mentem ' : praeclarum et
grave est. Quod Calvino Glaucia claudicanti, ' Ubi
est vetus illud : num claudicat ? at hic clodicat,'
hoc ridiculum est ; et utrumque ex eo, quod in

---

^a *Clodicare*, plebeian and rustic form of *claudicare*, *au*
being vulgarly pronounced *o*.

right occasion therefore for speaking out we shall
fix by our own wisdom and discretion : would that
we had some theory of the use of these qualities !
though intuition is the sovereign directress.

248   LXI. " Now let us summarize the essential natures Classifica-
of the chief sources of laughter. Let our first dis- tion of
verbal
tinction, then, be this, that a witty saying has its witticisms.
point sometimes in facts, sometimes in words, though
people are most particularly amused whenever
laughter is excited by the union of the two. But
remember this, that whatever subjects I may touch
upon, as being sources of laughing-matters, may
equally well, as a rule, be sources of serious thoughts.
The only difference is that seriousness is bestowed
austerely and upon things of good repute, jesting
upon what is a trifle unseemly, or, so to speak, uncouth ; for example, we can, in identical terms, praise
a careful servant, and make fun of one who is good-
for-nothing. There is humour in that old remark
of Nero's about a thievish servant, ' that he was
the only member of the household against whom
nothing was sealed up or locked away,' a description
frequently applied to a trusty servant also, and that
249 too word for word. In fact all kinds of remarks are
derived from identical sources. For his mother's
words to Spurius Carvilius, who was sadly lame from
a wound received on national service, and for that
reason shy of walking abroad, ' No no, my Spurius,
go out ! and let every step you take remind you
of your gallantry,' are noble and dignified. But
what Glaucia said to Calvinus, who was limping,
' Where is that old saying—Can he be hobbling ?
Nay, but he is wobbling,' [a] is merely absurd. Yet
both observations were derived from what the con-

claudicatione animadverti potuit, est ductum. ' Quid hoc Naevio ignavius?' severe Scipio. At in male olentem, ' Video me a te circumveniri,' subridicule Philippus. At utrumque genus continet verbi ad litteram immutati similitudo.

250 Ex ambiguo dicta vel argutissima putantur, sed non semper in ioco, saepe etiam in gravitate versantur. Africano illi superiori, coronam sibi in convivio ad caput accommodanti, cum ea saepius rumperetur, P. Licinius Varus, ' Noli mirari,' inquit, ' si non convenit : caput enim magnum est ' : laudabile et honestum. At ex eodem genere est : ' Calvus satis est, quod dicit parum.' Ne multa : nullum genus est ioci, quo non ex eodem severa et gravia sumantur.

251 Atque hoc etiam animadvertendum est, non esse omnia ridicula faceta. Quid enim potest esse tam ridiculum, quam sannio est ? Sed ore, vultu, imitandis moribus, voce, denique corpore ridetur ipso. Salsum hunc possum dicere, atque ita, non ut eiusmodi oratorem esse velim, sed ut mimum.

LXII. Quare primum genus hoc, quod risum vel maxime movet, non est nostrum : morosum, superstitiosum, suspiciosum, gloriosum, stultum ; naturae ridentur ipsae : quas personas agitare solemus, non

---

^a Professor Wilkins and others would sharpen the pun upon this name by substituting the less common form *Navius*.

^b This alleged joke seems to require the coinage of a word *hircumveniri*, *hircus* being Latin not only for " goat," but also for the very rank odour characteristic of that animal.

^c *Caput* is Latin for (1) a human cranium, (2) the Head of *e.g.* a body politic.

^d Baldness may be natural or metaphorical : the exact point of this pleasantry seems to have eluded the commentators.

templation of lameness might suggest. Scipio's pun,
'Is there an idler knave than this Naevius?'[a], was
intended for austerity. But there was a spark of
humour in the remark of Philippus to a malodorous
individual, 'I perceive that you are stinking me
out.'[b] Yet both kinds of pun lie in the verbal echo
that survives the change in a letter.

250 "Bons-mots prompted by an equivocation are (1) The
deemed the very wittiest, though not always con- ambiguous:
cerned with jesting, but often even with what is important. What Publius Licinius Varus said to the great
Africanus the elder, when he was adjusting a garland
to his head at a banquet, and it tore again and again,
was praiseworthy and creditable : 'Don't be astonished,' said he, 'if it does not fit, for it is on a Head
of vast capacity.'[c] Yet from the same category
comes, 'He is bald enough, seeing that he is bald
in diction.'[d] So, to bore you no further, there is
no source of laughing-matters from which austere
and serious thoughts are not also to be derived.

251 "There is also this to be noted, that all is not
witty that is laughable. For can there be anything
so droll as a pantaloon? Yet it is for his face, his
grimaces, his mimicry of mannerisms, his intonation,
and in fact his general bearing, that he is laughed
at. Humorous I am able to call him, but humorous
for a low comedian, and not in the sense in which I
would have an orator humorous.

LXII. "Accordingly this kind of wit, though raising as much laughter as any, is not at all our kind :
it caricatures peevishness, fanaticism, mistrust, pom-
posity and folly, characters which are laughed at for
their own sakes, masks which we do not put on, but

385

252 sustinere. Alterum genus est in imitatione admodum
ridiculum, sed nobis furtim tantum uti licet, si quando,
et cursim; aliter enim minime est liberale. Tertium,
oris depravatio, non digna nobis. Quartum, obscenitas, non solum non foro digna, sed vix convivio
liberorum. Detractis igitur tot rebus ex hoc oratorio
loco facetiae reliquae sunt, quae aut in re, ut ante
divisi, positae videntur esse aut in verbo. Nam quod,
quibuscumque verbis dixeris, facetum tamen est, re
continetur; quod mutatis verbis salem amittit, in
verbis habet leporem omnem.

253 Ambigua sunt in primis acuta atque in verbo posita,
non in re; sed non saepe magnum risum movent,
magisque ut belle et litterate dicta laudantur: ut in
illum Titium, qui, cum studiose pila luderet, et idem
signa sacra noctu frangere putaretur, gregalesque,
cum in Campum non venisset, requirerent, excusa-
vit Vespa Terentius, quod eum 'bracchium fregisse,'
diceret; ut illud Africani, quod est apud Lucilium :

Quid Decius? Nuculam an confixum vis facere? inquit.

Ut tuus amicus, Crasse, Granius, 'non esse sex-
254 tantis.' Et si quaeritis, is, qui appellatur dicax, hoc

---

a Was it his own or a holy statue's?
b The commentators are at fault here, for want of the
Lucilian context.
c Was he worth less or far more?

252 attack. Another kind, quite comical, consists in mimicry, but this we may employ only by stealth, if at all, and but momentarily, as fuller use of it does not befit the well-bred. A third kind is grimacing, which is beneath our dignity. A fourth is indecency, not only degrading to a public speaker, but hardly sufferable at a gentlemen's dinner-party. When all these modes, then, are withheld from this branch of oratory, the residue of wit depends apparently either on the facts or on the language, in accordance with the distinction I have already drawn. For the joke which still remains witty, in whatever words it is couched, has its germ in the facts ; that which loses its pungency, as soon as it is differently worded, owes all its humour to the language.

253 "The play upon equivocal words is particularly clever, and depends on language, not on facts ; but it seldom raises any considerable laughter, being chiefly praised as evidence of elegant scholarship : take, for example, that hit at the notorious Titius, who was devoted to ball-play and also under suspicion of mutilating the holy statues by night : when his associates missed him, as he had not come to the Playing Fields, Vespa Terentius apologized for his absence on the plea, 'He has broken an arm' [a] : or again, take the words of Africanus, preserved in Lucilius,

> "What of Decius? Do you wish to have Nucula spitted?"
>   said he. [b] !

Or you, Crassus, may take what your friend Granius

254 said, 'The man is not worth a farthing.' [c] And, if you wish to know, the jester who deals in so-called 'raillery' will chiefly shine in this kind of thing,

genere maxime excellet, sed risus movent alia
maiores. Ambiguum per se ipsum probatur id quidem, ut ante dixi, vel maxime ; ingeniosi enim
videtur vim verbi in aliud atque ceteri accipiant,
posse ducere ; sed admirationem magis quam risum
movet, nisi si quando incidit in aliud genus ridiculi.

255 LXIII. Quae genera percurram equidem. Sed
scitis esse notissimum ridiculi genus, cum aliud
exspectamus, aliud dicitur. Hic nobismet ipsis
noster error risum movet. Quod si admixtum est
etiam ambiguum, fit salsius : ut apud Novium videtur
esse misericors ille, qui iudicatum duci videns, per-
contatur ita : 'quanti addictus ?' 'Mille nummum.'
Si addidisset tantummodo : 'Ducas licet'; esset
illud genus ridiculi praeter exspectationem, sed quia
addidit : 'Nihil addo, ducas licet,' addito ambiguo,
altero genere ridiculi, fuit, ut mihi quidem videtur,
salsissimus. Hoc tum est venustissimum, cum in
altercatione arripitur ab adversario verbum, et ex eo,
ut a Catulo in Philippum, in eum ipsum aliquid, qui
256 lacessivit, infligitur. Sed cum plura sint ambigui
genera, de quibus est doctrina quaedam subtilior,
attendere et aucupari verba oportebit : in quo, ut ea

---

^a The piquant equivocation must lurk in 'nihil addo,'
which may mean, 'I say no more,' or (at an auction) 'I bid
no more.'

^b See the anecdote related supra, Book II, liv.

though other kinds raise louder laughter. Indeed
the play upon words wins really vast applause on its
own merits, as I said before, for the power to divert
the force of a word into a sense quite different from
that in which other folk understand it, seems to
indicate a man of talent ; yet the jest arouses wonder
rather than laughter, except when it also falls within
some other category of the laughable.

255   LXIII. " These categories I will certainly run over. (2) The
You know already, however, that the most familiar unexpected
of these is exemplified when we are expecting to (παρὰ προσ-
hear a particular phrase, and something different is δοκίαν);
uttered. In this case our own mistake even makes us
laugh ourselves. But, if there be also an admixture
of equivocation, the jest is rendered more pungent :
as, in that play of Novius, the man is apparently
moved by compassion when, on seeing a condemned
debtor taken away, he earnestly inquires the amount
of the judgement. He is told, ' A thousand sesterces.'
Had he then gone on to say merely, ' You may take
him away,' his rejoinder would have belonged to the
unexpected kind, but what he actually said was, ' No
advance from me ; you may take him away,' whereby
he brought in an element of equivocation, a different
category of the laughable, the result, in my opinion
at any rate, being piquancy in perfection.[a] This
playing on words is most delightful when, during a
wrangle, a word is snatched from an antagonist and
used to hurl a shaft at the assailant himself, as was
56 done by Catulus against Philippus.[b] But since
equivocation is of numerous kinds, and the teaching
as to these is somewhat abstruse, we shall have to
be watchful and lie in wait for the words : in this
way, while avoiding the feebler retorts (for we must

quae sint frigidiora, vitemus (etenim cavendum est,
ne arcessitum dictum putetur), permulta tamen acute
dicemus.

Alterum genus est, quod habet parvam verbi im-
mutationem, quod in littera positum Graeci vocant
παρονομασίαν, ut ' Nobiliorem, mobiliorem ' Cato ;
aut, ut idem, cum cuidam dixisset : ' Eamus deam-
bulatum ' : et ille : ' Quid opus fuit DE ? ' ' Immo
vero,' inquit, ' quid opus fuit te ? ' aut eiusdem responsio illa : ' Si tu et adversus et aversus impudicus
257 es.' Etiam interpretatio nominis habet acumen,
cum ad ridiculum convertas, quam ob rem ita quis
vocetur ; ut ego nuper Nummium divisorem, ut
Neoptolemum ad Troiam, sic illum in Campo Martio
nomen invenisse. Atque haec omnia verbo continentur.

LXIV. Saepe etiam versus facete interponitur, vel
ut est, vel paululum immutatus, aut aliqua pars
versus, ut Statius Scauro stomachanti : ex quo sunt
nonnulli, qui tuam legem de civitate natam, Crasse,
dicant :

St, tacete, quid hoc clamoris ? quibus nec mater, nec pater,
Tanta confidentia ? auferte istam enim superbiam.

Nam in Caelio sane etiam ad causam utile fuit tuum
illud, Antoni, cum ille a se pecuniam profectam

---

^a Fulvius Nobilior, consul in 189 B.C. Cato was evidently
attributing to him a certain instability of character.

^b Pyrrhus, son of Achilles, received the name of Neoptole-
mus, as being ' a new-comer to the (Trojan) war.' Caesar
facetiously derives the name ' Nummius ' from the coins
(*nummi*) which its bearer had distributed, in the course of
his duties as bribery agent at elections.

^c During the consulship of Crassus and Q. Mucius
Scaevola in 95 B.C. the *Lex Licinia Mucia de redigundis*

see to it that our bon-mot be not thought forced),
we shall still find ourselves delivering very many a
pointed remark.

"Another category, which uses a slight change in
spelling, the Greeks call 'assonance,' when the
variation is in a letter or two; for example, one
surnamed 'the Noble' [a] was referred to by Cato as
'the Mobile,' or again Cato said to a certain man,
'Let us go for a deambulation,' and, on the other
asking, 'What need of the "de—?",' Cato rejoined,
'Nay, rather, what need of thee?' or take that other
answer of the same Cato's, 'Whether you turn hither
257 or thither, you are filthy.' There is point also in the
explanation of a name, when you make fun of the
reason for a man being called as he is, as I said
the other day of Nummius, the voters' paymaster,
that he had found a name in the Election Field,[b] as
Neoptolemus had done at Troy. Now all such jests
hinge upon a word.

(3) play upon words or names;

LXIV. "Often too a verse, or some part of one, is
wittily introduced, either just as it stands or very
slightly varied, as when Statius quoted to an angry
Scaurus that passage from which, Crassus, some people
would have it that your own Nationality Act [c]
originated :—

(4) quotation of verses or proverbs;

> Hist! Silence! Why this din? Not overbold
> Should be the parentless! Have done with pride!

Doubtless, too, in the affair of Caelius, that jest of
yours, Antonius, helped your cause, when he gave
evidence of having parted with money and, as he

civibus was passed, apparently to prevent the usurpation of
Roman civic rights by Latins and Italians. The lines cited
seem to impute illegitimacy to the person or persons to
whom they were addressed.

diceret testis et haberet filium delicatiorem, abeunte
iam illo,

> Sentin senem esse tactum triginta minis ?

258 In hoc genus coniciuntur proverbia, ut illud Scipionis, cum Asellus omnes provincias stipendia
merentem se peragrasse gloriaretur, ' Agas asellum,'
et cetera. Quare ea quoque, quoniam mutatis verbis
non possunt retinere eandem venustatem, non in re,
sed in verbis posita ducantur.

259 Est etiam in verbo positum non insulsum genus ex
eo, cum ad verbum, non ad sententiam rem accipere
videare : ex quo uno genere totus est Tutor, mimus
vetus, oppido ridiculus. Sed abeo a mimis ; tantum
genus huius ridiculi insigni aliqua et nota re notari
volo. Est autem ex hoc genere illud, quod tu, Crasse,
nuper ei, qui te rogasset, num tibi molestus esset
futurus, si ad te bene ante lucem venisset : ' Tu
vero,' inquisti, ' molestus non eris.' ' Iubebis igitur
te,' inquit, ' suscitari ? ' Et tu : ' Certe negaram te
260 molestum futurum.' Ex eodem hoc vetus illud est,
quod aiunt Maluginensem illum Scipionem, cum
ex centuria sua renuntiaret Acidinum consulem
praecoque dixisset, ' Dic de L. Manlio ' ; ' Virum

---

[a] Antonius being prosecuted by Duronius on a charge of
corrupt practices, Caelius perhaps testified that he supplied
funds through his profligate son for use in bribery on behalf
of Antonius, whose defence may have insinuated that the
son obtained this money by a false pretence, and converted
it to his own use.

[b] *Asellus* is Latin for a little ass. The innuendo may be
that the boasted travels of Ti. Claudius Asellus were solely
attributable to compulsory military activity. The complete
saw is plausibly said to have been *Agas asellum ; cursum
non docebitur.*

had a rather voluptuous son, you remarked, on his leaving the witness-box,

> Seest thou the ancient, tapped for thirty pounds? [a]

258 " Old saws fall into this category, that for instance applied by Scipio, when Asellus was bragging that his military service had taken him all over every province ; whereupon Scipio quoted ' You may drive the ass's colt,' and the rest of it.[b] It follows moreover that such jests, since they must lose their charm directly the terms of expression are varied, should be regarded as depending on language, not on facts.

259 "There is another kind of joke, depending upon language and quite humorous, which proceeds from your seeming to understand an expression literally, and not in the sense intended : *The Guardian*, an ancient and exceedingly droll farce, was entirely made up of this sort of thing. But no more of farces ; I merely wish this type of laughing-matter to be illustrated by some prominent and familiar example. This too is the origin, Crassus, of your recent reply to the person who had asked you whether he would be a nuisance to you, if he were to visit you well before daylight : ' No,' you answered, ' you will not be a nuisance.' Upon this he said, ' Then you will give orders to call you ? ' And you rejoined, ' Surely I said you would not be a nuisance.'

(5) words taken literally;

260 From this same source comes that old pleasantry attributed to the famous Scipio Maluginensis, when announcing the vote of his own division to be for Acidinus as consul ; upon the crier demanding, ' What of Lucius Manlius ? ' Scipio replied, ' I take

bonum,' inquit, 'egregiumque civem esse arbitror.'
Ridicule etiam illud L. Nasica censori Catoni, cum
ille : ' Ex tui animi sententia tu uxorem habes ? '
'Non hercule,' inquit, 'ex mei animi sententia.'
Haec aut frigida sunt, aut tum salsa, cum aliud
est exspectatum.   Natura enim nos, ut ante dixi,
noster delectat error : ex quo, cum quasi decepti
sumus exspectatione, ridemus.

261   LXV. In verbis etiam illa sunt, quae aut ex immutata oratione ducuntur, aut ex unius verbi translatione, aut ex inversione verborum.   Ex immuta-
tione, ut olim, Rusca cum legem ferret annalem,
dissuasor M. Servilius : ' Dic mihi,' inquit, ' M. Pinari,
num, si contra te dixero, mihi male dicturus es, ut
262 ceteris fecisti ? '   ' Ut sementem feceris, ita metes,'
inquit.   Ex translatione autem, ut, cum Scipio ille
maior Corinthiis statuam pollicentibus eo loco, ubi
aliorum essent imperatorum, 'turmales' dixit 'dis-
plicere.'   Invertuntur autem verba, ut, Crassus apud
M. Perpernam iudicem pro Aculeone cum diceret,
aderat contra Aculeonem Gratidiano L. Aelius
Lamia, deformis, ut nostis ; qui cum interpellaret

---

a At the consular elections in the Comitia Centuriata,
voting being by centuries, the choice of each century was
reported to the presiding consul by its own spokesman.
Scipio, acting as one of these spokesmen, thought it humorous
wilfully to mistake the official question, as to his century's
decision on the candidature of L. Manlius Acidinus, for an
inquiry into his own personal opinion of the candidate.

b Bachelors were assessable to a special tax.   It is related

him for an honest man and a capital fellow-citizen.' *a*
Laughable again was the response of Lucius Nasica
to the interrogatory of Cato the censor, ' On your
conscience, are you satisfied that you are a married
man ? ' ' Married for certain,' returned Nasica, ' but
verily not to my entire satisfaction ! ' *b* Such jokes
may fall flat, being humorous only when some
different answer was expected. For, as I said before,
our own mistake naturally diverts us, so that, when
balked, as it were, of what we expected, we fall to
laughing.

261 LXV. " Jests dependent upon language further 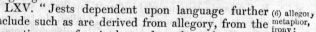(6) allegory
include such as are derived from allegory, from the metaphor,
figurative use of a single word, or from the ironical irony;
inversion of verbal meanings. Allegory as a source
was illustrated by Rusca long ago, in moving his
Limit of Age Bill,*c* when Marcus Servilius, an
opponent of the measure, said to him, ' Tell me,
Marcus Pinarius, if I speak against you, are you
going to revile me as you have done the others ? '
262 Rusca's reply was, ' You shall reap your sowing.'
Figurative use of one word occurred, for example,
when great Scipio the elder told the Corinthians,
who were promising him a statue among those of
the other commanders-in-chief, that ' he had no
liking for statues in troops.' And meanings were
ironically inverted when Crassus was representing
Aculeo before Marcus Perperna as arbitrator, and
Lucius Aelius Lamia, a cripple as you know, was for
Gratidianus against Aculeo, and kept on interrupting

that an unappreciative censor requited this untimely
pleasantry with temporary disfranchisement of the joker.
c Designed to fix a minimum age for candidates for any
political office.

odiose : ' Audiamus,' inquit, ' pulchellum puerum,'
Crassus. Cum esset arrisum, ' Non potui mihi,'
inquit Lamia, ' formam ipse fingere ; ingenium potui.'
Tum hic, ' Audiamus,' inquit, ' disertum.' Multo
etiam arrisum est vehementius.

Sunt etiam illa venusta, ut in gravibus sententiis,
sic in facetiis. Dixi enim dudum, materiam aliam esse
ioci, aliam severitatis ; gravium autem et iocorum
263 unam esse rationem. Ornant igitur in primis oratio-
onem verba relata contrarie, quod idem genus saepe
est etiam facetum, ut Servius ille Galba, cum iudices
L. Scribonio tribuno plebis ferret familiares suos, et
dixisset Libo, ' Quando tandem, Galba, de triclinio
tuo exibis ? ' ' Cum tu,' inquit, ' de cubiculo alieno.'
A quo genere ne illud quidem plurimum distat, quod
Glaucia Metello, ' Villam in Tiburte habes, cortem in
Palatio.'
264 LXVI. Ac verborum quidem genera, quae essent
faceta, dixisse me puto ; rerum plura sunt, eaque
magis, ut dixi ante, ridentur ; in quibus est narratio,
res sane difficilis ; exprimenda enim sunt et ponenda
ante oculos ea quae videantur et verisimilia, quod est
proprium narrationis, et quae sint, quod ridiculi pro-

---

a See Book II, lxi., *supra.*

b Although authority is scanty, it seems that, in certain
criminal proceedings, the defendant had the right to propose
a number of his judges, limited by a sufficient right of
challenge and exclusion on the part of the prosecution.

c Libo was his intending prosecutor on a charge of mis-
government.

d Libo evidently had a reputation for gallantry, in the
unenviable sense.

e The two properties would normally adjoin each other.
Glaucia seems to reflect upon the manners and morals of

vexatiously, until Crassus said, 'Let us hear the little beauty.' When the laughter at this had subsided, Lamia retorted, 'I could not mould my own bodily shape; my talents I could.' Thereupon Crassus remarked, 'Let us hear the eloquent speaker.' At this the laughter was far more uproarious.

"Such jests are delightful, whether the underlying thought be grave or gay. For I said before [a] that, though the fields of jesting and austerity lie wide apart, yet the methods of seriousness and jesting 263 are identical. So the opposition of verbal contra-dictories is one of the chief embellishments of diction, and this same device is often witty as well, as was shown by the well-known Servius Galba, when he was tendering to Lucius Scribonius, tribune of the commons, a list of his own cronies to serve on the tribunal,[b] and Libo [c] had commented, 'Galba, whenever will you go outside your own dining-room?' 'As soon as ever you come away from other people's bedrooms' was the reply.[d] To this kind of pleasantry Glaucia's words to Metellus bear some resemblance : 'You have your country-house at Tibur, your cattle-pen on the Palatine.' [e]

64 LXVI. "And now I think I have had my say re-garding the types of pleasantry which depend upon language. Those dependent upon facts are more numerous, and provoke heartier laughter, as I said before ; they include narrative, a really difficult sub-ject. For it must describe, and present to the mind's eye, such things as bear the semblance of truth, this being the peculiar function of narrative, and such also as are a trifle unseemly, this being the peculiar

the clients and hangers-on who thronged the town-house of Metellus.

(7) anti-thetical ex-pressions.

Wittiness of matter (*cf.* §§ 240 ff.): many varieties, especially—

prium est, subturpia : cuius exemplum, ut brevis-
simum, sit sane illud, quod ante posui, Crassi de
Memmio. Et ad hoc genus ascribamus etiam nar-
265 rationes apologorum ; trahitur etiam aliquid ex
historia, ut, cum Sex. Titius se Cassandram esse
diceret, ' Multos,' inquit Antonius, ' possum tuos
Aiaces Oileos nominare.'

Est etiam ex similitudine, quae aut collationem
habet aut tanquam imaginem : collationem, ut ille
Gallus olim testis in Pisonem, cum innumerabilem
Magio praefecto pecuniam dixisset datam, idque
Scaurus tenuitate Magii redargueret : ' Erras,'
inquit, ' Scaure ; ego enim Magium non conservasse
dico, sed tanquam nudus nuces legeret, in ventre
abstulisse ' ; ut ille M. Cicero senex, huius viri
optimi, nostri familiaris, pater, nostros homines
similes esse Syrorum venalium : ut quisque optime
Graece sciret, ita esse nequissimum.

266   Valde autem ridentur etiam imagines, quae fere in
deformitatem, aut in aliquod vitium corporis ducuntur cum similitudine turpioris : ut meum illud in
Helvium Manciam ' Iam ostendam cuiusmodi sis ' ;
cum ille ' Ostende, quaeso,' demonstravi digito
pictum Gallum in Mariano scuto Cimbrico sub Novis,

ᵃ See Book II, lix., *supra*.

ᵇ He meant that his prophecies of public disasters at Rome
had met with no more credit than those of Cassandra, King
Priam's daughter, at Troy, though they had proved as consistently true. After the fall of Troy the prophetess was
outraged by this Ajax. I follow Conington on *Aeneid* i. 46
in treating *Oileos* as a Greek genitive singular, not an accusa-
tive plural.

ᶜ The allegation is that the money has been squandered
in self-indulgence, after being received by Magius on behalf
of Piso, who is on trial for extortion.

function of joking ; as the shortest possible example
of this you may very well take Crassus's tale about
Memmius,[a] which I cited before. To this class we
265 may also refer the stories in the fables. Material is
derived too from history, as when Sextus Titius was
describing himself as a Cassandra,[b] and Antonius
commented, ' I can name many who played Ajax,
the son of Oileus, to your Cassandra.'

" Another source of such pleasantry is resemblance, comparison.
involving either comparison or something like por-
traiture. Comparison is illustrated by that Gallus,
who once upon a time gave evidence against Piso
that Piso's lieutenant Magius had received vast sums
of money, which testimony Scaurus was for contradicting by proving the straitened circumstances of
Magius, whereupon Gallus observed, ' You are
missing the point, Scaurus, for I do not assert that
Magius still has this fund, but that he has tucked it
away in his paunch, like a naked man who goes
nutting.' [c] To take another instance, the eminent
Marcus Cicero the elder, father of the best man of
our time, our own friend, said that our contemporaries
were like the Syrian slave-market : ' the better knowledge they had of Greeks, the more worthless were
their respective characters.'

266 " Caricatures also provoke loud laughter : as a rule caricature,
they are levelled against ugliness or some physical
defect, and involve comparison with something a little
unseemly ; an example was that remark of mine to
Helvius Mancia, ' I will now show what manner of
man you are,' to which he answered, ' Pray show
me,' whereupon I pointed out with my finger a Gaul
depicted on the Cimbrian shield of Marius,[d] which

[d] A shield captured by Marius in the Gallic War, 101 B.C.

399

distortum, eiecta lingua, buccis fluentibus ; risus est
commotus : nihil tam Manciae simile visum est ; ut
cum Tito Pinario mentum in dicendo intorquenti
' tum ut diceret, si quid vellet, si nucem fregisset.'

267   Etiam illa quae minuendi aut augendi causa ad
incredibilem admirationem efferuntur : velut tu,
Crasse, in concione, ' ita sibi ipsum magnum videri
Memmium ut in forum descendens caput ad for-
nicem Fabii demitteret.' Ex quo genere etiam
illud est quod Scipio apud Numantiam, cum
stomacharetur cum C. Metello, dixisse dicitur,
' si quintum pareret mater eius, asinum fuisse
parituram.'

268   Arguta est etiam significatio cum parva re et
saepe verbo res obscura et latens illustratur : ut,
cum C. Fabricio P. Cornelius, homo, ut existima-
batur, avarus et furax, sed egregie fortis, et bonus
imperator, gratias ageret quod se homo inimicus
consulem fecisset, bello praesertim magno et gravi :
' Nihil est quo mihi gratias agas,' inquit, ' si malui
compilari quam venire ' ; ut Asello Africanus, obi-

---

b The triumphal arch commemorating the success of
Fabius over the Allobroges was the loftiest so far erected in
Rome.
c Her four sons, of whom Gaius was the youngest,
apparently exhibited, in order of seniority, a diminuendo of
intelligence.
d Famous opponent of Pyrrhus and eminent type of the
old Roman morality.
e Better an extortionate magistrate than an incompetent

hung below the New Shops,[a] with the body twisted, the tongue protruding and the cheeks baggy : this raised laughter, for nothing so like Mancia was ever seen. Another instance was my telling Titus Pinarius, who kept twisting his chin when he was speaking, that the time for his observations, if he wished to say anything, would come when he had finished cracking his nut.

267 "Then again there are those intentional understatements or overstatements which are exaggerated to a degree of the astonishing that passes belief, such as your own assertion, Crassus, made in a speech before a public assembly, that Memmius thought himself so exalted an individual that, on his way down into the Market Place, he lowered his head in order to pass under the Arch of Fabius.[b] To this category also belongs the taunt said to have been uttered by Scipio at Numantia, when he was in a rage with Gaius Metellus, that ' if the mother of Metellus should bear a fifth time, she would be found to have borne an ass.'[c]

understatement,

268 "And a clever hint may be dropped when some hard and unintelligible saying is illuminated by some small detail, often by a word, as when Publius Cornelius, regarded as a covetous and dishonest man, but conspicuously brave and a competent military commander, thanked Gaius Fabricius[d] for having (though no friend of his) procured his election as consul, and that too in the course of an important and troublesome war. ' No need to thank me,' replied the other, ' for choosing to be plundered rather than sold into bondage.'[e] Compare with this the retort of

general, who would probably lead his followers to defeat, capture and the ancient fate of prisoners of war.

cienti lustrum illud infelix, ' Noli,' inquit, ' mirari ; is
enim qui te ex aerariis exemit lustrum condidit et
taurum immolavit.' [Tanta suspicio est ut religione
civitatem obstrinxisse videatur Mummius quod
Asellum ignominia levarit.]

269 LXVII. Urbana etiam dissimulatio est, cum alia
dicuntur ac sentias, non illo genere de quo ante dixi,
cum contraria dicas, ut Lamiae Crassus, sed cum
toto genere orationis severe ludas, cum aliter sentias ac loquare : ut noster Scaevola Septumuleio illi
Anagnino, cui pro C. Gracchi capite erat aurum
repensum, roganti ut se in Asiam praefectum duceret,
' Quid tibi vis,' inquit, ' insane ? tanta malorum est
multitudo civium ut tibi ego hoc confirmem, si Romae
manseris, te paucis annis ad maximas pecunias esse
270 venturum.'   In hoc genere Fannius in Annalibus suis
Africanum hunc Aemilianum dicit fuisse egregium et
Graeco eum verbo appellat εἴρωνα : sed, uti ferunt
qui melius haec norunt, Socratem opinor in hac ironia
dissimulantiaque longe lepore et humanitate omnibus
praestitisse.   Genus est perelegans et cum gravitate
salsum, cumque oratoriis dictionibus tum urbanis
271 sermonibus accommodatum.   Et hercule omnia haec
quae a me de facetiis disputantur non maiora forensium actionum quam omnium sermonum condimenta

---

ᵃ Africanus, as censor, in reciting the valedictory prayers
at the census, had taken a serious liberty with the ritual text.
ᵇ Africanus, as censor, had degraded Asellus to the class
of voteless taxpayers, but his colleague Mummius had refused
his necessary concurrence, and had thereby restored the
status quo of Asellus. Africanus suggests that this action of
Mummius left a taint upon the community.
ᶜ The bracketed passage is commonly regarded as a gloss.
ᵈ See Book II, lxv., *supra.*

Africanus, when Asellus taxed him with that unfortunate purification of his.[a] 'Do not be surprised,' said Africanus, 'for he who delivered you from disfranchisement completed the purification by sacrificing the bull.'[b] [So strong is mistrust that Mummius is thought to have laid the community under a religious obligation by having relieved Asellus from degradation.][c]

269 LXVII. "Irony too gives pleasure, when your words irony, differ from your thoughts, not in the way of which I spoke earlier, when you assert exactly the contradictory, as Crassus did to Lamia,[d] but when the whole tenor of your speech shows you to be solemnly jesting, what you think differing continuously from what you say ; as our friend Scaevola observed to the notorious Septumuleius of Anagnia (to whom its weight in gold had been paid for the head of Gaius Gracchus), when he prayed to be taken into Asia as his lieutenant, 'Madman,' said Scaevola, 'what would you have ? There is such a host of wicked citizens in Rome that I guarantee you, if you remain there, the attainment, 70 within a few years, of enormous wealth.' Fannius in his 'Chronicles' records that Africanus (the one named Aemilianus) was outstanding in this kind of thing, and describes him by the Greek word 'dissembler,' but, upon the evidence of those who know these subjects better than I do, my opinion is that Socrates far surpassed all others for accomplished wit in this strain of irony or assumed simplicity. This is a choice variety of humour and blended with austerity, and suited to public speaking as well as to 1 the conversation of gentlemen. And I vow that all this discourse of mine concerning types of pleasantry is as excellent sauce for general talk as for legal

sunt. Nam sicut quod apud Catonem est—qui multa
rettulit, ex quibus a me exempli causa multa ponun-
tur—per mihi scitum videtur, C. Publicium solitum
dicere, ' P. Mummium cuivis tempori hominem esse.'
Sic profecto res se habet nullum ut sit vitae tempus
in quo non deceat leporem humanitatemque versari.
Sed redeo ad cetera.

272 Est huic finitimum dissimulationi cum honesto
verbo vitiosa res appellatur : ut cum Africanus
censor tribu movebat eum centurionem qui in Pauli
pugna non adfuerat, cum ille se custodiae causa
diceret in castris remansisse quaereretque cur ab eo
notaretur, ' Non amo,' inquit, ' nimium diligentes.'

273 Acutum etiam illud est cum ex alterius oratione
aliud excipias atque ille vult ; ut Salinatori Maximus
cum Tarento amisso arcem tamen Livius retinuis-
set multaque ex ea proelia praeclara fecisset, cum
aliquot post annos Maximus id oppidum recepisset,
rogaretque eum Salinator ut meminisset opera sua se
Tarentum recepisse ; ' Quidni,' inquit, ' meminerim?
nunquam ego recepissem nisi tu perdidisses.'

274 Sunt etiam illa subabsurda, sed eo ipso nomine
saepe ridicula, non solum mimis perapposita, sed
etiam quodammodo nobis :

---

^a The victory over Perseus at Pydna in 168 B.C.
^b Quintus Fabius Maximus.
^c Marcus Livius Salinator, this cognomen being probably
a mistake of Cicero's for Macatus.

advocacy. For that phrase of Cato, who has recorded many such, several of which I cite in illustration, seems to me thoroughly fine, where he says that Gaius Publicius was fond of describing Publius Mummius as 'a man for any occasion whatever.' So certain is it, in the present connexion, that there is no occasion in life on which accomplished wit may not fittingly be displayed. But I return to what remains for my notice.

272 " A jest very closely resembles this ironical type when something disgraceful is called by an honourable epithet, as happened when Africanus as censor removed from his tribe that centurion who failed to appear at the battle [a] fought under Paulus, though the defaulter pleaded that he had stayed in camp on guard, and sought to know why he was degraded by the censor : ' I am no lover of the over-cautious,' was 273 the answer of Africanus. There is point too in taking some part of another's words in a sense differing from that which he intended, as Maximus [b] did with Salinator [c] when, after the loss of Tarentum, Livius had nevertheless held the citadel, and made a number of brilliant sallies from it, and Fabius, several years later, recaptured the town itself, whereupon Livius begged him to remember that the recapture of Tarentum had been due to his own achievement. ' To be sure, I shall remember that,' rejoined Fabius. ' I could never have recaptured the place had you not lost it.'

74 " Then there are jokes which are somewhat absurd, farcical but for that very reason often comical, and which jests, are appropriate not only to actors in farce, but also in some degree to us orators : examples of these are :

. . . Homo fatuus
Postquam rem habere coepit est emortuus.

Et

. . . Quid est tibi
Ista mulier ? — Uxor. — Similis me dius fidius.

Et

Quamdiu ad aquas fuit, nunquam est emortuus.

LXVIII. Genus hoc levius, et, ut dixi, mimicum,
sed habet nonnunquam aliquid etiam apud nos loci,
ut vel non stultus quasi stulte cum sale dicat aliquid :
ut tibi, Antoni, Mancia, cum audisset te censorem a
M. Duronio de ambitu postulatum, 'Aliquando,'
275 inquit, 'tibi tuum negotium agere licebit.' Valde
haec ridentur, et hercule omnia, quae a prudentibus
[quasi] per dissimulationem [non intellegendi] sub-
absurde salseque dicuntur. Ex quo genere est etiam
non videri intellegere quod intellegas ; ut Pontidius,
'Qualem existimas qui in adulterio deprehenditur ?'
—'Tardum.' Ut ego, qui in delectu, Metello,
cum excusationem oculorum a me non acciperet et
276 dixisset, 'Tu igitur nihil vides ?'—'Ego vero,' inquam, 'a porta Esquilina video villam tuam.' Ut
illud Nasicae, qui cum ad poetam Ennium venisset
eique ab ostio quaerenti Ennium ancilla dixisset

---

[a] Apparently a warning that luxury and avarice are likely
to engender disease.

[b] The innuendo seems to be, 'If you two are not married,
you ought to be.'

[c] Perhaps a hint to 'let well alone.' Compare the epitaph
to be read sixty years ago in a Devon churchyard :

'Here lies I and my two daughters,
All through drinking the Cheltenham waters ;
If we'd have stuck to Epsom salts,
We'd never have come to these here vaults.'

> The silly man,
> As soon as he was growing rich he died.[a]

Or

> And what to thee
> Is yonder dame?—My wife!—Like one, Faith help me![b]

Also

> As long as at the waters he remained,
> He never died.[c]

LXVIII. "A jest of this sort is rather trivial, and, as I said, fit for farces, but now and then even we orators find room for one of them, with the result that even a man who is no fool says something in the manner of a fool, but not without humour, as Mancia did to yourself, Antonius, on hearing that you were being prosecuted by Marcus Duronius for corrupt practices during your censorship ; ' At last,' said he, ' you will be able to attend to business of your own.' These jokes provoke hearty laughter, and so most assuredly does everything that is said ironically by the wise, and somewhat absurdly, but not without humour. Another jest from this class is pretending not to understand what you understand perfectly, as when Pontidius, being asked his opinion of the man who is taken in adultery, replied : ' He is a slowcoach,' or as when, at a muster of troops, Metellus rejected the excuse I pleaded of weak eyesight, and said to me, ' Can you then see nothing ? ', and I replied ' On the contrary, I can see your country-mansion from the Esquiline Gate.'[d] Another instance was that rejoinder of Nasica's : he had called upon the poet Ennius and, when he inquired for him at his front-

assumed simplicity,

---

[d] Said to be a reflection on the ostentatious size and splendour of the mansion.

domi non esse, Nasica sensit illam domini iussu
dixisse et illum intus esse ; paucis post diebus cum
ad Nasicam venisset Ennius et eum a ianua quaereret,
exclamat Nasica se domi non esse ; tum Ennius :
' Quid ? ego non cognosco vocem,' inquit, ' tuam ? '
Hic Nasica : ' Homo es impudens. Ego cum te
quaererem, ancillae tuae credidi te domi non esse ;
tu mihi non credis ipsi ? '

277   Est bellum illud quoque ex quo is qui dixit irride-
tur in eo ipso genere quo dixit : ut, cum Q. Opimius
consularis, qui adolescentulus male audisset, festivo
homini Egilio, qui videretur mollior nec esset, dixisset, ' Quid tu, Egilia mea ? quando ad me venis cum
tua colu et lana ? '—' Non pol,' inquit, ' audeo, nam
me ad famosas vetuit mater accedere.'

278   LXIX. Salsa sunt etiam quae habent suspicionem
ridiculi absconditam, quo in genere est Siculi illud,
cui cum familiaris quidam quereretur quod diceret
uxorem suam suspendisse se de ficu, ' amabo te,'
inquit, ' da mihi ex ista arbore quos seram surculos.'
In eodem genere est quod Catulus dixit cuidam
oratori malo : qui cum in epilogo misericordiam se
movisse putaret, postquam assedit, rogavit hunc
videreturne misericordiam movisse; ' ac magnam qui-

door, had been told by the housemaid that her master
was not at home, which reply Nasica perceived to
have been given by the master's order, he being in
fact in the house. A few days later Ennius called at
Nasica's, and asked for him at the entrance, whereupon Nasica called out that he was not at home.
'What?', cries Ennius, 'Do I not know your voice?'
To which Nasica rejoined, 'You are a shameless
fellow; when I asked for you, I believed your maid
when she said you were not at home; do you not
believe me when I tell you the same thing at first
hand?'

277 "It is delightful too when a jester is requited in the
identical vein in which he himself bantered, as when
Quintus Opimius, a past consul, but of bad repute in
his early manhood, said to a wit named Egilius, who
looked rather effeminate but was not so in fact, 'Well
now, my dear Egilia, when are you coming to visit me
with your distaff and wool?' 'Really I dare not
come,' replied the other, 'for mother told me never
to go near women of ill fame.'

278 LXIX. "Other witticisms are those that suggest hinted
a joke that is not quite on the surface; to this group ridicule,
belongs the quip of the Sicilian to whom a friend
was lamenting because, as he told him, his wife had
hanged herself from a fig-tree, and who replied,
'Do please let me have some cuttings from that
tree of yours to plant.' In the same group is the
remark made by Catulus to a poor speaker who,
after resuming his seat with the impression that his
concluding remarks had aroused the audience's pity,
inquired of Catulus whether he thought he had
been successful in arousing pity; 'Oh yes, and
plenty of it,' was the reply, 'for I can't imagine

dem,' inquit, 'neminem enim puto esse tam durum
279 cui non oratio tua miseranda visa sit.' Me quidem
hercule valde illa movent stomachosa et quasi sub-
morosa ridicula—non cum a moroso dicuntur ; tum
enim non sal sed natura ridetur ; in quo, ut mihi
videtur, persalsum illud est apud Novium :

> ' Quid ploras, pater ? '
> ' Mirum ni cantem ! condemnatus sum.'

Huic generi quasi contrarium est ridiculi genus
patientis ac lenti, ut, cum Cato percussus esset ab
eo qui arcam ferebat, cum ille diceret, ' Cave ! '
280 rogavit numquid aliud ferret praeter arcam. Est
etiam stultitiae salsa reprehensio, ut ille Siculus,
cui praetor Scipio patronum causae dabat hospitem
suum, hominem nobilem, sed admodum stultum :
' Quaeso,' inquit, ' praetor, adversario meo da istum
patronum, deinde mihi neminem dederis.' Movent
illa etiam quae coniectura explanantur longe aliter
atque sunt sed acute atque concinne : ut, cum
Scaurus accusaret Rutilium ambitus cum ipse consul esset factus, ille repulsam tulisset, et in eius
tabulis ostenderet litteras A. F. P. R. idque diceret
esse ' ACTUM FIDE P. RUTILII,' Rutilius autem ' ANTE
FACTUM, POST RELATUM,' C. Canius eques Romanus,
cum Rufo adesset, exclamavit[1] neutrum illis litteris

---

[1] *Rackham :* exclamat.

---

[a] No Scipio is known to us to have been praetor in Sicily.
[b] Apparently the presiding magistrate assigned such
assistance to a litigant who was a provincial and presumably
ignorant of Roman law.

410

anybody could be so hard-hearted as not to have
279 thought your speech a pitiable performance.' For
my own part I vow I am also much amused by those
pettish and rather ill-tempered jests—but not when
they are spoken by an ill-tempered person, for then
it is not his wit but his character that we laugh at;
and this point to my mind is very neatly put in the
lines in Novius :

'Sire, why dost thou lament?'
''Twere strange did I not sing, who am under sentence!'

A kind of jest that is just the opposite of this is the
tolerant and gentle sort—for example, Cato's when
he had been jostled by a man carrying a box, who
said 'Look out,' and he asked 'What, are you carry-
280 ing something else beside that box?' There is also
a neat way of reproving folly, for instance the remark
of the Sicilian to whom Scipio[a] when praetor was
assigning as counsel in a law-suit his host, a person
of position but rather stupid : 'Pray, Mr. Praetor,
assign that gentleman as counsel[b] to my opponent,
and then I will not ask you to assign any counsel to
me.' Also effective are conjectural explanations of
a document that are completely at variance with
the real meaning but are cleverly and wittily put :
as for instance, in the prosecution of Rutilius by
Scaurus on the charge of corrupt practices in the
election to the consulship which Scaurus himself had
won and Rutilius had lost, when Scaurus called attention to the entry A.F.P.R. in Rutilius's election
accounts, and said that they stood for 'Acting for
Pubilius Rutilius,' whereas Rutilius said they meant
'Allocated formerly, posted up recently,' Sir Gaius
Canius, who appeared for Rufus, called out that both

411

declarari; 'Quid ergo?' inquit Scaurus; 'Aemilius fecit, plectitur Rutilius.'

281 LXX. Ridentur etiam discrepantia. 'Quid huic
abest nisi res et virtus?' Bella etiam est familiaris
reprehensio quasi errantis; ut cum obiurgavit
Albium Granius quod, cum eius tabulis quiddam ab
Albucio probatum videretur, et valde absoluto Scaevola gauderet neque intellegeret contra suas tabulas
282 esse iudicatum. Huic similis est etiam admonitio in
consilio dando familiaris, ut, cum patrono malo
cum vocem in dicendo obtudisset suadebat Granius
ut mulsum frigidum biberet simul ac domum re-
disset, 'Perdam,' inquit, 'vocem, si id fecero';
283 'Melius est,' inquit, 'quam reum.' Bellum etiam
est cum quid cuique sit consentaneum dicitur; ut,
cum Scaurus nonnullam haberet invidiam ex eo quod
Phrygionis Pompei locupletis hominis bona sine
testamento possederat, sederetque advocatus reo
Bestiae, cum funus quoddam duceretur, accusator
C. Memmius: 'Vide,' inquit, 'Scaure, mortuus
284 rapitur, si potes esse possessor.' Sed ex his omnibus
nihil magis ridetur quam quod est praeter exspectationem, cuius innumerabilia sunt exempla, vel Appii
maioris illius, qui in senatu cum ageretur de agris

---

a Probably the grandfather of Cicero's enemy P. Clodius.

these interpretations of the initials were wrong. 'What do they mean then?' said Scaurus. 'Aemilius filched. Punish Rutilius.'

281   LXX. "A laugh is also scored by sentences that do not hang together : ' What does this gentleman lack —except cash and character ? ' Another pretty turn is a friendly criticism of an implied mistake, as when Granius reproved Albius because, when Albucius was held to have proved a statement on the evidence of Albius's accounts, Albius was not only much delighted by Scaevola's acquittal but actually failed to see that a verdict had been given against his own 282 accounts.   Also similar to this is giving a friendly hint by way of advice : for instance, when Granius was recommending an incompetent advocate who in the course of a speech had talked himself hoarse to have a drink of chilled wine and honey as soon as he got home, he answered ' If I do that, I shall ruin my voice,' and Granius retorted ' Better ruin your voice 283 than ruin your client.'   It is also a neat turn to point out what goes with anybody's individual characteristics ; as for instance, when Scaurus was somewhat under a cloud for having taken possession of the estate of a wealthy person named Pompeius Phrygio who had died intestate, and was appearing in court as an assessor on behalf of a defendant named Bestia, a funeral happened to pass by, and Gaius Memmius who was for the prosecution said, ' Look, Scaurus, there's a dead man being bundled out of the way—if 284 only you can get possession.'   But of all these devices nothing causes more amusement than an unexpected turn, of which there are countless instances—for example, the remark of old Appius senior,[a] who when there was a debate in the Senate about the

unexpected turns,

413

CICERO

publicis et de lege Thoria et premeretur Lucilius
ab eis qui a pecore eius depasci agros publicos
dicerent, 'Non est,' inquit, 'Lucilii pecus illud;
erratis'—defendere Lucilium videbatur—'ego
285 liberum puto esse: qua libet pascitur.' Placet
etiam mihi illud Scipionis illius qui Tib. Gracchum
perculit: cum ei M. Flaccus multis probris obiectis
P. Mucium iudicem tulisset, 'Eiero,' inquit, 'iniquus
est'; cum esset admurmuratum, 'Ah,' inquit,
'P. C., non ego mihi illum iniquum eiero, verum
omnibus.' Ab hoc vero Crasso nihil facetius: cum
laesisset testis Silus Pisonem quod se in eum audisse
dixisset, 'Potest fieri,' inquit, 'Sile, ut is unde te
audisse dicis, iratus dixerit.' Annuit Silus. 'Potest
etiam, ut tu non recte intellexeris.' Id quoque toto
capite annuit, ut se Crasso daret. 'Potest etiam
fieri,' inquit, 'ut omnino, quod te audisse dicis, nunquam audieris.' Hoc ita praeter exspectationem
accidit ut testem omnium risus obrueret. Huius
generis est plenus Novius, cuius iocus est familiaris
'Sapiens si algebis, tremes.' Et alia permulta.

286 LXXI. Saepe etiam facete concedas adversario id

---

^a Presumably the poet, *cf.* § 25.

414

lands in public ownership and the Lex Thoria, and Lucilius [a] was being attacked by members who asserted that his herd was being grazed on the lands in question, said 'No, that herd does not belong to Lucilius; you are making a mistake'—this sounded as if he were speaking in Lucilius's defence—'My own view is that it is a herd that's got free—it grazes freely 285 where it pleases.' I also like the remark of the Scipio who made away with Tiberius Gracchus: when Marcus Flaccus after a great many damaging objections had been made had carried Publius Mucius as a member of the jury, Scipio said 'I challenge him on oath: he is prejudiced!'; at this there was a murmur, but Scipio continued, 'Ah, gentlemen, I don't challenge him as prejudiced against myself, but as prejudiced against everybody.' From this point of view however nothing could be wittier than the remark of Crassus: serious damage had been done to the case of a certain Piso by a witness named Silus, who had said that he had heard something against him; 'It may be the case, Silus,' said Crassus, 'that the person whose remark you say you heard was speaking in anger.' Silus nodded assent. 'It is also possible that you misunderstood him.' To this also Silus nodded very emphatic assent, so putting himself into Crassus's hands. 'It is also possible,' he continued, 'that what you say you heard, you never really heard at all.' This was so entirely unexpected a turn that the witness was overwhelmed by a burst of laughter from the whole court. Novius is full of quips of this sort: everyone knows his jape, 'Even a philosopher like you, if he is cold, will shiver,' and a great many more.

286 LXXI. "Also you may often humorously yield to personal retorts.

ipsum quod tibi ille detrahit : ut C. Laelius, cum ei
quidam malo genere natus diceret indignum esse suis
maioribus, ' At hercule,' inquit, ' tu tuis dignus.'
Saepe etiam sententiose ridicula dicuntur, ut M.
Cincius, quo die legem de donis et muneribus tulit,
cum C. Cento prodisset et satis contumeliose
' Quid fers, Cinciole ? ' quaesisset, ' Ut emas,' in-
287 quit, ' Gai, si uti velis.'   Saepe etiam salse quae fieri
non possunt optantur : ut M. Lepidus, cum ceteris
in campo exercentibus in herba ipse recubisset :
' Vellem hoc esset,' inquit, ' laborare.' Salsum est
etiam quaerentibus et quasi percontantibus, lente
respondere quod nolint : ut censor Lepidus cum
M. Antistio Pyrgensi equum ademisset, amicique
cum vociferarentur et quaererent quid ille patri suo
responderet cur ademptum sibi equum diceret cum
optimus colonus, parcissimus, modestissimus, frugalis-
simus esset : ' Me istorum,' inquit, ' nihil credere.'
288 Colliguntur a Graecis alia nonnulla, exsecrationes,
admirationes, minationes, sed haec ipsa nimis mihi
videor in multa genera descripsisse ; nam illa quae
verbi ratione et vi continentur certa fere ac definita
sunt quae plerumque, ut ante dixi, laudari magis
289 quam rideri solent ; haec autem quae sunt in re ipsa

---

your opponent the very point that he is trying to make against you : for instance Gaius Laelius, when some low-born person told him he was not worthy of his ancestors, retorted ' But you *are* worthy of yours, I swear you are ! ' Also jests at the other's expense are often expressed in an epigrammatic form : for instance, on the day when Marcus Cincius carried a bill dealing with gifts and presentations, Gaius Cento came forward and asked in a rather insulting manner, ' What are you putting forward, my good Cincius ? ' And Cincius replied ' That if you want to use a thing, 287 Gaius,[a] you should pay for it ! ' Also it is often witty to wish for things that are impossible : as, for instance, when Marcus Lepidus was sprawling on the grass himself while everybody else was doing exercises in the field, he said ' I wish that hard work were what I am doing.' Also when people ask you something and keep on repeating the question it is witty gently to give the very reply they don't want : for example when the censor Lepidus had taken a horse from Marcus Antistius of Pyrgi and Antistius's friends made an outcry and kept asking him what answer he should give his father to explain why his horse had been taken away from him, a first-class farmer, and an extremely economical and moderate and thrifty person, he said his answer would be ' I 288 don't accept any of that ! ' The Greeks include some other varieties, execration, astonishment, threats, but I feel I have overdone my classification of these witticisms already ; for the notions contained in the meaning and force of a word are usually clear and definite, and most of them, as I said before,[b] usually 289 excite more applause than ridicule ; whereas the points comprised in the actual fact and meaning,

et sententia partibus sunt innumerabilia, generibus
pauca ; exspectationibus enim decipiendis et naturis
aliorum irridendis [ipsorum ridicule indicandis][1] et
similitudine turpioris et dissimulatione et subabsurda
dicendo et stulta reprehendendo risus moventur, itaque imbuendus est is qui iocose volet dicere quasi
natura quadam apta ad haec genera et moribus, ut
ad cuiusque modi genus ridiculi vultus etiam accom-
modetur ; qui quidem quo severior est et tristior, ut
in te, Crasse, hoc illa quae dicuntur salsiora videri
solent.

290   Sed iam tu, Antoni, qui hoc deversorio sermonis mei
libenter acquieturum te esse dixisti, tanquam in
Pomptinum deverteris, neque amoenum neque salu-
brem locum, censeo ut satis diu te putes requiesse et
iter reliquum conficere pergas.

Ego vero, atque hilare quidem a te acceptus,
inquit, et cum doctior per te, tum etiam audacior
factus iam ad iocandum ; non enim vereor ne quis
me in isto genere leviorem iam putet, quoniam quidem tu Fabricios mihi auctores, et Africanos, Maxi-
291 mos, Catones, Lepidos protulisti. Sed habetis ea
quae vultis ex me audire, de quibus quidem accuratius dicendum et cogitandum fuit : nam cetera
faciliora sunt, atque ex eis quae dicta sunt reliqua

---

[1] *secl. Wilkins.*

though falling into innumerable divisions, only belong to a few main classes ; what excites laughter is disappointing expectations and ridiculing other people's characters and imitating a baser person and dissembling and saying things that are rather silly and criticizing points that are foolish, and consequently a person who wants to speak humorously must be equipped with a disposition and character that is suited to artifices of this kind, so that even his expression of countenance may be adapted to each kind of variety of the ridiculous ; and indeed the sterner and gloomier a man's expression is, as in your case, Crassus, the more humorous as a rule his remarks are considered.

290   "Well, Antonius, you said you would be glad of a rest at this house of entertainment, which is what my discourse is, but you must imagine the resort you have visited to be in the Pomptine marshes, not a very agreeable or very salubrious locality, so I advise you to decide that you have had a sufficient rest and to push on to complete the remainder of your journey."

   "Yes, I will, and that after being amusingly entertained by you, and having, thanks to you, become not only a better scholar but also a more reckless jester ; for now I'm not afraid of anybody thinking me too frivolous in that line, inasmuch as you have supplied me with such authorities as Fabricius, and 291 also Africanus, Maximus, Cato and Lepidus. But now you have got the points you wanted to hear from me, points which did in fact require more careful statement and consideration, inasmuch as all the others are easier, and the points that remain all spring directly out of those that have been put.

Antonius resumes (from § 216) as to *inventio* : he begins with the strong points of his own case and his opponents'.

419

nascuntur omnia. LXXII. Ego enim cum ad causam
sum aggressus atque omnia cogitando quoad facere
potui persecutus, cum et argumenta causae et eos
locos quibus animi iudicum conciliantur et illos quibus
permoventur vidi atque cognovi, tum constituo quid
habeat causa quaeque boni, quid mali ; nulla enim
fere potest res in dicendi disceptationem aut controversiam vocari quae non habeat utrumque, sed
292 quantum habeat id refert ; mea autem ratio in
dicendo haec esse solet, ut boni quod habeat id
amplectar, exornem, exaggerem, ibi commorer, ibi
habitem, ibi haeream, a malo autem vitioque causae
ita recedam non ut me id fugere appareat sed ut
totum bono illo ornando et augendo dissimulatum
obruatur ; et, si causa est in argumentis, firmissima
quaeque maxime tueor, sive plura sunt sive aliquod
unum ; sin autem in conciliatione aut in permotione
causa est, ad eam me potissimum partem quae
maxime movere animos hominum potest confero.
293 Summa denique huius generis haec est, ut si in
refellendo adversario firmior esse oratio quam in
confirmandis nostris rebus potest, omnia in illum
tela conferam, sin nostra probari facilius quam illa
redargui possunt, abducere animos a contraria de-
294 fensione et ad nostram coner[1] deducere. Duo denique
illa quae facillima videntur, quoniam quae difficiliora

---

[1] *Rackham :* conor.

LXXII. For my part when I am launched on a case and have to the best of my ability passed all the facts under consideration, having discerned and ascertained the arguments that belong to the case and also the topics calculated to win the favour of the court and those adapted to arouse its emotions, I then decide what are the good and what the bad points in the case of each of the parties, as it is almost impossible for any matter to be brought under discussion or dispute which does not contain both—the thing that matters is *how much* of them it contains ;

292 but my own method in a speech usually is to take the good points of my case and elaborate these, embellishing and enlarging and lingering and dwelling on and sticking to them, while any bad part or weakness in my case I leave on one side, not in such a manner as to give the appearance of running away from it but so as to disguise it and entirely cover it up by embellishing and amplifying the good point referred to ; and if the case is one that turns on arguments, I maintain all the strongest among them in the fullest measure, whether they are several or only one, or if it is a matter of winning favour or arousing feeling, I concentrate particularly on the part of the case that is most capable of influencing

293 men's minds. In short, the chief thing in a case of this kind is, if my speech can be stronger in refuting our opponent than in proving our own points, for me to concentrate all my shafts upon him, but if on the contrary our points can be more easily proved than his can be refuted, to aim at drawing off their attention from our opponent's defence and directing it to

294 our own. Finally there are two lines that appear extremely easy—as the more difficult ones are beyond

sunt non possum, mihi pro meo iure sumo : unum ut
molesto aut difficili argumento aut loco nonnunquam
omnino nihil respondeam, quod forsitan aliquis iure
irriserit—quis enim est qui id facere non possit ?
sed tamen ego de mea nunc, non de aliorum facultate
disputo, confiteorque me si quae premat res vehementius ita cedere solere ut non modo non abiecto,
sed ne reiecto quidem scuto fugere videar, sed adhibere quamdam in dicendo speciem atque pompam
et pugnae similem fugam ; consistere vero in meo
praesidio sic ut non fugiendi hostis sed capiendi loci
295 causa cessisse videar ; alterum est illud quod ego
maxime oratori cavendum et providendum puto
quodque me sollicitare summe solet : non tam ut
prosim causis elaborare soleo quam ut ne quid
obsim ; non quin enitendum sit in utroque, sed
tamen multo est turpius oratori nocuisse videri causae
quam non profuisse.   LXXIII. Sed quid hoc loco vos
inter vos, Catule ?   An haec ut sunt contemnenda
contemnitis ?

Minime, inquit ille, sed Caesar de isto ipso quiddam
velle dicere videbatur.

my power—which I adopt as being entitled to do so : one is that, when I encounter a troublesome or difficult argument or topic, occasionally I make no reply to it at all : a method on which somebody will perhaps justly pour ridicule—for who is there who would not be capable of adopting it ? but all the same it is my own capacity and not that of other people which I am now discussing, and I frankly confess that I make it a practice, if some matter presses rather too forcibly upon me, to retire, but in such a manner as not to look as if I were running away even with my shield slung behind my back, much less after throwing it away, but to exhibit a certain seemliness and dignity in my delivery, and to execute a retreat that looks like a fight ; and when I come to a halt to stand on my guard in such a manner as to appear to have given ground for the sake of taking up a certain position, not for the sake of escaping the enemy ; the other line is one which I for my part think a speaker should only adopt with very great caution and preparation, and which regularly causes me an extreme amount of trouble : my practice is not to devote my efforts to further the advancement of my cases but to avoid doing them any damage ; not but what it is proper to use every effort in achieving both, but it is much more damaging to a speaker's reputation to be deemed to have done harm to his case than not to be thought to have advanced it.   LXXIII. But what are you whispering among yourselves at this point, Catulus ?   Do you despise these things as they deserve to be despised ? "

" By no means," he said, " but we thought that Caesar wanted to say something on just the point you are treating."

Me vero libente, inquit Antonius, dixerit sive refellendi causa sive quaerendi.

296 Tum Iulius : Ego mehercule, inquit, Antoni, semper is fui qui de te oratore sic praedicarem, unum te in dicendo mihi videri tectissimum, propriumque hoc esse laudis tuae, nihil a te unquam esse dictum quod obesset ei pro quo diceres ; idque memoria teneo, cum mihi sermo cum hoc ipso Crasso multis audientibus esset institutus Crassusque plurimis verbis eloquentiam laudaret tuam, dixisse me cum ceteris tuis laudibus hanc esse vel maximam, quod non solum quod opus esset diceres sed etiam 297 quod non opus esset non diceres : tum illum mihi respondere memini, cetera in te summe esse laudanda, illud vero improbi esse hominis et perfidiosi, dicere quod alienum esset et noceret ei pro quo quisque diceret ; quare non sibi eum disertum qui id non faceret videri sed improbum, qui faceret. Nunc, si tibi videtur, Antoni, demonstres velim quare tu hoc ita magnum putes, nihil in causa mali facere, ut nihil tibi in oratore maius esse videatur.

298 LXXIV. Dicam equidem, Caesar, inquit, quid intellegam, sed et tu, et vos omnes hoc, inquit, mementote, non me de perfecti oratoris divinitate quadam loqui sed de exercitationis et consuetudinis meae mediocritate. Crassi quidem responsum excel-

424

" Oh, as for me," said Antonius, " I should be delighted for him to speak, whether with the object of refuting me or of asking me a question."

296 " For my own part, Antonius," rejoined Julius, " I declare I have always taken the line of maintaining, in regard to your powers as a speaker, that in my view you were quite exceptionally guarded in your utterances, and that it was your special distinction that nothing had ever fallen from you that would damage the client you were defending ; and I clearly remember that when I was engaged in a debate with Crassus here, before a large audience, and Crassus extolled your eloquence at great length, what I said was that together with all your other claims to distinction the greatest one was that you not only said the proper thing but also avoided saying what was 297 not the proper thing ; and thereupon I remember Crassus rejoining that while all your other qualities were most deserving of praise, to say something untoward and damaging to one's client showed complete lack of principle and of loyalty, and consequently he did not consider a man to be a good speaker if he did not do so but an unprincipled person if he did. At this point, Antonius, if agreeable to you, I should like you to explain for what reason you put so high a value on this avoidance of doing any damage to one's case that you think it to be a speaker's most important qualification."

98 LXXIV. " I will tell you what my own view is, Caesar," he said, " but I must request you and all the rest of the company to bear in mind that I am not speaking of the inspired genius of a consummate orator but of the moderate level attained by practice and habituation in my own case. The answer given

lentis cuiusdam est ingeni ac singularis ; cui quidem
portenti simile esse visum est posse aliquem inveniri
oratorem qui aliquid mali faceret dicendo obessetque
299 ei quem defenderet ; facit enim de se coniecturam,
cuius tanta vis ingeni est ut neminem nisi consulto
putet quod contra se ipsum sit dicere ; sed ego non
de praestanti quadam et eximia sed prope de vulgari
et communi vi nunc disputo. Ita apud Graecos
fertur incredibili quadam magnitudine consili atque
ingeni Atheniensis ille fuisse Themistocles ; ad quem
quidam doctus homo atque in primis eruditus accessisse dicitur eique artem memoriae, quae tum
primum proferebatur, pollicitus esse se traditurum ;
cum ille quaesisset quidnam illa ars efficere posset,
dixisse illum doctorem ut omnia meminisset ; et
ei Themistoclem respondisse gratius sibi illum esse
facturum si se oblivisci quae vellet quam si
300 meminisse docuisset. Videsne quae vis in homine
acerrimi ingeni, quam potens et quanta mens fuerit ?
qui ita responderit ut intellegere possemus nihil ex
illius animo quod semel esset infusum unquam
effluere potuisse, cum quidem ei fuerit optabilius
oblivisci posse potius quod meminisse nollet quam
quod semel audisset vidissetve meminisse. Sed
neque propter hoc Themistocli responsum memoriae
nobis opera danda non est neque illa mea cautio et

by Crassus is of course the verdict of a quite outstanding and unrivalled intellect—of course he deems it miraculous that any speaker could be found whose oratory would actually damage and prejudice the 299 case of his client. This is because he judges from himself, being a person of such a strong intellect that he cannot imagine anybody saying anything to his own detriment, unless he did so on purpose. But I am not at the moment talking about some outstanding and exceptional ability but about ordinary average capacity. For instance, we are told that the famous Athenian Themistocles was endowed with wisdom and genius on a scale quite surpassing belief; and it is said that a certain learned and highly accomplished person went to him and offered to impart to him the science of mnemonics, which was then being introduced for the first time; and that when Themistocles asked what precise result that science was capable of achieving, the professor asserted that it would enable him to remember everything; and Themistocles replied that he would be doing him a greater kindness if he taught him to forget what he 300 wanted than if he taught him to remember. Do you observe what mental force and penetration the man possessed, what power and range of intellect? inasmuch as his answer brings home to us that nothing that had once been introduced into his mind had ever been able to pass out of it, inasmuch as he would rather have been able to forget something that he did not wish to remember than to remember everything that he had once heard or seen. But this reply of Themistocles must not cause us to neglect the training of the memory, and the exceptional intellectual powers of Crassus must not make us

timiditas in causis propter praestantem prudentiam
Crassi neglegenda est; uterque enim istorum non
mihi attulit aliquam sed suam significavit faculta-
301 tem. Etenim permulta sunt in causis in omni parte
orationis circumspicienda ne quid offendas, ne quo
irruas: saepe aliqui testis aut non laedit aut minus
laedit nisi lacessatur; orat reus, urgent advocati ut
invehamur, ut maledicamus, denique ut interroge-
mus: non moveor, non obtempero, non satisfacio—
neque tamen ullam assequor laudem, homines enim
imperiti facilius quod stulte dixeris reprehendere
302 quam quod sapienter tacueris laudare possunt. Hic
quantum fit mali si iratum, si non stultum, si non
levem testem laeseris! Habet enim et voluntatem
nocendi in iracundia et vim in ingenio et pondus in
vita. Nec, si hoc Crassus non committit, ideo non
multi et saepe committunt; quo quidem mihi turpius
videri nihil solet quam quod ex oratoris dicto aliquo
aut responso aut rogato sermo ille sequitur: 'Oc-
cidit.' 'Adversariumne?' 'Immo vero,' aiunt, 'se
303 et eum quem defendit.' LXXV. Hoc Crassus non
putat nisi perfidia accidere posse, ego autem saepissime video in causis aliquid mali facere homines
minime malos. Quid, illud quod supra dixi, solere
me cedere, et, ut planius dicam, fugere ea quae

ignore the caution and nervousness in pleading a case that I assigned to myself ; for neither Themistocles nor Crassus attributed any competence to me, 301 but indicated competence of their own. The fact is that in actions at law there are a great many precautions that you have to take in every part of your speech so as not to make a slip and run your head against some obstacle : frequently a witness does no damage, or less damage, if he is not challenged ; the defendant implores us and his supporters urge us to attack him, to abuse him, and finally to cross-examine him, but I pay no attention, I won't give way to them or oblige them—though all the same I do not get any praise for this, as ill-informed persons are more capable of criticizing one's foolish assertions than 302 one's wise omissions. In this department, how much harm is done if you fall foul of a witness who has lost his temper, and is no fool, and a person of consideration ! His anger supplies him with the wish to injure you, his ability with the power to do so, and his past record with influence. And even if Crassus does not make this mistake, it does not follow that it is not made by many people and frequently ; and for my part I always think nothing more disgraceful than when some statement or reply or question made by a speaker is followed by the remark ' He's done for it ! ' ' Done for his opponent ? ' ' Oh no,' they say, 303 ' done for himself and his client.' LXXV. Crassus holds the view that this can only happen through treachery, but I myself quite often see definite harm done in law-suits by persons who are not in the least malicious. Come, in regard to what I said previously, that I make a practice of giving way on, or to put it more plainly running away from, points that tell

Precaution against damaging one's own case.

valde causam meam premerent, cum id non faciunt
alii versanturque in hostium castris ac sua praesidia
dimittunt, mediocriterne causis nocent cum aut
adversariorum adiumenta confirmant aut ea quae
304 sanare nequeunt exulcerant ? Quid, cum personarum
quas defendunt rationem non habent, si quae sunt in
eis invidiosa non mitigant extenuando sed laudando
et efferendo invidiosiora faciunt, quantum est in eo
tandem mali ? Quid, si in homines caros iudicibusque
iucundos sine ulla praemunitione orationis acerbius
et contumeliosius invehare, nonne a te iudices
305 abalienes ? Quid, si quae vitia aut incommoda
sunt in aliquo iudice uno aut pluribus, ea tu in
adversariis exprobrando non intellegas te in iudices
invehi, mediocrene peccatum est ? Quid, si cum
pro altero dicas, litem tuam facias aut laesus
efferare iracundia, causam relinquas, nihilne noceas ?
In quo ego non quo libenter male audiam sed quia
causam non libenter relinquo nimium patiens et
lentus existimor ; ut cum te ipsum, Sulpici, obiur-
gabam quod ministratorem peteres, non adversarium ;
ex quo etiam illud assequor, ut si quis mihi maledicat
306 petulans aut plane insanus esse videatur. In ipsis
autem argumentis si quid posueris aut aperte falsum
aut ei quod dixeris dicturusve sis contrarium aut

heavily against my case : well, when other people
do not do this, and roam about inside the enemy's
camp and disband their own forces, is the damage
they do to their cases inconsiderable—when they
either strengthen their opponents' supports or aggra-
304 vate sores which they are unable to heal ? Come,
when they take no account of the characters of the
people they are defending, if they do not mitigate
any unpopular traits in them by minimizing their
importance but increase their unpopularity by praising and parading them, how much harm pray is there
in this ? Come, if without any preparatory forti-
fication of your position you deliver a rather bitter
and insulting attack on persons held in esteem and
popular with the court, do you not set the bench
305 against you ? Come, if you taunt your opponents
with vices or failings that are present in one or in
several of the judges without realizing that you are
delivering an attack on the bench, is it a trifling
mistake that you have committed ? Come, if when
speaking on behalf of a client you make yourself
morally responsible, or when provoked lose your
temper and let yourself go, losing sight of your case,
are you not doing any harm ? This is a matter in
which I myself am considered too tolerant and gentle,
not because I like being abused but because I do not
like abandoning my case—for instance, when I
taunted you yourself, Sulpicius, for attacking your
assistant and not your opponent ; and this method
also secures me the result that if somebody abuses
me, he appears to be making a wanton attack, or
306 else to be quite off his head. Then if your actual
arguments include something that is obviously untrue, or inconsistent with what you have said or are

431

genere ipso remotum ab usu iudiciorum ac foro, nihilne noceas ? Quid multa ? Omnis cura mea solet in hoc versari semper—dicam enim saepius—si possim, ut boni efficiam aliquid dicendo, sin id minus, ut certe ne quid mali.

307 LXXVI. Itaque nunc illuc redeo, Catule, in quo tu me paulo ante laudabas, ad ordinem collocationemque rerum ac locorum ; cuius ratio est duplex, altera quam affert natura causarum, altera quae oratorum iudicio et prudentia comparatur : nam ut aliquid ante rem dicamus, deinde ut rem exponamus, post ut eam probemus nostris praesidiis[1] confirmandis, contrariis refutandis, deinde ut concludamus atque 308 ita peroremus, hoc dicendi natura ipsa praescribit; ut vero statuamus ea quae probandi et docendi causa dicenda sunt quemadmodum componamus, id est vel maxime proprium oratoris prudentiae. Multa enim occurrunt argumenta, multa, quae in dicendo profutura videantur ; sed eorum partim ita levia sunt ut contemnenda sint, partim, etiam si quid habent adiumenti, sunt nonnunquam eiusmodi ut insit in eis aliquid viti, neque tanti sit illud quod prodesse 309 videatur ut cum aliquo malo coniungatur ; quae autem utilia sunt atque firma, si ea tamen, ut saepe fit, valde multa sunt, ea quae ex eis aut levissima

---

[1] [praesidiis] *Vassis.*

going to say, or intrinsically out of keeping with the practice of the courts and with public life, would you be doing no harm ? In short, the whole of my efforts are always regularly devoted to this—for I will go on repeating it—if possible to do some good by speaking, or if that is not possible, at all events not to do any harm.

307   LXXVI. "Accordingly I now return to the point in respect of which, Catulus, you were praising me just now, the question of the order and arrangement of one's facts and topics. In respect of this there are two rules of procedure, one arising from the nature of the cases and the other contributed by the discretion and the wisdom of the speakers : for to make some prefatory remarks, then to set out our case, afterwards to prove it by establishing our own points with arguments in their favour and refuting our adversary's points, then to wind up our case and so to come to our conclusion—this is the procedure 308 enjoined by the very nature of oratory ; but to decide how to arrange the statements that have to be made for the purpose of establishing and explaining our case—that is in the highest degree a task for professional skill. For many arguments occur to us, and many considerations that appear likely to be of use to us in speaking ; but some of these are so unimportant as not to deserve notice, and some, even if they offer some amount of assistance, are occasionally of such a nature that they contain some flaw and that the amount of assistance they seem to provide is not of such value as to be used in conjunction with 309 a definitely detrimental point ; while if nevertheless, as frequently happens, there are numerous advantages and strong arguments, in my judgement those

Arrangement:

433

sunt aut aliis gravioribus consimilia, secerni arbitror
oportere atque ex oratione removeri : equidem
cum colligo argumenta causarum, non tam ea
310 numerare soleo quam expendere. LXXVII. Et
quoniam, quod saepe iam dixi, tribus rebus homines
ad nostram sententiam perducimus, aut docendo aut
conciliando aut permovendo, una ex tribus his rebus
res prae nobis est ferenda, ut nihil aliud nisi docere
velle videamur, reliquae duae, sicuti sanguis in
corporibus, sic illae in perpetuis orationibus fusae
esse debebunt. Nam et principia et ceterae partes
orationis, de quibus paulo post pauca dicemus,
habere hanc vim magnopere debent, ut ad eorum
mentes apud quos agetur movendas pertinere
311 possint ; sed his partibus orationis quae, et si nihil
docent argumentando, persuadendo tamen et com-
movendo proficiunt plurimum, quanquam maxime
proprius est locus et in exordiendo et in perorando,
digredi tamen ab eo quod proposueris atque agas
permovendorum animorum causa saepe utile est ;
312 itaque vel re narrata et exposita saepe datur ad
commovendos animos digrediendi locus, vel argumentis nostris confirmatis vel contrariis refutatis vel
utroque loco vel omnibus, si habet eam causa
dignitatem atque copiam, recte id fieri potest ;
eaeque causae sunt ad augendum et ad ornandum

---

a §§ 326, 333.

among them that are the least weighty or that closely resemble others that are weightier ought to be discarded and left out of the speech : in my own case when I am collecting arguments for my cases I make it my practice not so much to count them as to weigh
310 them. LXXVII. And because (as I have repeatedly said already) there are three methods of bringing people to hold our opinion, instruction or persuasion or appeal to their emotions, one of these three methods we must openly display, so as to appear to wish solely to impart instruction, whereas the two remaining methods should be interfused throughout the whole of the structure of our speeches like the blood in our bodies. For as for the exordium and the other divisions of a speech, about which we shall make a few remarks a little later,[a] it is essential that they should have the power of being able to exert this
311 influence in stirring the minds of the audience ; but in regard to the portions of a speech that in spite of proving no point by means of argument, nevertheless have a very great effect in persuading and arousing emotion, although the most appropriate place for them is in the introduction and the conclusion, nevertheless it is often useful to digress from the subject one has put forward and is dealing with, for the pur-
312 pose of arousing emotion ; and accordingly very often either a place is given to a digression devoted to exciting emotion after we have related the facts and stated our case, or this can rightly be done after we have established our own arguments or refuted those of our opponents, or in both places, or in all the parts of the speech, if the case is one of this importance and extent ; and the cases that are the weightiest and fullest for amplification and embellishment are those

places for appeals to emotion ;

gravissimae atque plenissimae quae plurimos exitus
dant ad eiusmodi digressionem, ut eis locis uti liceat
quibus animorum impetus eorum qui audiunt aut
313 impellantur aut reflectantur. Atque etiam in illo
reprehendo eos qui quae minime firma sunt ea
prima collocant ; in quo illos quoque errare arbitror
qui, si quando—id quod mihi nunquam placuit—plures
adhibent patronos, ut in quoque eorum minimum
putant esse, ita eum primum volunt dicere : res enim
hoc postulat, ut eorum exspectationi qui audiunt
quam celerrime succurratur ; cui si initio satisfactum
non sit, multo plus sit in reliqua causa laborandum,
male enim se res habet quae non statim ut dici
314 coepta est melior fieri videtur. Ergo ut in oratore
optimus quisque, sic in oratione firmissimum quodque sit primum, dum illud tamen in utroque teneatur, ut ea quae excellent serventur etiam ad
perorandum si quae erunt mediocria—nam vitiosis
nusquam esse oportet locum—in mediam turbam
315 atque in gregem coniciantur. Hisce omnibus rebus
consideratis tum denique id quod primum est dicendum postremum soleo cogitare, quo utar exordio ;
nam si quando id primum invenire volui, nullum mihi
occurrit nisi aut exile aut nugatorium aut vulgare
aut commune. LXXVIII. Principia autem dicendi
semper cum accurata et acuta et instructa sententiis,

436

that give the greatest number of openings for a digression of this kind, so allowing the employment of the topics which either stimulate or curb the

313 emotions of the audience. And in regard to arrangement I also censure the people who place their weakest points first ; and I think a mistake is also made in this respect by those who on occasions when they have several supporters to bring forward—a thing which I have never approved of doing—ask the particular one among them whom they think least influential to speak first ; for the situation demands that the anticipation of the audience should be gratified as quickly as possible, and if it is not satisfied at the start, a great deal more work has to be put in during the remainder of the proceedings, for a case is in a bad way which does not seem to become

314 stronger as soon as it begins to be stated. Consequently as in the choice of speaker the best man on each occasion should come first, so in arrangement of the speech the strongest point should come first, provided nevertheless that in both cases the rule be kept to reserve one's outstanding resources to the actual peroration, while collecting into a general medley in the middle any points of moderate importance—bad points must not be given a place any-

315 where. Well, not till I have attended to all these matters, then finally my practice is to consider last of all the thing that has to come first in the speech— what introduction to employ : for whenever I have chosen to begin by ascertaining this, nothing has occurred to me that was not either bald or trifling or hackneyed or undistinctive. LXXVIII. But one's opening remarks, though they should always be carefully framed and pointed and epigrammatic and

strongest points should come first;

tactful introduction;

437

apta verbis, tum vero causarum propria esse debent ;
prima est enim quasi cognitio et commendatio orationis in principio, quaeque continuo eum qui audit
316 permulcere atque allicere debet. In quo admirari
soleo non equidem istos qui nullam huic rei operam
dederunt, sed hominem in primis disertum atque
eruditum, Philippum, qui ita solet surgere ad dicendum ut quod primum verbum habiturus sit nesciat ; et
ait idem, cum brachium concalefecerit, tum se solere
pugnare ; neque attendit eos ipsos unde hoc simile
ducat primas illas hastas ita iactare leniter ut et
venustati vel maxime serviant et reliquis viribus suis
317 consulant. Neque est dubium quin exordium dicendi vehemens et pugnax non saepe esse debeat, sed
si in ipso illo gladiatorio vitae certamine quo ferro
decernitur tamen ante congressum multa fiunt quae
non ad vulnus sed ad speciem valere videatur, quanto
hoc magis in oratione est spectandum, in qua non vis
potius quam delectatio postulatur ! Nihil est denique
in natura rerum omnium quod se universum pro-
fundat et[1] totum repente evolvat—sic omnia quae
fiunt quaeque aguntur acerrime lenioribus principiis
318 natura ipsa praetexuit. Haec autem in dicendo non
extrinsecus alicunde quaerenda sed ex ipsis visceribus
causae sumenda sunt ; idcirco tota causa pertemptata

---

[1] *Kayser :* et quod.

suitably expressed, must at the same time be appropriate to the case in hand ; for the opening passage contains the first impression and the introduction of the speech, and this ought to charm and attract the 316 hearer straight away. This is a point in respect of which I am constantly surprised, not indeed at people who have given no attention to oratory, but at Philip, a person of outstanding and accomplished eloquence, whose habit it is to get up to make a speech without knowing what is to be the first word he will utter ; what he says about it is that his way is to warm up his biceps first and then start fighting—not observing that even the professionals from whom he derives this metaphor when throwing the spear deliver their first throws gently, so as to make their movements as graceful as possible and also to economize the re-317 mainder of their strength. Nor is there any doubt that the opening passage of a speech ought not as a rule to be of a forcible, fighting character ; but if in an actual fight to the death between gladiators, where the decision is made by the steel, nevertheless before closing a number of strokes are made that seem not to be intended to inflict a wound but to be done for the sake of appearance, how much more proper is it for this to be taken into consideration in making a speech, where what is asked for is not so much force as entertainment ! In conclusion, nothing exists in the physical universe that emerges as a whole and develops completely all in a moment : so true is it that all processes and actions of extreme rapidity have been provided by Nature herself with more 318 gentle commencements. But the opening passage in a speech must not be drawn from some outside source but from the very heart of the case ; consequently

atque perspecta, locis omnibus inventis atque instructis
319 considerandum est quo principio sit utendum. Sic ut[1]
facile reperientur—sumentur enim ex eis rebus quae
erunt uberrimae vel in argumentis vel in eis partibus
ad quas dixi digredi saepe oportere—ita momenti
aliquid afferent, cum erunt paene ex intima defensione deprompta et apparebit ea non modo non esse
communia nec in alias causas posse transferri sed
penitus ex ea causa quae tum[2] agatur effloruisse.
320 LXXIX. Omne autem principium aut rei totius
quae agetur significationem habere debebit aut
aditum ad causam et communitionem aut quoddam
ornamentum et dignitatem; sed oportet, ut aedibus
ac templis vestibula et aditus, sic causis principia pro
portione rerum praeponere ; itaque in parvis atque
infrequentibus causis ab ipsa re est exordiri saepe
321 commodius ; sed cum erit utendum principio, quod
plerumque erit, aut ex reo aut ex adversario aut ex
re aut ex eis apud quos agetur sententias duci licebit.
Ex reo—reos appello quorum res est—quae signifi-
cent bonum virum, quae liberalem, quae calamitosum,

---

[1] *Warmington :* et.   [2] tum *om. edd.*

our case must first be thoroughly considered and examined as a whole, and all our topics thought out
and arranged, before we consider what opening to
319 employ. In this way just as openings will be easily
discovered—for they will be taken from the subjects
that will prove most fertile either in the argumenta-
tive passages or in the digressions upon which I said
we must frequently enter—, so also they will contribute an element of movement, as they will be
taken from almost the most essential part of the
defence, and it will be felt not merely that they are
not generalities and capable of being transferred into
another case, but that they are essentially the natural
outcome of the case under consideration. LXXIX.
320 Every introduction will have to contain either a
statement of the whole of the matter that is to be
put forward, or an approach to the case and a preparation of the ground, or else to possess some element
of ornament and dignity ; but the opening passage
put at the beginning of a case should be in due propor-
tion to the importance of the facts, just as a forecourt
or an entrance should be properly proportioned to
the mansion or temple to which it belongs ; and
consequently in petty cases and ones not attracting
much attention it is often more suitable to start
321 straight away with the actual charge ; whereas when
it is proper to employ a formal opening, as will mostly
be the case, it will be possible to draw subjects either
from one's client or from one's opponent or from the
charge or from the members of the court before
whom it is to be brought. Points drawn from one's
client—by clients I mean the persons concerned in
the matter—are considerations showing him to be a
man of high character, a gentleman, a victim of mis-

quae misericordia dignum, quae valeant contra falsam
criminationem ; ex adversario eisdem ex locis fere
322 contraria ; ex re, si crudelis, si nefanda, si praeter
opinionem, si immerito, si misera, si ingrata, si in-
digna, si nova, si quae restitui sanarique non possit ;
ex eis autem apud quos agetur, ut benevolos beneque
existimantes efficiamus, quod agendo efficitur melius
quam rogando. Est id quidem in totam orationem
confundendum nec minime in extremam ; sed tamen
323 multa principia ex eo genere gignuntur. Nam et
attentum monent Graeci ut principio faciamus iudicem et docilem, quae sunt utilia, sed non prin-
cipii magis propria quam reliquarum partium ;
faciliora etiam in principiis, quod et attenti tum
maxime sunt cum omnia exspectant et dociles magis
in initiis esse possunt ; illustriora enim sunt quae
in principiis quam quae in mediis causis dicuntur aut
324 arguendo aut refellendo. Maximam autem copiam
principiorum ad iudicem aut alliciendum aut inci-
tandum ex eis locis trahemus qui ad motus animorum
conficiendos inerunt in causa, quos tamen totos
explicare in principio non oportebit, sed tantum
impelli iudicem primo leviter, ut iam inclinato re-
325 liqua incumbat oratio. LXXX. Connexum autem
442

fortune deserving of compassion, and any facts that
will tell against a false charge; from one's opponent,
more or less the contrary assertions derived from the
322 same topics; from the matter charged, in case it
is cruel or outrageous or improbable or undeserved
or pitiable or showing ingratitude or unworthy or unprecedented or not admitting of compensation or
remedy; from the members of the court, considerations designed to make them favourable and well-
disposed towards us, which is better achieved by
developing our case than by making a request for
goodwill. Conciliation of the audience must indeed
permeate the whole of the speech, and especially the
peroration, but nevertheless this class of consideration does supply a great many modes of opening.
323 For the Greeks advise us to use the opening passage
for securing the attention of the judge and making
him receptive, and these are valuable things, though
they do not belong more to the introduction than to
the other parts of a speech; moreover they are easier
in the introduction, because the audience are most
attentive when they have the whole of the speech to
look forward to, and also they are more receptive at
the start, for statements made at the beginning,
whether aimed at proof or at refutation, stand out
clearer than those made in the middle of a case.
324 But we shall derive our greatest supply of openings
designed either to conciliate or to stimulate the judge
from topics contained in the case that are calculated
to produce emotions, though it will not be proper to
develop these fully at the start, but only to give a
slight preliminary impulsion to the judge, so that the
remainder of our speech may find him already biassed
325 in our direction. LXXX. But the opening passage

narration of circumstances;

CICERO

ita sit principium consequenti orationi ut non tamquam citharoedi prooemium affictum aliquid sed cohaerens cum omni corpore membrum esse videatur.
Nam non nulli, cum illud meditati ediderunt,
sic ad reliqua transeunt ut audientiam fieri sibi non
velle videantur. Atque eiusmodi illa prolusio debet
esse, non ut Samnitium, qui vibrant hastas ante pugnam quibus in pugnando nihil utuntur, sed ut ipsis
sententiis quibus proluserint vel pugnare possint.

326   Narrare vero rem quod breviter iubent, si brevitas
appellanda est cum verbum nullum redundat, brevis
est L. Crassi oratio ; sin tum est brevitas cum
tantum verborum est quantum necesse est, aliquando
id opus est, sed saepe obest vel maxime in narrando,
non solum quod obscuritatem affert sed etiam quod
eam virtutem quae narrationis est maxima, ut
iucunda et ad persuadendum accommodata sit, tollit.
Videant illa

    nam is postquam excessit ex ephebis . . .

327 quam longa est narratio ! Mores adolescentis ipsius
et servilis percontatio, mors Chrysidis, vultus et
forma et lamentatio sororis, reliqua pervarie iucundeque narrantur. Quodsi hanc brevitatem quaesisset :

      [a] Terence, *Andria* 51.

should be so closely connected with the speech that
follows as to appear to be not an appendage, like
the prelude to a piece of music, but an integral
part of the whole structure. For some musicians
play their prelude after due practice, but pass on
to the remainder of the work in such a manner
as to seem not really to want to be listened to.
Also the preliminary passage must not be like the
skirmishing of Samnite gladiators, who before a fight
brandish their spears which they are not going to
make any use of in the actual encounter, but must
be of such a character as to enable the combatants
to employ in the real encounter the very ideas which
they have made play with in the introduction.

326   " As for their rule that the narration of the case
must be brief, if the term brevity may be used to
denote the absence of a single word that is superfluous,
Lucius Crassus's style has brevity ; but if brevity
means employing only the absolutely essential minimum of words, this is required occasionally, but often
it is actually very detrimental in stating the facts of
the case, not only because it causes obscurity but
also because it does away with a quality that is
the greatest merit in narrative, that of entertaining
and convincing. Let people consider the passage
beginning

For ever since the day he came of age . . .[a]

327 what a long story it is ! The young man's own
character, the slave's inquiry, the death of Chrysis,
her sister's face and figure and her mourning, and all
the rest of it—all agreeably narrated in every variety
of style ! Whereas if he had really sought for brevity
in this style :

Effertur, imus, ad sepulcrum venimus,
In ignem imposita est,

fere[1] decem versiculis totum conficere potuisset;
quamquam hoc ipsum ' effertur, imus ' concisum est
ita ut non brevitati servitum sit sed magis venustati.
328 Quodsi nihil fuisset nisi ' in ignem imposita est,'
tamen res tota cognosci facile potuisset; sed et
festivitatem habet narratio distincta personis et
interpuncta sermonibus, et est et probabilius quod
gestum esse dicas cum quemadmodum actum sit
exponas, et multo apertius ad intellegendum est si
constituitur aliquando ac non ista brevitate percur-
329 ritur.   Apertam enim narrationem tam esse oportet
quam cetera, sed hoc magis in hac elaborandum est,
quod et difficilius est non esse obscurum in re narranda quam aut in principio aut in argumentando
aut in perorando, et maiore etiam periculo haec
pars orationis obscura est quam ceterae, vel quia,
si quo alio in loco est dictum quid obscurius, tantum
id perit quod ita dictum est, narratio obscura totam
occaecat orationem, vel quod alia possis, semel si
obscurius dixeris, dicere alio loco planius, narrationis
unus est in causa locus.   Erit autem perspicua
narratio si verbis usitatis, si ordine temporum ser-
330 vato, si non interrupte narrabitur.   LXXXI. Sed
quando utendum sit aut non sit narratione, id est

---

[1] fere om. codd. opt.

[a] Terence, *Andria* 117.

> The funeral—we start, we reach the tomb,
> The corpse is placed upon the pyre—[a]

he could have completed the whole affair in a matter of ten verses ! although the actual phrase ' The funeral—we start,' though very concise, nevertheless achieves not brevity but rather grace of style. 328 Supposing it had merely run ' She was placed on the pyre,' the whole of the facts could have been easily understood nevertheless ; but the narrative gains liveliness when it brings in several characters and is broken up with speeches, and also one's statement of what took place is both more convincing when one explains how it was done and much clearer to understand if occasionally a halt is called and the story 329 does not run right on with that curt brevity. The narrative ought to be as clear as all the other parts of the speech, but more pains must be taken to achieve clarity in this part because in narrating the facts of the case it is more difficult to avoid obscurity than in either the introduction or the proof or the peroration, and also obscurity is even more dangerous in this part of a speech than in the others, either because an obscure expression in any other place only causes the point obscurely expressed to be lost, but obscurity in the narrative blacks out the entire speech, or else because, whereas with other points if you have expressed them rather obscurely at one time you can express them more clearly in another place, there is only one place in a case for the narration. But clearness in the narration will be attained if it employs ordinary language, and if it keeps to the chronological order of events and is not broken by digres- 30 sions. LXXXI. But when to use and when not to use narrative is a matter for consideration : narra-

consilii ; neque enim si nota res est nec dubium quid
gestum sit narrare oportet nec si adversarius narravit, nisi si refellemus; ac si quando erit narran-
dum, nec illa quae suspicionem et crimen efficient
contraque nos erunt acriter persequemur et quicquid potuerit detrahemus, ne illud quod Crassus,
si quando fiat, perfidia, non stultitia fieri putat, ut
causae noceamus accidat. Nam ad summam totius
causae pertinet, caute an contra demonstrata res
sit, quod omnis orationis reliquae fons est narratio.

331   Sequitur ut causa ponatur, in quo videndum est
quid in controversiam veniat ; tum suggerenda sunt
firmamenta causae coniuncte et infirmandis contrariis et tuis confirmandis. Namque una in causis
ratio quaedam est eius orationis quae ad probandam
argumentationem valet, ea autem et confirmationem
et reprehensionem quaerit ; sed quia neque reprehendi quae contra dicuntur possunt nisi tua confirmes, neque haec confirmari nisi illa reprehendas,
idcirco haec et natura et utilitate et tractatione con-
332 iuncta sunt. Omnia autem concludenda sunt plerumque vel[1] rebus augendis vel inflammando iudice
vel mitigando ; omniaque cum superioribus orationis

---

[1] vel *add. Reid.*

tive should not be employed if the facts are known
and there is no doubt what occurred, nor yet if
they have been narrated by our opponent, unless
we are going to refute his account of them ; and
on occasions when narrative is necessary we shall
not lay very great stress on points that will cause
suspicion and occasion accusation, and will tell
against us, and we shall minimize anything that
might have had this effect, for fear lest it may result
in our injuring our own case—a thing which if it ever
does occur is in Crassus's opinion invariably due to
treachery and not to folly. For it touches the main
issue of the whole suit whether the case has been set
out with circumspection or the opposite, because the
narrative is the fountain head from which the whole
remainder of the speech flows.

331 "Next comes the statement of the case, a section in *rules for*
which the precise point at issue must be envisaged ; *statement*
and then the case must be supported by proofs, *of case and*
which is effected by conjointly demolishing your *conclusion.*
opponent's arguments and establishing your own.
For in cases at law the pleading that serves to prove
the line adopted may be said to have only a single
principle, though it aims at both proof and refutation ;
but inasmuch as it is neither possible to refute statements made against you unless you prove your own,
nor to prove your own statements without refuting
your opponent's, it follows that these proceedings are
connected together not only by nature but also in
respect of their value for your case and the method
332 of handling them. But all these arguments must as
a rule be rounded off either by enlarging on your
points or by arousing the feelings of the judge or
calming them down ; and all of them both in the

locis tum maxime extremo ad mentes iudicum quam
maxime permovendas et ad utilitatem nostram vo-
candas conferenda sunt.

333 Neque sane iam causa videtur esse cur secerna-
mus ea praecepta quae de suasionibus tradenda
sunt aut laudationibus, sunt enim pleraque communia ; sed tamen suadere aliquid aut dissuadere
gravissimae mihi personae videtur esse, nam et sapi-
entis est consilium explicare suum de maximis rebus
et honesti et diserti, ut mente providere, auctoritate
probare, oratione persuadere possis. LXXXII. Atque haec in senatu minore apparatu agenda sunt ;
sapiens enim est consilium multisque aliis dicendi
relinquendus locus, vitanda etiam ingeni ostenta-
334 tionis suspicio: contio capit omnem vim orationis et
gravitatem, varietatemque desiderat. Ergo in sua-
dendo nihil est optabilius quam dignitas ; nam qui
utilitatem petit, non quid maxime velit suasor sed
quid interdum magis sequatur videt. Nemo est
enim, praesertim in tam clara civitate, quin putet
expetendam maxime dignitatem, sed vincit utilitas
plerumque cum subest ille timor ea neglecta ne
335 dignitatem quidem posse retineri. Controversia
autem est inter hominum sententias aut in illo, utrum
sit utilius, aut etiam cum id convenit certatur

earlier parts of the speech and most of all at the end must be directed towards influencing the minds of the judges as much as possible and attracting them in the direction of our advantage.

333 "Again, there seems to be no reason why we should keep separate the rules that are to be imparted on the subject of advisory speeches or of panegyrics, as they are for the most part common to both ; but nevertheless to give advice for or against a course of action does seem to me to be a task for a person of the greatest weight of character, for to expound one's advice on matters of high importance calls for both wisdom and ability and eloquence, to enable one to make an intelligent forecast, give an authoritative proof and employ persuasive eloquence. LXXXII. And these ends can be achieved with less apparatus in the Senate, as that is a wise deliberative body, and one should leave room for many others to speak, beside avoiding any suspicion of a display of talent, 334 whereas a public meeting permits of the full employment of powerful and weighty oratory, and requires variety. Consequently in an advisory speech nothing is more desirable than dignity ; for a man who demands mere expediency does not see his adviser's main purpose but only his more immediate aim for the time being. For there is nobody, especially in a famous state like ours, who does not think that moral worth is the highest object of ambition, but for the most part expediency wins the day when there is a covert fear lest if expediency be neglected worth 335 will also have to be abandoned. But differences of opinion arise either on the question which of two alternatives is more expedient, or even supposing there is agreement about this, it is disputed whether

Advisory speeches on public affairs:

utrum honestati potius an utilitati consulendum sit ;
quae quia pugnare inter se saepe videntur, qui utilitatem defendet enumerabit commoda pacis, opum,
potentiae, vectigalium, praesidi militum, ceterarum
rerum quarum fructum utilitate metimur, itemque
incommoda contrariorum : qui ad dignitatem im-
pellet, maiorum exempla quae erant vel cum periculo gloriosa colliget, posteritatis immortalem memoriam augebit, utilitatem ex laude nasci defendet
336 semperque eam cum dignitate esse coniunctam. Sed
quid fieri possit aut non possit quidque etiam sit
necesse aut non sit in utraque re maxime est quaerendum ; inciditur enim omnis iam deliberatio si
intellegitur non posse fieri aut si necessitas affertur,
et qui id docuit non videntibus aliis, is plurimum
337 vidit. Ad consilium autem de republica dandum
caput est nosse rempublicam, ad dicendum vero
probabiliter nosse mores civitatis, qui quia crebro
mutantur, genus quoque orationis est saepe mutan-
dum ; et quamquam una fere vis est eloquentiae,
tamen quia summa dignitas est populi, gravissima
causa rei publicae, maximi motus multitudinis, genus
quoque dicendi grandius quoddam et illustrius esse
adhibendum videtur ; maximaque pars orationis ad-
movenda est ad animorum motus non numquam aut

---

^a Aristotle, *Rhet.* I. iv. 2.

the chief consideration should be integrity or expediency ; and as these two considerations often seem to conflict, the champion of expediency will reel off a list of the advantages of peace and wealth and power and revenue and military strength and all the other things whose value we measure by expediency, and also the disadvantages of their opposites, whereas one who urges us on the path of moral worth will collect examples of our ancestors' achievements that were glorious even though involving danger, and will magnify the value of an undying memory with posterity and maintain that glory engenders advantage

336 and moral worth is invariably linked with it. But in both departments it is of the greatest importance to inquire what is possible and what is impossible of achievement, and also what is inevitable or the reverse ; for all debate is at once cut short by the realization that a thing is impossible or if it is proved to be inevitable, and the philosopher [a] who taught this truth, which others did not discern, showed the

337 greatest insight. But the chief essential for giving counsel on affairs of state is a knowledge of the constitution of the state, whereas the thing that is essential for persuasive speaking is a knowledge of the national character ; and as this frequently alters, it is often necessary also to alter the style of speaking employed ; and although the fundamental nature of eloquence practically does not vary, nevertheless in view of the exalted dignity of the nation, the supreme importance of politics, and the violent passions of the crowd, it would seem that an oratorical style of more than average grandeur and brilliance is required ; and the greatest part of a speech must occasionally be directed to arousing the emotions of the

cohortatione aut commemoratione aliqua aut in spem aut in metum aut ad cupiditatem aut ad gloriam concitandos, saepe etiam a temeritate, iracundia, spe, iniuria, invidia, crudelitate revocandos. LXXXIII.

338 Fit autem ut, quia maxima quasi oratoris scaena videatur contionis esse, natura ipsa ad ornatius dicendi genus excitemur; habet enim multitudo vim quandam talem ut, quemadmodum tibicen sine tibiis canere, sic orator sine multitudine audiente

339 eloquens esse non possit. Et cum sint populares multi variique lapsus, vitanda est acclamatio adversa populi, quae aut orationis peccato aliquo excitatur si aspere, si arroganter, si turpiter, si sordide, si quo animi vitio dictum esse aliquid videtur, aut hominum offensione vel invidia, quae aut iusta est aut ex criminatione atque fama, aut res si displicet, aut si est in aliquo motu suae cupiditatis aut metus multitudo. His quattuor causis totidem medicinae opponuntur : tum obiurgatio, si est auctoritas ; tum admonitio, quasi lenior obiurgatio ; tum promissio si audierint probaturos ; tum deprecatio, quod est

340 infirmum sed nonnunquam utile. Nullo autem loco plus facetiae prosunt et celeritas et breve aliquod dictum nec sine dignitate et cum lepore ; nihil enim tam facile quam multitudo a tristitia et saepe ab acerbitate commode et breviter et acute et hilare dicto deducitur.

audience, by means of exhortation or of some form of reminder, to either hope or fear or desire or ambition, and often also to calling them back from rashness, anger or hope and from injustice, envy or cruelty.

338 LXXXIII. But as the orator's chief stage seems to be the platform at a public meeting, it naturally results that we are stimulated to employ the more ornate kind of oratory ; for the effect produced by numbers is of such a kind that a speaker can no more be eloquent without a large audience than a 339 flute-player can perform without a flute. And as there are a number of different ways of falling foul of the public, one must be careful not to arouse the disapproving outcries of the people, who are aroused either by some error in the speech, if a remark is thought to be harsh or arrogant or base or mean or to show some fault of character, or by personal annoyance or dislike that is either deserved or arises from slander and rumour, or if the subject is un-popular, or if the public is in a state of excitement arising out of some desire or alarm that it feels. These four causes of unpopularity can be met by as many remedies : sometimes by reproof, if one possesses authority, sometimes by admonition, which may be called a gentle form of reproof, sometimes by promising that if they will hear us out they will agree with us, and sometime, by apology, which is not a strong line to take, but is sometimes useful. 340 And in no other place is there more to be gained by using facetious turns and a rapid style and epigram-matic remarks expressed in a dignified and attractive way ; for nothing is so easy as to divert a crowd from gloominess and often from bitter feeling by means of a neat and terse and pointed and amusing phrase.

the style appropriate for public speaking.

455

LXXXIV. Exposui fere ut potui vobis in utroque genere causarum quae sequi solerem, quae fugere, quae spectare quaque omnino in causis ratione versari. 341 Nec illud tertium laudationum genus est difficile quod ego initio quasi a praeceptis nostris secreveram ; sed et quia multa sunt orationum genera et graviora et maioris copiae de quibus nemo fere praeciperet, et quod nos laudationibus non ita multum uti soleremus, totum hunc segregabam locum. Ipsi enim Graeci magis legendi et delectationis aut hominis alicuius ornandi quam utilitatis huius forensis causa laudationes scriptitaverunt ; quorum sunt libri quibus Themistocles, Aristides, Agesilaus, Epaminondas, Philippus, Alexander aliique laudantur ; nostrae laudationes quibus in foro utimur aut testimonii brevitatem habent nudam atque inornatam aut scribuntur ad funebrem contionem, quae ad orationis laudem minime accommodata est. Sed tamen, quoniam est utendum aliquando, nonnunquam etiam scribendum, velut Q. Tuberoni Africanum avunculum laudanti scripsit C. Laelius vel ut nosmet ipsi ornandi causa Graecorum more si quos velimus laudare possimus, sit a 342 nobis quoque tractatus hic locus. Perspicuum est

LXXXIV. "I have practically completed giving you an account, to the best of my ability, of the rules that I am accustomed to follow, and the faults which I try to avoid and the objects which I have in view in both kinds of cases, and generally of the method that
341 I adopt in law-suits. Nor is there any difficulty about Panegyrics. the third class, consisting of panegyrics, which I had excluded from our set of instructions at the outset. But there are a great many kinds of oratory that are both more dignified and wider in scope, which virtually nobody lays down rules about, and also we Romans do not much practise the custom of panegyrics, so consequently I put this department entirely on one side. For the Greeks themselves have constantly thrown off masses of panegyrics, designed more for reading and for entertainment, or for giving a laudatory account of some person, than for the practical purposes of public life with which we are now concerned : there are Greek books containing panegyrics of Themistocles, Aristides, Agesilaus, Epaminondas, Philip, Alexander and others ; whereas our Roman commendatory speeches that we make in the forum have either the bare and unadorned brevity of evidence to a person's character or are written to be delivered as a funeral speech, which is by no means a suitable occasion for parading one's distinction in rhetoric. But nevertheless, as laudatory speeches must be delivered occasionally and sometimes even written out, either as Gaius Laelius wrote a panegyric for Quintus Tubero to deliver on his uncle Africanus, or in order that we ourselves may be able if we wish to praise certain persons in an honorific speech in the Greek manner,
42 let us also treat of this topic. Well then, it is clear

igitur alia esse in homine optanda, alia laudanda;
genus, forma, vires, opes, divitiae, cetera quae fortuna[1] dat aut extrinsecus aut corpori, non habent in
se veram laudem, quae deberi virtuti uni putatur;
sed tamen quod ipsa virtus in earum rerum usu ac
moderatione maxime cernitur, tractanda in laudationibus etiam haec sunt naturae et fortunae bona,
in quibus est summa laus non extulisse se in
potestate, non fuisse insolentem in pecunia, non se
praetulisse aliis propter abundantiam fortunae, ut
opes et copiae non superbiae videantur ac libidini
sed bonitati ac moderationi facultatem et materiam
343 dedisse. Virtus autem, quae est per se ipsa lauda-
bilis et sine qua nihil laudari potest, tamen habet
plures partes, quarum alia est alia ad laudationem
aptior. Sunt enim aliae virtutes quae videntur in
moribus hominum et quadam comitate ac beneficentia
positae, aliae quae in ingeni aliqua facultate aut
animi magnitudine ac robore; nam clementia, iustitia, benignitas, fides, fortitudo in periculis com-
344 munibus iucunda est auditu in laudationibus, omnes
enim hae virtutes non tam ipsis qui eas habent quam
generi hominum fructuosae putantur: sapientia et
magnitudo animi qua omnes res humanae tenues ac
pro nihilo putantur et in excogitando vis quaedam
ingeni et ipsa eloquentia admirationis habent non
minus, iucunditatis minus; ipsos enim magis videntur quos laudamus quam illos apud quos laudamus

---

[1] *Wilkins:* ceteraque quae *aut* cetera quaeque.

that the qualities that are desirable in a person are
not the same as those that are praiseworthy : family,
good looks, bodily strength, resources, riches and
the rest of the external or personal gifts of fortune
do not in themselves contain any true ground for
praise, which is held to be due to virtue alone ; but
nevertheless, as it is in the employment and wise
management of these that virtue itself is very largely
discerned, a panegyric must also treat of these goods
of nature and of fortune in which the highest praise
is not to have been puffed up in office or insolent
in wealth, or to have put oneself in front of others
because of fortune's bounty—so that wealth and
riches may seem to have provided opportunity and
occasion not for pride and licence but for beneficence
343 and temperance. But virtue, which is praiseworthy
in itself and is a necessary element in anything that
can be praised, nevertheless contains several divisions,
one of which is more fit to be praised than another.
For there are some virtues that are manifested as
qualities of people's behaviour and by a sort of kindness and beneficence, while others consist in intellectual ability or in highmindedness and strength of
character ; inasmuch as mercy, justice, kindness,
fidelity, courage in common dangers are acceptable
344 topics in a panegyric, since all these virtues are
thought to be beneficial not so much to their
possessors as to the human race in general, whereas
wisdom, and magnanimity that counts all human
fortunes slight and worthless, and strength and
originality of intellect, and eloquence itself are not
less admired it is true but give less pleasure, because
they seem to grace and to safeguard the subjects of
our panegyrics themselves rather than the persons

ornare ac tueri. Sed tamen in laudando iungenda
sunt etiam haec genera virtutum, ferunt enim aures
hominum cum illa quae iucunda et grata, tum
etiam illa quae mirabilia sunt in virtute laudari.

345 LXXXV. Et quoniam singularum virtutum sunt
certa quaedam officia ac munera et sua cuique virtuti
laus propria debetur, erit explicandum in laude iusti-
tiae quid cum fide, quid cum aequabilitate, quid
cum eiusmodi aliquo officio is qui laudabitur fecerit,
itemque in ceteris res gestae ad cuiusque virtutis
346 genus et vim et nomen accommodabuntur. Gratis-
sima autem laus eorum factorum habetur quae sus-
cepta videntur a viris fortibus sine emolumento ac
praemio ; quae vero etiam cum labore ac periculo
ipsorum, haec habent uberrimam copiam ad laudandum, quod et dici ornatissime possunt et audiri
facillime ; ea enim denique virtus esse videtur
praestantis viri quae est fructuosa aliis, ipsi aut
laboriosa aut periculosa aut certe gratuita. Magna
etiam illa laus et admirabilis videri solet tulisse casus
sapienter adversos, non fractum esse fortuna, re-
347 tinuisse in rebus asperis dignitatem ; neque tamen
illa non ornant, habiti honores, decreta virtutis
praemia, res gestae iudiciis hominum comprobatae ;
in quibus etiam felicitatem ipsam deorum immor-

before whom they are delivered. But nevertheless virtues of these kinds also should be introduced in a panegyric, since an audience will accept the bestowal of praise on the aspects of virtue that call for admiration as well as on those that give pleasure and gratification.

345   LXXXV. "And since particular virtues have their own definite duties and functions and each virtue has an appropriate form of commendation that is due to it, in giving praise for justice it will be necessary to recite actions of the subject of our panegyric that exhibited fidelity and fairness, and any right conduct of that nature ; and similarly under the other heads our account of his actions will be fitted in to each successive class and meaning and designation of
346 virtue. But the most welcome praise is that bestowed on deeds that appear to have been performed by brave men without profit or reward ; while those that also involve toil and personal danger supply very fertile topics for panegyric, because they admit of being narrated in a most eloquent style and of obtaining the readiest reception from the audience ; for it is virtue that is profitable to others, and either toilsome or dangerous or at all events not profitable to its possessor, that is deemed to mark a man of outstanding merit. Also it is customarily recognized as a great and admirable distinction to have borne adversity wisely, not to have been crushed by misfortune, and not to have lost dignity in a difficult
347 situation ; and distinction is also conferred by offices filled, rewards of merit bestowed, and achievements honoured by the judgement of mankind ; in these matters moreover it is proper to a panegyric to attribute what is merely good fortune to the verdict

talium iudicio tribui laudationis est. Sumendae autem res erunt aut magnitudine praestabiles aut novitate primae aut genere ipso singulares ; neque enim parvae neque usitatae neque vulgares admira-
348 tione aut omnino laude dignae videri solent. Est etiam cum ceteris praestantibus viris comparatio in laudatione praeclara. De quo genere libitum est mihi paulo plura quam ostenderam dicere, non tam propter usum forensem, qui est a me omni hoc ser-mone tractatus, quam ut hoc videretis, si laudationes essent in oratoris officio, quod nemo negat, oratori virtutum omnium cognitionem sine qua laudatio
349 effici non possit esse necessariam. Iam vituperandi praecepta contrariis ex vitiis sumenda esse perspicuum est ; simul est illud ante oculos, nec bonum virum proprie et copiose laudari sine virtutum nec impro-bum notari ac vituperari sine vitiorum cognitione satis insignite atque aspere posse. Atque his locis et laudandi et vituperandi saepe nobis est utendum in omni genere causarum.

350   Habetis, de inveniendis rebus disponendisque quid sentiam ; adiungam etiam de memoria, ut labore Crassum levem neque ei quidquam aliud de quo disserat relinquam nisi ea quibus haec exornentur.

LXXXVI. Perge vero, inquit Crassus, libenter

of divine wisdom. And one must select achievements that are of outstanding importance or unprecedented or unparalleled in their actual character ; for small achievements or those that are not unusual or out of the ordinary are not as a rule felt to be specially admirable or to deserve praise at all. Moreover a splendid line to take in a paneygric is to compare the subject with all other men of high distinction. And the spirit has moved me to enlarge rather more fully on this class of topic than I had promised to do, not so much for the purpose of its employment in the courts, which has been my subject in the whole of this discourse, as to bring home to you the fact that if the functions of a speaker include the delivery of panegyrics, which nobody denies, a speaker is bound to possess, as an indispensable means for the construction of a panegyric, a knowledge of all the virtues. Then, it is clear that the rules for assigning blame have to be developed out of the vices that are the opposites of these virtues ; at the same time it is obvious that it is impossible either to praise a good man appropriately and fully without a knowledge of the virtues or to brand and blame a wicked man in a sufficiently impressive and crushing manner without a knowledge of the vices. And these topics of praise and blame we shall frequently have occasion to employ in every class of law-suit.

"I have given you my view in regard to the discovery and the arrangement of topics ; I will also add something on the subject of memory, in order to lighten the task of Crassus and to leave him nothing else to discuss except the method of elaborating these subjects."

LXXXVI. "Oh, pray continue," said Crassus, " I

enim te cognitum iam artificem aliquandoque evolutum illis integumentis dissimulationis tuae nudatumque perspicio ; et quod mihi nihil aut quod non multum relinquis, percommode facis, estque mihi gratum.

351 Iam istuc quantum tibi ego reliquerim, inquit Antonius, erit in tua potestate : si enim vere me[1] agere volueris, omnia tibi relinquo ; sin dissimulare, tu quemadmodum his satisfacias videris. Sed, ut ad rem redeam, non sum tanto ego, inquit, ingenio quanto Themistocles fuit, ut oblivionis artem quam memoriae malim ; gratiamque habeo Simonidi illi Cio quem primum ferunt artem memoriae protulisse.

352 Dicunt enim cum cenaret Crannone in Thessalia Simonides apud Scopam fortunatum hominem et nobilem cecinissetque id carmen quod in eum scripsisset, in quo multa ornandi causa poetarum more in Castorem scripta et Pollucem fuissent, nimis illum sordide Simonidi dixisse se dimidium eius ei quod pactus esset pro illo carmine daturum : reliquum a suis Tyndaridis quos aeque laudasset peteret si ei

353 videretur. Paulo post esse ferunt nuntiatum Simonidi ut prodiret : iuvenes stare ad ianuam duos quosdam qui eum magnopere evocarent ; surrexisse illum, prodisse, vidisse neminem ; hoc interim spatio conclave illud ubi epularetur Scopas concidisse ; ea ruina ipsum cum cognatis oppressum suis interiisse ;

---

[1] me *add. Rackham.*

[a] See § 299.

am delighted to see you at last known as a master of the theory, finally unmasked and stripped of the veil of your pretended ignorance ; and it is extremely obliging of you to leave little or nothing to me, and I am grateful for it."

351   "Oh, as for that," said Antony, "the amount I shall have left to you will be for you to decide ; if you want complete candour, what I leave to you is the whole subject, but if you want me to keep up the pretence, it is for you to consider how you may satisfy our friends here.   But to return to the subject," he continued, "I am not myself as clever as Themistocles[a] was, so as to prefer the science of forgetting to that of remembering ; and I am grateful to the famous Simonides of Ceos, who is said to have first invented

352 the science of mnemonics.   There is a story that Simonides was dining at the house of a wealthy nobleman named Scopas at Crannon in Thessaly, and chanted a lyric poem which he had composed in honour of his host, in which he followed the custom of the poets by including for decorative purposes a long passage referring to Castor and Pollux ; whereupon Scopas with excessive meanness told him he would pay him half the fee agreed on for the poem, and if he liked he might apply for the balance to his sons of Tyndareus, as they had gone halves in the pane-

353 gyric.   The story runs that a little later a message was brought to Simonides to go outside, as two young men were standing at the door who earnestly requested him to come out ; so he rose from his seat and went out, and could not see anybody ; but in the interval of his absence the roof of the hall where Scopas was giving the banquet fell in, crushing Scopas himself and his relations underneath the ruins and

465

quos cum humare vellent sui neque possent obtritos
internoscere ullo modo, Simonides dicitur ex eo quod
meminisset quo eorum loco quisque cubuisset de-
monstrator uniuscuiusque sepeliendi fuisse; hac tum
re admonitus invenisse fertur ordinem esse maxime
354 qui memoriae lumen afferret. Itaque eis qui hanc
partem ingeni exercerent locos esse capiendos et ea
quae memoria tenere vellent effingenda animo atque
in eis locis collocanda : sic fore ut ordinem rerum
locorum ordo conservaret, res autem ipsas rerum
effigies notaret, atque ut locis pro cera, simulacris pro
355 litteris uteremur. LXXXVII. Qui sit autem oratori
memoriae fructus, quanta utilitas, quanta vis, quid
me attinet dicere ? tenere quae didiceris in acci-
pienda causa, quae ipse cogitaris ? omnes fixas esse
in animo sententias ? omnem descriptum verborum
apparatum ? ita audire vel eum unde discas vel eum
cui respondendum sit ut illi non infundere in aures
tuas orationem sed in animo videantur inscribere ?
Itaque soli qui memoria vigent sciunt quid et quatenus et quomodo dicturi sint, quid responderint, quid
supersit : eidemque multa ex aliis causis aliquando a

killing them; and when their friends wanted to
bury them but were altogether unable to know
them apart as they had been completely crushed,
the story goes that Simonides was enabled by his
recollection of the place in which each of them had
been reclining at table to identify them for separate
interment; and that this circumstance suggested to
him the discovery of the truth that the best aid to
clearness of memory consists in orderly arrangement.
354 He inferred that persons desiring to train this faculty
must select localities and form mental images of the
facts they wish to remember and store those images
in the localities, with the result that the arrangement
of the localities will preserve the order of the facts,
and the images of the facts will designate the facts
themselves, and we shall employ the localities and
images respectively as a wax writing tablet and the
355 letters written on it. LXXXVII. But what business
is it of mine to specify the value to a speaker and
the usefulness and effectiveness of memory? of re-
taining the information given you when you were
briefed and the opinions you yourself have formed?
of having all your ideas firmly planted in your
mind and all your resources of vocabulary neatly
arranged? of giving such close attention to the
instructions of your client and to the speech of the
opponent you have to answer that they may seem
not just to pour what they say into your ears but to
imprint it on your mind? Consequently only people
with a powerful memory know what they are going to
say and for how long they are going to speak and in
what style, what points they have already answered
and what still remains; and they also can remember
from other cases many arguments which they have

356 se acta, multa ab aliis audita meminerunt. Quare confiteor equidem huius boni naturam esse principem, sicut earum rerum de quibus ante locutus sum omnium : sed haec ars tota dicendi, sive artis imago quaedam et similitudo est, habet hanc vim, non ut totum aliquid cuius in ingeniis nostris pars nulla sit pariat et procreet, verum ut ea quae sunt orta iam in 357 nobis et procreata educet atque confirmet ; verumtamen neque tam acri memoria fere quisquam est ut non dispositis notatisque rebus ordinem verborum omnium aut sententiarum complectatur neque vero tam hebeti ut nihil hac consuetudine et exercitatione adiuvetur. Vidit enim hoc prudenter sive Simonides sive alius quis invenit, ea maxime animis effingi nostris quae essent a sensu tradita atque impressa ; acerrimum autem ex omnibus nostris sensibus esse sensum videndi ; quare facillime animo teneri posse ea quae perciperentur auribus aut cogitatione si etiam commendatione oculorum animis traderentur ; ut res caecas et ab aspectus iudicio remotas conformatio quaedam et imago et figura ita notaret ut ea quae cogitando complecti vix possemus intuendo 358 quasi teneremus. His autem formis atque corporibus, sicut omnibus quae sub aspectum veniunt sede[1] opus est, etenim corpus intellegi sine loco non potest. Quare (ne in re nota et pervulgata multus et insolens

---

[1] *v.l.* veniunt admonetur memoria nostra atque exercitatur sede.

---

[a] After ' view ' some inferior MSS. insert ' serve to prompt and stimulate our memory.'

previously advanced and many which they have
356 heard from other people. And consequently for
my own part I confess that the chief source of this
endowment, as of all the things I have spoken of
before, is nature ; but the efficacy of the whole
of this science, or perhaps I should say pseudo-
science, of rhetoric, is not that it wholly originates
and engenders something no part of which is already
present in our minds, but that it fosters and
strengthens things that have already sprung to birth
357 within us ; though nevertheless hardly anybody
exists who has so keen a memory that he can retain
the order of all the words or sentences without having
arranged and noted his facts, nor yet is anybody so
dull-witted that habitual practice in this will not give
him some assistance. It has been sagaciously discerned by Simonides or else discovered by some
other person, that the most complete pictures are
formed in our minds of the things that have been
conveyed to them and imprinted on them by the
senses, but that the keenest of all our senses is the
sense of sight, and that consequently perceptions
received by the ears or by reflexion can be most
easily retained in the mind if they are also conveyed
to our minds by the mediation of the eyes, with the
result that things not seen and not lying in the field
of visual discernment are earmarked by a sort of outline and image and shape so that we keep hold of as
it were by an act of sight things that we can scarcely
358 embrace by an act of thought. But these forms and
bodies, like all the things that come under our view *a*
require an abode, inasmuch as a material object
without a locality is inconceivable. Consequently (in
order that I may not be prolix and tedious on a sub-

sim) locis est utendum multis, illustribus, explicatis, modicis intervallis; imaginibus autem agentibus, acribus, insignitis, quae occurrere celeriterque percutere animum possint; quam facultatem et exercitatio dabit, ex qua consuetudo gignitur, et similium verborum conversa et immutata casibus aut traducta ex parte ad genus notatio et unius verbi imagine totius sententiae informatio pictoris cuiusdam summi ratione et modo formarum varietate locos distin-
359 guentis. LXXXVIII. Sed verborum memoria, quae minus est nobis necessaria, maiore imaginum varietate distinguitur; multa enim sunt verba quae quasi articuli connectunt membra orationis quae formari similitudine nulla possunt; eorum fingendae nobis sunt imagines quibus semper utamur; rerum memoria propria est oratoris; eam singulis personis bene positis notare possumus ut sententias imaginibus,
360 ordinem locis comprehendamus. Neque verum est quod ab inertibus dicitur, opprimi memoriam imaginum pondere et obscurari etiam id quod per se natura tenere potuisset; vidi enim ego summos homines et divina prope memoria, Athenis Charmadam, in Asia, quem vivere hodie aiunt, Scepsium Metrodorum, quorum uterque tanquam litteris in cera sic se aiebat imaginibus in eis locis quos haberet quae meminisse vellet perscribere. Quare hac

---

[a] The phrase denotes what we call 'perspective.'

[b] Cato's rule was *Rem tene, verba sequentur.*

[c] Prepositions and conjunctions are specially meant.

ject that is well known and familiar) one must employ
a large number of localities which must be clear and
defined and at moderate intervals apart, and images
that are effective and sharply outlined and distinctive,
with the capacity of encountering and speedily penetrating the mind ; the ability to use these will be
supplied by practice, which engenders habit, and by
marking off similar words with an inversion and altera-
tion of their cases or a transference from species to
genus, and by representing a whole concept by the
image of a single word, on the system and method
of a consummate painter distinguishing the positions
of objects by modifying their shapes.[a] LXXXVIII.
359 But a memory for words, which for us is less essential,[b]
is given distinctness by a greater variety of images ;
for there are many words [c] which serve as joints
connecting the limbs of the sentence, and these
cannot be formed by any use of simile—of these we
have to model images for constant employment ; but
a memory for things is the special property of the
orator—this we can imprint on our minds by a skilful
arrangement of the several masks that represent
them, so that we may grasp ideas by means of images
360 and their order by means of localities. Nor is it true,
as unscientific people assert, that memory is crushed
beneath a weight of images and even what might
have been retained by nature unassisted is obscured ;
for I have myself met eminent people with almost
superhuman powers of memory, Charmadas at Athens
and Metrodorus of Scepsis in Asia, who is said to be
still living, each of whom used to say that he wrote
down things he wanted to remember in certain ' localities ' in his possession by means of images, just as if
he were inscribing letters on wax. It follows that

471

exercitatione non eruenda memoria est si est nulla
naturalis, sed certe si latet evocanda est.

361   Habetis sermonem bene longum hominis utinam
non impudentis ! Illud quidem certe, non nimis vere-
cundi, qui quidem cum te, Catule, tum etiam
L. Crasso audiente de dicendi ratione tam multa dixerim ; nam istorum aetas minus me fortasse movere
debuit. Sed mihi ignoscetis profecto, si modo quae
causa me ad hanc insolitam mihi loquacitatem im-
pulerit acceperitis.

362   LXXXIX. Nos vero, inquit Catulus, etenim pro
me hoc et pro meo fratre respondeo, non modo tibi
ignoscimus sed te diligimus magnamque tibi habemus gratiam ; et cum humanitatem et facilitatem
agnoscimus tuam, tum admiramur istam scientiam et
copiam. Equidem etiam hoc me assecutum puto,
quod magno sum levatus errore et illa admiratione
liberatus quod multis cum aliis semper admirari
solebam unde esset illa tanta tua in causis divinitas ;
nec enim te ista attigisse arbitrabar quae diligentissime cognosse et undique collegisse usuque doctum
partim correxisse video, partim comprobasse ; neque

363 eo minus eloquentiam tuam et multo magis virtutem

---

this practice cannot be used to draw out the memory if no memory has been given to us by nature, but it can undoubtedly summon it to come forth if it is in hiding.

361 "There is a fairly long lecture for you from a person whom I hope you will not think conceited! Though not over-modest I am sure you must think me, for having discoursed at such length on the theory of rhetoric before an audience including not only you, Catulus, but also Lucius Crassus—for no doubt I was right in not troubling so much about hearers of the age of our friends here. But I am sure you will forgive me if only I explain to you the motive that has urged me on to a talkativeness for me unusual."

Conclusion : Crassus complimented and requested to speak on ornaments of style. Debate adjourned to afternoon.

362 LXXXIX. "Oh, as for us," said Catulus, "inasmuch as I am making this answer for myself and for my brother, not only do we forgive you but we hold you in high esteem and are extremely grateful to you ; and we recognize your courtesy and kindness, and also are filled with admiration for the knowledge and the fluency that you have displayed. For my own part I feel I have scored the further advantage that I have been cured of a great mistake and have been set free from the wonder that I spoke of,[a] as to a matter that has always been a constant puzzle to me and many others as well,—where you obtained the mastery, amounting to genius, which you display in law-suits ; in fact I used to imagine that you had never embarked on the subjects that you have been dealing with, to which I now see that you have given the most diligent study, collecting them from all sources and employing the teaching of experience 363 partly to correct and partly to confirm them ; nor do I feel less admiration for your eloquence, and much

473

et diligentiam admiror et simul gaudeo iudicium animi mei comprobari quod semper statui neminem sapientiae laudem et eloquentiae sine summo studio et labore et doctrina consequi posse. Sed tamen quidnam est quod dixisti fore ut tibi ignosceremus si cognossemus quae te causa in sermonem impulisset ? Quae est enim alia causa nisi quod nobis et horum adolescentium studio, qui te attentissime audierunt, morem gerere voluisti ?

364 Tum ille : Adimere, inquit, omnem recusationem Crasso volui quem ego paulo ante sentiebam[1] vel pudentius vel invitius, nolo enim dicere de tam suavi homine fastidiosius, ad hoc genus sermonis accedere. Quid enim poterit dicere ? Consularem se esse hominem et censorium ? Eadem nostra causa est. An aetatem afferet ? Quadriennio minor est. An se haec nescire ? Quae ego sero, quae cursim arripui, quae subsicivis operis, ut aiunt, iste a puero, summo studio, summis doctoribus. Nihil dicam de ingenio, cui par nemo fuit ; etenim me dicentem qui audiret, nemo unquam tam sui despiciens fuit quin speraret aut melius aut eodem modo se posse dicere : Crasso dicente nemo tam arrogans, qui similiter se unquam dicturum esse confideret. Quam ob rem ne frustra hi tales viri venerint, te aliquando, Crasse, audiamus.

[1] *Kayser:* sciebam.

---

[a] Actually three, see p. xiii n. *a*; but 140 B.C. would be spoken of as the *fourth* year after 143.

more admiration for your energy and industry, and
at the same time I rejoice in the confirmation of my
own conviction, which I have always held, that no
one can achieve high distinction for wisdom and
eloquence without a very great amount of zeal
and industry and study. But all the same, what
exactly did you mean by saying that we should
forgive you if we knew the motive that had led you
to deliver a discourse ? What other motive can it
be except a desire to oblige us and to satisfy the
interest of these young people, who have given you
a most attentive hearing ? "

364 " Oh," he replied, " I wanted to deprive Crassus
of all excuse for crying off, having noticed a little
earlier that he was too modest, or too reluctant—for
in regard to such an agreeable person I will not say
too fastidious—about entering on this kind of debate.
For what will he be able to say ? That he is a person
who has held the offices of consul and of censor ? We
can make the same plea. Or will he adduce his age ?
He is four[a] years our junior. Or that he does not
know these subjects ? Why, I took them up late and
casually and as an occupation for odd moments, as
the phrase is, whereas our friend has studied them
from boyhood with the greatest industry and under
the best masters. I will say nothing about his ability,
which nobody has ever rivalled : in fact whereas no
one who has heard me speaking has ever held so low
an opinion of himself as not to hope he was capable of
speaking better, or at all events as well, when Crassus
speaks nobody was ever so conceited as to believe
that he would ever speak as well. Therefore, so that
these distinguished gentlemen may not have come
here to no purpose, let us at last, Crassus, hear you."

365   XC. Tum ille : Ut ita ista esse concedam, inquit,
Antoni, quae sunt longe secus, quid mihi tandem
hodie aut cuiquam homini quod dici possit reliquisti ?
Dicam enim vere, amicissimi homines, quod sentio :
saepe ego doctos homines, quid dico saepe ? immo
nonnunquam, saepe enim qui potui, qui puer in
forum venerim neque inde unquam diutius quam
quaestor abfuerim ? sed tamen audivi, ut heri dice-
bam, et Athenis cum essem doctissimos viros et in
Asia istum ipsum Scepsium Metrodorum cum de
his ipsis rebus disputaret ; neque vero mihi quisquam
copiosius unquam visus est neque subtilius in hoc
genere dicendi quam iste hodie esse versatus : quod
si esset aliter et aliquid intellegerem ab Antonio praetermissum, non essem tam inurbanus et paene in-
humanus ut in eo gravarer quod vos cupere sentirem.

366   Tum Sulpicius : An ergo, inquit, oblitus es, Crasse,
Antonium ita partitum esse tecum ut ipse instrumentum oratoris exponeret, tibi eius distinctionem
atque ornatum relinqueret ?

Hic ille : Primum quis Antonio permisit, inquit,
ut et partes faceret et utram vellet prior ipse
sumeret ? Deinde, si ego recte intellexi cum valde
libenter audirem, mihi coniuncte est visus de utraque
re dicere.

Ille vero, inquit Cotta, ornamenta orationis non

476

365 XC. " Granted, Antonius," rejoined Crassus, " that I allow something to be the case which is in reality quite otherwise, what pray have you to-day left to me, or to anybody, that can possibly be said ? For, my very good friends, I will give you my true opinion : I have heard learned persons often—why do I say ' often ' ? rather let me say ' occasionally,' for how could I possibly have heard them often, having gone to the bar as I did while a mere lad, and having never had a longer absence from it than my period of office as quaestor ? but be that as it may, I have, as I was saying yesterday, heard very learned men, both when I was at Athens, and in Asia your Metrodorus of Scepsis himself, discussing these very subjects ; but nevertheless I have never thought that anybody discoursed with greater fullness or with greater penetration in this class of debate than our friend here to-day ; and even if this were not the case, and if I detected some point that Antonius had passed over, I should not be so uncivil and I may say so inhuman as to make a difficulty about what I feel to be your strong desire."

366 " Have you then forgotten, Crassus," rejoined Sulpicius, " the apportionment arranged with you by Antonius, for him to expound the speaker's stock-in-trade himself while he left its elaboration and embellishment to you ? "

Hereupon, " In the first place," said Crassus, " who gave Antonius leave to divide the subject up into shares and himself to have the first choice ? And next, if I understood him rightly, listening as I was with great pleasure, he seemed to me to be discussing both the two subjects conjointly."

" As a matter of fact," said Cotta, " he did not

attigit neque eam laudem ex qua eloquentia nomen suum invenit.

Verba igitur, inquit Crassus, mihi reliquit Antonius, rem ipse sumpsit.

367 Tum Caesar : Si quod difficilius est id tibi reliquit, est nobis, inquit, causa cur te audire cupiamus : sin quod facilius, tibi causa non est cur recuses.

Et Catulus : Quid quod dixisti, inquit, Crasse, si hodie apud te maneremus te morem nobis esse gesturum, nihilne ad fidem tuam putas pertinere ?

Tum Cotta ridens : Possem tibi, inquit, Crasse, concedere ; sed vide ne quid Catulus attulerit religionis : hoc opus censorium est, id autem committere vide[1] quam homini censorio conveniat.

Agite vero, inquit,[2] ut vultis. Sed nunc quidem, quoniam est id temporis, surgendum censeo et requiescendum : post meridiem, si ita vobis est commodum, loquemur aliquid, nisi forte in crastinum differre mavultis.

Omnes se vel statim vel si ipse post meridiem mallet, quam primum tamen audire velle dixerunt.

[1] *Reid:* vides.   [2] *v.l.* ille inquit.

touch on the embellishment of oratory, nor the accomplishment from which eloquence has derived its name."

"If that is so," said Crassus, "Antony left the words to me and took the matter for himself."

367 "If he left you the harder part," interposed Caesar, "we have good reason for wanting to hear you, and if the part he left you is the easier one, you have no reason for refusing."

And Catulus said, "What about your promise, Crassus, that if we stayed on at your house to-day you would gratify our wish? Don't you think you are bound in honour to do so?"

"I might possibly give way to you, Crassus," rejoined Cotta with a smile, "but mind we don't have Catulus introducing a point of moral obligation; this is a job for a censor's attention, but mind how it can be proper for a former censor to commit it."

"Oh well," said Crassus, "do as you please. But now, seeing what the time is, I move that the house do adjourn for a rest; and if it is agreeable to you we will say something in the afternoon, unless perhaps you would prefer to postpone it till to-morrow."

They all said they wanted to hear him at once, or at all events, if he himself preferred the afternoon, as early as possible.

APPENDIX

Book I, § 41 (p. 30). *qui aut interdicto . . . temere irruisses.*
In legal disputes as to possession the *interdictum* was a preliminary order of the praetor intended to secure for one of the litigants interim possession of the disputed property, so as to make him defendant in the subsequent real action and cast the burden of proof upon the other as plaintiff. *Consertio manus* was the stage in the real action at which the parties simulated the physical struggle of lawless times, by laying hands together upon the property and making claim and counterclaim to the ownership. In the case of land this formality took place out of court.

Book I, § 42 (pp. 30-32). *Agerent enim tecum lege . . . non liceret.* *Legis actiones*, of five types, were the remedies at the earliest stage of developed Roman legal procedure : they involved a rigid and elaborate ritual, in which the slightest slip was fatal to the blunderer's case. *Sacramentum* was one of these types, involving a pecuniary deposit by each litigant. The winner of the action recovered his *sacramentum*, while the loser's was forfeited to the State.

Book I, § 178 (p. 122). *defendebamus . . . praestare debere.*
By this time Roman Law had apparently evolved the rule that a vendor of immovable property warrants the purchaser against all such material defects in his title as he does not disclose. The English rule is the same.

Book I, § 180 (p. 124). *antequam in suam tutelam venisset.*
A boy emerged from guardianship at the age of fourteen. In this famous *causa Curiana* a testator had left his estate to his expected posthumous child, with a gift over to Curius in the event of such child dying under age. After all no child was born. Was the condition of death under age fulfilled by the default of birth? Crassus successfully maintained the affirmative, and Curius took under the will.

Printed in Great Britain by R. & R. CLARK, LIMITED, *Edinburgh*

THE LOEB CLASSICAL LIBRARY

VOLUMES ALREADY PUBLISHED

LATIN AUTHORS

AMMIANUS MARCELLINUS. J. C. Rolfe. 3 Vols. (*3rd Imp. revised.*)

APULEIUS : THE GOLDEN ASS (METAMORPHOSES). W. Adlington (1566). Revised by S. Gaselee. (*7th Imp.*)

ST. AUGUSTINE : CITY OF GOD. 7 Vols. Vol. I. G. E. McCracken.

ST. AUGUSTINE, CONFESSIONS OF. W. Watts (1631). 2 Vols. (Vol. I *7th Imp.*, Vol. II *6th Imp.*)

ST. AUGUSTINE : SELECT LETTERS. J. H. Baxter. (*2nd Imp.*)

AUSONIUS. H. G. Evelyn White. 2 Vols. (*2nd Imp.*)

BEDE. J. E. King. 2 Vols. (*2nd Imp.*)

BOETHIUS : TRACTS AND DE CONSOLATIONE PHILOSOPHIAE. Rev. H. F. Stewart and E. K. Rand. (*6th Imp.*)

CAESAR : ALEXANDRIAN, AFRICAN AND SPANISH WARS. A. G. Way.

CAESAR : CIVIL WARS. A. G. Peskett. (*6th Imp.*)

CAESAR : GALLIC WAR. H. J. Edwards. (*11th Imp.*)

CATO AND VARRO : DE RE RUSTICA. H. B. Ash and W. D. Hooper. (*3rd Imp.*)

CATULLUS. F. W. Cornish ; TIBULLUS. J. B. Postgate ; and PERVIGILIUM VENERIS. J. W. Mackail. (*13th Imp.*)

CELSUS : DE MEDICINA. W. G. Spencer. 3 Vols. (Vol. I *3rd Imp. revised*, Vols. II and III *2nd Imp.*)

CICERO : BRUTUS AND ORATOR. G. L. Hendrickson and H. M. Hubbell. (*3rd Imp.*)

CICERO : DE FATO ; PARADOXA STOICORUM ; DE PARTITIONE ORATORIA. H. Rackham. (With De Oratore, Vol. II.) (*2nd Imp.*)

1

CICERO: DE FINIBUS. H. Rackham. (4th Imp. revised.)

CICERO: DE INVENTIONE, etc. H. M. Hubbell.

CICERO: DE NATURA DEORUM AND ACADEMICA. H. Rackham. (3rd Imp.)

CICERO: DE OFFICIIS. Walter Miller. (7th Imp.)

CICERO: DE ORATORE. E. W. Sutton and H. Rackham. 2 Vols. (2nd Imp.)

CICERO: DE REPUBLICA, DE LEGIBUS, SOMNIUM SCIPIONIS. Clinton W. Keyes. (4th Imp.)

CICERO: DE SENECTUTE, DE AMICITIA, DE DIVINATIONE. W. A. Falconer. (6th Imp.)

CICERO: IN CATILINAM, PRO MURENA, PRO SULLA, PRO FLACCO. Louis E. Lord. (3rd Imp. revised.)

CICERO: LETTERS TO ATTICUS. E. O. Winstedt. 3 Vols. (Vol. I 7th Imp., Vols. II and III 4th Imp.)

CICERO: LETTERS TO HIS FRIENDS. W. Glynn Williams. 3 Vols. (Vols. I and II 4th Imp., Vol. III 2nd Imp. revised and enlarged.)

CICERO: PHILIPPICS. W. C. A. Ker. (4th Imp.)

CICERO: PRO ARCHIA, POST REDITUM, DE DOMO, DE HARUSPICUM RESPONSIS, PRO PLANCIO. N. H. Watts. (3rd Imp.)

CICERO: PRO CAECINA, PRO LEGE MANILIA, PRO CLUENTIO, PRO RABIRIO. H. Grose Hodge. (3rd Imp.)

CICERO: PRO CAELIO, DE PROVINCIIS CONSULARIBUS, PRO BALBO. R. Gardner.

CICERO: PRO MILONE, IN PISONEM, PRO SCAURO, PRO FONTEIO, PRO RABIRIO POSTUMO, PRO MARCELLO, PRO LIGARIO, PRO REGE DEIOTARO. N. H. Watts. (3rd Imp.)

CICERO: PRO QUINCTIO, PRO ROSCIO AMERINO, PRO ROSCIO COMOEDO, CONTRA RULLUM. J. H. Freese. (3rd Imp.)

CICERO: PRO SESTIO, IN VATINIUM. R. Gardner.

[CICERO]: RHETORICA AD HERENNIUM. H. Caplan.

CICERO: TUSCULAN DISPUTATIONS. J. E. King. (4th Imp.)

CICERO: VERRINE ORATIONS. L. H. G. Greenwood. 2 Vols. (Vol. I 3rd Imp., Vol. II 2nd Imp.)

CLAUDIAN. M. Platnauer. 2 Vols. (2nd Imp.)

COLUMELLA: DE RE RUSTICA; DE ARBORIBUS. H. B. Ash, E. S. Forster, E. Heffner. 3 Vols. (Vol. I 2nd Imp.)

CURTIUS, Q.: HISTORY OF ALEXANDER. J. C. Rolfe. 2 Vols. (2nd Imp.)

THE LOEB CLASSICAL LIBRARY

FLORUS. E. S. Forster; and CORNELIUS NEPOS. J. C. Rolfe. (2nd Imp.)

FRONTINUS: STRATAGEMS AND AQUEDUCTS. C. E. Bennett and M. B. McElwain. (2nd Imp.)

FRONTO: CORRESPONDENCE. C. R. Haines. 2 Vols. (3rd Imp.)

GELLIUS. J. C. Rolfe. 3 Vols. (Vol. I 3rd Imp., Vols II and III 2nd Imp.)

HORACE: ODES AND EPODES. C. E. Bennett. (14th Imp. revised.)

HORACE: SATIRES, EPISTLES, ARS POETICA. H. R. Fairclough. (9th Imp. revised.)

JEROME: SELECT LETTERS. F. A. Wright. (2nd Imp.)

JUVENAL AND PERSIUS. G. G. Ramsay. (8th Imp.)

LIVY. B. O. Foster, F. G. Moore, Evan T. Sage, A. C. Schlesinger and R. M. Geer (General Index). 14 Vols. Vols. I-XIII. (Vol. I 5th Imp., Vol. V 4th Imp., Vols. II-IV, VI, VII, IX-XII 3rd Imp., Vol. VIII 2nd Imp. revised.)

LUCAN. J. D. Duff. (4th Imp.)

LUCRETIUS. W. H. D. Rouse. (7th Imp. revised.)

MARTIAL. W. C. A. Ker. 2 Vols. (Vol. I 5th Imp., Vol. II 4th Imp. revised.)

MINOR LATIN POETS: from PUBLILIUS SYRUS to RUTILIUS NAMATIANUS, including GRATTIUS, CALPURNIUS SICULUS, NEMESIANUS, AVIANUS, with "Aetna," "Phoenix" and other poems. J. Wight Duff and Arnold M. Duff. (3rd Imp.)

OVID: THE ART OF LOVE AND OTHER POEMS. J. H. Mozley. (4th Imp.)

OVID: FASTI. Sir James G. Frazer. (2nd Imp.)

OVID: HEROIDES AND AMORES. Grant Showerman. (7th Imp.)

OVID: METAMORPHOSES. F. J. Miller. 2 Vols. (Vol. I 11th Imp., Vol. II 10th Imp.)

OVID: TRISTIA AND EX PONTO. A. L. Wheeler. (3rd Imp.)

PETRONIUS. M. Heseltine; SENECA: APOCOLOCYNTOSIS. W. H. D. Rouse. (9th Imp. revised.)

PLAUTUS. Paul Nixon. 5 Vols. (Vol. I 6th Imp., Vol. II 5th Imp., Vol. III 4th Imp., Vols. IV and V 2nd Imp.)

PLINY: LETTERS. Melmoth's translation revised by W. M. L. Hutchinson. 2 Vols. (Vol. I 7th Imp., Vol. II 6th Imp. revised.)

PLINY : NATURAL HISTORY. 10 Vols. Vols. I-V and IX.
H. Rackham. Vols. VI and VII. W. H. S. Jones.
(Vols. I-III 3rd Imp., Vol. IV 2nd Imp.)

PROPERTIUS. H. E. Butler. (7th Imp.)

PRUDENTIUS. H. J. Thomson. 2 Vols.

QUINTILIAN. H. E. Butler. 4 Vols. (Vols. I and IV 4th
Imp., Vols. II and III 3rd Imp.)

REMAINS OF OLD LATIN. E. H. Warmington. 4 Vols.
Vol. I (Ennius and Caecilius). Vol. II (Livius, Naevius,
Pacuvius, Accius). Vol. III (Lucilius, Laws of the XII
Tables). Vol. IV (Archaic Inscriptions). (2nd Imp.)

SALLUST. J. C. Rolfe. (4th Imp. revised.)

SCRIPTORES HISTORIAE AUGUSTAE. D. Magie. 3 Vols.
(Vol. I 3rd Imp., Vols. II and III 2nd Imp. revised.)

SENECA : APOCOLOCYNTOSIS. Cf. PETRONIUS.

SENECA : EPISTULAE MORALES. R. M. Gummere. 3 Vols.
(Vol. I 4th Imp., Vols. II and III 3rd Imp. revised.)

SENECA : MORAL ESSAYS. J. W. Basore. 3 Vols. (Vol. II
3rd Imp. revised, Vols. I and III 2nd Imp. revised.)

SENECA : TRAGEDIES. F. J. Miller. 2 Vols. (Vol. I 4th
Imp., Vol. II 3rd Imp. revised.)

SIDONIUS : POEMS AND LETTERS. W. B. Anderson. 2 Vols.
(Vol. I 2nd Imp.)

SILIUS ITALICUS. J. D. Duff. 2 Vols. (Vol. I 2nd Imp.,
Vol. II 3rd Imp.)

STATIUS. J. H. Mozley. 2 Vols. (2nd Imp.)

SUETONIUS. J. C. Rolfe. 2 Vols. (Vol. I 7th Imp., Vol. II
6th Imp.)

TACITUS : DIALOGUS. Sir Wm. Peterson ; and AGRICOLA
AND GERMANIA. Maurice Hutton. (7th Imp.)

TACITUS : HISTORIES AND ANNALS. C. H. Moore and J.
Jackson. 4 Vols. (Vols. I and II 4th Imp., Vols. III and
IV 3rd Imp.)

TERENCE. John Sargeaunt. 2 Vols. (Vol. I 8th Imp., Vol.
II 7th Imp.)

TERTULLIAN : APOLOGIA AND DE SPECTACULIS. T. R. Glover ;
MINUCIUS FELIX. G. H. Rendall. (2nd Imp.)

VALERIUS FLACCUS. J. H. Mozley. (3rd Imp. revised.)

VARRO : DE LINGUA LATINA. R. G. Kent. 2 Vols. (3rd
Imp. revised.)

VELLEIUS PATERCULUS AND RES GESTAE DIVI AUGUSTI.
F. W. Shipley. (2nd Imp.)

THE LOEB CLASSICAL LIBRARY

VIRGIL. H. R. Fairclough. 2 Vols. (Vol. I 19th Imp., Vol. II 14th Imp. revised.)

VITRUVIUS: DE ARCHITECTURA. F. Granger. 2 Vols. (Vol. I 3rd Imp., Vol. II 2nd Imp.)

GREEK AUTHORS

ACHILLES TATIUS. S. Gaselee. (2nd Imp.)

AELIAN: ON THE NATURE OF ANIMALS. A. F. Scholfield. 3 Vols. Vols. I and II.

AENEAS TACTICUS, ASCLEPIODOTUS AND ONASANDER. The Illinois Greek Club. (2nd Imp.)

AESCHINES. C. D. Adams. (3rd Imp.)

AESCHYLUS. H. Weir Smyth. 2 Vols. (Vol. I 7th Imp., Vol. II 6th Imp. revised and enlarged.)

ALCIPHRON, AELIAN AND PHILOSTRATUS: LETTERS. A. R. Benner and F. H. Fobes.

APOLLODORUS. Sir James G. Frazer. 2 Vols. (3rd Imp.)

APOLLONIUS RHODIUS. R. C. Seaton. (5th Imp.)

THE APOSTOLIC FATHERS. Kirsopp Lake. 2 Vols. (Vol. I 8th Imp., Vol. II 6th Imp.)

APPIAN'S ROMAN HISTORY. Horace White. 4 Vols. (Vol. I 4th Imp., Vols. II-IV 3rd Imp.)

ARATUS. Cf. CALLIMACHUS.

ARISTOPHANES. Benjamin Bickley Rogers. 3 Vols. (5th Imp.) Verse trans.

ARISTOTLE: ART OF RHETORIC. J. H. Freese. (3rd Imp.)

ARISTOTLE: ATHENIAN CONSTITUTION, EUDEMIAN ETHICS, VIRTUES AND VICES. H. Rackham. (3rd Imp.)

ARISTOTLE: GENERATION OF ANIMALS. A. L. Peck. (2nd Imp.)

ARISTOTLE: METAPHYSICS. H. Tredennick. 2 Vols. (4th Imp.)

ARISTOTLE: METEOROLOGICA. H. D. P. Lee.

ARISTOTLE: MINOR WORKS. W. S. Hett. " On Colours," " On Things Heard," " Physiognomics," " On Plants," " On Marvellous Things Heard," " Mechanical Problems," " On Indivisible Lines," " Situations and Names of Winds," " On Melissus, Xenophanes, and Gorgias.' (2nd Imp.)

ARISTOTLE: NICOMACHEAN ETHICS. H. Rackham. (6th Imp. revised.)

THE LOEB CLASSICAL LIBRARY

ARISTOTLE: OECONOMICA AND MAGNA MORALIA. G. C. Armstrong. (With Metaphysics, Vol. II.) (*4th Imp.*)

ARISTOTLE: ON THE HEAVENS. W. K. C. Guthrie. (*3rd Imp.*)

ARISTOTLE: ON THE SOUL, PARVA NATURALIA, ON BREATH. W. S. Hett. (*2nd Imp. revised.*)

ARISTOTLE: ORGANON—THE CATEGORIES. ON INTERPRETATION. H. P. Cooke; PRIOR ANALYTICS. H. Tredennick. (*3rd Imp.*)

ARISTOTLE: ORGANON—POSTERIOR ANALYTICS. H. Tredennick; TOPICS. E. S. Forster.

ARISTOTLE: ORGANON—SOPHISTICAL REFUTATIONS. COMING-TO-BE AND PASSING-AWAY. E. S. Forster. ON THE COSMOS. D. J. Furley.

ARISTOTLE: PARTS OF ANIMALS. A. L. Peck; MOTION AND PROGRESSION OF ANIMALS. E. S. Forster. (*3rd Imp.*)

ARISTOTLE: PHYSICS. Rev. P. Wicksteed and F. M. Cornford. 2 Vols. (Vol. I *2nd Imp.*, Vol. II *3rd Imp.*)

ARISTOTLE: POETICS AND LONGINUS. W. Hamilton Fyfe; DEMETRIUS ON STYLE. W. Rhys Roberts. (*5th Imp. revised.*)

ARISTOTLE: POLITICS. H. Rackham. (*4th Imp.*)

ARISTOTLE: PROBLEMS. W. S. Hett. 2 Vols. (*2nd Imp. revised.*)

ARISTOTLE: RHETORICA AD ALEXANDRUM. H. Rackham. (With Problems, Vol. II.)

ARRIAN: HISTORY OF ALEXANDER AND INDICA. Rev. E. Iliffe Robson. 2 Vols. (*3rd Imp.*)

ATHENAEUS: DEIPNOSOPHISTAE. C. B. Gulick. 7 Vols. (Vols. I-IV, VI and VII *2nd Imp.*, Vol. V *3rd Imp.*)

ST. BASIL: LETTERS. R. J. Deferrari. 4 Vols. (*2nd Imp.*)

CALLIMACHUS: FRAGMENTS. C. A. Trypanis.

CALLIMACHUS: HYMNS AND EPIGRAMS, AND LYCOPHRON. A. W. Mair; ARATUS. G. R. Mair. (*2nd Imp.*)

CLEMENT OF ALEXANDRIA. Rev. G. W. Butterworth. (*3rd Imp.*)

COLLUTHUS. *Cf.* OPPIAN.

DAPHNIS AND CHLOE. *Cf.* LONGUS.

DEMOSTHENES I: OLYNTHIACS, PHILIPPICS AND MINOR ORATIONS: I-XVII AND XX. J. H. Vince. (*2nd Imp.*)

DEMOSTHENES II: DE CORONA AND DE FALSA LEGATIONE. C. A. Vince and J. H. Vince. (*3rd Imp. revised.*)

DEMOSTHENES III: MEIDIAS, ANDROTION, ARISTOCRATES, TIMOCRATES, ARISTOGEITON. J. H. Vince. (*2nd Imp.*)

THE LOEB CLASSICAL LIBRARY

DEMOSTHENES IV-VI : PRIVATE ORATIONS AND IN NEAERAM.
A. T. Murray. (Vol. IV 3rd Imp., Vols. V and VI 2nd Imp.)
DEMOSTHENES VII : FUNERAL SPEECH, EROTIC ESSAY,
EXORDIA AND LETTERS. N. W. and N. J. DeWitt.
DIO CASSIUS : ROMAN HISTORY. E. Cary. 9 Vols. (Vols.
I and II 3rd Imp., Vols. III-IX 2nd Imp.)
DIO CHRYSOSTOM. 5 Vols. Vols. I and II. J. W. Cohoon.
Vol. III. J. W. Cohoon and H. Lamar Crosby. Vols. IV
and V. H. Lamar Crosby. (Vols. I-IV 2nd Imp.)
DIODORUS SICULUS. 12 Vols. Vols. I-VI. C. H. Oldfather.
Vol. VII. C. L. Sherman. Vols. IX and X. Russel M.
Geer. Vol. XI. F. R. Walton. (Vols. I-IV 2nd Imp.)
DIOGENES LAERTIUS. R. D. Hicks. 2 Vols. (Vol. I 5th Imp.,
Vol. II 4th Imp.)
DIONYSIUS OF HALICARNASSUS : ROMAN ANTIQUITIES. Spel-
man's translation revised by E. Cary. 7 Vols. (Vols.
I-V 2nd Imp.)
EPICTETUS. W. A. Oldfather. 2 Vols. (3rd Imp.)
EURIPIDES. A. S. Way. 4 Vols. (Vols. I and IV 7th Imp.,
Vol. II 8th Imp., Vol. III 6th Imp.) Verse trans.
EUSEBIUS : ECCLESIASTICAL HISTORY. Kirsopp Lake and
J. E. L. Oulton. 2 Vols. (Vol. I 3rd Imp., Vol. II 5th Imp.)
GALEN : ON THE NATURAL FACULTIES. A. J. Brock. (4th
Imp.)
THE GREEK ANTHOLOGY. W. R. Paton. 5 Vols. (Vols. I-
IV 5th Imp., Vol. V 3rd Imp.)
THE GREEK BUCOLIC POETS (THEOCRITUS, BION, MOSCHUS).
J. M. Edmonds. (7th Imp. revised.)
GREEK ELEGY AND IAMBUS WITH THE ANACREONTEA. J. M.
Edmonds. 2 Vols. (Vol. I 3rd Imp., Vol. II 2nd Imp.)
GREEK MATHEMATICAL WORKS. Ivor Thomas. 2 Vols.
(3rd Imp.)
HERODES. Cf. THEOPHRASTUS : CHARACTERS.
HERODOTUS. A. D. Godley. 4 Vols. (Vol. I 4th Imp., Vols.
II and III 5th Imp., Vol. IV 3rd Imp.)
HESIOD AND THE HOMERIC HYMNS. H. G. Evelyn White.
(7th Imp. revised and enlarged.)
HIPPOCRATES AND THE FRAGMENTS OF HERACLEITUS. W. H. S.
Jones and E. T. Withington. 4 Vols. (Vol. I 4th Imp.,
Vols. II-IV 3rd Imp.)
HOMER : ILIAD. A. T. Murray. 2 Vols. (7th Imp.)
HOMER : ODYSSEY. A. T. Murray. 2 Vols. (8th Imp.)

THE LOEB CLASSICAL LIBRARY

Isaeus. E. S. Forster. (*3rd Imp.*)

Isocrates. George Norlin and LaRue Van Hook. 3 Vols. (*2nd Imp.*)

St. John Damascene : Barlaam and Ioasaph. Rev. G. R. Woodward and Harold Mattingly. (*3rd Imp. revised.*)

Josephus. H. St. J. Thackeray and Ralph Marcus. 9 Vols. Vols. I-VII. (Vol. V *4th Imp.*, Vol. VI *3rd Imp.*, Vols. I-IV, VII *2nd Imp.*)

Julian. Wilmer Cave Wright. 3 Vols. (Vols. I and II *3rd Imp.*, Vol. III *2nd Imp.*)

Longus : Daphnis and Chloe. Thornley's translation revised by J. M. Edmonds ; and Parthenius. S. Gaselee. (*4th Imp.*)

Lucian. A. M. Harmon. 8 Vols. Vols. I-V. (Vols. I and II *4th Imp.*, Vol. III *3rd Imp.*, Vols. IV and V *2nd Imp.*)

Lycophron. *Cf.* Callimachus.

Lyra Graeca. J. M. Edmonds. 3 Vols. (Vol. I *5th Imp.*, Vols. II (*revised and enlarged*) and III *4th Imp.*)

Lysias. W. R. M. Lamb. (*3rd Imp.*)

Manetho. W. G. Waddell ; Ptolemy : Tetrabiblos. F. E. Robbins. (*3rd Imp.*)

Marcus Aurelius. C. R. Haines. (*4th Imp. revised.*)

Menander. F. G. Allinson. (*3rd Imp. revised.*)

Minor Attic Orators. 2 Vols. K. J. Maidment and J. O. Burtt. (Vol. I *2nd Imp.*)

Nonnos : Dionysiaca. W. H. D. Rouse. 3 Vols. (*2nd Imp.*)

Oppian, Colluthus, Tryphiodorus. A. W. Mair. (*2nd Imp.*)

Papyri. Non-Literary Selections. A. S. Hunt and C. C. Edgar. 2 Vols. (*2nd Imp.*) Literary Selections (Poetry). D. L. Page. (*3rd Imp.*)

Parthenius. *Cf.* Longus.

Pausanias : Description of Greece. W. H. S. Jones. 5 Vols. and Companion Vol. arranged by R. E. Wycherley. (Vols. I and III *3rd Imp.*, Vols. II, IV and V *2nd Imp.*)

Philo. 10 Vols. Vols. I-V. F. H. Colson and Rev. G. H. Whitaker ; Vols. VI-IX. F. H. Colson. (Vol. IV *4th Imp.*, Vols. I, II, V-VII *3rd Imp.*, Vols. III, VIII, IX *2nd Imp.*)

Two Supplementary Vols. Translation only from an Armenian Text. Ralph Marcus.

Philostratus : The Life of Apollonius of Tyana. F. C. Conybeare. 2 Vols. (Vol. I *4th Imp.*, Vol. II *3rd Imp.*)

THE LOEB CLASSICAL LIBRARY

PHILOSTRATUS: IMAGINES; CALLISTRATUS: DESCRIPTIONS.
A. Fairbanks. (2nd Imp.)

PHILOSTRATUS AND EUNAPIUS: LIVES OF THE SOPHISTS.
Wilmer Cave Wright. (2nd Imp.)

PINDAR. Sir J. E. Sandys. (8th Imp. revised.)

PLATO I: EUTHYPHRO, APOLOGY, CRITO, PHAEDO, PHAEDRUS.
H. N. Fowler. (11th Imp.)

PLATO II: THEAETETUS AND SOPHIST. H. N. Fowler. (4th
Imp.)

PLATO III: STATESMAN, PHILEBUS. H. N. Fowler; ION.
W. R. M. Lamb. (4th Imp.)

PLATO IV: LACHES, PROTAGORAS, MENO, EUTHYDEMUS.
W. R. M. Lamb. (3rd Imp. revised.)

PLATO V: LYSIS, SYMPOSIUM, GORGIAS. W. R. M. Lamb.
(5th Imp. revised.)

PLATO VI: CRATYLUS, PARMENIDES, GREATER HIPPIAS,
LESSER HIPPIAS. H. N. Fowler. (4th Imp.)

PLATO VII: TIMAEUS, CRITIAS, CLITOPHO, MENEXENUS, EPI-
STULAE. Rev. R. G. Bury. (3rd Imp.)

PLATO VIII: CHARMIDES, ALCIBIADES, HIPPARCHUS, THE
LOVERS, THEAGES, MINOS AND EPINOMIS. W. R. M. Lamb.
(2nd Imp.)

PLATO: LAWS. Rev. R. G. Bury. 2 Vols. (3rd Imp.)

PLATO: REPUBLIC. Paul Shorey. 2 Vols. (Vol. I 5th Imp.,
Vol. II 4th Imp.)

PLUTARCH: MORALIA. 14 Vols. Vols. I-V. F. C. Babbitt;
Vol. VI. W. C. Helmbold; Vol. VII. P. H. De Lacy and
B. Einarson; Vol. X. H. N. Fowler; Vol. XII. H.
Cherniss and W. C. Helmbold. (Vols. I-VI, X 2nd Imp.)

PLUTARCH: THE PARALLEL LIVES. B. Perrin. 11 Vols.
(Vols. I, II, VI, VII and XI 3rd Imp., Vols. III-V and
VIII-X 2nd Imp.)

POLYBIUS. W. R. Paton. 6 Vols. (2nd Imp.)

PROCOPIUS: HISTORY OF THE WARS. H. B. Dewing. 7 Vols.
(Vol. I 3rd Imp., Vols. II-VII 2nd Imp.)

PTOLEMY: TETRABIBLOS. Cf. MANETHO.

QUINTUS SMYRNAEUS. A. S. Way. (3rd Imp.) Verse trans.

SEXTUS EMPIRICUS. Rev. R. G. Bury. 4 Vols. (Vol. I 4th
Imp., Vols. II and III 2nd Imp.)

SOPHOCLES. F. Storr. 2 Vols. (Vol. I 10th Imp., Vol. II
6th Imp.) Verse trans.

STRABO: GEOGRAPHY. Horace L. Jones. 8 Vols. (Vols. I,

THE LOEB CLASSICAL LIBRARY

V and VIII 3rd *Imp.*, Vols. II-IV, VI and VII 2nd
Imp.)

THEOPHRASTUS : CHARACTERS. J. M. Edmonds ; HERODES,
etc. A. D. Knox. (3rd *Imp.*)

THEOPHRASTUS : ENQUIRY INTO PLANTS. Sir Arthur Hort.
2 Vols. (2nd *Imp.*)

THUCYDIDES. C. F. Smith. 4 Vols. (Vol. I 5th *Imp.*, Vols.
II and IV 4th *Imp.*, Vol. III 3rd *Imp.*)

TRYPHIODORUS. *Cf.* OPPIAN.

XENOPHON : CYROPAEDIA. Walter Miller. 2 Vols. (Vol. I
4th *Imp.*, Vol. II 3rd *Imp.*)

XENOPHON : HELLENICA, ANABASIS, APOLOGY, AND SYMPO-
SIUM. C. L. Brownson and O. J. Todd. 3 Vols. (Vols. I
and III 3rd *Imp.*, Vol. II 4th *Imp.*)

XENOPHON : MEMORABILIA AND OECONOMICUS. E. C. Marchant. (3rd *Imp.*)

XENOPHON : SCRIPTA MINORA. E. C. Marchant. (3rd *Imp.*)

VOLUMES IN PREPARATION

GREEK AUTHORS

ARISTOTLE : HISTORY OF ANIMALS. A. L. Peck.
PLOTINUS. A. H. Armstrong.

LATIN AUTHORS

BABRIUS AND PHAEDRUS. B. E. Perry.

DESCRIPTIVE PROSPECTUS ON APPLICATION

CAMBRIDGE, MASS.   LONDON
HARVARD UNIV. PRESS   WILLIAM HEINEMANN LTD
Cloth $2.50   Cloth 15s.